Urban Elections

in Democratic

Latin America

Urban Elections

in Democratic

Latin America

EDITED BY

Henry A. Dietz
and
Gil Shidlo

A Scholarly Resources Inc. Imprint
Wilmington, Delaware

Scholarly Resources Inc.
104 Greenhill Avenue
Wilmington, DE 19805-1897

Library of Congress Cataloging-in-Publication Data

Urban elections in democratic Latin America / edited by
  Henry A. Dietz and Gil Shidlo.
        p.   cm. — (Latin American silhouettes)
    Includes bibliographical references and index.
    ISBN 0-8420-2627-4 (cloth : alk. paper). — ISBN 0-8420-2628-2
(pbk. : alk. paper)
    1. Local elections—Latin America. I. Dietz, Henry A.
II. Shidlo, Gil, 1956–   . III. Series.
JS2061.U73   1997
324.98'09173'209045—DC21   97-13454
                                                                CIP

⊗The paper used in this publication meets the minimum requirements of the American National Standard for permanence of paper
for printed library materials, Z39.48, 1984.

About the Editors

HENRY A. DIETZ is professor of government at the University of Texas. His major research focuses on urban poverty and political participation, especially in Peru. He has also written on civil-military relations and on voting behavior.

GIL SHIDLO is a research associate with the Government Department at the London School of Economics. He has written on public housing in Brazil and on Third World militaries as well as the Persian Gulf War. He has taught or done research at Tel Aviv University, the University of Texas at Austin, the University of Pittsburgh, and the University of Maryland.

Contents

Introduction, **ix**
Henry A. Dietz and Gil Shidlo

Abbreviations of Political Parties, **xix**

1   Urban Electoral Politics in Argentina, **2**
       Peter A. Calvert

2   Municipal Elections in Bolivia, **21**
       Eduardo A. Gamarra

3   Local Urban Elections in Democratic Brazil, **63**
       Gil Shidlo

4   Urban Electoral Behavior in Colombia, **91**
       Gary Hoskin

5   Urban Elections in the Dominican Republic, 1962–1994, **117**
       Christopher Mitchell

6   National and Local Elections in El Salvador, 1982–1994, **141**
       Ricardo Córdova Macías and Andrew J. Stein

7   Opening the Electoral Space in Mexico: The Rise of the
       Opposition at the State and Local Levels, **163**
       Victoria E. Rodríguez

8   Urban Elections in Peru, 1980–1995, **199**
       Henry A. Dietz

9   Why Are There No Local Politics in Uruguay? **225**
       Aidan Rankin

10 Venezuelan Local and National Elections, 1958–1995, **243**
        Angel E. Alvarez

Conclusion, **279**
Henry A. Dietz and Gil Shidlo

About the Contributors, **282**

Index, **291**

Introduction

Henry A. Dietz and Gil Shidlo

Electoral politics in Latin America has become a way of life since most countries returned to (or established) civilian procedures during the 1980s. Before that decade of democratic renewal, there were notable exceptions: Costa Rica has been holding elections since 1949, both Venezuela and Colombia have been democratic polities since 1958, and Mexico has developed its own brand of civilian authoritarianism since the 1930s. In addition, the Dominican Republic has been holding elections since 1966. Starting around 1980, however, virtually all countries of Latin America came under civilian governance: Ecuador in 1979, Peru in 1980, Honduras and Bolivia in 1982, Argentina in 1983, Brazil, El Salvador, Uruguay, and Nicaragua in 1984, Guatemala in 1985, and Chile and Paraguay in 1989. Thus, as Latin America entered the 1990s, its governments (except for Cuba) were civilian and electoral, each with its own array of institutions, processes, and problems.

This transformation to and search for consolidation of democracy has generated a significant amount of literature. But political scientists (O'Donnell, Schmitter, and Whitehead, 1987; Malloy and Seligson, 1987; Diamond, Linz, and Lipset, 1989; Higley and Guenther, 1992; Weiner and Ozbudun, 1987) have concentrated almost entirely upon the national level and upon presidential elections when they have examined elections at all. Local politics (parties, candidates, or issues) have received scant attention.

Such a state of affairs is not appropriate. The transition and consolidation of democracy do not depend solely upon presidential elections and their national results. While such contests take center court, the auxiliary political arenas of local elections offer much of interest and in many ways allow understandings and analyses of the democratic process that are blurred or hidden at the national level. Thus, while much has been written about necessary and sufficient conditions for democracy to take hold, as well as the processes by which authoritarian regimes yield power, the several roles that electoral politics play remain largely terra incognita. One aspect that is especially uninvestigated is urban elections. Only a few studies have examined elections in specific cities, and there has been no effort to develop a series of cross-national studies that offer readily comparable examinations of electoral behavior in Latin America's major urban areas.

The lack of any examination of subnational elections, and of any specific focus on urban areas, is perhaps surprising, since urban centers and their politics play several crucial roles in democratic polities generally. Latin America is no exception to this rule. Today, as a world region, it is about 70 percent urban, meaning that more than three hundred million people inhabit the area's cities. Moreover, two of the world's three largest cities are now in Latin America: the metropolitan areas of Mexico City (with about twenty-two million) and São Paulo, Brazil (with about eighteen million). In addition to such demographic and geographic reasons, the cities of Latin America comprise essential settings for the political process.

During the extended period of democratic consolidation following a normally rather abrupt transition (usually brought about through presidential and legislative elections), many individuals may become seriously and personally involved in the democratic political process through neighborhood or city politics. Such involvement can act as a primary socializing experience for newly enfranchised or young citizens who, because of extended military rule, may have no experience in electoral politics. Local issues and candidates may thus inculcate a citizenry with political tolerance and with other norms and values critical to sustaining a democracy.

In addition to individual citizens learning about politics in local races, political parties may first come into being within and because of cities. Since cities by definition contain large numbers of people in small areas, political parties find them essential for electoral success, especially if one or two urban areas contain a sizable proportion of a nation's total population as well as its electorate (for example, Montevideo in Uruguay, Buenos Aires in Argentina, Lima in Peru). Moreover, cities offer candidates and parties, especially smaller or lesser ones, a chance to develop themselves and their policies and ideological stances and to see what citizen reactions might be elicited at the polls.

More than three decades ago Karl Deutsch (1961) posited the importance of urbanization in the overall process of social mobilization, noting that an urban setting is by its very nature more political than a traditional rural context. In particular, he argued that individuals and groups residing in cities are open and available to a variety of political stimuli that either do not operate at all in rural areas or operate cumulatively in urban settings in ways that they cannot in the countryside. These stimuli include the presence of political parties, labor unions, social movements of various kinds (for instance, neighborhood associations and religious groups), and the mass media, electronic as well as print. In a similar vein, Samuel Huntington (1968, 1991) argued that such stimuli create what are best described as politicized needs, expectations, and demands that grow in number and variety as urbanization increases, thus creating severe difficulties for the capacity of the state to respond to such demands.

As many observers have noted, Latin America has come to conform to Deutsch's and Huntington's analyses. Its cities contain a wide variety of politically relevant parties, trade unions, social movements, and other stimuli that act upon their ever-growing numbers of inhabitants. Such stimuli tend to create precisely these politicized demands and expectations—that is, more and more demands and wants and needs on the part of more and more people, all of whom expect the political system (the state) to provide those needs and answer those demands.

The nature and structure of cities comprises an additional factor. If a nation's capital city makes up the dominant political arena, what goes on in that city influences national politics, and vice versa. In Latin America, many countries have "primate cities" —that is, cities that dominate their nations by their overwhelming size and importance. Mexico City, for example, is at least eight times larger than Mexico's second largest city, Monterrey; Lima is close to ten times larger than Peru's second city, Arequipa, and so on: Santo Domingo in the Dominican Republic, virtually all of the capital cities in Central America, and Caracas in Venezuela. While there are exceptions (for instance, Ecuador and Brazil both have two major cities, Quito and Guayaquil, and São Paulo and Rio de Janeiro, respectively, and Colombia has several large cities), urban primacy is a critical fact of political life for many Latin American countries.

Such primacy exists not only in demographic terms but in other forms as well. For example, Lima's seven million inhabitants constitute about one-third of Peru's total population. But Lima also contains well over one-third of the country's total electorate, produces three-fifths of its industrial output and four-fifths of its consumer goods, holds over one-half of the labor force employed in commerce and two-thirds of that in industry, and accounts for over 90 percent of all financial transactions and associated activities. Given such multifaceted primacy, political parties and candidates must focus their attention on the area's capital cities if they are to make a serious run at national office. They also must try to attract the financial backing of urban-based elites and mass movements if they are to carry on what have become increasingly expensive and sophisticated campaigns, which utilize the mass media and try to activate and direct the political stimuli discussed above.

Not surprisingly, therefore, many aspiring leaders learn their political skills in local urban political arenas, and a variety of Latin American political movements and parties have had their genesis in the cities. The Brazilian Workers' Party (PT) is one such example. It was formed in 1979 in São Bernardo de Campos, an industrial city in the state of São Paulo, as a result of the military government's willingness to permit growth in union activity. The PT's electoral experience started in 1982 when the military allowed competitive elections for all political offices except that of president.

Although the results of the 1982 elections were a profound shock and disappointment to the PT, two of its mayoral candidates were elected as well as seventy-eight municipal council members in thirty-nine municipalities. The running of candidates in all but one state capital in the 1985 municipal elections laid the groundwork for the presidential elections in 1989. In the Dominican Republic, some of the mayors of the capital city, Santo Domingo, entered office with presidential ambitions. PRD mayor Pedro Franco Badia (1978–1982) hoped to succeed President Antonio Guzmán, and the next mayor, José Francisco Peña Gomez, ran hard for the PRD's presidential nomination in 1986. Prior to the transition to democracy, some Latin American nations under military rule (Brazil is the major example) held local elections well before national or presidential ones were allowed. Thus, the urban setting became the source of political movements that later moved on, or at least attempted to move on, to the national level.

Economically, Latin America in general suffered through the 1980s to such an extent that major international agencies such as the World Bank and the Inter-American Development Bank concluded that the period had to be labeled a "lost decade." High rates of inflation, substantial losses of purchasing power, and increasing foreign debts and the need to pay them all combined to deepen and widen poverty and to limit whatever means that governments had to combat the economic crisis. Rising frustration over such conditions contributed to the downfall of many military regimes, but their civilian successors were bequeathed a difficult legacy.

These economic hard times produced two interrelated results. First, the urban masses in particular were acutely vulnerable to macroeconomic hardships and crisis, since they operated within a monetary economy, while their rural counterparts, though perhaps poorer in absolute terms, could cushion the impact through subsistence farming. Therefore, the urban masses (and the middle classes, for that matter) were immediately and intimately affected by rising inflation, decreasing purchasing power, and escalations in the cost of living (especially for staple items and transportation) in ways that rural populations were not.

Second, these economic hardships fomented widespread grass-roots efforts among the urban poor, sometimes as protest movements, sometimes as religious ecclesial base communities, and other times as soup kitchens and sustenance providers. Regardless of the type, these "informal" movements all served in varying ways to empower low-income groups. As electoral democracies assumed control, governments often found that previously marginal groups were no longer willing to be led passively but instead were determined to have a voice in their own futures. Indeed, the disastrous economic performance of the 1980s may have contributed to increased levels of political participation outside the formal electoral arena, meaning that new civilian leaders found themselves heading societies with deep cleavages between the formal and the informal sectors. In some countries (especially those with substantial indigenous populations such as Mexico, Guatemala, and the Andean nations of Ecuador, Peru, and Bolivia), these economic cleavages were exacerbated by ethnic, racial, linguistic, and cultural traits.

In another vein, examining the urban electoral arena has potential benefits for understanding national politics. Local elections can reveal strengths and weaknesses of parties that are evident in a presidential race; for example, there are several cases in Latin America where traditionally dominant parties have had difficulties in the capital (AD in Caracas, the PRI in Mexico City, APRA in

Lima). Or a party that appears solid in terms of aggregate results can show upon analysis that it has trouble in carrying the urban middle class or the popular masses. Urban elections also can highlight or identify regional differences within a nation.

Furthermore, many Latin American countries at least have discussed, if not implemented, policies directed toward the decentralization or the devolution of political power. Such policies aim at reversing what are generally centuries of centralized control on the national level. While different countries have taken different paths and have encountered different levels of success (Cheema and Rondinelli, 1983), it is impossible to think of decentralization in meaningful terms without local elections being firmly in place.

To consider either singly or jointly the specific roles of cities in these several areas—the consolidation of democracy, the process of socialization into politics, the arena for new political parties and movements as well as various politically relevant groups, the emergence of a complex informal economy, the key for political and economic decentralization—would require an entire series of large-scale, configurative monographs.* The scope and intent of this volume is much less ambitious in that it consists of a series of comparable chapters that examine electoral structures, institutions, and behavior in major Latin American cities. The authors all address the following clusters of questions.

Intraurban politics. What have been the patterns of electoral results in the major urban areas since the restoration, or creation, of civilian politics, roughly during the 1980s? In these major urban areas (understood to include generally the capital and the next largest three or four cities), have electoral results been more or less parallel? Has the capital city shown itself to be something of a maverick, or have provincial cities tended to act in such ways? Does local urban politics reflect significant regional loyalties?

Urban-national politics. In what ways have local elections either paralleled or diverged from national (that is, presidential) elec-

---

*This volume does not attempt to cover in any systematic fashion areas such as local governance—that is, how cities are governed—or how a specific mayoral regime confronted problems in a specific city. Nor is it concerned with local urban finance (tax laws, local budgetary autonomy), or questions of administrative centralization. Finally, this study does not undertake an investigation of patronage as such. Local elections as a means of political advancement are, however, a matter of concern in certain countries, for example, the Dominican Republic.

toral patterns? Does it appear to make any difference if local elections are held simultaneously with national elections, or not? Why, and in what ways? What is the role or influence of minority parties and candidates in local elections? What factors prevent such minority parties from attaining national significance? Under what conditions can such minority parties affect national politics without countrywide electoral appeal or strength?

Formal-informal politics. What has been the effect of "informal politics"—for example, new social movements, community organizations, politically relevant grass-roots movements—on local electoral politics in Latin America's major urban areas? Do formal parties attempt to co-opt, repress, embrace, reject, incorporate, accede to, or replace such movements? And do the leaders and members of such movements attempt to make them electorally relevant by running candidates or by merging with or competing against and allowing co-optation by formal parties?

To carry out this investigation, the editors, along with nine contributors, wrote their chapters following a specific outline derived from these three clusters of questions. Obviously, each chapter has its own idiosyncracies; for example, some questions may be irrelevant in one national setting, or they may take on specific forms or contours in another.

Two explanatory notes are necessary here. First, we selected the ten countries through the use of one major criterion: the presence (at the time of writing) of at least two democratic local elections in the nation under investigation. This criterion explains, for example, the absence of Chile from this volume. Chile returned to democratic rule in 1989 but held its first set of local elections in mid-1992. The two-election criterion allows each contributor to discern patterns over time and to draw conclusions that simply could not be done on the basis of a single election.

Second, not every country that fits the two-election rule has been included. Especially notable are some absences within Central America. Costa Rica, for example, has had competitive local elections every four years since 1953. The only explanation possible is that contributors for these countries were not available, for a variety of reasons. Nevertheless, the ten chapters cover all of the large Latin American countries that qualified at the time of writing, and the inclusion of several of the small countries offers enough variation to allow generalizations to be drawn from the cases.

The contributors address three basic areas. First, they discuss the background of the country and cities in question including (but not confined to) electoral experience under military regimes, the degree to which present elections are competitive and open (that is, the degree of "democraticness" of the electoral system), and the nature of the party system (for instance, single-party dominant, two-party competitive, or multiparty). Also included are figures on the frequency of local elections, electoral results over the past two or more democratic local contests, and voter turnout.

Second, they examine the electoral experience on the local scene, including the results of local versus national turnout levels. In addition, the contributors analyze campaigns and personalities and discuss national-local linkages between parties and issues, the impact of polls and media, changes over time in voter preferences, and the differences in voter preference by social class, ethnic or racial cleavages, or income levels as relevant. The roles of informal organizations and social movements in influencing the electoral process are also included.

Finally, in concluding statements, each contributor focuses on identifying patterns in the electoral arena and on the importance of local elections in the democratic life of the nation. Some of the questions asked earlier are raised again, such as: What is the effect of national or international issues on future local electoral activity? And, if local elections were held during authoritarian rule, what was the impact of that experience on the democratic electoral experiment?

Each chapter will have different emphases; factors crucial to determining electoral outcomes in one country may have little effect in another, and one of the major purposes of each contribution is to point out these idiosyncracies for each city and nation. In an effort to generalize from the cases, however, the editors' conclusions generate some findings that cut across national boundaries to offer some global answers to the three basic questions that initially sparked interest in this volume.

Whatever its limitations, what cannot be overemphasized is the fact that compelling reasons now exist for this book. Two or three decades ago the mere notion of examining local elections in Latin America would have produced a puzzled look and a simple question: Why? Elections of any sort were limited and suspect if they occurred at all, and local elections were for the vast majority of countries nonexistent: mayors were appointees under both civilian and military regimes. The fact that this situation no longer applies, and that local elections are now meaningful throughout the region, is mute testimony to the breadth and depth of the political change that has taken place in Latin America.

References

Cheema, G. Shabbir, and Dennis Rondinelli, eds. 1983. *Decentralization and Development: Policy Implementation in Developing Countries.* Beverly Hills, CA: Sage.

Deutsch, Karl. 1961. "Social Mobilization and Political Development." *American Political Science Review* 55, no. 3 (September): 493–514.

Diamond, Larry, Juan Linz, and Seymour Martin Lipset, eds. 1989. *Democracy in Developing Countries: Latin America.* Boulder, CO: Lynne Reinner.

Higley, John, and Richard Guenther, eds. 1992. *Elites and Democratic Consolidation in Latin America and Southern Europe.* New York: Cambridge University Press.

Huntington, Samuel. 1968. *Political Order in Changing Societies.* New Haven: Yale University Press.

———. 1991. *The Third Wave.* Norman: University of Oklahoma Press.

Malloy, James, and Mitchell Seligson, eds. 1987. *Authoritarians and Democrats: Regime Transition in Latin America.* Pittsburgh: University of Pittsburgh Press.

O'Donnell, Guillermo, Philippe Schmitter, and Lawrence Whitehead, eds. 1987. *Transitions from Authoritarian Rule: Latin America.* Baltimore: Johns Hopkins University Press.

Weiner, Myron, and Ergun Ozbudun, eds. 1987. *Competitive Elections in Developing Countries.* Durham, NC: Duke University Press.

Abbreviations of Political Parties

AD	Acción Democrática (Democratic Action), Venezuela
AD-M-19	Alianza Democrática-M-19 (Nineteenth of April Democratic Alliance), Colombia
ADN	Acción Democrática y Nacionalista (Nationalist Democratic Action), Bolivia
ANAPO	Alianza Nacional Popular (National Popular Alliance), Colombia
AP	Acuerdo Patriótico (Patriotic Accord), Bolivia
AP	Acción Popular (Popular Action), Peru
APRA	Alianza Popular Revolucionaria Americana (American Popular Revolutionary Alliance), Peru
ARENA	Alianca Renovadora Nacional (National Renovating Alliance), Brazil
ARENA	Alianza Republicana Nacionalista (Nationalist Republican Alliance), El Salvador
CCN	Cruzada Cívica Nacionalista (National Civic Crusade), Venezuela
CD	Convergencia Democrática (Democratic Convergence), El Salvador
CFI	Confederación Federalista Independiente (Independent Federalist Confederation), Argentina
CM	Consejo Municipal (Municipal/City Council), Mexico
CODE	Convergencia Democrática (Democratic Convergence), Peru
CONDEPA	Conciencia de Patria (Conscience of the Fatherland), Bolivia
COPEI	Comité de Organización Política Electoral Independiente (Committee of Independent Electoral Political Organization), Venezuela

FA	Frente Amplio (Broad Front), Uruguay
FARC	Fuerzas Armadas Revolucionarias de Colombia (Revolutionary Armed Forces of Colombia), Colombia
FDN	Frente Democrático Nacional (National Democratic Front), Mexico
FDP	Frente Democrática Popular (Popular Democratic Front), Venezuela
FELCN	Fuerza Especial de Lucha contra el Narcotráfico (Special Forces of the Struggle against Drug Traffic), Bolivia
FMLN	Farabundo Martí Liberación Nacional (Farabundo Martí National Liberation Front), El Salvador
FND	Frente Nacional Democrático (National Democratic Front), Venezuela
FPU	Frente del Pueblo Unido (United People's Front), Bolivia
FREDEMO	Frente Democrático (Democratic Front), Peru
FREJUDEPA	Frente Justicialista de la Patria (Justicalist Front of the Fatherland), Argentina
FREJULI	Frente Justicialista de Liberación (Justicialist Liberation Front), Argentina
FREJUPO	Frente Justicialista Popular (Peronist Popular Justicialist Front), Argentina
FRENETRACA	Frente Nacional de Trabajadores y Campesinos (National Workers and Peasants Front), Peru
FREPASO	Frente para un País en Solídaridad (Front for a Country in Solidarity), Argentina
FSB	Falange Socialista Boliviana (Bolivian Socialist Falange), Bolivia
FUP	Frente Unido del Pueblo (United Front of the People), Colombia
ICC	Independientes Con el Cambio (Independents for Change), Venezuela
IPFN	Independientes para un Frente Nacional (Independents for a National Front), Venezuela
IU	Izquierda Unida (United Left), Bolivia
IU	Izquierda Unida (United Left), Peru
LCR	La Causa Radical (The Radical Cause), Venezuela

MAC   Movimiento Auténtico Cristiano (Authentic
           Christian Movement), El Salvador
MAS   Movimiento al Socialismo (Movement to Social-
           ism), Venezuela
MBL   Movimiento Bolivia Libre (Free Bolivia Move-
           ment), Bolivia
MDB   Movimento Democrático Brasileiro (Brazilian
           Democratic Movement), Brazil
MEP   Movimiento Electoral del Pueblo (Electoral
           Movement of the People), Venezuela
MIN   Movimiento de Integración Nacional (National
           Integration Movement), Venezuela
MIR   Movimiento de Izquierda Revolucionaria
           (Movement of the Revolutionary Left), Bolivia
MIR   Movimiento de Izquierda Revolucionaria
           (Movement of the Revolutionary Left),
           Venezuela
MIR-BL   Movimiento de Izquierda Revolucionaria-
           Bolivia Libre (Movement of the Revolutionary
           Left-Free Bolivia), Bolivia
MIR-NM   Movimiento de Izquierda Revolucionaria-
           Nueva Mayoría (Movement of the Revolu-
           tionary Left-New Majority), Bolivia
MIR-Masas Movimiento de Izquierda Revolucionaria
           (Labor faction), Bolivia
MLN   Movimiento de Liberación Nacional (National
           Liberation Movement), Uruguay
MNR   Movimiento Nacionalista Revolucionario (Revo-
           lutionary Nationalist Movement), Bolivia
MNR   Movimiento Nacionalista Revolucionario
           (National Revolutionary Movement), El
           Salvador
MNRH   Movimiento Nacionalista Revolucionario
           Histórico (Historic Revolutionary Nationalist
           Movement), Bolivia
MNRI   Movimiento Nacionalista Revolucionario
           Izquierdista (Revolutionary Nationalist
           Movement of the Left), Bolivia
MODIN   Movimiento para Dignidad e Independencia
           (Movement for Dignity and Independence),
           Argentina

MOPOF	Movimiento Popular Fuegino (Fuegino Popular Movement), Argentina
MPP	Movimiento Patria Profunda (Profound Fatherland Movement), Bolivia
MPSC	Movimiento Popular Social Cristiano (Popular Social Christian Movement), El Salvador
MRTK	Movimiento Revolucionario Tupac Katari (Tupac Katari Revolutionary Movement), Bolivia
MSN	Movimiento de Solidaridad Nacional (National Solidarity Movement), El Salvador
MST	Movimiento Socialista de los Trabajadores (Socialist Movement of the Workers), Bolivia
MU	Movimiento de Unidad (Unity Movement), El Salvador
NE	Nuevo Espacio (New Space), Uruguay
NFD	Nueva Fuerza Democrática (New Democratic Force), Colombia
NGD	Nueva Generación Democrática (New Democratic Generation), Venezuela
ORA	Organización Renovadora Auténtica (Authentic Renovating Organization), Venezuela
PAISA	Partido Auténtico Institucional Salvadoreño (Salvadoran Authentic Institutional Party), El Salvador
PAN	Partido Acción Nacional (National Action Party), Mexico
PARM	Partido Auténtico de la Revolution Mexicana (The Authentic Party of the Mexican Revolution), Mexico
PC	Partido Colorado (Colorado Party), Uruguay
PCB	Partido Comunista Boliviano (Bolivian Communist Party), Bolivia
PCB	Partido Comunista Brasileiro (Brazilian Communist Party), Brazil
PCdoB	Partido Comunista do Brasil (Communist Party of Brazil), Brazil
PCN	Partido de Conciliación Nacional (National Conciliation Party), El Salvador
PCU	Partido Comunista Uruguayo (Uruguayan Communist Party), Uruguay

PCV	Partido Comunista Venezolano (Venezuelan Communist Party), Venezuela
PDB	Partido Democrático Boliviano (Bolivian Democratic Party), Bolivia
PDC	Partido Democrático Cristão (Christian Democratic Party), Brazil
PDC	Partido Demócrata Cristiano (Christian Democratic Party), Bolivia
PDC	Partido Demócrata Cristiano (Christian Democratic Party), El Salvador
PDM	Partido Demócrata Mexicano (Mexican Democrat Party), Mexico
PDS	Partido Democrático Social (Social Democratic Party), Brazil
PDT	Partido Democrático Trabalhista (Democratic Labor Party), Brazil
PFL	Partido Frente Liberal (Party of the Liberal Front), Brazil
PFCRN	Partido Frente Cardenista de Reconstrucción Nacional (Cardenista Front for National Reconstruction), Mexico
PI	Partido Intransigente (Intransigents Party), Argentina
PJ	Partido Justicialista (Justicialist Party), Argentina
PL	Partido Liberal (Liberal Party), Brazil
PLD	Partido de la Liberación Dominicana (Dominican Democratic Liberation Party), Dominican Republic
PMDB	Partido Movimento Democrático Brasileiro (Party of the Brazilian Democratic Movement), Brazil
PMN	Partido da Mobilização Nacional (National Mobilization Party), Brazil
PNRD	Partido Nacionalista Revolucionario Democrático (Democratic Nationalist Revolutionary Party), Dominican Republic
PPC	Partido Popular Cristiano (Popular Christian Party), Peru
PPS	Partido Popular Socialista (Socialist Popular Party), Brazil

PPS	Partido Popular Socialista (Socialist Popular Party), Mexico
PR	Partido Reformista (Reformist Party), Dominican Republic
PRD	Partido de la Revolución Democrática (Party of the Democratic Revolution), Mexico
PRD	Partido Revolucionario Dominicano (Dominican Revolutionary Party), Dominican Republic
PRI	Partido Revolucionario Independiente (Independent Revolutionary Party), Dominican Republic
PRI	Partido Revolucionario Institucional (Institutional Revolutionary Party), Mexico
PRN	Partido da Reconstrucão Nacional (Party for National Reconstruction), Brazil
PRS	Partido das Reformas Sociais (Party for Social Reforms), Brazil
PRSC	Partido Reformista Social Cristiano (Christian Social Reformist Party), Dominican Republic
PS-1	Partido Socialista-Uno (Socialist Party-One), Bolivia
PSB	Partido Socialista Brasileiro (Brazilian Socialist Party), Brazil
PSC	Partido Social Cristão (Social Christian Party), Brazil
PSC	Partido Social Cristiano (Social Christian Party), Bolivia
PSD	Partido Social Democrática (Democratic Social Party), Brazil
PSD	Partido Social Democrática (Social Democratic Party), El Salvador
PSDB	Partido da Social Democrácia Brasileiro (Party of the Brazilian Social Democracy), Brazil
PST	Partido Socialista de los Trabajadores (Worker's Socialist Party), Mexico
PST	Partido Social Trabalhista (Social Labor Party), Brazil
PSU	Partido Socialista del Uruguay (Uruguayan Socialist Party), Uruguay
PT	Partido del Trabajo (Labor Party), Mexico

PT	Partido dos Trabalhadores (Workers' Party), Brazil
PTB	Partido Trabalhista Brasileiro (Brazilian Labor Party), Brazil
PTR	Partido Trabalhista Renovador (Renovating Labor Party), Brazil
UCEDE	Unión del Centro Democrático (Union of the Democratic Center), Argentina
UCN	Unión Cívica Nacional (National Civic Union), Dominican Republic
UCR	Unión Cívica Radical (Radical Civic Union), Argentina
UCS	Unidad Cívica Solidaridad (Solidarity Civic Union), Bolivia
UDN	Unión Democrática Nacionalista (Nationalist Democratic Union), El Salvador
UDP	Unidad Democrática y Popular (Democratic Popular Union), Bolivia
UNO	Unión Nacional de Oposición (National Opposition Union), Colombia
UP	Unión Patriótica (Patriotic Union), Colombia
UPA	Unión para Avanzar (United to Advance), Venezuela
URD	Unión Republicana Democrática (Democratic Republican Union), Venezuela
US	Unidad Socialista (Socialist Unity), Argentina
VR-9	Vanguardia Revolucionaria 9 de Abril (Revolutionary Vanguard of April 9), Bolivia

ATLANTIC
OCEAN

MEXICO

Mexico
City

DOMINICAN REPUBLIC
Santo
Domingo

EL SALVADOR
San Salvador

Caracas

VENEZUELA

Bogotá

COLOMBIA

PERU

BRAZIL

Lima

Brasilia

PACIFIC
OCEAN

ARGENTINA
URUGUAY

Buenos
Aires
Montevideo

LATIN AMERICA

0   500 miles

0   400   800 kilometers

1

Urban Electoral Politics in Argentina*

Peter A. Calvert

Politics in Argentina since 1945 has been dominated by one main theme, the rise and continued survival of Peronism, a political doctrine emphasizing a cross-class alliance under "verticalist" leadership. Within this tradition the centrality of the urban working class has given a particular significance to the urban-rural divide.

The success of Raúl Alfonsín and the Radical Civic Union (UCR) in 1983 was primarily the result of a massive reaction to eight years of military rule and to the Process of National Reorganization, more commonly known now as the Dirty War. It was achieved by the Radicals uniting "a rather heterogeneous coalition, including the ideological Left, the mass of the Right of Center voters (who deserted their parties) and some disillusioned Peronists" (Di Tella, 1984). Personalities played an important part: a dull Peronist candidate was opposed for the presidency by a relatively charismatic Radical. But Alfonsín, with questionable taste, owed much of his electoral success to none-too-subtle hints of a possible alliance between the Peronist trade unions and the armed forces. If the electorate did not necessarily believe that the military wanted the Peronists (which, given their past track record, seems distinctly improbable), they did not find it hard to accept that "a Peronist

*Fieldwork on which this chapter is based was conducted in Buenos Aires in July 1991 and March 1993. I would like to acknowledge gratefully the financial support of the Committee for Advanced Studies and the Department of Politics of the University of Southampton, and the assistance of Janet and Maudie Duncan, Lic. Raúl Alberto Gática, Joyce McNair, Lic. Ricardo G. Parera, Michael Soltys, Nicholas Tozer, and the staff of the Instituto Torcuato Di Tella.

victory would be just a stepping stone to chaos and a new military coup" (Neilson, 1983; Botna et al., 1985).

Since that time a strong two-party system has emerged in Argentina. Voting is compulsory, so participation levels are high. It is hardly surprising, therefore, that the tide of national opinion exercises a major influence on the outcome of municipal elections, although, since elections are staggered and provinces do not vote simultaneously, the effects can be hard to assess. So, too, the effects of competition for governorships or membership in the federal Senate or Chamber of Deputies influence midterm and provincial elections. The major parties are well organized and well funded, and the ruling Peronists have successfully established close links with business, which gives them an assured source of income that they can use to great effect (N'haux, 1993). A third set of influences comes from the operation of Argentina's federal system, which gives so much power to the provinces that they can be, and have been argued to be, sovereign and not merely autonomous (Cano, 1936). However, the evident dominance of the federal government in nearly every aspect of the national life is most emphatically shown by the ability of the president to "intervene" a provincial or local government—that is, to suspend its operation by the appointment of a federal intervenor. Alfonsín prided himself on being the first president in Argentina's history not to make use of this power; President Carlos Menem, on the other hand, has used it at both the provincial and municipal levels.

Intraurban Politics

Three factors reduce public interest in intraurban politics. First, all politics, as on many past occasions, was effectively suspended between 1976 and 1983, with such powers as were left to the municipalities being exercised by the mayors (*intendentes*). After 1983 some old personalities were discredited and new ones had to emerge. Second, ever since the 1930s, and even more since the rise of Juan Perón, municipalities have had to struggle, unsuccessfully, against the federal government for areas of competence such as the supply of electricity, water, gas, transportation, and food (Mouchet, 1969). In the prevailing climate of economic liberalism in Argentina, powers lost by the municipalities in the past to the federal government are not being returned to them. Instead, they have additionally to compete for favor with the newly privatized industries on whose services they will increasingly depend. And third, municipal politics is generally seen to be even more corrupt than other aspects of Argentine public life. For whichever reason, urban electoral politics seems since 1983 to have attracted only limited attention from Argentine researchers (and then as incidental to the national scene), while aspects of the community power structure, for example, have attracted very keen interest (see, for example, Díaz de Landa and Parmigiani de Barbará, 1994).

In the municipal hierarchy, pride of place inevitably goes to Greater Buenos Aires, in which some two-fifths of the population live. Politically, the conurbation is divided into the Federal Capital, the seat of government, with a population of 2,908,000 (1980 census), and the surrounding nineteen municipalities located in the northern part of the Province of Buenos Aires, covering a total area of 3,880 sq. km. and having a population in 1980 of 10,070,000, or some 37 percent of the total population of the country (Buenos Aires, 1980).

The Federal Capital (as it is often called, to avoid confusion with the Province of Buenos Aires) has a unique status, being both a federal district and thus the seat of national government, and a *municipio*, with its own elected legislature but (until 1994) with a mayor who was only indirectly elected and held his office effectively at the will of the president. The city is in every sense the center of Argentine national life. In the late 1980s the Radicals came forward with an imaginative plan to move the capital to a new site in the extreme south of the Province of Buenos Aires, at Viedma or Carmén de Patagones, but it came to nothing (Reboratti, 1987).

The Federal Capital was created in 1880 under Article 3 of the 1853 Constitution and was extended by the cession of Flores in 1884 and Belgrano in 1887. The metropolitan region, the urbanized area of the Province of Buenos Aires surrounding the capital, also has been modified from time to time. It was defined in 1964 by Decree 1907/969 as consisting of the capital and twenty-five provincial municipalities, including the substantial rural area of the Paraná Delta (Mouchet, 1969; Smith, 1989:54–55). Buenos Aires is by far the largest of the provinces and has its seat of government at La Plata, Argentina's fourth largest city, fifty-six kilometers (or about an hour's drive) from the capital on the edge of the estuary of the Río de la Plata. This area and the two neighboring riverside municipalities of Ensenada and Berisso are not regarded as part of Greater Buenos Aires.

In the period under review, two places have alternated as Argentina's second city: Rosario (properly Rosario de Santa Fe), in the Province of Santa Fe, a major grain port and railway junction; and Córdoba, the university city and the capital of the province of the same name, midway between Buenos Aires and the Andes, some two hours' flying time to the northwest of the Federal Capital. Both have a population of about 800,000. Other major urban areas in order of size are Tucumán (properly San Miguel de Tucumán) with 326,000; Mar del Plata in the Province of Buenos Aires, with 320,000; and Santa Fe, with 312,000. Other smaller cities such as Mendoza (120,000) and Salta owe much of their importance to their role as provincial capitals, although Mendoza, like Rosario, has a significant regional extension, and Rosario, once the national capital of the Argentine Federation before Buenos Aires joined it, is not even a provincial capital, despite its importance in all other respects.

The pattern of electoral results in the major urban areas since the restoration of civilian politics in 1983 shows that electoral results in the capital and the next largest cities have been more or less parallel, but with significant differences. In this respect it is the capital city itself (and to a lesser extent Greater Buenos Aires) that has been something of a maverick. In the 1983 presidential race the voters of the Federal Capital cast 1,269,352 ballots (66.0 percent) for Alfonsín (UCR) and only 540,389 for Italo Luder (PJ), with the balance going to the Intransigents (PI) (4.6 percent) and the center-right Union of the Democratic Center (UCEDE) (1.3 percent). In 1989 there was a hairline plurality for Carlos Menem, candidate of the Peronist Popular Justicialist Front (FREJUPO) (36.7 percent), over the Radical governor of Córdoba, Eduardo Angeloz (UCR) (36.3 percent). The Alianza de Centro (12.3 percent) led the remainder of the eight candidates in the field. However, these results disguise the fundamental conservatism of the urban electorate.

Far from being the hotbed of Peronism the Federal Capital is disputed territory. In addition, as the economic center of the nation, it is to a much lesser extent a stronghold of the (economic) liberals, the UCEDE, founded and formerly led by Alvaro Alsogaray, and their friends in the Alianza del Centro who, despite their national significance as allies of the present government, have negligible electoral support outside the capital and the surrounding province.

Elections for city councillors (*concejales*) show these trends clearly, although from 1983 to 1993 the Deliberative Council was consistently dominated by the UCR, whose Facundo Suárez Lastra served as mayor throughout Alfonsín's term, from 1983 to 1989. In 1985 the Renewal Peronists, led by Carlos Grosso, made a respectable showing and gained some 25 percent of the vote. In the 1987 elections the UCR, despite recording a very substantial vote in the Federal Capital, lost 10 Council seats. They ended up with only 28 seats to 16 for the PJ and 10 for the UCEDE, the remaining 6 being shared between the Intransigents (3), the Federal Party (2), and the Pensioners (1). Yet their plurality proved to be enough to give them effective control.

In 1989, UCR representation fell to only 23 seats to 19 for the PJ and 12 for the Alianza de Centro. With the remaining 6 seats going to six other parties, the UCEDE ended up holding the balance of power. Immediately the new leader of the Peronist group, Jorge Argüello, in conjunction with the Radical mayor, sought to oust the Radical council chair, Juan Carlos Farizano (*Buenos Aires Herald*, henceforth *BAH*, May 20, 1989). Grosso, the Peronist candidate for mayor, was a clear winner. So much turbulence followed that in December 1989 President Menem ordered the intervention (that is, suspension) of the Council. While discussions on the resumption of normal service continued, the building was cordoned off and surrounded by heavily armed policemen wearing bullet-proof jackets as demonstrations took place outside.

Intraurban politics in the Federal Capital, therefore, is very much part of the national scene. Otherwise, intraurban politics displays very similar characteristics throughout the country. The mayoralty of an important city is in itself a significant prize, and those who hold such positions can make a contribution to national politics. Where the province is dominated by a rival party, the influence of the mayor is likely to increase. Since the revival of democracy in 1983, local government has clearly become an important training ground for future leaders.

Urban-National Politics

In what ways have local elections either paralleled or diverged from national electoral patterns? It will be seen that the major influence on electoral politics in the Federal Capital comes from national politics. Thus, a pattern of dominance by the Radicals within the urban-national context in the 1980s and their displacement by the Peronists at the end of the decade is confirmed by elections for federal deputies in the capital. The UCR won the first three elections, despite a slow erosion of their support, mostly to the UCEDE. The Peronist vote hardly changed between 1983 and 1987, when the Radicals won 13 seats to 7 for the PJ, 4 for the UCEDE, and 1 for the PI.

As elsewhere in the nation, however, this picture changed sharply in 1989 under the impact of financial crisis, hyperinflation, and the evident incapacity of the UCR to deal with either. The UCR vote fell by 10 percent, from 38.7 percent (779,399 votes) in 1987 to 28.1 percent (570,138) in 1989 , and the Peronist vote rose, though not so steeply, from 23.7 percent (477,617 votes) to 31.1 percent (631,905 votes). The UCEDE gained about 3 percent and polled a substantial 21.8 percent (442,027 votes) to take third place. The results in terms of seats still gave the Radicals the lead, the outcome being UCR 10 seats, PJ (FREJUPO) 8, Alianza de Centro 6, and the CFI (allied with the UCR) 1. It can hardly have helped that the head of the UCR slate in the capital was Dante Caputo, who had no experience of elective office and owed his position as foreign minister (1983–1989) to the fact that he was a personal friend of President Alfonsín.

In 1991 the UCEDE lost two of the three seats they were contesting: one to the Peronists and one, surprisingly, to the Socialist Alfredo Bravo. The Peronists, despite a small drop in their vote to 538,872 (28.1 percent), therefore gained one seat; and the Radicals, who regained almost all of their 1987 vote (750,710 votes, or 39.19 percent), remained the same (Fraga and Malacrida, 1989:63; Fraga, 1992:70). The tendency for fragmentation—even more marked in 1991, when both the Peronists and the UCEDE were split, than in 1987—prolonged the period of Radical dominance and enabled the Radicals to make substantial gains. They pushed their vote in the capital up from 28 to 40 percent, while the Peronists fell from 38 to 28 percent. The Radicals used their success to demand direct elections for the mayoralty (*BAH*, September 11, 1991).

However, Mayor Grosso, one of the founders of Renewal Peronism as well as one of the key members of the wing of the party that included Antonio Cafiero, José Luis Manzano, and the president of the PJ in Mendoza, José Manuel de la Sota (*La Nación*, March 28, 1993), was accused of corruption and removed from office in 1992. He was replaced by Saúl Bauer, who subsequently was accused of insider trading by Minister of the Economy Domingo Cavallo in February 1993.

The Radicals failed to capitalize on this scandal. In the 1993 elections they concentrated on national issues and failed to take full advantage of recent memories of the Carlos Grosso adminis-tration (*BAH,* October 10, 1993). Instead, in 1993 the national Peronist ticket secured a "sensational win" in Buenos Aires, which was reflected at the local level. The PJ won 42.3 percent of the votes cast overall and 126 seats in the Federal Congress. The Radicals (UCR) won 83 seats, a loss of 1 (*BAH,* October 10, 1993). In the capi-tal, where the Peronists won for the first time, the campaign had been led by António Ermán González. He had resigned as defense minister and was replaced by former Foreign Minister Oscar Camilión on April 5.

The Olivos Pact of December 1993, by which the Radicals agreed to accept the revision of the Constitution, split the party. In the elec-tions for the Constituent Assembly in April 1994 the Radicals fur-ther lost ground in the capital, when Fernando de la Rúa, an opponent of the pact, withdrew from the Radical primary. With the Peronist slate led by Legal and Technical Secretary Carlos Corach (appointed minister of the interior in 1995), who lacked charisma, both major parties did badly; and the left-wing Frente Grande, fo-cusing its attack on government corruption, scored a surprise win in the capital, where Jorge Domínguez was elected mayor. In the infighting for the postponed 1995 mayoral elections, Socialist Unity councilman Norberto La Porta claimed that the Peronists were try-ing to impose their candidate (generally believed to be Revenue Secretary Carlos Tacchi) to regain control of City Hall, "which in these past years they have run as if it were a farm with a foreman receiving orders from the Pink House."* (*BAH,* May 28, 1995).

The pattern in Greater Buenos Aires reflects the same trends throughout the country. In the 1983 elections the Radical victory nationally was attended by unexpected defeats for the Peronists in many of their former strongholds in the metropolitan area. Even Avellaneda, the birthplace of the Peronist candidate for governor of the province, Herminio Iglesias, went to the Radicals by a sub-stantial margin, 96,340 to 63,887. The Peronists retained only four

*Casa Rosada, in which are found the offices of the president, in Buenos Aires.

of the nineteen metropolitan municipalities: Berazategui, Florencio Varela, La Matanza, and Lomas de Zamora (*BAH*, November 1, 1983).

The Radicals improved their position in 1985, carrying all but two of the nineteen municipalities, General Sarmiento and Florencio Varela, both of which were carried by the FREJUDEPA, the Peronist faction supporting Provincial Governor Antonio Cafiero. However, this victory was deceptive, since in ten of the seventeen areas which they won, the UCR was outvoted by the combined totals of the Frente Justicialista de la Patria (FREJUDEPA) and the rival FREJULI, supporters of Iglesias (*BAH*, November 4, 1985). The Radicals had lost votes in the middle-class areas, where they expected to do best, and gained in working-class areas, where they did not; but in neither case had they done well enough to outweigh their disappointing performance in the capital itself. "Still, the Radicals' marginal over-all performance in the Federal Capital prevented the party from winning big" (Hatch, 1985).

Two years later the Province of Buenos Aires went to Cafiero (PJ), who gained 2,799,250 votes to 2,363,008 for Juan Manuel Casella (UCR), a plurality of over 400,000. Compared with 1983, the 1987 results represented a swing of some 1 million votes to the Peronists. Although, in part, the outcome was affected by the devastating flooding of that year, it did prove to foreshadow the massive Peronist victory nationwide in 1989. Of the nineteen municipalities of Greater Buenos Aires, all went to the Peronists except Avellaneda, San Isidro, and Vicente López, won by the Radicals, and Tigre, won by the local civic action party, the Union Vecinal (*BAH*, September 9, 1987; Soltys, 1987).

In the presidential election year of 1989 the Peronists carried all but three of the Greater Buenos Aires municipalities. Only Vicente López voted for the UCR, which gained 38.35 percent of the vote to 29.84 percent for the Peronists. Otherwise, only in Avellaneda, Morón, and San Isidro did the Peronists draw less than 50 percent of the votes cast, and in Almirante Brown, Florencio Varela, La Matanza, and Moreno they received more than 60 percent (*BAH*, May 17, 1989).

At the next midterm elections in 1991 the Radical vote collapsed in the Province of Buenos Aires. Former hardliner Aldo Rico had campaigned hard for the governorship—every tree in La Plata had the word "Rico" painted on it in bold white letters. In the event, however, the former junior officer and hero of the Malvinas War received only 9 percent of the vote, while Vice President Eduardo Duhalde (PJ) was an easy victor over the rather uninspiring Radical Juan Carlos Pugliese. Many of these ballots were cast in the shantytowns of Greater Buenos Aires, where his Peronist followers gained 3 seats in the Chamber of Deputies. Michael Soltys commented: "The jetsam of Menem's economic revolution seemed less attracted by socialist ideology than a Perón imitator, a military man open to the poor" (Soltys, 1991).

At the local level, the Peronists retained their traditional strength in the suburbs. The PJ carried seventeen of twenty-one districts in the Buenos Aires area. The Radical mayors of San Isidro (Melchor Posse) and Vicente López (Enrique García) held their seats. But the Radicals lost Avellaneda to the Peronists, led by Baldomero "Chacho" Alvarez, and the Peronists lost Moreno to an independent. The independent Unión Vecinal candidate also retained Tigre (*BAH*, September 10, 1991).

Again, we find local politics an important training ground for future national leaders. Duhalde, governor of the Province of Buenos Aires, owes his later political career to his initial success in municipal electoral politics. In the crucial elections of 1983, in which his party did so unexpectedly badly, he was confirmed as the Peronist mayor of the metropolitan municipality of Lomas de Zamora after four recounts, obtaining a plurality of only 771 votes (101,872 to 101,101) (*BAH*, November 3, 1983).

This margin was all the more striking since, outside the metropolitan area in the Province of Buenos Aires, the Radicals established a commanding position in the 1983 elections. Not only did they carry the provincial capital, La Plata, by a lop-sided majority (159,457 to 95,798), but also neighboring Ensenada and such well-known places as Mar del Plata and Bahía Blanca (*BAH*, November 1, 1983). President Alfonsín's own origins (he still lives in his hometown of Chascomús, an early settlement about 120 kilometers southeast of the capital) was a strong plus for the provincial Radicals. They maintained their position in 1985, when province-wide they polled some 39.34 percent of the votes cast. Votes for the Peronists were divided between 22.78 percent for the FREJUDEPA and 11.39 percent for the hardline FREJULI. However, with only 19 of their seats in the Chamber of Deputies up for reelection, the FREJUDEPA held all of them, while FREJULI won 17 without a contest. The Radicals, with many more to defend, lost 3, the Peronists overall ending up with 56 to 51 for the UCR (*BAH*, November 6, 1985).

In 1987, the year in which the Peronists under Cafiero ousted the Radicals from the provincial governorship, there was violence at Mar del Plata when Mario Russak, who had been mayor from 1978 to 1980 under the military government, went to Radical headquarters to congratulate the party's victorious candidate, Angel Roig. In 1991, Russak, now running under the UCEDE banner, successfully ousted the Radicals from the mayoralty. At the same time they lost La Plata to the Peronists, who had made sweeping gains in the presidential year 1989. Radical mayor Osvaldo Pozzio, who had held office since 1983, was narrowly defeated by Julio Alak (*BAH*, September 10, 1991).

In 1995, despite their massive defeat at the national level, the Radicals retained thirty-seven mayoralties in the province while Frente para un País en Solidaridad (FREPASO) secured none. As Soltys pointed out, a vote for Menem was a vote for stability and continuity—"indeed, not to put too fine a point on it, every man and his dog seems to have been reelected. Thus, some mayors, like Melchor Posse in San Isidro or Manuel Quindimil in Lanús, are well on their way to overtaking the new French President Jacques Chirac's 18-year stint as mayor of Paris" (Soltys, 1995).

Does it appear to make any difference whether local elections are held simultaneously with national elections, or not? The coincidence of local elections with all other levels up to the presidency occurs only every twelve years. In 1995 it happened for the first time since 1983. But other midterm elections do coincide with congressional and gubernatorial ones. So the answer to the question is that it does; who heads the local ticket appears to have a considerable effect both on the turnout and the result. Interpreting the results, however, is complicated. Since 1987, when they obtained 41 percent of the congressional vote, the Peronists' bid for Congress has remained steady at just over 40 percent, with a slight increase to 46 percent in the past presidential election year of 1989. Hence, local variance often owes more to what the other 60 percent does, and in particular to that rather low fraction of it that habitually is cast for the small parties.

One important aspect of the Federal Capital's unique constitutional position is that, unlike the provinces, where they are nominated by the legislature, it indirectly elects its own two (now three) senators. In 1983 there was an easy victory for the Radicals, one of whose candidates, Fernando de la Rúa, had held the same post from 1973 to 1976 after running as vice presidential candidate to Ricardo

Balbín in 1973 (Norgués, 1989:91). However, in 1989, when de la Rúa came up for reelection, the Intransigents (PI), who had gained 6 percent of the vote in 1983, did not contest the elections; and in a three-cornered race there was a marked shift back toward the PJ and to the third party, the UCEDE, and its allies. Hence, though de la Rúa won the support of twenty-two of the fifty-four electors, an alliance between the PJ (19) and the Centrists (11) elected Eduardo Vaca (PJ) to the vacant seat. Vaca, a protégé of Italo Luder, had served as a federal deputy for the capital since 1985. De la Rúa was subsequently elected a federal deputy in 1991 and returned to national public life as the elected leader of the Radical caucus in the Chamber. In 1992 elections for fifty-four electors to choose a replacement to Juan Trilla (UCR) were contested by three alliances and six political parties. The result was a substantial victory for de la Rúa, who thus emerged as the leading Radical candidate for the presidency in 1995, having demonstrated his effectiveness in lead-ing the local ticket (*BAH*, June 28, 1992; Fraga, 1992:79).

De la Rúa's slate was defeated in the Federal Capital on Octo-ber 3, 1993, for two reasons. The Radical ticket was headed not by an experienced politician but by the writer Martha Mercader, and many votes were lost to the left-wing Frente Grande. At the same time the collapse of the UCEDE benefited principally its former allies, the Peronists (*BAH*, October 10, 1993). As a result the na-tional UCR was divided; and having earlier nominated Federico Storani as its presidential candidate, it replaced him in November 1994 with Horacio Massaccesi, governor of Río Negro, who went on to score a poor third place in the presidential elections of May 1995, the party's worst result since 1916. Meanwhile, as noted above, the Frente Grande won a surprise victory in the Federal Capital in April 1994, the first for the left there since 1961 (Soltys, 1994); and in the 1995 presidential elections it was Senator José Bordón of Mendoza who ran against President Menem, with his center-left Front for a Country in Solidarity (FREPASO), allied with the Frente Grande, picking up support both from the Radicals and dissident Peronists to gain second place.

The election for a third senator for the capital, held in October 1995, had additional interest as a pointer to the possible result of the elections for mayor, to take place under new constitutional ar-rangements in 1996. The victor was Deputy Graciela Fernández Meijide of the center-left FREPASO-Frente Grande alliance, which had carried the city in three preceding elections, and she obtained over 45 percent of the votes cast to outpoll the two major parties by a margin of more than 100,000 votes (*BAH*, October 15, 1995).

The role and influence of minority candidates locally can be considerable, therefore, in both national and local elections. The special significance of the UCEDE in the Federal Capital has already been noted. As is usual with minor parties, personalities have been very important. The UCEDE was, after all, very much the personal creation of its founder, Alvaro Alsogaray, and contributes two of the few women deputies in the Chamber: María Julia Alsogaray (elected in 1985), subsequently secretary and minister for the environment in President Menem's government in 1995; and Adelina Dalesio de Viola (elected in 1989). Although the significance of the capital is such that the Deliberative Council is seldom left to get on with its work uninterrupted, the rise of the latter demonstrates that it can be and is a route to political preferment. Sra. Dalesio de Viola came to public attention when she served as a councillor from 1985 to 1987 (Nogués, 1989:88–89), and she has since emerged as one of the two leaders of UCEDE as it has fragmented following the retirement of its founder.

In 1993 the smaller parties' successes came mainly in the metropolitan region. Aldo Rico's right-wing Movement for Dignity and Independence or Movimiento para Dignidad e Independencia (MODIN) won 7, a gain of 3; the liberal UCEDE only 5, a loss of 4; 5 went to Socialist Unity (US) and 2 to provincial parties. The decline of the UCEDE has clearly been to the benefit of the ruling Peronists. In fact, the powerful attraction of the two main parties is the principal factor preventing such minority parties from attaining national significance. Although MODIN nominated Rico for the presidency in 1995, it gained only 1.8 percent of the national vote, well short of the 9 percent it had been able to achieve at the provincial level.

It would be fair to say, however, that Argentina does have a clear pattern of regional politics in which minority parties have been able to some extent to affect national politics without attaining either electoral appeal or strength countrywide. Elections in provincial cities show significant regional variations. For instance, during the 1980s, Rosario, the capital of the Province of Santa Fe, temporarily lost its status as Argentina's second city to Córdoba, but it has since regained it and is much larger than the city from which the province takes its name. The city's importance as a railway junction make it a key element in the Peronist coalition established after 1946, but the province voted Radical in 1958, 1961, and 1963 before switching to the Peronists in the two elections of 1973 (Fraga, 1992:97). After the restoration of democracy in 1983, the Province of Santa Fe had two successive Peronist administrations in 1983 and 1987 and elected a third under former racing car driver Carlos Reutemann in the 1991 elections.

Rosario, however, elected as mayor a Radical, Horacio Usandizaga, who resigned dramatically in 1989 on learning of the news of the national Peronist victory (*BAH*, May 16, 1989). Usandizaga, who was succeeded as interim mayor by Council chair Carlos Martínez, pending a special election, was unsuccessful as a candidate for governor in 1991 when he failed to gain the support of a substantial fraction of his own party (*BAH*, May 17, 1989; September 15, 1991). Meanwhile, although the PJ won thirty-two of the forty-eight municipalities in the province in the elections of 1991, Rosario itself was won by a pro-Menem Socialist candidate, Héctor Cavallero. In 1995 the September 3 poll in the Province of Santa Fe was marred by conflicting claims and a suspicious computer "failure." After thirty-seven days, victory in the gubernatorial race went to the Peronist mayor of Santa Fe, Jorge Obeid. Although he obtained only 325,037 votes to 464,270 for Usandizaga, the Radical former mayor of Rosario, under the province's Uruguayan-style *lema* system, or double simultaneous vote, was elected because the aggregated total for all Peronist candidates was higher than that for the Radical-Progressive Democrat-Popular Socialist coalition. Moreover, the Peronist mayor of Rosario, Cavallero, failed to poll as many votes as had been expected in his much larger home town (*BAH*, October 15, 1995).

Córdoba's vote in 1991 is typical. It is a Radical province. Governor Eduardo Angeloz had a majority of 68,000 in 1987. The spectacular increase in this majority to 220,000 in 1991 no doubt was largely, if not entirely, the result of the governor's national prominence as a would-be presidential candidate. In 1991 the Radicals held 140 of the 249 municipalities, to 89 for the PJ, 5 for the UCEDE and 15 for local groups.

The 1991 election was marred when two days beforehand, on his way home from a Radical rally, former provincial senator Regino Maders was shot and killed by an unknown assailant (*BAH*, September 8, 1991). The mystery surrounding his death has never been cleared up, although it was reported (and widely believed) that he was killed as a result of his inquiries into corruption in the province.

In 1993 the Radicals held Córdoba, despite all expectations. There, the PJ campaign had been led by Minister of the Economy Cavallo, who had received plaudits for the successful stabilization of the economy. The party's defeat in a key province was a severe blow to his electoral prestige and effectively ended his chances of succeeding President Menem (*BAH*, October 10, 1993). However, the province also offers one of the most striking examples of the value of municipal experience to a political career. Ramón Mestre, mayor of the city of Córdoba for the eight years from 1983 to 1991, was elected in May 1995 with over 58 percent of the vote to succeed Angeloz as governor of the province. When he did so five months early, in July 1995, it was because the province was so insolvent that almost daily disturbances in the streets had forced Angeloz to resign after nearly twelve years, putting an end to his hopes of succeeding Alfonsín as president of the Radical Party. Sensibly, Mestre lost no time in accepting the federal revenue-sharing program that Angeloz had spurned (*BAH*, July 9 and 16, 1995).

In 1991, Peronists swept the Province of Mendoza, which had been predicted as a close contest. They increased their majority from 67,000 to 150,000. The outgoing governor, José Bordón, emerged as the leading Peronist candidate to challenge former Vice President Duhalde for the party's nomination for president in 1995. The PJ held fourteen of the eighteen municipalities in the province. However, the Radicals kept control of the provincial capital, the city of Mendoza, with Víctor Fayad as mayor. He proved to be highly successful and was chosen by his party as gubernatorial candidate in 1995, only to go down to defeat by 37,000 votes when he received the endorsement of Senator Bordón, now the FREPASO candidate.

Argentina's smallest province, Tucumán, has a violent history. Indeed, some of the worst atrocities of the so-called *proceso* took place there. In the 1983 elections four of the five people wounded in election violence were attacked in Tucumán; in 1987 two Peronists activists were killed there on the eve of the vote. The fact that the Radical candidate for governor of Tucumán in 1987 was Ruben Chabaia, former mayor of the provincial capital, San Miguel de Tucumán, was generally credited with giving the Radicals as many as twenty-two of the state's sixty electoral votes. The PJ, which was as divided as it had been elsewhere, took only seventeen electoral votes. As a result, minor parties had the opportunity significantly to affect the outcome. Eleven electoral votes went to the supporters of former military governor Gen. Antonio Bussi and his right-wing Fuerza Republicana. However, his challenge from the right failed, because ten went to former Provincial Minister of the Economy Osvaldo Cirnigliano, candidate of the Provincial Action Party, a Peronist splinter group (*BAH*, September 13, 1987). Consequently, the vote in the electoral college went to the Peronists.

In the 1991 gubernatorial election the reunited Peronists more than regained their 1983 vote to elect as governor a former popular singer, Ramón "Palito" Ortega, with Bussi's Fuerza Republicana coming in a very close second. But the picture at the municipal level was rather different. In the 1989 elections the PJ won twelve of the province's eighteen municipalities, the UCR five and the Fuerza Republicana one. In 1991 the PJ and the UCR both lost one to the Fuerza Republicana, which was not nearly as well represented in terms of seats as in terms of votes.

In the Constituent elections of April 1994, however, the dominant theme was distrust of the Olivos Pact and of both major parties, and Bussi's Fuerza Republicana carried Tucumán. Local parties also scored significant victories in other provinces for a variety of reasons: the left-wing Frente Grande carried Neuquén as well as the Federal Capital; in Jujuy where, as in neighboring Salta, there had been riots in 1993, victory went to María Cristina Guzmán's Jujuy Popular Movement; and the Province of Corrientes went to the locally based Autonomist-Liberal Pact (Soltys, 1994). In July 1995, Bussi was finally successful in Tucumán with some 46 percent of the votes cast, despite the fact that in this case federal funds were forthcoming early to pay the May provincial salaries.

At the first elections in 1991 in Argentina's newest and most southerly province, Tierra del Fuego, José Estabillo of the Movimiento Popular Fueguino (MOPOF) seized the governorship by a margin of only two hundred votes. In September 1995, however, against the national trend, he won easily against a challenge from the Peronist mayor of Ushuaia, Mario Daniele (*BAH*, October 1, 1995).

These circumstances were exceptional. In fact, two main conclusions about provincial municipal politics may be drawn. First, despite the size of the country, the national two-party contest is replicated throughout the Republic. Even in 1994, seventeen of the twenty-three provinces chose the same party as the winner of the

1991 gubernatorial elections. And second, the minority parties and other local interest groups are, where possible, co-opted by the national parties, usually by way of the complex electoral alliances that are constructed locally.

In the provinces, as in the metropolitan area, moreover, we find that key urban areas do perform a number of important roles in the Argentine political system although the provinces themselves form the essential link within the pattern of urban-national politics. Both municipal and provincial elections offer the opportunity for new political figures and for members of the large number of very small parties to make their mark and to attract future support. In some cases neighborhood organizations successfully contest control of municipalities. But the national parties devote a considerable amount of time and money contesting local campaigns as part of their national drive for power, and the system of electoral alliances enables them to co-opt significant fractions of support.

Formal-Informal Politics

A predictable result of national two-party politics is that the effect of "informal politics"—new social movements, community organizations, ecological groups, and other grass-roots politically relevant organizations—is relatively limited. The tradition of such movements in Argentina is weak. At the same time, the formal parties are eager to woo such movements and lose no time in adjusting their appeal, either by candidate selection or by the choice of platform, in order to co-opt them. The 1991 decision to require each party to nominate women for 30 percent of all positions being contested has as yet produced few high-profile candidates, but it has undoubtedly increased female representation. The Peronists have traditionally worked hard to woo in-migrants to the metropolitan areas, and their success is confirmed by the fact that in 1995 only Greater Buenos Aires and Bahía Blanca gave President Menem more than 45 percent of the vote.

Attempts of the movements themselves to become more electorally relevant have not proved particularly successful. In the midterm elections of 1993, ninety mayoralties and 2,623 Council seats were contested. In the absence of either a presidential or a gubernatorial contest, interest tended in the main to be low. Democracy has not restored to the municipalities the powers that they have lost over decades of military rule.

A major new issue with electoral significance is the effect of deregulation and privatization. A continuing irritation in the Greater Buenos Aires region has been the government's wish to impose highway tolls. Not only did high charges create ill will, but the theoretical advantage of tolls as a source of income for a better maintained network of roads was being lost, and the impact of toll evaders using previously quiet residential neighborhoods as alternative routes to escape payment caused strong resentment (*BAH*, February 7, 1993). Privatization, too, has failed to deliver on its early promises. When 51 percent of the capital's electricity utility, SEGBA, was sold in August 1992 to two separate consortia trading as two companies, EDENOR and EDESUR (*International Herald Tribune*, September 1, 1992), it was widely thought that the service could hardly be worse. By 1994 the failure of these two companies to maintain uninterrupted service led to heavy fines for the privatized utilities, and it may be significant that in securing reelection the Peronists did not do as well as neoliberal parties in neighboring Brazil and Peru.

The role of Argentina's vigorous and critical press and, to a lesser extent, its recently privatized television service in airing these and other grievances is significant. On June 17, 1995, for example, *Diario Popular* published an article claiming that one in six of the inhabitants of the capital are "chronically poor" and that the shantytowns erected under throughways or on vacant lots, so characteristic of the military period, were again on the increase (*BAH*, June 18, 1995). However, the limited powers of municipal governments should not be forgotten. Local authorities lack economic resources, because local taxation is so easy for residents to evade. The rich northern suburb of San Isidro recently cleared a substantial shantytown after building public housing into which to relocate the population, but few other municipalities can afford such action.

Electoral Behavior since 1995

The municipal elections of 1995 took place under the shadow of widespread provincial unrest. Austerity measures had led to strikes, culminating in a one-day general strike on April 21. However, the strike failed to bring the country to a halt and in the municipal elections held on May 14, the Peronists held on surprisingly well in an election dominated by the national contest. Opinions differed on the reasons why. The people, in the words of the electoral analyst Rosendo Fraga, "voted for continuity and stability." The political scientist Roberto Cortes Conde, however, regarded their action in a more positive light: "People are evaluating an administration which, despite its pros and cons, has brought them significant progress" (*BAH*, May 16, 1995).

In the province of Buenos Aires, controlled by Peronist Governor Eduardo Duhalde, the Peronists won ninety-one of the one hundred thirty-four municipalities. Despite complaints by the Radicals at alleged electoral irregularities in Florencio Varela, Lanús, and Lomas de Zamora, the UCR won thirty-seven municipalities— a loss of four. For the first time since 1983, they lost control of Chascomús, the hometown of former President Alfonsín, but gained Mar del Plata, a major prize. The Radical mayor of San Isidro, Melcho Posse, was critical of his party's leadership and called for Alfonsín's resignation. In the Federal Capital, FREPASO emerged as the main contender to the Peronists, winning five places in the Chamber of Deputies to three each for the Peronists and Radicals. Nationally, the only good news for the Radicals was the reelection of Ramón Mestre in Córdoba (*BAH*, May 16, 1995). However the news for the PJ was not all good, the rural-urban divide being particularly evident. Among the cities, only Greater Buenos Aires (outside the Federal Capital) and Bahia Blanca voted Peronist.

However, in May the fiscal crisis in the provinces had yet to have its full impact, as funds dried up and staff was laid off. Ironically, the Radicals were the main victims. In Córdoba, the largest province controlled by the opposition, rioting broke out on June 22–23, and over one hundred people were injured, forcing at the beginning of July the premature resignation of Governor Eduardo Angeloz. Similar disturbances in Río Negro between September 22 and 25 forced the resignation of Governor Horacio Massaccesi. Discontent at the high level of unemployment was reflected on October 8 in the easy victory of Graciela Fernández Mejide, in the contest for the new third Senate seat for the Federal Capital, thus confirming FREPASO as the main rivals nationally to the ruling Peronists if not yet a serious threat locally to the previously dominant Radicals.

This rivalry was soon to be put to the test in the first direct election for the mayoralty of Buenos Aires, a post previously held by presidential appointment. In the election on June 30, 1996, the PJ candidate came in a poor third to both the Radicals and

FREPASO, the results being: Fernando de la Rua (UCR) 731,863 (39.9 percent), Norberto de la Porta (FREPASO) 486,919 (26.5 percent), Jorge Domínguez (PJ) 341,594 (18.6 percent). The dissident Gustavo Béliz, a former Peronist cabinet minister, who had refused to join FREPASO and ran under the banner of New Leadership (ND), gained a very respectable 149,426 votes (13.1 percent) (BAH, July 2, 1996).

One year later, in May 1997, even the pro-Peronist Clarín was gloomy about the prospects for the elections scheduled for October. Votes for the PJ had been in "free fall" since 1993 (Clarín, May 13, 1997). In the presidential opinion polls, Carlos "Chacho" Alvarez of FREPASO was leading all other candidates with 26 percent—six points ahead of the Radical Rodolfo Terragno and nineteen points ahead of any Peronist. De la Rua, the new mayor of Buenos Aires has given the Radicals a plausible vote-getting candidate for 1999, as well as a platform for his views. However, he will remain dependent on state funding and is likely to find that President Menem is not very cooperative in providing it.

Conclusion

In Argentina, as elsewhere, national opinion exercises a major influence on the outcome of municipal elections. Moreover, despite the country's two-party system, or perhaps because of it, local and regional alliances are not only significant at the municipal level but also have the potential to influence provincial and thus national politics. With the consolidation of democracy, municipal government has been increasingly important as a recruiting ground for higher office. However, the powers and resources of municipal government remain weak and inadequate. In almost all respects, the national capital remains an exception, though one of unique importance.

References

Botana, Natalio R., et al. 1985. *La Argentina electoral*. Buenos Aires: Editorial Sudamericana.
Buenos Aires, Municipalidad de la Ciudad de. 1980. *Estadistica 1980*. Buenos Aires: City of Buenos Aires.
Cano, Guillermo. 1936. *Soberania de los estados (provincias) miembros de una federacion*. Mendoza.

Di Tella, Torcuato S. 1984. "The October 1983 Elections in Argentina." *Government and Opposition* 19, pt. 2 (Spring), 188–92.

Díaz de Landa, Martha, and M. Consuelo Parmigiani de Barbará. 1994. *Organized Business and the Community Power Structure in an Argentinian City: From Authoritarian to Democratic Regimes*. Paper presented at Sixteenth World Congress of the International Political Science Association, Berlin, August 21–15.

Fraga, Rosendo. 1992. *Argentina en las urnas, 1931–1991*. Buenos Aires: Editorial Centro de Estudios Unión para la Nueva Mayoría.

———, and Gabriela Malacrida. 1989. *Argentina en las urnas, 1916–1989*. Buenos Aires: Editorial Centro de Estudios Unión para la Nueva Mayoría.

Hatch, George. 1985. "A Lucid Message from the Electorate." *Buenos Aires Herald*, November 10.

Mouchet, Carlos. 1969. *Buenos Aires: Organización y planificación del area metropolitana*. Buenos Aires: Municipalidad de la Ciudad de Buenos Aires. Paper presented at Fifth Congreso Hispano-Luso Americano-Filipino de Municipios, Santiago, Chile, November.

Munck, Ronaldo. 1992. "The Democratic Decade: Argentina since Malvinas." *Bulletin of Latin American Research* 11, no. 2 (May):205–16.

Neilson, James. 1983. "Polls Result Puts Peronism's Future in Doubt." *Buenos Aires Herald*, November 6.

N'haux, Enrique. 1993. *Menem-Cavallo: El poder mediterráneo*. Buenos Aires: Ediciones Corregidor.

Nogués, Germinal, ed. 1989. *Diccionario biográfico de políticos argentinos*. Buenos Aires: Editorial Planeta.

Reboratti, Carlos. 1987. *Nueva capital, viejos mitos: La geopolítica criolla o la razón extraviada*. Buenos Aires: Sudamericana-Planeta.

Schoultz, Lars. 1983. *The Populist Challenge: Argentine Electoral Behavior in the Postwar Era*. Chapel Hill: University of North Carolina Press.

Smith, William C. 1989. *Authoritarianism and the Crisis of the Argentine Political Economy*. Stanford, CA: Stanford University Press.

Soltys, Michael. 1987. "How Lame-Duck a President is Alfonsín?" *Buenos Aires Herald*, September 13.

———. 1991. "Peronism Is Dead, Menemism Born?" *Buenos Aires Herald*, September 15.

———. 1993. "More of the Same in Every Sense." *Buenos Aires Herald*, October 10.

———. 1994. "Menemstroika Meets Its Glasnost." *Buenos Aires Herald*, April 17.

———. 1995. "Menem between Perón and Thatcher." *Buenos Aires Herald*, May 21.

2

Municipal Elections in Bolivia

Eduardo A. Gamarra

Open and competitive municipal elections have been held in Bolivia since 1987, nearly five years after the military was forced to
relinquish power.[1] Local electoral politics has become essential to
understanding the national political scene and in many ways is giving new meaning to the old American adage that all politics is local. Municipal elections filled crucial roles such as the recruitment
of new leaders. Since 1987 they have served as a launching pad for
several nontraditional political leaders. Beginning in 1985, the
mayor's office of the city of La Paz has been occupied by a radio
station owner, a prominent businessman with a Scottish last name,
a former member of the Communist Party, and the wife of the radio station owner.

This study focuses on four elections (December 1987, December 1989, December 1991, and December 1993) held in La Paz, the
capital and largest urban center. With about one million inhabitants, La Paz has been the primary witness to the battles between
the military governments of the 1970s and early 1980s and to the
forces of civil society that eventually succeeded in establishing a
democratic system. When Bolivia fell from a grave economic crisis
to a complete collapse of its economy in 1985, the most significant
political battles also converged on La Paz. For better or worse, the
city has been a true barometer of politics in the country.

Municipal elections in Bolivia were last held in 1943. Owing to
the fact that all kinds of voter restrictions existed at the time, such
elections were not open or competitive until 1987. Between 1952
and 1964 the ruling Movimiento Nacionalista Revolucionario
(MNR) routinely appointed mayors of major cities and towns as a
way to reward loyal followers and to keep control over dissent.

This practice was continued between 1964 and 1982 by both military and civilian rulers alike. Under the military, prominent civilians drawn mainly from the private sector were appointed to the mayor's office.

Although no reliable data exist to certify this claim, individuals who served as mayors of La Paz during the military dictatorships frequently enjoyed a great deal of popularity. Mario Mercado and Armando Escobar, for example, were able to mobilize widespread popular support.[2] Their attempts to parlay this popularity into a political base were nipped in the bud by the military authorities. The popular appeal of these two men was based largely on the perception that they were the ones who got things done. Whether a bridge had to be constructed, a road paved, or a new sewer installed, public works programs have been the most important mechanism for building political support. Mayors elected since 1987 learned a lot from their de facto predecessors. In any given electoral period, candidates attempted to outdo each other with promises of specific improvements in infrastructure or public works.

Beginning in 1985, elections have been held every two years, usually on the first Sunday in December. The election for mayor, however, is not direct. The electorate votes only for a municipal council that, in turn, elects a mayor through a simple majority.[3] Owing to the multiparty system that prevails at the local level, electing a mayor has been a complex procedure. Council members are elected under proportional representation laws that ensure minority representation in the municipal council. But this system means that it has been extremely difficult to secure even a simple majority. In many ways, the election of a mayor in the major cities has reproduced the difficulties that the national system faces every four years to elect a president. It is not only difficult to become mayor, but it is also difficult to govern the city of La Paz without stable political pacts. Municipal councils have become miniparliaments where political alliances are crucial to running the city. In the past seven years, local municipal councils have tested electoral and governing pacts and alliances established by political parties. For the moment, at least, pacts formed by political parties to govern Bolivia, such as the Pacto por la Democracia (1985–1989) and the Acuerdo Patriótico (1989–1993), were crucial to the stability of municipal governments as well.

Political Parties and Municipal Elections

To understand municipal elections in the city of La Paz, an overview of the principal parties is warranted.[4] The survey presented below is not comprehensive and describes only the most relevant ones that have contested elections in La Paz since 1987. A few general characteristics are noteworthy. First, political parties at the local level depend entirely on the national party organization and are only superficially autonomous. Second, candidates for municipal government are usually selected by national party leaders behind closed doors. There are no conventions or internal elections to select candidates for these posts. In recent years, political parties recruited individuals from regional civic organizations to run for mayor and the municipal council. The council has become an important place for the recruitment of future national leaders.

The Left

Owing mainly to its disastrous experience in office between 1982 and 1985, the left in Bolivia suffered a tremendous defeat (Gamarra and Malloy, 1995). The end of the Cold War delivered a near fatal blow to the few parties that still ventured to call themselves Marxist. Faced with this uncertainty, parties on the left have generally been forced to run together in weak alliances or to shift to the right and join with more traditional parties. Both strategies have been used at the municipal level. The most significant alliance on the left was the Frente del Pueblo Unido (FPU), formed to contest the 1985 national elections. It included the Bolivian Communist Party (PCB) and the MIR-Bolivia Libre, among others. After contesting the 1985 elections, the FPU virtually disintegrated and had all but disappeared by 1987.

The FPU gave way, however, to the emergence of a so-called Alianza Patriótica as the principal leftist political front in 1987. The Alianza Patriótica achieved some success in the latter part of the 1980s in attracting leftist parties to form a united front to contest municipal elections. In 1987 it managed to bring together the MBL (the former MIR-BL, analyzed below), the PCB, dissidents of the Socialist Party (PS-1), and dissidents of the MIR (MIR-Masas). As has been the case with all leftist fronts, the Alianza did not last long owing not only to internal disputes but also to the emergence of neopopulist parties. In contrast, the Izquierda Unida (IU), an even smaller alliance founded in 1985, made a significant comeback in the early 1990s when it filled the vacuum left by the Alianza Patriótica. Nevertheless, the IU's significance in municipal and national elections was minimal.

Movimiento Nacionalista Revolucionario (MNR)

Founded in 1941 by Víctor Paz Estenssoro, Hernán Siles Zuazo, and Walter Guevara Arze, among others, the MNR is far and away the most important political party in twentieth-century Bolivia. After leading the April 9, 1952, revolution, the MNR ruled until 1964, when it was overthrown by a military junta. Throughout its history it has been afflicted by internal disputes and factionalism, which in large measure accounted for its overthrow in 1964 by military officers allied with certain segments of the party.

For the next twenty years the party suffered even more serious splits. When Bolivia lurched toward democracy in the late 1970s, at least thirty MNR factions were identifiable. Only two were significant: the Historic MNR (MNRH), led by Paz Estenssoro, and the MNR of the Left (MNRI), headed by Siles Zuazo. Between 1982 and 1985, Siles's MNRI governed the country in a weak coalition called the Unidad Democrática y Popular (UDP) with the Bolivian Communist Party, the Movement of the Revolutionary Left (MIR), and the Christian Democratic Party (PDC). The UDP experience proved catastrophic for the MNRI, which has all but disappeared as a result. In contrast, Paz Estenssoro was able not only to control his faction but also to exert enough power to recast his party in a significantly different light. Factional disputes arose as he launched the New Economic Policy (NPE) in 1985 and joined General Hugo Banzer Suárez's Acción Democrática y Nacionalista (ADN) in the Pacto por la Democracia. Old party stalwarts who resisted the MNR's new image formed a variety of so-called Comités de Defensa del MNR. These groups lacked any real power but did generate a significant degree of internal turmoil.

The naming of Gonzalo Sánchez de Lozada, a prominent businessman credited with the design and implementation of the 1985 NPE, as the party's candidate added to the turmoil. After the 1989 elections, Sánchez de Lozada's failure to secure the presidency after winning the elections prompted the Comités de Defensa del MNR to challenge his grip on the party. These groups remained active but failed in their bid to form a new "true" MNR. In 1993 the MNR appeared to have controlled these dissident groups and rallied under the successful presidential bid of Sánchez de Lozada. Although the party has historically been a La Paz institution, success in open, competitive municipal elections in the capital city has eluded it.

Acción Democrática y Nacionalista (ADN)

ADN was founded in March 1979 by General Banzer in an attempt to create a civilian political group that could defend him and his collaborators against charges of corruption and human rights violations during his seven-year term (1971–1978) as president of Bolivia. The party performed extremely well in national elections— placing third in 1980, winning in 1985, and placing second in 1989 and again in 1993. To its members, ADN and Banzer have been instrumental in the consolidation of democracy in Bolivia. In 1985 the general supported the MNR government by entering into a "pact for democracy," and then in 1989 it entered into a coalition dubbed the Acuerdo Patriótico (AP) with the MIR to govern the country. The party, however, has suffered a series of internal splits that may lead to its demise in the mid-1990s. Its first serious rift came after members of the party who served the García Meza government were expelled to demonstrate that ADN had had no linkages to that controversial period. Several of these members were welcomed back into the party in 1985 and now hold several prominent posts within it.

In 1985, Eudoro Galindo, a former vice presidential candidate and ADN founder, left the party to establish the Partido Democrático Boliviano (PDB) when ADN joined the MNR in the Pacto por la Democracia. Paradoxically, the PDB then joined the MNR in 1989 for the elections. More recently, splits in the party have taken on a decidedly regional and generational tone. Ronald Maclean, a young technocrat, former mayor of La Paz, and former minister of foreign affairs, was generally perceived as the leader of the modernizing generation. His faction was confronted by Guillermo Fortún and others in the party linked to the traditional political class. In 1993, Maclean lost the critical internal struggle within ADN and was pushed aside despite having served three highly successful terms as mayor of the capital. ADN's younger generation turned to Fernando Kieffer, a veteran member of the

National Congress, to direct their battles with the Old Guard. In mid-1991 a new group led by Jorge Landívar, a former president of the Santa Cruz Civic Committee, appeared to assert some influence within the party.

These three groups fought for ADN's leadership, especially after Banzer resigned as party chief in November 1993. Internal disputes continued throughout 1994 and 1995 and threatened to destroy the party. Only Banzer's return to ADN in 1995, and his apparent candidacy in 1997, ended the succession controversy. In sum, this dispute demonstrated that ADN has not overcome its caudillo and is not prepared to deliver a successor to the old general.

Movimiento de Izquierda Revolucionaria (MIR)

Founded in 1971 by Jaime Paz Zamora, Oscar Eid Franco, and Antonio Araníbar, among others, the MIR achieved political prominence in the early 1980s when it entered into the UDP that governed Bolivia between 1982 and 1985. This experience resulted in serious internal turmoil. In 1983, Walter Delgadillo split from the main party and founded the MIR-Masas, a labor faction. In 1985 a major split occurred in the party: Araníbar left it and founded the MIR-Bolivia Libre. Owing to a decision by the National Electoral Court, the MIR-BL became the Movimiento Bolivia Libre (MBL) in 1986. Araníbar initially stuck to the orthodox Marxism of the original MIR but by the early 1990s moved the MBL to a more fashionable social democratic stance. In 1993 the MBL joined the MNR in a so-called Pact for Change and helped the government policies that it once fought.

Meanwhile, Paz Zamora's MIR became the MIR-Nueva Mayoría when middle-class professionals and factions of the MNR and the left joined the party to contest the 1989 general election. The unexpected election of Paz Zamora to the presidency in August 1989 opened a rift as members of the Nueva Mayoría left the party when the MIR entered into a ruling alliance with General Banzer's ADN. By the early 1990s the MIR also faced generational splits. In 1991 a group of young members demanded a greater role in the party. This group, derogatorily referred to as the *abogansters*, exerted enough pressure to secure governmental posts. Other splits occurred during the 1993 general elections, whose outcome raised serious doubts about the future of the MIR. Out of office, Paz Zamora initially announced the founding of another party to separate himself from accusations of widespread corruption by the MIR. His attempt to groom himself for the 1997 general elections was suddenly aborted when he and several top members of the MIR were formally accused by the Fuerza Especial de Lucha contra el Narcotráfico (FELCN) of linkages with narcotraffickers. These charges have all but ended the MIR's chances of an electoral comeback. However, in Bolivia the possibility of a return by even the most discredited politicians should never be dismissed.

Neopopulist Parties: CONDEPA and UCS

Public perception regarding the nature of the three principal parties has been key to the emergence of two leader-dominated and populist-style parties, Conciencia de Patria (Conscience of the Fatherland, or CONDEPA) led by Carlos Palenque, and Unidad Cívica Solidaridad (Solidarity Civic Union, or UCS), headed by Max Fernández. As in other Latin American countries, these neopopulist parties emerged outside of the political mainstream and carried out an antipolitics message. Because they are led by charismatic strongmen, both are also reminiscent of old-style Bolivian caudillismo. It is probably a mistake, however, to explain their emergence solely as a result of the inability of the traditional parties to channel the interests of marginal sectors of the population. The reasons are more complex and varied.[5]

One possible explanation is suggested by Guillermo O'Donnell's notion of "delegative democracy" (O'Donnell, 1990). Owing to the state's incapacity to enforce the law, the popular classes become disenchanted with the ineffectiveness of democratic institutions to resolve their problems. This disenchantment translates into political withdrawal and mass apathy. As these groups become more marginal, they "delegate" their grievances to new leaders whose commitment to representative democracy is suspect. Through traditional mechanisms such as clientelism and appeals to populism, these new leaders convey to the citizenry that participation within the framework of representative democracy is obsolete and undesirable. Moreover, they offer a more direct and unmediated channel of representation as well as new hope for the displaced sectors. O'Donnell's description, derived mainly from a consideration of Peru, Brazil, and Argentina, is worth pondering in examining Bolivia's emerging neopopulist leaders.

In Bolivia, region, class, ethnicity, and even old-fashioned per-
ceptions of the charisma of the leaders are all significant factors
influencing voter identification with CONDEPA and UCS.
CONDEPA has been successful mainly due to the appeal of its
founder, a popular radio and television announcer revered by the
Aymara-speaking working classes of La Paz. Palenque's nickname,
El Compadre, revealed that, although this was a new party, the basic
logic of the country's party system was still patrimonial. CONDEPA
made huge inroads in the lower-class sectors of the capital city. In
many ways these sectors have "delegated" their demands to
Palenque. Through his Radio y Televisión Popular (RTP), for example, he offers a unique alternative to Bolivia's often discrimina-
tory administration of justice. Palenque's RTP programs, especially
one called "La Tribuna del Pueblo," provide a quick "resolution"
to the myriad social problems afflicting recent non-Spanish-speak-
ing arrivals to the capital, domestic servants, and the vast population of the informal sector that encircles La Paz. Palenquismo (as
Jorge Lazarte has called it) provides the only linkage these groups
have to the system (Lazarte, 1989).

Palenquismo appeared on the scene as a regional phenomenon
in 1988. Since the 1989 elections, Palenque attempted to develop a
broader cross-regional, cross-class, and interethnic base of support.
After demonstrating his party's ability to win municipal elections
(in 1989, for example, CONDEPA defeated all three major parties
in La Paz and again won the mayor's race in December 1991),
Palenque moved decisively on several fronts. First, he expanded
his base of local La Paz support by recruiting prominent defectors
from the left such as Julio Mantilla, who went on to become mayor
of the city (1991–1993). He also attracted many members of the old
nationalist right. The most significant support was drummed up
through the airwaves of RTP. Finally, to contest the national elections, he courted prominent members of Santa Cruz's business sector. In 1993, to prevent another humiliating experience with rejection
from the more traditional Santa Cruz elite, Palenque signed Ivo
Kuljis, a young and prominent businessman, as his vice presidential candidate. While Palenque lost the general election, his showing nationally was impressive. More important, CONDEPA easily
won La Paz again. In any event, the nature of Palenquismo has
evolved considerably from its beginnings in 1988.

Another significant player was Fernández and his UCS. In a
short period he transformed UCS into a mechanism to deliver prom-

ises to vast and remote sectors of Bolivia. The slogan "Max obras" became more than a simple political statement. Throughout the country, Fernández built hospitals and schools, paved roads, and handed out sporting equipment and generators.

Fernández first appeared as a public figure in 1986 when he purchased enough stock to control the Cervecería Boliviana Nacional (CBN), the country's largest brewery. A Cochabamba native of humble background, he claimed that his business skills enabled him to establish a monopoly over the commercialization and distribution of beer in Santa Cruz, which he then used to control the entire company.[6] This control was a highly profitable venture. During the hyperinflationary period of 1984–85, for example, rumor had it that the government could only pay its salaries after the CBN paid its taxes.

Much speculation surrounded the origins of Fernández's fortune. Until recently, the U.S. embassy in La Paz was obsessed with his alleged ties to the narcotics traffic. Little evidence to indict him was available; however, unsubstantiated charges were often made that Fernández is tied to the so-called Cartel de los Techos, Bolivia's prominent drug cartel based in Santa Ana de Yacuma. As his political base grew, embassy officials considered it imprudent to go after him, primarily because of the increase in his popular support and his connection since 1993 to the MNR.[7]

Because Fernández's UCS was not allowed to run in the 1989 elections, it held no seats in the National Congress until 1993.[8] The government and the opposition parties used this lack of representation as an excuse to exclude him and his party from all major and minor negotiations. This exclusion ended abruptly in December 1991 when UCS showed its strength on a national scale. Since then, UCS has been a part of every attempt to negotiate reforms to the electoral laws.

Fernández ran UCS in an authoritarian manner and, in classic populist style, controlled his political party by his capacity to deliver. His wealth enabled him to establish a wide network based on old-style vertical and hierarchical patron-clientelism. Fernández named the party leadership; no assemblies or elections were held to elect the governing body of UCS. Most striking, however, was his rather unappealing personality. He lacked charisma, spoke Spanish poorly, and was unable to articulate any party platform. To overcome these shortcomings, Fernández hired prominent members of the political class to present UCS campaign promises.

As Lazarte argues, however, Fernández resembles Sánchez de Lozada in many ways. Both are entrepreneurs, pragmatic, and men of action rather than words (Lazarte, 1991). Because both appeal to the same social sectors (the lower middle classes and the urban proletariat), Fernández's humble social origins may give him an electoral advantage. Most appealing to the working classes was Fernández's innovative employee relations at the CBN. Workers in the brewery enjoy high wages and other benefits not available to blue-collar employees elsewhere in the private or public sector. On one occasion when the government decreed a wage increase, Fernández doubled salaries. Periodically, newspapers carry declarations from grateful workers who defend him from his political opponents.[9]

Fernández has attracted a number of experienced political hacks who have become his advisers and candidates for office. Over the course of the past two years, dozens of dissidents from major and minor parties have flocked to UCS.[10] All of the traditional parties— ADN, MIR, and the MNR— courted Fernández at one time or another. Contacts with the MNR culminated in July 1993 with the signing of a "governability pact" that exchanged congressional support for the MNR for a prominent cabinet post. Since 1993 the relationship between the MNR and UCS has been extremely rocky. Fernández threatened to quit the ruling coalition several times (he effectively abandoned the pact between December 1994 and June 1995) but always returned.

Tragedy struck UCS in November 1995, however, when Fernández was killed in an airplane accident during the middle of a campaign trip to a small *altiplano* town. His death may have sparked a good showing in the 1995 municipal elections by UCS, but there is no guarantee that his party can survive without its leader.

Fernández and Palenque used patrimonial methods to mobilize support during elections. Like all other parties in the system, however, the central objective of CONDEPA and UCS is to penetrate the system and obtain access to state patronage through the formation of alliances with the three principal parties. The irony is that while these new populist parties emerged partially in response to the patrimonial practices of the traditional ones, Fernández and Palenque utilize the same methods. Maxismo and Palenquismo, in fact, may share the same constituency and electoral battles at the national and municipal level. As a result, they have often faced each other in bitter confrontations. Palenque, and not the traditional parties, for example, raised the allegations of linkages to the drug cartel. Fernández slapped a libel suit on Palenque and announced that if he won it, he would donate U.S.$10 million to homeless children and senior citizens.

In any event, the important issue is that both Palenquismo and Maxismo may have succeeded because of public disdain for the inability of the three principal parties to aggregate the demands of the popular sectors. However, they have become key local and national political options that will not disappear. Many analysts are concerned that the actions, rhetoric, and personal histories of both Palenque and Fernández demonstrate only a vague commitment to democratic values. Lazarte (1992) notes that the social bases of both UCS and CONDEPA are also antidemocratic. In his view, the social sectors which support both parties are only superficially committed to democracy because no other option is available. Of course, the same could be said about nearly every social sector and political group in the country. Commitment to democratic values on the part of any actor in Bolivia is still incipient. Lazarte argues, however, that Palenquistas and Maxistas have organized neither in favor nor against representative democracy but outside of the democratic process. Hence, although they can play a positive role by attempting to integrate these excluded sectors into the institutions of the democratic process, they may also tilt the balance against democracy. Furthermore, Lazarte warned that in 1992

> precisely because (Max and Palenque) lack democratic convictions, one can assume that the principal motivation of their actions will not be the necessity to preserve the democratic political system but the preservation of their leadership among the masses that support them. The probability exists that if these two variables conflict with one another, these new leaders would opt for the latter; thus, they will place the system at risk (Lazarte, 1992:606).

In short, it is probably worthwhile to heed Lazarte's warning. The popular sectors attracted to Palenquismo and Maxismo may be reticent to accept the logic of representative democracy and may also be swayed by the promises of a more direct form of democracy. Uncomfortable with the mediation of parties, these sectors in Bolivia have historically displayed an affinity for a direct relationship with the leader. It is important to note, however, that

Palenquismo and Maxismo have played a crucial role in the stability of democracy and may have become the only mitigating force which has prevented the emergence of radical groups among the marginal sectors of Bolivia.

Municipal Elections in La Paz, 1987–1993

December 1987

On December 6, 1987, the first open municipal elections in Bolivian history were held. Local voters could cast their ballots directly for mayors and members of city councils independent of national party lists. In this sense, candidates campaigned specifically on issues relating directly to the city and not tied to the national political agenda of any given party.[11] Great uncertainty surrounded these elections. An adequate law to regulate them was lacking, a number of towns and counties around the country were ill prepared to hold the contest, and, owing to poor voter registration, a large number of rural people were unable to vote.

The elections were held during a particularly significant period. In some measure they constituted a referendum on the Nueva Política Económica introduced by the MNR in August 1985 to end hyperinflation. The NPE had introduced one of the most draconian stabilization programs ever implemented in Bolivia. So harsh was it that it altered the political economy of the nation (Gamarra, 1995). To implement these reforms, the MNR entered into a crucial alliance, the Pacto por la Democracia, with General Banzer's ADN. Although the MNR and the ADN ran separate candidates, the municipal elections of 1987 provided a preliminary examination of the strength of the Pacto por la Democracia in an electoral setting.

Owing to an agreement among all political parties with congressional representation, broader electoral reforms passed in May 1986 were used to regulate the municipal elections (Baldivia and Sáinz, 1987). A new municipal government law, however, did not make it through the National Congress. As a result, the new local governments would be bound by laws that predated the 1952 revolution. Consequently, many of the problems of the political system at the national level appeared in a more extreme form in the newly elected municipal councils. For example, the dilemmas of stand-offs in legislative assemblies, a common occurrence in the National

Congress, now showed up at the local level. Yet, the experience of elected local governments played a positive role in legitimating the democratic process in Bolivia.

In La Paz, Walter Mur, the MNR's candidate for mayor and a deputy in the National Congress with little popular appeal, suffered a humiliating defeat. On a countrywide scale, the results revealed that the MNR had lost in every major city and that its overall support had dropped from 26 percent to less than 12 percent. The outcry within the party was immediate. Led by Guillermo Bedregal, the old populist guard demanded the purging of the technocrats from the cabinet and a reversal of NPE policies (Bedregal, 1987a, 1987b). In turn, the technocrats blamed the politicos in charge of the campaign for running unappealing candidates and for poor campaign management.

Paz Estenssoro commissioned a poll to uncover the reasons for the MNR's electoral failure. According to government officials, he found an underlying support for the basic premises of the NPE. The poll suggested that the electoral results had little to do with the social impact of stabilization and more to do with poor candidate selection by the political wing of the party.[12] In response, Paz created a national commission to renovate and modernize the party. He also called for the democratization of the party, a move that threatened to tear down clientelistic structures developed over the years.

The new "restructuring" commission was superimposed on the party's directorate elected during its 1985 convention. Paz's message to the populist wing was very clear: the NPE would be consolidated and the pact with ADN would remain. Discontent became evident as the younger guard moved to replace old party stalwarts. During the first six months of 1988, the new commission proposed reforms and plotted the path for the MNR en route to the May 1989 election.

Evidence that the NPE did not affect the outcome of the poll was ADN's remarkable showing. It is important to note, however, that its constituency favored the types of policies pursued by the NPE. The electoral results showed that, on a national scale, ADN retained about the same level of support as in 1985. Like the MNR, however, ADN was plagued by internal disputes over the NPE and whether or not to join the pact. Since the split that forced Galindo and his followers from the party, Banzer loyalists (Banzeristas) established a tight grip over the party apparatus.

ADN attracted an important group of young professionals who cleaned up the party's image. Its officials put forth their party as the only one not plagued by internal disputes and job-hungry politicians. The pact with the MNR has been justified as an unselfish act that demonstrated the commitment of ADN and its members to democratic values. Whatever the reasons for entering into the pact, ADN was able to sell this image to the electorate. During the municipal elections,it ran candidates with long-established local ties throughout Bolivia's major cities. In La Paz, the most important race, it had the advantage of running an incumbent, Maclean, a Harvard-educated businessman who had been elected in 1985 and who had run the municipal government like a well-managed business enterprise. Maclean's record of fiscal responsibility, however, was not enough to hold off the challenge from the MIR.

One of the principal beneficiaries of the apparent MNR burnout was the MIR. The results of the 1987 municipal elections demonstrated that this relatively young party was a rising political force. In the three previous years Paz Zamora had transformed it into a mainstream social democratic party and put much effort into improving its international image. The MIR's image as a young and more socially progressive version of the MNR had wide appeal in contemporary Bolivia. Especially among the younger sectors of the middle class who perceived that the party might transcend the MNR and its generation, the MIR made great progress. Its success during the municipal elections, however, rested more on its ability to attract dissident MNR factions and individuals.

The key to the MIR's electoral success was to recruit individuals with strategic local ties. In the La Paz race, for example, the MIR attracted Raúl Salmón, a popular former mayor of La Paz (1979–1981) and owner of one of the city's largest radio stations, to run against Maclean. Salmón became a formidable opponent to Mayor Maclean; when the popular vote was counted, he had defeated the incumbent.

The left, divided and discredited by the Siles period, could only forge a weak alliance called the Alianza Patriótica. Drawing on the left's symbols and myths for the La Paz election, the Alianza named Ema Obleas de Torres, widow of the late populist General Juan José Torres, as its candidate. Although she ran a disappointing campaign, she managed to win an important seat on the La Paz city council. In Sucre, Bolivia's legal capital city, the victory of the Movimiento Bolivia Libre (Free Bolivia Movement, or MBL), a wing of the MIR led by Araníbar that split in 1985, was surprising. The MBL developed a significant political base in the departments of Chuquisaca and Potosí that proved to be a key long-term survival strategy.

The results of the municipal elections in La Paz illustrate the problems and dilemmas confronted by the institutions of Bolivian democracy. The outcome revealed the obstacles facing the party system; specifically, the results provided a measure as to the strength of the Pacto por la Democracia in an electoral setting.

Table 1. Municipal Elections in the City of La Paz, December 1987

Party	Votes	Percentage
ADN	86,648	36.8
MIR	95,737	40.6
MNR	11,874	5.0
AP	15,255	6.5
VR-9	7,970	3.9
PS-1	5,621	2.4
MBL	3,179	1.3
FSB	2,469	1.0
Valid Votes	228,753	100.0

Source: National Electoral Court.
Due to the rounding of figures, percentages do not equal one hundred percent.

The La Paz results reflected many of the dilemmas of Bolivian democracy at the national level. In the national elections, if the winner fails to attain 50 percent plus 1 of the popular vote, the National Congress, whose members are elected by proportional representation, decides among the top three contenders. The indirect nature of the municipal elections mimicked the impasses that occurred in 1979 and 1985 at the national level.

Table 2. The La Paz Municipal Council, 1987–1989

Party	Candidate	Seats
MIR	Raúl Salmón	5
ADN	Ronald Maclean	5
AP	Ema O. de Torres	1
MNR	Walter Mur	1
Total		12

Source: National Electoral Court.

Raúl Salmón of the MIR defeated Maclean by a slight plurality; as a result, each party won five council seats. The MNR and AP split the two remaining seats in the twelve-member assembly. A foregone conclusion was that the Pacto por la Democracia would go into operation and the MNR would support Maclean. By the same token, it was assumed that Ema Obleas of AP would support the MIR's Salmón over ADN's Maclean. A standoff was inevitable. ADN appeared to score an early knockout when Carlos Miranda, a MIR councilman, defected in return for a promise to become president of the council. The MNR's Mur, however, refused to go along with his party's directives to support Maclean. He soon defected to the MIR and was promptly expelled from the MNR. In any event, the result was a standoff, punctuated by occasional brawls, that lasted through March 1988.

Much like the scenarios that developed in the National Congress following elections, with the mediation of the Church, the major political parties bargained, manipulated, and negotiated. Finally, in early March, a way out was found. The MIR and ADN resolved that Salmón would serve as mayor of La Paz until December 1988 and Maclean would finish out the term in December 1989. As was the case with national elections, this interim solution resolved a particular problem but did not address the deeper structural issues that were at stake.

Salmón's tenure as mayor of La Paz illustrated the benefits and disadvantages of recruiting candidates. One the one hand, he was able to bolster the image of the MIR by carrying out more projects than his predecessor, mainly in the form of creating small parks, paving sidewalks and streets, and constructing a new, grand Central Park and an avenue surrounding the city. On the other hand, the new mayor's projects turned into a financial disaster for the municipal government as contractors went unpaid for their labor. Moreover, Salmón's tenure proved disastrous for the MIR from a political standpoint. Almost from the outset, he attempted to dictate policy within the MIR. He also established his own political base independent from the party.[13] In December, when his term was about to expire, he pressured the MIR to renege on its agreement with ADN. This precipitated another standoff in the municipal council in late December that was resolved only through the mediation of the Church. In the end, the MIR stood by its agreement with ADN while Salmón conveniently moved to the MNR. Salmón died prematurely of a heart attack in 1989.

Maclean finished off Salmón's term with a bang. In the short ten months he served as mayor, he tackled several thorny issues, especially the legacy of corruption left by Salmón and the MIR. Loaded with projects and ideas, Maclean aimed to leave his personal mark on the La Paz municipality. Some of his projects were so successful that, according to Maclean, they became textbook cases on local management at Harvard University.[14] Moreover, his anticorruption drive was crucial in winning the support of business sectors, especially construction, which no longer had to pay onerous "commissions" to bid on a project.

In 1987 and 1988, Bolivia was in the midst of profound political, social, and economic changes. A political realignment appeared evident from the election results. Many observers argued that these elections marked a giant step toward democratization and heralded the possibility of resolving a host of problems (Soruco 1988). An important conclusion was drawn from the 1987 experience. While the elections and their aftermath served as a prelude to a scenario that developed in the National Congress in May-July 1989 after the Pacto por la Democracia broke down in February 1989, they were also a critical first step toward the institutionalization of a tradition of local politics.

December 1989

Barely four months after the unusual election of Paz Zamora to the presidency, with the support of General Banzer, municipal elections were held.[15] These elections served to measure the strength of the new Acuerdo Patriótico government and were the key to determining the future of the ruling alliance, which brought together a strange mix between the MIR and ADN, until then on opposite sides of the ideological spectrum. Maclean was again nominated to run for mayor of La Paz. Throughout Bolivia, a single candidate was presented by the AP in an attempt to test the electorate's response to the ruling alliance.

The 1989 municipal elections were held under rather odd circumstances. Problems in the organization of the elections, such as delays in the deadlines established by the National Electoral Court and late disbursements of funds by the court, threatened to postpone the election. Moreover, the electorate appeared exhausted after the intensity of the national elections and the three-month-long negotiations that followed. Voter disinterest and apathy were apparent as was widespread confusion over registration requirements. Only those voters who registered for the May 1989 general election could cast their ballots, leading some observers to ask why as many as 50 percent of the electorate could not vote. Municipal elections were seen as a fraudulent process that did little to contribute to the welfare of the population.

Owing to several questionable practices by the National Electoral Court during the general elections, voter confidence in the court dropped significantly.[16] Nevertheless, a new set of electoral mechanisms was put in place, and the government signed a new law that raised the number of council members in the city of La Paz from twelve to thirteen. The objective of the increment was to prevent the recurrence of impasses, as had occurred following the 1987 elections, in the municipal council.

By October 19, fifteen parties registered their candidates with the National Electoral Court. The most significant were the ruling AP, the MNR, CONDEPA, and UCS. The MNR's candidate this time was Guido Capra Jamio, a well-known engineer and rector of the state university in La Paz. Unlike the party's candidate in 1987, Capra had been active in civic organizations and was an attractive alternative for the La Paz middle class.

Clearly, the most interesting contender was CONDEPA's Palenque, who represented a major threat to the AP's Maclean for a number of reasons that had mainly to do with social class. Maclean appealed to the middle and upper classes not only because of his European looks and his Harvard training but also because, while in office, he was able to deliver services to those sectors. Under his tenure Maclean was credited with securing foreign financing for a series of public works programs, including a very visible bridge, pompously named the Puente de las Américas, that linked two La Paz middle-class neighborhoods. In contrast, El Compadre came onto the political scene rather precipitously, owing mainly to the June 1988 closing of his radio and television stations. CONDEPA did well in the national elections and was expected to sweep the La Paz mayoral elections in December 1989 because the more populous working-class sectors of the city were diehard supporters. Owing to the number of contestants, however, an outright victory by either Palenque or Maclean was unlikely; hence, the new mayor of La Paz would once again be elected by the municipal council.

The fourth relevant candidate was Jorge Burgoa of UCS. While Burgoa was an unknown, his boss Max Fernández, the UCS party chief, was not. Fernández resorted to the old-fashioned distribution of favors and incentives throughout the country to secure votes.

UCS had been prevented from competing in the national elections by the National Electoral Court; thus, in December it aimed to prove that it had countrywide appeal despite U.S. embassy allegations that the party boss was linked to the cocaine trade. While Burgoa was given no chance of winning the La Paz election, UCS hoped to obtain at least one council seat. This gain would be a significant victory for Fernández, who desperately sought recognition through the electoral process.

The 1989 municipal elections, however, were held under extraordinary circumstances that raised questions about the government's intentions and the continuity of Bolivian democracy. Facing a month-long hunger strike by a teachers' union, President Paz Zamora decreed a state of siege throughout Bolivia on November 15. In the government's view, the state of siege was a "measured response to a general strike and hunger strike perpetrated by Bolivian teachers, which has disrupted public order and threatens the economic and financial stability of the country" (*Presencia*, November 15, 1989).

Faced with criticism from the opposition political parties, Paz Zamora announced that municipal elections would be held on December 3, and respect for the political rights of both Bolivian citizens and their political parties participating in the electoral process would be maintained (*Presencia*, November 15, 1989). At the same time, police forces detained a majority of the strikers in La Paz, Cochabamba, Oruro, Trinidad, and other cities. At least three of the leaders who initiated the hunger strike went into a state of coma and were transferred by ambulances to a clinic in La Paz for medical attention. The other strikers were banished to Puerto Rico or to remote towns in the Bolivian Amazon (*Presencia*, November 15, 1989).

For the MNR-led opposition, the declaration of a state of siege by the Bolivian government signaled its inability to deal with labor unrest. Claiming that it needed to contain popular protest to guarantee municipal elections, the government responded to demands for social and economic justice with police dogs and tear gas (Moldiz Mercado, 1989). The prefect of La Paz, Fernando Cajías, issued a decree prohibiting political meetings of any sort, in compliance with a so-called Decree of Good Government. In addition, he announced that the government would adopt other measures relating to the political campaign preceding the December municipal elections. According to Cajías, the state of siege was to "prevent violence against public institutions, as well as against people and their property, as the elections approach" (*El Diario*, November 16, 1989).

The leader of the MNR, Sánchez de Lozada, argued that municipal elections could not take place under the restrictions imposed by a state of siege and the suspension of civil liberties. Sánchez de Lozada called for mediation by the Catholic Church and international observers. Now, another questionable practice by the government was at issue. Resorting to a congressional maneuver of dubious constitutionality, the AP coalition managed to call a congressional recess, thus preventing any public discussion of the state of siege. In short, the government granted itself dictatorial powers for a ninety-day period.[17] The municipal elections went on anyway.

The municipal elections of 1989 were held on December 3 despite the protests against the state of siege and accusations that the AP coalition would stage fraudulent elections. Again, no clear winner emerged from the contest, and a horse-trading round in the municipal council replaced the public voting. CONDEPA won a plurality, but Palenque lacked the clout with the MNR and other parties to be elected mayor of La Paz. Given the poor relations between Palenque and the MNR, even Capra announced that he could become the next mayor. Palenque called on the municipal council to respect the will of the majority in La Paz. Another impasse appeared inevitable as the top three each claimed the mayor's office. The Bolivian political system was becoming accustomed to these situations at both the national and municipal level. To many people, they were a dangerous habit that delegitimized democracy; how-

Table 3. Municipal Elections in the City of La Paz, December 1989

Party	Votes	Percentage
MNR	26,698	13.32
MIR-ADN	74,537	37.18
UCS	10,738	5.36
IU	4,341	2.17
CONDEPA	81,000	40.41
VR-9	835	0.42
MST	2,321	1.16
Valid votes	200,470	93.51
Blank	3,790	1.77
Null	10,129	4.72
Votes cast	214,389	100.00

Source: National Electoral Court.

ever, these rounds forced political parties to compromise and negotiate.

In the end, Maclean was reelected with the votes of the MNR and UCS. The outcome reflected the notion that interparty agreements forged after the first electoral round had changed the preelectoral correlation of forces, thus blocking the control of many municipal governments by the official MIR-ADN coalition. Thanks to arrangements worked out with the MNR during the December 1989 municipal elections, however, UCS was able to occupy the office in the mayoralties of Cochabamba, Oruro, Trinidad, and several provinces in each of those departments.

Table 4. The La Paz Municipal Council, 1989–1991

Party	Candidate	Seats
ADN-MIR	Ronald Maclean	5
CONDEPA	Carlos Palenque	5
MNR	Guido Capra	2
UCS	Jorge Burgoa	1

Source: National Electoral Court.

December 1991

The December 1991 municipal elections were reminiscent of 1987. They served as a referendum on the performance of an incumbent government. In this instance they gauged Paz Zamora's performance and voter sentiment regarding the deepening process of neoliberal adjustment. Among the traditional parties, no surprises were expected since a predictable slate of candidates was on the ballot. The ruling Acuerdo Patriótico's candidate ratified the candidacy of Maclean. The MNR once again went with Capra, who had gained a great deal of municipal experience in the council since 1989. Known as a technocrat linked to Sánchez de Lozada, Capra appealed to political independents and vast sectors of the middle class. Most of these voters chose to vote for Maclean or for Julio Mantilla, CONDEPA's candidate. The MNR's strategy in La Paz was not to win a majority but simply to get a large enough number of votes to make a difference in the council.

Real surprises, however, came in CONDEPA and UCS. CONDEPA drafted Mantilla, a Mexico-trained sociologist and former member of the Communist Party, who brought some degree of intellectual coherence to the party's *modelo endógeno* that called "for a self-sustaining economy, the generation of an internal market and productive capacity based on the strengthening of artisans and small producers, and relied on many of the principles of revolutionary nationalism of the 1950s" (Mesa Gilbert, 1992:15).

Mantilla was one of many middle-class intellectuals drafted by CONDEPA. Prior to 1991, these former leftist intellectuals looked with disdain upon CONDEPA because of its unsophisticated style. By drafting Mantilla and others, Palenque bypassed some of the founding members. The new arrivals were immediately promoted to high-ranking posts within CONDEPA, much to the chagrin of older party members. Ethnic tensions within the party were also evident as these late-arriving middle-class professionals displaced working-class individuals with indigenous names such as Mamani, Quispe, and Condori (Archondo, 1991). Many within the party complained that the intellectuals had taken over and captured El Compadre. The intellectuals, however, were able to sell CONDEPA more effectively through the manipulation of Andean symbols and rituals displayed prominently throughout the electoral campaign.[18]

A few important contextual issues determined the 1991 municipal elections. First, they were held after a crucial February agreement among the key political parties that established the basis for a new electoral law and a new electoral court. In many ways, these elections were the first truly honest ones in Bolivia at any level. These accords, however, were the result of a debilitating political crisis that pitted the ruling AP against the MNR and other members of the opposition and that put into question the very legitimacy of the Paz Zamora government. Despite promises to the contrary, the AP held out until the last moment before it agreed to modify the electoral law and to relinquish its grip over the electoral court. Moreover, the government failed in its bid to control the judiciary by prosecuting eight members of the Supreme Court. In short, the municipal elections were a first test of a redefined consensus among the largest political parties.

Broadly speaking, three broad options were available to the La Paz electorate in December 1991. The first followed the neoliberal agenda established in 1985 and included the AP and the MNR. While they agreed with the broad premises of neoliberalism, personal antagonisms between Banzer and Sánchez de Lozada prevented the recomposition of any type of alliance. The second option was more populist in orientation and included CONDEPA and UCS, which both contested for the votes of the same social classes, although CONDEPA's appeal was limited mainly to La Paz. The main difference in their campaign strategy was that CONDEPA provided a well-structured political platform embodied in its *modelo endógeno*.

The leftist option was provided by the IU and the MBL. The IU was made up largely of members of the PCB who failed to modernize in the midst of the global changes affecting socialism. It also included holdovers of the defunct Partido Socialista and a few other smaller leftist parties. In contrast, in 1991 the MBL revealed that it had modernized, replacing its old Marxist dogma with more fashionable social democratic statutes. Since 1987 the MBL had concentrated on building a political base in the departments of Chuquisaca and Cochabamba. Its significance in La Paz, however, was still small.

Several problems were clearly evident as the municipal elections approached. One report, for example, noted that an undetermined number of citizens would not be allowed to vote because the towns in which they lived did not "legally exist" and were not recognized by the National Electoral Court to elect municipal authorities (*Informe R*, 11, no. 227: 3). Yet, as the election date approached, it became evident that the abstention rate would be low. The impact of economic reforms on migration patterns in Bolivia was also a significant factor affecting voter turnout. Entire communities became ghost towns as populations moved toward coca-growing zones. When the results were known, the Acuerdo Patriótico had won at the national level with 27 percent of the vote to the MNR's 23 percent. Nationally, UCS made a remarkable showing with 21 percent, CONDEPA with 11.5 percent, the MBL with 5.3 percent, and the IU with barely 3.7 percent. The results for La Paz are presented in Table 5.

One way of interpreting the results is that they reflected a solid 50 percent support for the economic policies in place since 1985. More important, however, the results revealed a considerable decline in support for the AP government. In 1989 it won 30 percent nationally. Moreover, the AP coalition won in only four departments (Potosí, Cochabamba, Chuquisaca, and Pando). Taking into account that the opposition effectively blocked the election of AP mayors in each city council, the government's performance in the elections was dismal. Despite the poor showing in the municipal elections by the AP parties, Paz Zamora was able to sustain high levels of popular support. In 1991 the president was more popular than the parties which made up his ruling coalition.

Table 5. Municipal Elections in the City of La Paz, December 1991

Party	Votes	Percentage
MNR	62,107	23.15
AP	64,135	23.91
IU	6,012	2.24
UCS	50,621	18.8
MBL	12,030	4.48
CONDEPA	73,381	27.35
Valid votes	268,286	
Blank	4,642	
Null	9,205	
Votes cast	282,133	99.93*

Source: National Electoral Court.
*Due to the rounding of figures, percentages do not equal 100 percent.

Both ADN and the MNR believed that they could obtain a victory in La Paz because they sensed that support for CONDEPA had declined considerably. Polls conducted by these parties did not take into account the nature of the population in the peripheral areas of the city. Because a high proportion of voters was made up of recent arrivals to La Paz, some analysts believed that their answers to polling questions about candidate preference were unreliable. Given the long history of racial discrimination, respondents aimed to please the pollster. When the results were announced, it became clear that CONDEPA's support had not declined.

Table 6. The La Paz Municipal Council, 1991–1993

Party	Candidate	Seats
ADN-MIR (AP)	Ronald Maclean	3
CONDEPA	Julio Mantilla	4
MNR	Guido Capra	3
UCS	Juan Ayoroa	2
MBL	Germán Monroy	1

Source: National Election Court.

One of the most significant developments in the postelection hoopla was Maclean's announcement that the AP would vote for Mantilla as La Paz's next mayor. On the same day of the election, when the results were barely in, Maclean burst into a television studio where Mantilla was being interviewed to congratulate the winner and to announce that "we will keep our promise of respecting the first majority to strengthen democracy because the citizens deserve all our respect" (*Hoy Internacional* 7, no. 406: 23). Maclean's support for Mantilla contrasted sharply with ADN's refusal in the 1989 general elections to vote for the MNR's Sánchez de Lozada in the National Congress despite his victory at the polls.

German ("Chaza") Chazarreta of the MBL also voted for Mantilla. The MNR and UCS, however, were less forthcoming. Throughout Bolivia, those two parties agreed to distribute mayorships among themselves. In contrast, for the first time since open elections for the La Paz municipal council and mayors were reinstituted, there was no prolonged battle to determine the next mayor.

The 1991 results were the culmination of CONDEPA's efforts in the city of La Paz and gave credence to the party's cry of *jach'a uru* (the great day will arrive). Moreover, they suggested several trends in the national political alignments. UCS improved its showing, winning in Oruro and Sucre. CONDEPA won in La Paz and El Alto, the MNR in Santa Cruz, Trinidad, and Tarija. These victories, by parties which to varying degrees opposed the neoliberal economic policies in force since 1985, suggested that public opinion about neoliberalism was shifting (*Presencia*, December 2, 1991). This trend would become evident as the national elections of 1993 approached.

In his two years as mayor of La Paz, Mantilla developed a political base that both projected him as national leader and challenged Palenque's direction of CONDEPA. Mantilla, after all, was an intellectual with technical skills that enabled him to manage the city in ways that were reminiscent of Maclean's efficiency. Moreover, Mantilla was able to take credit for completing a great many projects, such as the Puente de las Américas, initiated under Maclean's tenure, but he was also able to deliver his own set of projects funded largely by foreign loans. These projects were visible especially in the working- and lower-middle-class sectors of La Paz. Mantilla took credit, for example, for building an underground tunnel that ended rush-hour traffic at the Plaza San Francisco, one of the busiest intersections in the city. His appeal was also largely ethnic. Fluent in Aymara, the new mayor flaunted his command of the language and delivered major speeches while touring the most marginal sectors of the city. He demonstrated a capacity to discuss in Aymara practical solutions for a shantytown on one occasion and to engage in Spanish long-winded academic explanations of his plans for La Paz at another.

He also wasted few opportunities to embarrass his predecessor. For example, Mantilla ordered the U.S. ambassador to move or tear down a huge concrete security wall that had been built to protect the new embassy building. The permit for raising the wall had been granted under Maclean's watch despite the fact that it violated city codes. In the meantime, Maclean had become foreign minister and was in the uncomfortable position of having to mediate between the ambassador and Mantilla. In the end, Mantilla won; the U.S. embassy was forced to move the wall.

December 1993

The elections of December 1993 echoed many of the themes that had prevailed in 1989. Four months after the swearing-in of a new president, local elections would serve as a ninety-day referendum on the performance of the national government. In 1993 the municipal elections would serve to gauge the first months of Gonzalo Sánchez de Lozada's MNR government. Elected in June under great expectations, "Goni," as he is popularly called, capitalized on an anticorruption sentiment and a general sense that neoliberal reforms should be toned down to minimize their accompanying social cost. To win the elections, Sánchez de Lozada and the MNR recruited Víctor Hugo Cárdenas, an Aymara intellectual and leader of the Movimiento Revolucionario Tupac Katari. To ensure their election by the National Congress, the MNR entered into a "governability pact" with Fernández's UCS and a "pact for change" with Araníbar's MBL.

Having established these alliances, the MNR controlled two-thirds of the National Congress and appeared ready to govern with few problems. Thus, in August, expectations were that the MNR would sweep the municipal elections and be poised to become the only party of significance in Bolivia. The first four months of the new government, however, proved to be difficult. Sánchez de Lozada's economic cabinet team fired 10,000 government employees and imposed other austerity policies; furthermore, attempts to attract foreign investment were met with lukewarm reactions abroad. Finally, despite the presence of Cárdenas, the government also pressed ahead with coca eradication programs and other polices aimed at the indigenous sectors of the population.

These rocky first four months occurred at a particularly auspicious time for the MNR, since other parties could not muster enough strength to challenge it regionally or nationally. Severe internal crises in the MIR, ADN, and UCS led to predictions that these parties would disappear. Perhaps the most serious crisis was within ADN. General Banzer's retirement from politics in November left at least three identifiable contenders for the party's leadership. Splits in the party reflected both generational and regional disputes. Fernando Kieffer from La Paz headed a group of younger party members based in that city. Jorge Landívar, an industrialist from Santa Cruz, was the anointed successor, but he demonstrated no skill in controlling dissenters. Finally, Guillermo Fortún, a former party subchief, headed efforts by the older La Paz-based *banzeristas* to control ADN. For the election, Fortún's faction tapped Luis Alberto "Chito" Valle, a member of the Old Guard, as the party's candidate in La Paz.

A similar crisis afflicted the MIR. Since leaving office in August, the party had had no real leader. Paz Zamora devoted most of his time to distancing himself from the MIR in an effort to cultivate a fledgling international image. Oscar Eid Franco, the former party chief, dedicated some of his time to become a political consultant for Max Fernández. Finally, the party was rocked by the indictment in Cuba of two up-and-coming members of the younger generation who were allegedly involved in a hit-and-run drunk-driving incident during a brief official visit in 1990. More significantly, however, the MIR underwent a severe crisis as the Fuerza Especial de Lucha contra el Narcotráfico accused Paz Zamora, Eid Franco, and other high-ranking MIR officials of dealings with one of Bolivia's most notorious drug traffickers. These accusations resulted in congressional hearings and the subsequent indictment and jailing of Eid Franco.

Fernández discovered that his party could not survive with one foot in the government. Granted the Ministry of Defense, UCS essentially became absorbed by the MNR despite Fernández's repeated attempts to distance himself and his party from the government. In a telling incident in November, for example, when he announced his party's withdrawal from the ruling coalition, the minister of defense refused to step down. Fernández proved to be an impossible coalition partner, and he and his party were forced out in December 1994.

The MBL, on the other hand, proved to be a loyal ally, but it ran the risk of losing its electoral appeal. In the first two months in office, the party essentially supported all the economic and political initiatives that it had once denounced as the opposition. Clearly, the most serious violation was to endorse the arrival of fifty-five U.S. military officers to train Bolivia's counternarcotics forces. Nevertheless, the MBL announced that Chazarreta, one of its younger leaders, would run for mayor of La Paz. Few gave him more than an outside chance of securing a council seat.

Despite Goni's weak performance as president, the MNR was the only party with a national power base. This vantage point did not make it disciplined, however. On the contrary, splits were also evident as Sánchez de Lozada struggled to control internal dissent. Observers noted in jest that he had pacted with UCS and the MBL but had forgotten to pact with the MNR.

The MNR appeared as well to have dealt CONDEPA a definitive blow by luring Mantilla, the former mayor of La Paz, who had developed a significant political following. Mantilla was involved in a serious battle for CONDEPA's leadership with Palenque and other less prominent members of the party when the MNR offer was forwarded. The MNR assumed that Mantilla could both bring with him support from the social sectors traditionally linked to CONDEPA and simultaneously attract middle- and upper-class support. However, the MNR misread the situation within CONDEPA. In fact, despite the defections, CONDEPA was the only party that kept intact its following after the June 6 national elections. Owing to the appeal of Palenque's RTP programs, CONDEPA was able to preserve its strength with its constituent base. Yet it had to fight for its constituency, as it was affected most severely by the defection to the MNR of Mantilla, whose popularity had soared during his time in office. Mantilla's falling-out with CONDEPA caused a serious internal crisis that gave rise to speculation that the party would not survive the mass defection of its prominent members.

To prevent lasting damage, Palenque announced that his wife, Mónica Medina, also known as La Comadre Mónica, would run for mayor of La Paz. CONDEPA's campaign was extremely well orchestrated. Medina's principal challenge was not to scare the middle and upper sectors who continued to fear an invasion of *cholos* (half-breeds). These classes of La Paz society rejected Medina for the same reasons that they had rejected her husband in past elections. CONDEPA is the party of domestic servants, construction workers, the unemployed, and the *cholo* masses that live in the shantytowns surrounding La Paz. The strategy employed by Palenque and Medina against Mantilla and the MNR worked extremely well in these social sectors and unmasked Mantilla's erroneous assumption that he would be able to lure these sectors away from CONDEPA.

Mónica Medina's campaign embodied the several culturally significant symbols that solidified support among these sectors. The *compadre* and *comadre* in many ways was akin to the old Andean masculine and feminine conception (Mama Ocllo and Manco Kapac, for example). Moreover, Mantilla was called a Judas who had been bought for a few coins by the MNR. His description of Palenque as the anti-Christ, in turn, played well among the middle- and upper-class housewives who always held that opinion of the pompous *compadre* anyway. This strategy had no real impact, however, among electorally significant sectors.

The results of the municipal elections revealed support for the MNR in a majority of the country's districts. It won in La Paz, Santa Cruz, Potosí, Beni, and Pando, although it was not able to win enough seats to secure the mayor's office. The MIR won only in Oruro, while ADN did not win in any city; in most cities it did not finish in the top three. The principal loser, according to most analysts, was Fernández's UCS. Save for CONDEPA, the opposition was unable to capitalize on the MNR's rather unfortunate first four months in office. The MNR's performance had given it the right to claim that the electorate support its Plan de Todos, especially a move to transfer health and educational services to municipal governments.

The principal winner was CONDEPA. To the surprise of most parties, its electoral base transcended La Paz. On a national scale El Compadre's party placed second only to the MNR. CONDEPA remained, however, largely a regional *altiplano* phenomenon. Its appeal is mostly ethnically based and is concentrated in La Paz, Oruro, and Potosí departments where there is a large concentration of Aymaras and Quechuas.

There was much talk about the possibility of establishing yet another party by local political figures in several key cities. Rumors circulated that the MNR "borrowed" Germán Gutierrez Gantier in Sucre, Percy Fernández in Santa Cruz, and Manfred Reyes Villa and Julio Mantilla in La Paz to form a new party. The fact that the Bolivian electorate is divided between traditional parties and CONDEPA did little to quell these rumors.

The results in La Paz demonstrated interesting and ironic twists. Paradoxically, Mantilla had become the candidate of the upper classes, despite his previous antineoliberal background and his acceptance of the *modelo endógeno,* not to mention his own ethnic background. Mantilla's 40 percent was comprised mainly of voters from the upper and middle classes. He was also able to garner the support of a specific lower-middle-class sector. In past elections these social sectors were decidedly Adenista voters; more specifically, this was Ronald Maclean territory. Valle was able to retain some of ADN's traditional support.

Based on exit poll interviews, Mantilla declared himself the new mayor of La Paz. He erroneously assumed that the MNR had won 6 seats to CONDEPA's 4, giving it a clear-cut victory if the MBL followed through with its commitment at the national level. When the electoral returns from the working-class suburbs were counted, however, a 5-to-5 tie in council seats emerged.

With the support of the MIR and ADN, at age thirty La Comadre Mónica became the first woman mayor of La Paz. Her principal challenge—besides not scaring the middle and upper sectors who continued to fear an invasion of *cholos*—was to govern the capital city without unleashing the wrath of the MNR, which could ostensibly block life-sustaining foreign assistance to the municipal government (Moldiz Mercado, 1993).

Table 7. **Municipal Elections in the City of La Paz, December 1993**

Party	Votes	Percentage
MNR	98,241	39.98
ADN	12,992	5.29
MBL	12,399	5.05
CONDEPA	93,700	38.13
FRI	1,691	0.69
ASD	3,743	1.52
EJE	1,407	0.57
UCS	8,296	3.38
MIR-NM	10,268	4.18
FSB	2,970	1.21
Valid votes	245,707	100.00
Blank	3,112	1.21
Null	8,218	3.20
Votes cast	257,037	

For two years Medina served as mayor of La Paz. Predictably her tenure was marked by a great deal of controversy, but she also became a significant political personage. During her time in office, she put the finishing touches on a number of public works programs that had been on the books for a long time. While Medina had not secured funding for them, she took credit for finishing roads, bridges, and other costly projects. The new mayor proved once again that the important issue is not who secures the funding but who is in office when the job is completed. Paradoxically, she took credit for the completion of highways and bypasses that mainly benefited the upper-class neighborhoods of the city. Construction of her most ambitious project, a beltway surrounding the capital, was initiated but not completed.

Table 8. **The La Paz Municipal Council, 1993–1995**

Party	Candidate	Seats
ADN	Luis Alberto Valle	1
MNR	Julio Mantilla	5
MIR	Fernando Cajías	1
CONDEPA	Mónica Medina de Palenque	5
MBL	Germán Monroy	1
Total		13

Source: National Electoral Court.

A poll conducted by the Political Science Department of the Universidad Mayor de San Andrés in June 1994 reflected Medina's relative success. According to the survey, she had a 51 percent approval rating; moreover, in comparison to her two immediate predecessors, Maclean and Mantilla, her ranking on a confidence scale was higher (Carrera de Ciencias Políticas, 1994). Her popularity transcended Bolivia, mainly because of the fact that she was a woman who had made it to office in a predominantly macho society. She toured Europe, visited the United States, and made *Newsweek*'s list of Latin America's most powerful women. Her international reputation added a great deal of muscle to her domestic agenda, but she was eventually unable to sustain the political coalition that had put her in office. Medina developed close ties with CONDEPA's constituency and used every opportunity to attack both the ruling MNR and the other opposition parties, including those who had helped elect her. This strategy proved both effective and costly. It was effective because her popularity among CONDEPA's constituency grew considerably. Medina's reelection hopes were pinned on the prospect of a landslide victory in the 1995 municipal election. At the same time, however, the strategy proved destabilizing as she antagonized other parties and attempted to bully them into following CONDEPA's municipal agenda, which included the firing of workers not linked to her own party.

Within a few months after assuming office, efforts were under way to undermine the new mayor's plan of action. A few were directly related to everyday political battles within the municipal council. Accusations of corruption and patronage were notable.[19] However this period is examined, the real issue rested with the inability of any mayor to hold onto a ruling coalition and maintain any discipline within the municipal council. These tensions between mayor and council were evidence of the institutional characteristics at the local level that essentially reproduced the confrontations between executive and legislative branches at the national one. Thus, in this situation, holding onto a ruling coalition to secure policy implementation is crucial. Medina and CONDEPA proved that they could not hang onto the allies who had brought them to power.

Medina faced other serious obstacles to governing the city. The impact of the MNR's "popular participation" program that affected all municipal governments in the country was not felt in La Paz, where it would have been most visible. The Popular Participation Law (LPP), promulgated on April 21, 1994, radically changed the territorial, economic, and democratic conditions of local government in Bolivia.[20] The transfer of political and economic power to municipal governments, along with increased social participation, would be a revolutionary process equivalent to the 1952 transformation of the country. Territorially, the new law defined the municipality as a section of a province and placed every rural and urban square inch of the nation under the political-administrative jurisdiction of one of about three hundred municipal governments. It also provided a relatively large amount of financial resources to these municipal governments on a per capita basis. In short, the LPP may eventually ensure that national resources that have been accumulating in the Central Bank since early July 1994 will be disbursed to the newly constituted municipalities. Moreover, it granted legal status to traditional citizens' groups at the grass-roots level, arguing that it would facilitate their participation in and oversight of municipal government.

During the law's first year, 308 municipal governments were established. These replaced 1,100 local ones. With the resources that they receive from the state, these municipal governments have initiated the construction of over one thousand schools, health-care clinics, roads, and public restrooms. The national government claimed that eight thousand such projects were completed in 1995. The most recent data available showed that as of April 1995, some three thousand communities and neighborhood associations had been recognized, with an additional seven thousand pending. The LPP proved to be popular internationally as extensive media coverage of its implementation painted a positive picture of a law intended to empower local government and allow citizens to decide how revenues would be spent.

Domestically, the law stirred only a bit of controversy. The principal accusation was that the so-called territorial base communities and vigilance committees were less instruments of accountability and more MNR mechanisms to control local government. The truth probably lies somewhere in between; however, the opposition, especially CONDEPA, used this as a rallying cry against the government. Moreover, the LPP appeared to go against the grain of previous administrative decentralization initiatives and bypassed the powerful civic committees in each city and department who considered the new law a threat to their vision of decentralization. Civic committees called for an elected prefect in each department and a weaker municipal council. In April 1995 this debate came to a head with a sharp confrontation with regional civic committees from Tarija, Santa Cruz, and elsewhere demanding the implementation of a decentralization law. While the LPP had a huge impact throughout Bolivia, La Paz was not a direct beneficiary since its provisions were not enforced in the capital. The reasons for this lack are not entirely clear.

Suffice it to say that Popular Participation became a significant issue that showed up dramatically in the campaign against Medina. Nevertheless, she was able to complete her term with a great degree of popular support among those sectors of the capital that had been strong backers of CONDEPA over the past eight years. Moreover, she played a critical role in expanding the role of women in Bolivian politics. In 1995 two other women were recruited by the MNR and MIR to run against her. At the same time, however, Medina managed to stir up a great deal of anti-CONDEPA sentiment among the principal political parties. It was not surprising, therefore, that the main premise of the 1995 electoral campaign among ADN, the MNR, the MBL, and others was to forge a coalition to end CONDEPA's grip on the La Paz city government.

The 1995 Municipal Elections

The December 1995 elections were perceived as an important gauge of the popularity of the MNR at the national level and CONDEPA at the municipal level in La Paz. Overall, the message was clear in urban centers: the MNR lost in most mayoral cities, although it obtained the most votes at the national level. President Sánchez de Lozada argued that the importance of the elections was not necessarily rooted in the MNR's performance but in that of the MBL and UCS, the other parties of the national ruling coalition. The latter two won surprising victories in the cities of Cochabamba and Santa Cruz, respectively. In Cochabamba, the MBL won by recruiting a charismatic former ADN member named "Bombon." In Santa Cruz, the MBL won largely as a result of a sympathy vote for UCS after

Table 9. Municipal Elections in the City of La Paz, December 1995

Party	Votes	Percentage
ADN	60,959	20.17
CONDEPA	114,910	38.22
EJE	1,177	0.39
FRI	2,753	0.92
IU	2,822	0.94
MBL	25,023	8.32
MIR	9,949	3.31
MNR	45,807	15.23
MPP	18,423	0.42
MRTKL	1,262	0.42
UCS	14,354	4.77
VR-9	3,253	1.08
Valid votes	300,692	
Blank	3,188	1.02
Null	8,194	2.63
Votes cast	312,074	
Absent	144,745	31.69
Registered	456,819	
Actas	1,913	

Source: National Electoral Court, final results.

Fernández's death in the plane accident in November. Fernández's son Johnny became the new mayor of Bolivia's second largest city.

Table 10. The La Paz Municipal Council, 1995-2000

Party	Candidate	Seats
MNR	Gabriela Candia	2
CONDEPA	Mónica Medina de Palenque	11
ADN	Ronald Maclean	2
MBL	Rodolfo Galvez	1
MIR	Mabel Cruz	0
MPP	Julio Mantilla	1
UCS	Alfonso Gosalvez	1

Source: National Electoral Court.

The results in La Paz ratified the relative stability of support for CONDEPA. Mónica Medina won the elections with 38.2 percent of the popular vote. In contrast, the MNR, which had carried the 1993 elections with 39.9 percent, barely achieved 15.2 percent despite having recruited Gabriela Candia, a talented young economist with a degree from Columbia University, as its candidate. The MIR also attempted to challenge Medina by recruiting another young professional woman, Mabel Cruz, but Cruz could barely muster 3.3 percent of the vote. While the MBL did not recruit a woman, it attempted to emulate yet another CONDEPA legacy. This former Marxist party tapped Rodolfo Galvez, a popular radio talk-show host. Almost immediately, Galvez became a significant anti-corruption crusader, and he did well enough to get on the municipal council.

In this context, ADN became the party that benefited most from the results, despite an 18-point difference between its candidate, Ronald Maclean, and Mónica Medina (ADN obtained 20 percent of the vote.) Noting that nearly 60 percent of the population had voted against Medina, Maclean set out to craft a coalition that would elect him to the mayor's office for a fourth time. Maclean's efforts centered on the MNR and its allies at the national level. On December 7 an agreement between the principal opposition parties ended Medina's claim to office.[21] The so-called Declaración de La Paz signed by the MNR, the MBL, UCS, and ADN returned Maclean to the mayor's office for another four years. Under the terms of the agreement, the MNR's Candia would serve as president of the council, the UCS's Gosalvez would be vice president, and the MBL's Galvez would be secretary general until the year 2000. The La Paz

Declaration was public ratification of an unwritten agreement between all opposition parties to not vote for Medina under any circumstances.

In his first few months back in office, Maclean devoted a great deal of his efforts to push for the implementation of the LPP in La Paz and pledged to complete the numerous projects left undone since he left office in 1991. Maclean and his MNR allies also unleashed charges of corruption against Medina, claiming that her tenure was one of the most corrupt in La Paz history. While a great deal of evidence has been put forward, the fact remains that CONDEPA and Medina are still extremely popular in La Paz and will remain significant contenders in years to come.

Conclusion

This survey of municipal elections in La Paz has highlighted a few general trends that are worth reiterating. At most, these observations should be taken as preliminary thoughts on politics at the local level in Bolivia. Much work, both quantitative and qualitative, is required to determine if the patterns noted here hold over time.

The first general observation is that the old adage that all politics is local has also shaped the electoral battles in La Paz. The success of CONDEPA demonstrates that, in contrast to the traditional parties, this party paid a great deal of attention to its "district." As have the voters in any Boston precinct, the dwellers of La Paz's *villas* have voted for the candidate who does not forget about them, who knocks on their doors to ask for their votes, and who speaks their language. The trade-off for CONDEPA was simple: success in La Paz versus failure at the national level. CONDEPA's third consecutive municipal victory in December suggests that it may now be safe to make a move nationally.

Max Fernández's UCS provides an interesting contrast. Blessed with more resources, UCS focused on a national strategy aimed at winning general elections. In the process, however, it revealed that it had no home base. Electoral and polling data suggest that UCS was quickly overtaken by CONDEPA and even the MNR among working-class voters. But this is only half the story. CONDEPA's success in La Paz has a lot to do with its appeals to race, class, and nationalism. In many ways, this mix is ominously familiar. With some degree of correctness, CONDEPA has stirred fear in the minds of the upper-middle classes of La Paz. These classes, however, should not worry. CONDEPA has behaved in many ways like other traditional parties: in its administration of the mayor's office, the party revealed that it was interested more in distributing patronage to its followers and fitting into the political system. Its great day (*jach'a uru*) has indeed arrived.

Moreover, CONDEPA reflects that old habits die slowly. Municipal elections in La Paz reveal the persistence of patrimonialism and the tenacity of regional caudillos. Carlos Palenque's appeal as El Compadre is based largely on his ability to deliver promises to his *ahijados* (godchildren) by resolving basic problems of *villa* dwellers. His radio and television programs have served as an alternative, and more efficient, administration of justice. Citizens' everyday problems ranging from wife abuse to lost children have been targeted by El Compadre and CONDEPA. The general perception of voters is that CONDEPA's control over the municipal government will only mean greater attention to their everyday problems.

CONDEPA has served as a major stabilizing force for La Paz and for the neighboring city of El Alto and the surrounding *altiplano*. The social sectors that it has attracted are the natural constituency for more radical options. By bringing them into the political system, CONDEPA has become an important buffer against the spread of radical guerrilla alternatives. Through CONDEPA, displaced sectors believe that they have a voice in the system that not only protects them but also delivers its promises.

A second general conclusion about La Paz municipal elections is that campaigns have not been dominated by political or partisan disputes, although these have been present, especially among the traditional parties. For the most part, the parties responded to the electorate's demands for solutions to everyday problems. In other words, the average voter at the local level demands better sewers, garbage collection, potable water, electrical service, and paved streets. Voters do not appear to be concerned with internal partisan disputes. In a city of one million inhabitants where potable water, electric service, and sewer services barely reach one-half of the population, it is not surprising that the electorate is concerned more with these issues than with political ideology.

Municipal elections in La Paz have acted as an important recruitment mechanism for the political system. Since 1985 its municipal council has produced at least four major personalities who have already or will go on to become important political contenders at the national level. Julio Mantilla and Ronald Maclean are only the most outstanding. It is noteworthy that Palenque himself has been recruited into the political process through his party's success in the La Paz municipal elections. Moreover, all parties have actively recruited individuals with strong ties to civic committees and other local organizations. Individuals such as Raúl Salmón and Fernando Cajías, for example, were recruited by the MIR because of their well-known civic work for La Paz.

On a more institutional level, it is clear that municipal elections in La Paz reproduce the basic problems of the national political system. This situation is especially true in the indirect procedure used to elect a mayor. While protecting minority party representation, Bolivia's multiparty and proportional representation system prevents the formation of solid majorities, thereby making more difficult the election of a mayor in the city council. Although political pacts at the national level between ruling parties, such as the Pacto por la Democracia and Acuerdo Patriótico, have done well in the local councils, they are often not strong enough to prevent the second- or even third-place finisher from contesting the mayor's office.

To prevent impasses such as the one following the 1987 elections, the size of the municipal council was increased to thirteen, yet this action has done little to prevent the threat of another stalemate. In 1991 only Maclean's early concession kept another long battle from happening in the council. As of mid-1996 the council faces the threat of an impasse. The December 1993 adoption of an amendment granting seven seats to the winner of a simple majority appears to be one way of resolving the recurrence of this problem. At the same time, however, it betrays the best features of proportional representation by reducing representation by smaller parties. Finally, for all the negative traits attributed to the current system, the fact remains that it has forced political parties to bargain, to compromise, and to govern the city jointly. In many ways, the system at the local level is parliamentary—that is, the head of government is elected by a parliamentary body (city council), and he or she may be forced to resign at the discretion of this body. In some measure, this parliamentary feature has contributed to the stability of local politics.

References

Archondo, Rafael. 1991. *Compadres al micrófono: La resurrección metropolitana del ayllu*. La Paz: HISBOL.

Baldivia, José Baldivia. 1988. *Balance y perspectivas: Elecciones municipales*. La Paz: Instituto Latinoamericano de Investigaciones Sociales.

————, and Leticia Sáinz. 1987. *Elecciones municipales: Candidatos y propuestas*. La Paz: Instituto Latinoamericano de Investigaciones Sociales.

Bedregal, Guillermo. 1987a. "Comité de Rescate del MNR." *Presencia*. December 9.

————. 1987b. "El MNR y el resultado de las elecciones municipales de 1987." *Presencia*. December 20.

Carrera de Ciencias Políticas. 1994. "Encuesta." La Paz: Universidad Mayor de San Andres. Mimeo.

El Diario. 1987–1994, various issues.

Gamarra, Eduardo. 1989. "Mass Elections and Elite Arrangements: Elections and Democracy in Bolivia." Paper presented at the Fifteenth Congress of the Latin American Studies Association, Miami, Florida. December.

————. 1995. "Market-Oriented Reforms and Democratization in Bolivia," in Joan Nelson and Marcelo Cavarozzi, eds. *The Precarious Balance: Democratic Consolidation and Economic Reform in Latin America and Eastern Europe*. Washington, DC: International Center for Economic Growth.

————, and James Malloy. 1995. "The Patrimonial Dynamics of Party Politics in Bolivia," in Scott Mainwaring and Timothy Scully, eds. *Building Democratic Institutions: Parties and Party Systems in Latin America*. Stanford, CA: Stanford University Press.

Hoffman, Renata. 1988. *A propósito de las elecciones municipales*. La Paz: Instituto Latinoamericano de Investigaciones Sociales.

Hoy Internacional. Various issues.

Informe R. Various issues.

Laserna, Roberto. 1992. "1989: Elecciones y democracia en Bolivia." *Revista Mexicana de Sociología* 52, no. 4 (October–December): 205–26.

Lazarte, Jorge. 1989. *Movimiento obrero y procesos políticos en Bolivia*. La Paz: Editorial Offset, 1989.

————. 1991. "Partidos, democracia, problemas de representación e informalización de la política: El caso de Bolivia." Unpublished manuscript.

————. 1993. *Bolivia, cerlezas in certidumbres de la democracia*. Cochabamba: ILDIS: Los Amigos del Libro, 1993.

Malloy, James, and Eduardo Gamarra, eds. 1988. *Revolution and Reaction: Bolivia, 1964–1985*. New Brunswick, NJ: Transaction.

Mayorga, Fernando. 1992. *Max Fernández: La política del silencio*. La Paz: Instituto Latinoamericano de Investigaciones Sociales.

Mesa Gilbert, Carlos. 1992. "Bolivia municipales del '91, neoliberalismo vs. populismo." *Nueva Sociedad* 117 (January–February): 15–19.

Moldiz Mercado, Hugo. 1989. "Las dos caras des estado de sitio." *Aqui*. November 18.

———. 1993. "Despues de las elecciones, un doble desafío: CONDEPA romper el cerco del temor, el MNR evitar el enfrentamiento." *Ultima Hora*. December 12.

O'Donnell, Guillermo. 1990. "Delegative Democracy?" University of Notre Dame, Kellogg Institute Working Paper 172. December 1990.

Presencia. 1986–1995, various issues.

San Martín Arzabe, Hugo. 1991. *El Palenquismo: Movimiento social, populismo, informalidad política*. La Paz: Editorial Los Amigos del Libro.

Saravia, Joaquín, and Godofredo Sandoval. 1991. *Jach'a Uru: La esperanza de un pueblo?* La Paz: Instituto Latinoamericano de Investigaciones Sociales.

Soruco, Juan Carlos. 1988. "Bolivia: Ocaso de un ciclo histórico." *Nueva Sociedad* 94 (March–April): 13–21.

Notes

1. Prior to 1987, municipal elections were tied to national elections. For a general survey of Bolivian politics at the national level, see Malloy and Gamarra (1988).

2. Mario Mercado was mayor of La Paz in the 1970s under the dictatorship of General Hugo Banzer Suárez. Armando Escobar Uría was a popular mayor in the late 1960s under the presidency of General René Barrientos Ortuño.

3. Until 1989 the municipal council was composed of twelve members. In that year the number was raised to thirteen in an attempt to prevent a stalemate. In 1983 the number was lowered to eleven.

4. For a more comprehensive history of contemporary political parties in Bolivia, consult Gamarra and Malloy (1995).

5. The best studies on the parties and their leaders can be found in Lazarte (1989, 1992), Saravia and Sandoval (1991), Mayorga (1992), Archondo (1991), and San Martín Arzabe (1991).

6. Author's interview with Max Fernández, La Paz, March 3, 1989.

7. Author's interview with U.S. embassy officials, La Paz, July 1991.

8. Fernández missed the deadline to register his new party in the National Electoral Court and was kept from running for office. He claimed that U.S. embassy pressure on the court prevented the registration of his party.

9. In one instance, for example, workers defended Don Max against charges of ties to the drug industry from Guillermo Lora, Bolivia's oldest

Trotskyite leader. Lora was subsequently jailed following a lawsuit for defamation and libel brought against him by Fernández's lawyers.

10. In early 1991, for example, several hundred ADN militants from Cochabamba publicly announced their support for UCS.

11. For an excellent comparison of the 1985 and 1987 elections, consult Baldivia (1988) and Hoffman (1988).

12. Personal communication from former Minister of Finance Juan Cariaga, La Paz, June 1994.

13. In his attempt to exert control over the MIR, Salmón pressured Jaime Paz Zamora to name him vice presidential candidate and to surrender seven slots on the party's legislative lists. Personal communication with MIR party officials, Miami, December 1988.

14. Author's interview with Ronald Maclean, La Paz, December 12, 1992.

15. The MNR won a plurality in the 1989 general elections, but Article 90 of the Constitution dictates that in the event no candidate has won 50 percent plus 1, it is up to the National Congress to elect the next president from the top three vote-getters. In 1989, Banzer's ADN voted for Jaime Paz Zamora and the MIR in what most consider the political turnaround of the century. For a discussion of the 1989 general elections, see Gamarra (1989) and Laserna (1992).

16. The National Electoral Court was composed of representatives of the MNR, the MIR, and ADN. Together the MIR and ADN controlled 4 out of the 7 seats on the court. The MNR charged that the MIR and ADN used this majority—facetiously labeled *la banda de los cuatro*—to commit fraud in the recounting of ballots following the May 1989 election. Because the same court was in place to regulate the December 1989 municipal election, fears on the part of the opposition were presumably justified.

17. For a powerful indictment of the government's motives, see the letter sent to the vice president of Bolivia and the president of the National Congress by five MBL deputies entitled "En defensa del estado de derecho." *Presencia*, November 19, 1989.

18. CONDEPA took as its own the Aymara multicolored flag called Wiphala.

19. Political jokes, a Bolivian national sport, became focused on Mónica Medina. As might be expected in a very *machista* society, most had a sexist twist.

20. The law was signed by President Gonzalo Sánchez de Lozada on April 20, 1994, and published in the Official Gazette of Bolivia as Law No. 1551 on April 21. Its most profound structural changes include the establishment of 308 municipalities and the redistribution of economic resources to these on a per capita basis in each provincial section. Fifty percent of all investment will occur, in theory, at the municipal level.

21. It is important to reiterate that under the new municipal laws, the La Paz council has 11 seats and a winning candidate must secure 50 percent plus 1 to become mayor. In the event that no candidate achieves a majority, the council must vote for mayor.

3

Local Urban Elections in Democratic Brazil

Gil Shidlo

The years 1988 and 1992 saw the first elections free from military intervention that allowed the selection of mayors in major cities in Brazil. Prior to that time, during the two decades of military rule, there were no real contests in major municipalities defined as important to national security, since mayors were appointed by the national government. Local elections were held only in medium-sized and small cities, although in 1982 the military permitted voters to choose at every level except the presidential one.[1]

Unlike other Latin American countries, national politics and elections are not reflected by what happens in the capital, Brasília. Brazil is highly urbanized, with 75 percent of its population living in cities in 1988. According to the 1970 census, there were five cities with more than one million inhabitants; in 1987 the number had risen to 11 million. In 1991 the ten major metropolitan regions accounted for 49.1 million inhabitants, or one-third of the total population (147 million). These major metropolitan regions are São Paulo (16.5 million), Rio de Janeiro (10.4 million), Belo Horizonte (4.6 million), Pôrto Alegre (3.7 million), Salvador (3.1 million), Recife (2.9 million), Fortaleza (2.35 million), Curitiba (2.32 million), Belém (1.62 million), and Brasília (1.6 million).

Over the last fifty years or so there have been major changes in the distribution of population between states due to migration. This demographic redistribution has traditionally favored urban centers and, more recently, new regions of agricultural production, such as Rondônia and Pará in the north, Paraná in the south, and all the states in the center west. The scale of migration has been substantial, with more than 24 million people moving from their place of birth during the 1970s. Preliminary 1991 census data for the ten largest states and the Federal District of Brasília show that urbanization has continued throughout the 1980s. However, the two largest metropolitan areas—São Paulo and Rio de Janeiro—are experiencing "demetropolization" with people dispersing into smaller cities and towns outside these two giant metropolises.

In 1991 the metropolitan region, which includes São Paulo (the largest city and a traditional magnet for immigration), experienced its first net out-migration since the 1940s. This trend is predicted to accelerate over the next five years, possibly stabilizing by the turn of the century. The cities continuing to grow are mainly in the northeast. During the decade from 1980 to 1991 cities such as Salvador and Fortaleza had higher annual median growth rates (2.72 percent and 2.77 percent, respectively) than São Paulo and Rio de Janeiro (1.15 percent and 0.66 percent, respectively).

Local elections took place in 1972, 1976, and 1982 under military rule and in 1985, 1988, and 1992 under democratic conditions.[2] And while results from rural areas will be discussed here, state capitals receive most of the attention, since data are more complete and more accessible. Nevertheless, rural results are important in identifying party strengths and weaknesses.

Urban Social Movements and Local Elections

In the 1970s, a period of economic growth but also a decade when state repression was at its worst, new forms of neighborhood associations came into being.[3] These neighborhood associations were most often linked to Comunidades Eclesias de Base (CEBs, or ecclesial base communities) and were part of an organized and vocal popular movement with an eclectic array of different elements, including labor unions, professional organizations, and religious groups. These popular movements were important because they provided a measure of resistance to the military regime, played a prominent role in the organization of a number of large-scale public protests, and eventually formed the basis for a new political party, the Partido dos Trabalhadores (PT), in 1979.

The CEBs arose out of a renewal taking place within the Catholic Church in Brazil in the 1960s. They aimed to enact communitarian ways of life embodying Christian values of equality and solidarity. Without the help of political parties, and often inspired by basic Christian communities, localized pressure groups began to appear throughout Brazil. The Church created political space for issues as diverse as living conditions for the poor, workers' rights, the cost of living, illegal land subdivisions, landownership for squatters, and direct elections for the presidency. Specific examples of popular movements include the Movimento da Saúde (Health Movement, formed originally in 1973 and directed at improved medical services); Movimento da Favela (Squatter Settlement Movement, created in 1976 to secure land titles and improve services and infrastructure); and Movimento dos Desempregados (Unemployed Movement, formed in 1983 to solve immediate problems of joblessness through demands for unemployment benefits). A main feature of these popular urban social movements in Brazil is the role of women in their formation and organization. Since the 1970s the number of women in such organizations increased rapidly and constituted in the late 1980s, on average, 80 percent of participants. While women tended to be heavily underrepresented in political parties and trade unions, their roles as leaders in urban social movements was unmistakable (Corcoran-Nantes, 1990).

During the final years of the military regime, and in the context of the increasing importance of electoral politics, some public agencies began to encourage contact between public officials and the population targeted by social service policies. At the same time opposition parties, such as the PT, Partido Movimento Democrático Brasileiro (PMDB), and Partido Comunista do Brasil (PCdoB), supported the dialogue between civil society and the state, thereby reinforcing these popular demand-driven groups. But leftist political parties gave the most support to the new urban social movements, "seeing them as healthy indicators of the popular sectors' strength. And perhaps this explains why they try to enlist the most militant popular leaders, creating a double militancy for them. Still, as members of local associations, these leaders have to continually reaffirm the nonpartisan nature of their interventions" (Cardoso, 1992:297).

Still, Ruth Cardoso (1992) concludes from her research in São Paulo that urban social movements supported specific congress members who could help them channel particular demands. "The groups are more likely to choose those politicians who encourage greater popular participation and are willing to subordinate themselves to the movements' guidelines, whereupon they serve as intermediaries to set up appointments with mayors or state authorities" (Cardoso, 1992). In some instances these organizations sought access to politicians who were opposed to popular movements but who had connections to the executive.

The PDT, the PT, and Neighborhood Associations

In Rio de Janeiro the Partido Democrático Trabalhista (PDT) won the elections in 1982 under the leadership of Leonel Brizola. The emergence of the PDT as a major political force in Rio cost the PMDB control of the state and its municipal government. Throughout the election campaign, the PDT made a clear commitment to Rio's *favelas* (squatter settlements), thereby generating substantial support for Brizola in 1982. But his victory also raised expectations among the leadership of the *favelas* that, once in office, the PDT would favor popular participation in government. In fact, the PDT probably did more for the *favelas* than any other administration in Rio, in terms of both its various programs and the accessibility that leaders of *favela* neighborhood associations had to the state (Gay, 1994).

For example, soon after the PDT took office in 1983, it developed programs to provide or improve urban and social services to the *favelas*. The most important of these programs, which became a political issue in the 1986 campaign, was the construction of high schools designed to keep children in school all day and to provide food, health care, and physical recreation. Another important program was the distribution by the state of titles of landownership to *favela* dwellers.

> The PDT's strategy was to carry out public works projects in a small but highly visible part of the largest number of favelas in Rio. In most cases these projects would also be carried out in stages. The rationale behind these strategies was twofold. First, these projects, no matter how small, would in themselves generate support for the party. Second, conducting these projects in stages encouraged those who might have voted to vote for the PDT, for fear that the projects would be discontinued if the party was not returned to office (Gay, 1994:31).

At the same time, however, the PDT embarked on a strategy to co-opt Rio's *favela* leaders. Those of the FAFERJ (Favela Neighborhood Associations of Rio de Janeiro) were frequently seen in state and municipal administrative offices, thus creating the impression that the PDT encouraged popular participation. Furthermore, presidents of *favela* neighborhood associations were invited by the PDT to work as advisers to the state agencies responsible for implementing the urban and social programs. Such acts by the PDT made it difficult for the leaders of the *favelas* to maintain their independence from the party. The PDT municipal government of Rio also provided FAFERJ with rent-free offices and employed some of its directors as political advisers.

To complicate matters further, several directors of FAFERJ were nominated as PDT candidates in local elections. For instance, the election of Roberto Saturino Braga as mayor of Rio de Janeiro in 1985 improved relations between the PDT and the *favela* neighborhood movement, since his running mate was the former president of FAMERJ (Federação de Associacoes de Moradores do Estado de Rio de Janeiro, a federation of middle-class neighborhood groups). One of Braga's most important initiatives, once in office, was the creation of local government-community councils, whose objective was to determine priorities in state investment in each of Rio's regions. But the community councils were headed by administrators nominated on the basis of allegiance to the PDT and not by democratic elections. This whole operation by the PDT was regarded by critics as a decentralization of the problems without decentralizing the power to solve them.

Participation and decentralization were central themes in PT's electoral platform. The direct election of Gilson Menezes as mayor of Diadema (São Paulo) in 1982 brought new opportunities to democratize municipal administration. But while the newly elected PT government in Diadema considered consulting delegates elected from each of the neighborhoods, the Diadema city officials soon realized that they lacked the organization required to sustain such a form of direct democracy and turned to the promotion of other venues of popular participation. Due to friction between municipal executives, local party leaders, the local legislature, and the mayor, the PT's first attempt at popular government failed (Keck, 1992). Its lack of experience in city management was one of the main reasons for this failure.

Popular Participation in Municipal Governance

In 1988, after the municipal elections in which the PT won in São Paulo, popular participation would again be a major challenge.

Mayor Luiza Erundina, during her first year in office (1989), promoted "popular participation" by mandating that the twenty regional administrations serve as participatory channels. However, sectoral city agencies simultaneously started their own decentralization and participation programs, resulting in inefficiencies and considerable confusion, and the following year Mayor Erundina decided to decrease these activities to a consultative character.

In the early 1990s a new Organic Law of Municipality was formulated, which foresaw the establishment of city councils involved in sectoral planning as well as the creation of subprefectures with financial and budgetary autonomy. Thus, the PT administration in São Paulo, abandoned the notion of people's councils and instead adopted another mechanism created by the new Organic Law: a council of representatives to monitor the subprefectures. At the same time, the PT encouraged Paulistas to participate through public meetings in debates on the budget, the city master plan, and the Organic Law (Assies, 1993).

In other large cities, such as Vitória (Espírito Santo) and Pôrto Alegre (Rio Grande do Sul), PT governments encouraged popular participation in decisions concerning the municipal budget. The PT administration in Vitória invited social movements as well as the general population to discuss the 1989 budget. In 1990 a commission was established with representatives from popular movements, nongovernment organizations, and the municipality. Initial meeting were held at the neighborhood level where demands were noted and delegates elected. These delegates took part in meetings where regional priorities were defined as well as discussed the budget with the Planning Department and other city departments. Although neighborhood and social movements held a meeting of delegates to vote on the budget, the municipal council had the final voice.

A different strategy for popular participation was initiated by the PT in Pôrto Alegre in 1989. Meetings were held to discuss the budget and to elect representatives in sixteen newly created microregions in the city. The delegates took part in the Forum of Representatives, established by the PT administration of Pôrto Alegre. But participation in the formulation of the budget was rather limited, and the delegates shifted their attention to specific investment items and the planning of public works. Nevertheless, the Forum of Representatives was widely publicized and contributed to the PT's winning local elections again in 1992.

The Military and Urban Elections

Although a number of studies have investigated the significance of elections under military regimes, few relate directly to local elections (Diniz, 1982; Lamounier, 1986; Shidlo, 1990b.). For many years, analysts tended to treat the existence of elections, parties, and the Congress in authoritarian Brazil as a meaningless facade. Even though local elections were held from 1964 to 1985, it was only in 1982 that direct local elections took place. Until the 1982 contests, the military imposed a two-party system composed of a government party, Alianca Renovadora Nacional (ARENA), and an official opposition party, Movimento Democrático Brasileiro (MDB).

ARENA was given the full backing of the state and, not surprisingly, dominated the elections of 1972 and 1976. Yet, in spite of its advantages, ARENA did not win the landslide expected in 1976. On the contrary, the party won only a 5 percent margin over the MDB. In 1972 the MDB won mayoral elections and gained control of the city councils in only thirty-one of the one hundred largest cities. In 1976 it won fifty-nine.

The direct municipal, congressional, and gobernatorial elections of November 1982 were the most open since 1962 and occurred during a period of economic hardship and after the postponement of municipal elections from 1980 to 1982. "According to many observers, they were the first truly free elections in twenty years, the first unhampered by the ominous presence of an institutional act that had overridden the Brazilian constitution" (Soares, 1986, p. 292). The 1982 elections were as crucial to the *abertura* (opening toward democracy) as they were to the creation of an electoral college, consisting of members of the Congress and delegates from state legislatures who were to elect a new president in 1985. On November 15 the country elected new state governors, federal senators and deputies, state legislators, municipal councilors, and (except in areas falling under the national security regulations) new mayors.

Five "new" parties competed in the 1982 elections. Theoretically, only those that had never competed in previous elections were allowed to participate. The use of labels from the old two-party system was not allowed by the military regime. In practice, as many observers pointed out, the new government party, the Partido Democrático Social (PDS), was simply ARENA with a new name. The opposition MDB then became the PMDB.

Three small parties appeared as well. First, the PT whose origins go back only to the 1978 ABC region (Santo André, São Bernardo do Campo, and São Caetano do Sul) metalworkers' strikes in São Paulo, in which its leader, Luís Ignacio da Silva ("Lula"), then a union president, attained national fame. Through cooperation with the more assertive unions and the Church's CEBs, the PT established directorates and drew up slates of candidates for the 1982 elections all over Brazil. Second, the Partido Trabalhista Brasileiro (PTB), which tried unsuccessfully to revive a popular party label from the pre-1964 electoral period. It relied on the mystical image of Getulio Vargas that was revived by his grandniece and party leader Ivete Vargas. The PTB entered into various coalitions with the PDS but eventually pulled out. With the death of Ivete Vargas in 1984, the PTB's future was placed in jeopardy. And third, the PDT, led by the legendary politician Leonel Brizola. His base has been almost exclusively limited to the states of Rio de Janeiro, where he was elected governor, and Rio Grande do Sul, his home state.

These three small parties were created from scratch after the two-party system was disbanded by the military in 1979. A provision by the military government required that each party field candidates for all offices being contested in a given municipality. If a party failed to comply, it was barred altogether from the ballot. This provision was intended to force opposition parties to run their own candidates in each municipality and to compete against each other. Of the three small parties, only the PT fielded a slate of candidates in all municipalities. "Perhaps the most significant aspect of the PT campaign was its ability to open the political process to marginalized sectors of the population who had never before been active in political organizations and parties" (Alves, 1985:225).

A highly restrictive electoral "package" issued in November 1981 brought an abrupt halt to the optimistic aspirations of the opposition. This measure weakened the opposition parties' chances just as their collective standings in the polls looked strong. To reduce opposition strength and prop up the waning official PDS, party alliances were prohibited, straight-ticket voting was made mandatory, and all parties were required to submit candidates for all posts within a state in order to present a slate at all.

An additional electoral measure instituted a ballot without party and candidate names, requiring voters to write in all their candidates (a possible total of six) separately by name or number.

This measure was aimed directly at the opposition parties, since presumably only the PDS had sufficient local organization to ensure that its voters would learn to fill out their ballots correctly (Skidmore, 1989).

The results of the 1982 municipal elections were ambiguous enough to give both government and opposition reasons to celebrate. Neither side received a crippling setback. The PDS won nearly two-thirds of the country's municipalities, over one-half of the state governorships, two-thirds of the Senate, and 52.6 percent of the electoral college as well as a near-simple majority of the Chamber of Deputies. Yet the opposition won a substantial number of governorships and showed strength in the larger cities, in the most developed regions of the country, and with the middle class. In specific terms, the PMDB won seventy-five of the one hundred largest cities, while the PDS took seventeen, the PDT four, and the PTB and PT each one. The opposition won city council majorities in nineteen of the twenty-three state capitals and extended its control of municipalities from 12.7 percent to 34.8 percent of the total of 4,085.

Nationally, the success of the PDS inversely correlated with urbanization and overall development. In the state of São Paulo, for example, the PDS won only 22.5 percent of the valid party vote for federal deputies. Even in the northeast the PMDB won council majorities in seven of the nine capital cities, while overwhelming PDS majorities were rolled up mainly in the interior.

The 1982 elections were especially important to the PT, Brazil's most authentic left-wing party. During the 1982 campaign the PT not only succeeded in registering in every state but also built networks of local supporters who would be crucial in future elections. The results of the 1982 elections were disappointing. The PT did not meet the law's minimum goal of 5 percent nationally and 3 percent in each of the nine states; it won over 3 percent only in São Paulo and Acre. Yet the mayoral PT candidates who won, as well as the seventy-eight council members in thirty-nine municipalities in São Paulo, gained political and administrative experience that would be valuable when they entered national elections.

Urban Elections under a Transitional Regime

The military president of Brazil, General Joãs Baptista Figueiredo, along with the PDS leadership, was determined to control the 1985 presidential elections. But huge nationwide demonstrations favoring direct election of the president revealed the public's impatience with the slow pace of *abertura*. The PMDB's presidential candidate, Minas Gerais governor Tancredo Neves, was on good terms with the military and well suited to carry out the transition. He appealed as well to PDS backers without whose support he could not win, since the PMDB was by 1985 a minority party (Skidmore, 1989). The PDS nominee was former São Paulo governor Paulo Salim Maluf. Dissident members of the PDS accused Maluf of trying to buy the election and bolted from the party in July 1984, forming the Partido Frente Liberal (PFL) and issuing their own election manifesto. Maluf's arrogance and electioneering tactics alienated key members of the PDS, who defected and joined the PMDB to create the Alianca Democrática. This coalition supported Neves for president and José Sarney for vice president.

The Neves-Sarney ticket secured 480 votes to Maluf's 180 in the electoral college balloting in January 15, 1985. Although Brazil now seemed ready for direct elections for president, full powers to Congress, the writing of the new constitution, and free local elections throughout the country, the death of Neves on the eve of his inauguration found Sarney, a former PDS senator, sworn in as acting president. A traditional northeastern politician, he had been one of the leaders of the party that supported the military government.

In the 1985 elections, the first in two decades with a civilian government in office, the PMDB emerged as the dominant party, winning in seventeen of the country's twenty-three state capitals and in the two territorial capitals (see Table 1). Despite its successes the PMDB suffered some unexpected setbacks in some of the largest urban centers, losing in São Paulo, Rio de Janeiro, Pôrto Alegre, and Recife. Former President Janio Quadros (PTB/PFL) won by a small margin in São Paulo on a right-wing law-and-order platform. The PMDB tried unsuccessfully to form a coalition with the PFL, which had been created by dissidents of the PDS. Another explanation to the PMDB's loss in São Paulo was that the electorate no longer perceived it as the opposition, since quite a few state governors were PMDB party members. Indeed, in São Paulo, both the governor and the mayor belonged to the PMDB. Further, the inability of PMDB elected officials on national, state, and local levels to make substantial improvement in the economy resulted in a frustrated electorate. And finally, the PMDB was attacked from the left by the PT and from the right by the conservative bloc led by Quadros.

Table 1. Urban Electoral Results in State Capitals, 1985–1992

	1985	1988	1992
North			
Rondônia	PMDB	PTB	PSDB
Acre	PMDB	PDS	PT
Amazonas	PMDB[b]	PSB	PDC
Pará	PMDB	PTB	PFL
Roraima	PMDB[b]	PMDB	PDS
Amapá	PMDB	PSB	PSDB
Tocantins[a]	—	—	PDC
Northeast			
Maranhão	PDS	PDT	PSB
Piauí	PMDB	PMDB	PSDB
Ceará	PT	PMDB	PMDB
Rio Grande do Norte	PMDB[c]	PDT	PSB
Paraíba	PMDB[b]	PDT	PDT
Pernambuco	PSB[c]	PFL	PMDB
Alagoas	PMDB[c]	PFL	PSB
Sergibe	PMDB[b]	PSB	PDT
Bahia	PMDB[c]	PMDB	PSDB
Southeast			
Minas Gerais	PMDB	PSDB	PT
Espírito Santo	PMDB	PT	PSDB
Rio de Janeiro	PDT	PDT	PMDB
São Paulo	PTB[b]	PT	PDS
South			
Paraná	PMDB	PDT	PDT
Santa Catarina	PMDB	PDS	PPS
Rio Grande do Sul	PDT	PT	PT
Center West			
Mato Grosso	PMDB	PFL	PDT
Mato Grosso do Sul	PMDB	PTB	PMDB
Goiás	PMDB[c]	PMDB	PT
Distrito Federal	—	—	—

Source: Adapted from O *Estado de São Paulo*, various years.
[a]Tocantins is a new state created in 1988 by subdivision of the former state of Goias.
[b]In alliance with either the PFL, or PFL and PDS.
[c]In alliance with left-wing parties (PSC, PSB, PDT).

The 1985 municipal campaign issues in São Paulo were dictated by one candidate, Janio Quadros, who had been president of Brazil before the 1964 coup d'état and had run on a slogan of "Honesty, Employment, and Security." The reference to employment did not in any way suggest that Quadros would create new jobs but rather that, if elected mayor, he would reduce the number of city employees. His slogan also referred to the need for better security in the city. Quadros's direct attack on the performance of the incumbent PMDB government resulted in the attempt by the PMDB to claim that it was solving the problems raised by Quadros (Lamounier, 1986). There was also an attempt to shift the campaign to the level of national economic issues.

The PDT, under Brizola's leadership, won in both Rio de Janeiro and Pôrto Alegre. The emergence of Quadros in Paulista urban politics and the growth of Brizola's influence suggest that many voters still responded more to personalities than to parties. One study pointed out that a certain segment of the electorate—older people and those with a lower level of education—responded more to the Janista myth than to an identification with a party. According to Bolívar Lamounier and Judith Muszynski, less than one-third of the electorate in São Paulo knew to which party Quadros belonged, while 52 percent associated Eduardo Suplicy with the PT and Fernando Henrique Cardoso with the PMDB (Lamounier and Muszynski, 1986). The most interesting conclusion of this study is that the Janista voters were those who could least associate a candidate with his party.

For the PT the 1985 elections were an important turnaround: "The PT's strong performance in the mayoral elections in state capitals in 1985 gave it a new lease on life and suddenly projected it onto the national stage as a viable and growing political force" (Keck, 1992:154). PT candidates ran in all but one state capital, winning over 5 percent in twelve of them and 3 percent in two others. For the first time, a PT candidate was elected mayor in a major city—Maria Luiza Fontanelle in Fortaleza, the capital of Ceará in the northeast. In three other state capitals the PT's candidates came in second place—Goiânia, Espírito Santo, and Aracaju—while in São Paulo its candidate won nearly one-fifth of the votes.

In summary, the 1985 municipal elections saw the PDS, the military's old base of support, virtually disappear from the large urban areas. At the same time, the PMDB, the former opposition party during the military government, succeeded in carrying 33.9 percent of all votes nationwide, although it failed to capitalize on the electorate's dissatisfaction. This discontent was expressed by voting for the new political parties that emerged. The PDT, PT, and PSB (Partido Socialista Brasileiro), parties that represented the left, won elections in Rio de Janeiro, Recife, and Fortaleza. Together these three parties won 26.5 percent of all votes nationwide. On the right of the political spectrum, conservative parties took 28.2 percent of all votes across Brazil. Janios Quadros of the PTB was one of the candidates with a rightist position:

> This was the beginning of a period of rough turbulence for the party system, which had previously managed to strengthen the identification between voters and parties, albeit through the protest vote. From then on the party of the military regime, the PDS would constantly be rejected by voters, and simultaneously oppositionism spread beyond the boundaries of what had been formerly its main channel of expression, the PMDB, extending to the new parties that began to take shape as of the 1979 party reform legislation (Moises, 1993:589).

Urban Elections under a Democratic Regime

Brazil conducted nationwide mayoral elections in 1988.

> Previously, the military regime had imposed officials on large cities and on certain municipalities it classed as "strategically important," so the 1988 election was the first since the 1964 military takeover in which all municipalities elected their own mayors and councils. Nineteen different parties elected mayors in more than 4,000 municipalities. The major parties (PT, PDT, PMDB, PSDB, PDS, PTB, and PFL) elected a total of 3,164 mayors (Ames, 1994:97).

The 1988 municipal elections were a massive repudiation for the PMDB government. The PMDB lost control of all the capitals in the important southern states, including São Paulo to the PT and Rio de Janeiro to the PDT. The key to the collapse of the PMDB was clearly the government's mismanagement of the economy (inflation ran 1000 percent in 1988), the social crisis, and the proliferation of corruption at all levels of the administration. Not surprisingly, the electorate turned to the opposition candidates.

Thirty-one political parties participated in the 1988 elections. In a record turnout of 75 million voters, the results clearly indicated a shift of the axis to the center-left:

> The 1988 mayoral elections were the first clear sign that the electorate was intent upon a massive rejection of the status quo. The

PMDB became the status quo party, following in the tracks of ARENA and PDS before it and losing ground in the more industrialized center and south of the country, while maintaining a position in the northeast, and losing the large cities while winning in the interior (Keck, 1992:157).

No state governor succeeded in getting his candidate for mayor elected in the state capitals. Even in São Luís, the capital of the state of Maranhão, the candidate for mayor, who had President Sarney's support (Maranhão is Sarney's home state), lost to the PDT.

The PMDB, in spite of its electoral decline, won in Salvador, Fortaleza, Teresina, Boa Vista, Rio Branco, Goiânia, and in 1,200 of 4,307 municipalities, totaling 38 percent of the votes. The PMDB did not retain any of the state capitals in the more developed regions of south and southeastern Brazil. It is important to point out that although we can see a substantial rise in the voting for the left and center-left, the more conservative parties (PMDB, PFL, and PDS) collected a high percentage of the votes, especially in the interior of the states.

One of the biggest surprises was the victory of the PT in Greater São Paulo as well as in thirty other municipalities. The PT, which previously had won only two municipalities (one after the 1982 election and another after the 1985 election), thus had to govern thirty-one city halls, among them three state capitals: São Paulo, Vitória (Espírito Santo), and Pôrto Alegre (Rio Grande do Sul). The PT also won in three other large cities in the state of São Paulo: Santo André, Diadema, and São Bernardo do Campo. Although the PT won mostly in urban centers, "a number of the smaller municipalities where the PT won were rural districts where struggles over land tenure during the 1980s had been particularly virulent, and where the PT worked closely with the landless movement and/or the rural labor organization" (Keck, 1992:156). Luiza Erundina, a social worker, became the first female mayor of the city of São Paulo after emerging from third place in the polls to oust the PDS's Paulo Maluf, the former presidential candidate and the favorite.

The proximity of the 1988 municipal elections to the first direct presidential elections (1989) inspired many references to national political issues during the campaign for mayors by the parties that were planning to field presidential candidates in the following year. Erundina's political campaign consisted primarily of visits to the *favelas* of Greater São Paulo, whose population is considered to be the largest Nordestino settlement in Brazil. Because of the opposition within the PT to Erundina's candidacy for mayor, financial support for her campaign was rather limited. In fact, the leader of the PT, Lula, had supported a different candidate for the municipal election. The 70 million *cruzados* allocated to Erundina were not only less than the funds available to the other candidates but also substantially less than those for several of the PT's candidates for federal deputies. More than one-half of the 70 million *cruzados* was used to pay for her television campaign.

The PDT, led by its founder, Leonel Brizola, kept control of Rio de Janeiro and won the important city of Curitiba; the PDT also won several major towns, including Volta Redonda, and in the northeast the important towns of Natal and São Luís. As a result of the voters' switch to the left, the right-wing PDS won in only one state capital, Florianópolis. The PTB won in the north and centerwest regions: Belém, state capital of Pará; Pôrto Velho, state capital of Rondônia; and Campo Grande, state capital of Mato Grosso do Sul. In the northeast the PFL continued to dominate and even succeeded in ousting the left-wing mayor of Recife; PFL candidates also gained Maceió, João Pessoa, and Cuiabá. The PSDB, a newly formed social democratic party, won only in one state capital, Belo Horizonte. The PSB won in the north and northeast in Manaus, the state capital of Amazonas; Macapá, the state capital of Amapá; and Aracaju, the state capital of Sergipe.

The 1988 municipal elections continued the trend started in 1985. The electorate's disillusionment with politicians would be expressed by voting for new parties. The PMDB won only five mayoralties in state capitals, the same number as those won by the PDT and only two more that those won by the PT; the remaining ten were divided among the PSDB, PSB, PDS, and PTB (Moises, 1993).

Local Elections and the 1988 Constitution

In 1988 the new constitution for the first time contained an article on urban policies. The constitution profoundly modified the position of the municipalities by considering them components of the federal structure:

> Article 1 declared that the Federal Republic of Brazil is formed by a indisolvable union of states, municipalities, and the Federal District. Article 18 declares that the political administrative organization of the Federal Republic of Brazil is composed of the

Union, the States, the Federal District, and the Municipalities, all
of them autonomous in the terms of this Constitution (Ferreira,
1993:59).

For the first time in Brazilian history, municipalities were recognized as integral political administrative and financial entities. It
is only because of the 1988 constitution that they achieved autonomy
through legislation guaranteeing this autonomy.

For example, for the first time since 1964 all mayors, deputy
mayors, and city council members would be chosen through direct
and simultaneously held elections for a period of four years. No
cities would be considered vital for "national security," as they had
been under the military. Candidates for mayor, deputy mayor, and
city council had to be residents of the municipality, whose resource
base was broadened by bringing two more taxes under its authority and by modifying the redistribution of tax revenues. The
municipalities would eventually receive 21 percent of total tax revenues, the state government 42 percent, and federal government
36 percent. The new constitution also stipulated that approval of
municipal organic laws was the task of the city councils instead of
the state legislatures.

In addition to the 1988 constitution, new and more specific legislation that regulated the 1992 local elections was initiated by Senator Mario Covas (PSDB-SP), who had been the mayor of São Paulo.
This legislation, Electoral Law No. 8214 (7–24–1991), initiated many
basic changes:

1) Simultaneous elections were to be held for council mem-
    bers, mayors, and deputy mayors. A second round was
    to be held but only in municipalities with at least 200,000
    voters.
2) Candidates had to be affiliated with a political party at least
    six months prior to the elections and had to reside in the
    municipality for at least one year prior to local elections
    (the 1988 constitution had not specified the length of resi-
    dency prior to candidacy).
3) All candidates were obliged to declare and register all of
    their personal assets in the Office of Titles and Deeds.
4) Each party could register up to double the number of can-
    didates for the municipal council corresponding to the num-
    ber of vacancies to be filled. If two parties decided to form

a coalition, then the number of candidates eligible for registration equaled up to three times the vacancies available.

5) Campaigning through the media had to be prepaid; only
one-eighth of a newspaper page and one-quarter of a magazine page could be used for campaigning.

6) Only up to 50 percent of the available "outdoor" advertising space in a municipality was allowed to be used for
campaign advertising.

7) In cities of 100,000 voters or more, polling stations and
ballot counting would be carried out in the same location.

8) Agencies that conducted a public opinion poll had to divulge to the regional electoral tribunal, at least three days
prior to its official publication, the name of the persons or
the party that solicited the poll and sources of financing as
well as methodology and other relevant information.

9) Persons who prior to registering as candidates were radio
or television anchors had to quit their employment.

10) Electoral candidates were not allowed to be linked to or
associated with widely publicized projects.

11) No electoral program would be censored or suspended.

12) Candidates who claimed slander or defamation by the media had the right to respond by using the same medium
(newspaper, magazine, loudspeaker, television, or radio)
(Ferreira, 1992).

This important legislation was implemented for the first time in
1992.

The Local Elections of 1992

On September 29, 1992, Brazil's Chamber of Deputies voted overwhelmingly to seek President Fernando Collor de Mello's impeachment on corruption charges. The move came only halfway through
Collor's five-year term as the country's first freely elected president in three decades. This was the first time in over a century as a
republic that a president of Brazil was removed by constitutional
means, other than election. An informed and highly demonstrative
public made it clear that it would defeat legislators who supported
the president in the face of overwhelming evidence of corruption.
Previously, other major political figures involved in corrupt behavior, such as President Sarney, had escaped punishment:

Several unusual circumstances contributed to the effective public mobilization against Collor: economic distress caused by
Collor's policies; the timing of municipal elections, scheduled
almost immediately after the vote; and the decision to broadcast
deputies' votes on television. In their absence, it is not at all certain that two-thirds of Brazil's deputies would have voted to begin impeachment proceedings (Geddes and Neto, 1992:644).

The impeachment cleared the way for a trial on charges that the
president's family and friends had accepted huge bribes in return
for government favors.

The impeachment of Collor occurred just before the municipal
elections. The PMDB, PT, PDT, and PDS pressured Deputy Ibsen
Pinheiro to approve the impeachment before the election on October 3, since opposition parties such as the PT were certain that they
would benefit electorally from the impeachment. Elections were
held in 4,963 municipalities for the third time since the return to
democracy. But it was clear that since the reestablishment of democracy, there had never been such a lack of interest in municipal
elections due to Collor's impeachment and to the routine process
of elections.

Apathy was therefore the mark of the 1992 contests. Nearly one-
third of the electorate in São Paulo preferred not to vote for any of
the nine candidates for mayor and opted to vote in blank or abstain (in 1988 the rate had been 24.5 percent). Candidates identified with the government—either federal, state, or municipal—
confronted an electorate that was thoroughly disillusioned with
Collor. A poll carried out in September in twelve state capitals
showed that 63 percent of those interviewed declared that they
would not vote for someone who had Collor's support (ISTOE,
9/30/1992:28). In the first round of the elections the majority of
governors and mayors of state capitals did not see their candidates
win, although some would have a second chance. PMDB candidates won the elections in nearly 2,000 cities out of the total 4,963,
due largely to its well-organized national party organization. Its
candidates also won in one-half of the 625 municipalities in the
state of São Paulo. The PMDB, however, lost in the majority of the
twenty largest municipalities in the state of São Paulo, winning only
in six of them. Still, the PMDB remained the largest single party,
controlling one-third of the Brazilian towns, followed by the PFL,
which won 19 percent but only one state capital. No other party

gained more than 10 percent of the country's towns, thereby underlining growing party fragmentation.

The PMDB candidates won in four state capitals: Campo Grande (Mato Grosso do Sul), Fortaleza (Ceará), Recife (Pernambuco), and Rio de Janeiro (see Table 2). The PSDB (Tucanos) candidates gained Bahia (Salvador), Vitória (Espírito Santo), Teresina (Piauí), Macapá (Amapá), and Pôrto Velho (Rondônia), while the PFL won mostly in the state of Bahia. The PDS won elections mainly in the interior of São Paulo state; Maluf, its candidate for mayor of Greater São Paulo, went on to participate in the second round. Collor's disgrace caused the PRN (Partido da Reconstrução Nacional) virtually to disappear from the electoral map in every state capital. The PPS, the heir to the PCB, won in Florianópolis. The PT won forty-six mayoral races, one of them a state capital (Rio Branco in Acre)

Table 2. State Capitals and Local Elections in 1992

Capital	Party	Mayor
São Paulo PDS	Paulo Maluf	
Rio de Janeiro	PMDB	César Maia
Vitória	PSDB	Paulo Hartung
Salvador	PSDB	Lídice da Mata
Aracaju	PDT	Jackson Barreto
Recife	PMDB	Jarbas Vasconcelos
João Pessoa	PDT	Francisco Franca
Natal	PSB	Aldo Tinoco Filho
Fortaleza	PMDB	Antônio Cambraia
Teresina	PSDB	Wall Ferraz
São Luís	PSB	Conceição Andrade
Macapá	PSDB	João Bosco Papaleo
Belém	PFL	Hélio Gueiros
Maceio	PSB	Ronaldo Lessa
Boa Vista	PDS	Maria Teresa S. Juca
Manaus	PDC	Amazonino Mendes
Pôrto Velho	PSDB	José Guedes
Rio Branco	PT	Jorge Viana
Cuiabá	PDT	Dante de Oliveira
Palmas	PDC	Eduardo S. Campos
Campo Grande	PMDB	Juvêncio Fonseca
Goiânia	PT	Darci Accorsi
Belo Horizonte	PT	Patrus Ananias
Pôrto Alegre	PT	Tarso Genro
Florianópolis	PPS	Sérgio Grande
Curitiba	PDT	Rafael Greca

Source: O Estado de São Paulo, November 17, 1992.

but lost in two critical cities (São Bernardo do Campo and Santo André); it also won in Pôrto Alegre, in Goiânia, and in the important state capital, Belo Horizonte, in the southern region. But overall the PT won in small cities that "have an electorate that is traditionally more interested in electing mayors that promise to construct bridges or pave roads than being involved in great national questions" (ISTOE, 14/10/1992). Finally, the PDC won in the capitals of two center-west states, Palmas (Tocantins) and Manaus (Amazonas).

In most of the largest cities no candidate won a simple majority, and a second round was held on November 15. In Greater São Paulo, Eduardo Suplicy of PT and Paulo Maluf of the PDS ran against each other. A politician of legendary deal-making skill, Maluf enjoyed considerable popularity in São Paulo and his PDS controlled hundreds of municipalities across the nation (Ames, 1994). Appointed governor of São Paulo by the military in 1979, he won over two million votes, giving him 48.8 percent in the first round. Also during the first round, Maluf, whose party had two highly placed representatives in the Collor government, declared himself in favor of impeachment and convinced his fellow members of the PDS to vote against the president. In the second round, Maluf won the election in Latin America's second largest city with a clear margin of 15 percent over Suplicy, who drew 2 million votes as opposed to Maluf's 2.8 million.

The 1992 local elections saw four parties increase the number of state capitals under their control. The PSDB moved from one to five; the PT increased from three to four; the PDC, which had not won in any state capital, now controlled two; and the PPS, also previously shut out, won one race. Four other parties—the PDT, PDS, PFL, and PTB—saw reductions in the number of state capitals under their control.

Intergovernmental Relations

Brazil is an example of a country where there are various levels of government, each with political autonomy as well as autonomy over expenditures and revenues but with no clearly defined functional responsibility. Throughout most of its history, except during the military regime, municipalities have enjoyed a high degree of political autonomy. Mayors and councils are chosen through competitive local elections; local government officials have autonomy in spending and freedom over the rates of taxes that have been transferred to them from the state and central governments. Municipalities are assigned a fixed 20 percent share of the proceeds of the value-added tax without restrictions on its use.

The two major types of transfer of state and federal monies to the local level are State and Local Participation Funds (FPE and FPM) and negotiated transfers, or *convênios*. The Participation Funds are unconditional bloc tax transfers, which states and municipalities are free to use except for a constitutional mandate that requires them to devote at least 25 percent of their revenues to educational expenditures. These bloc grants are calculated on the basis of population and per capita income. *Convênios* are allocated according to the budgetary process and are subject to political manipulation. According to William Dillinger, "no attempt has been made, however, to define the functional responsibilities of each tier of government in Brazil. Both state and municipal governments may operate primary schools, health services, road construction and maintenance programs, or any other public service simultaneously within the same jurisdiction" (Dillinger, 1994).

This lack of a clear distinction between the functional responsibilities of state and municipal governments means that local governments cannot be easily held responsible for problems in service delivery to their constituents. The need exists to reform the structure of municipal service delivery so that mayors will assume responsibility for performing specific services rather than simply being lobbyists before the central government. In addition, there is uncertainty over the degree of state and municipal governments' compliance with constitutional provisions that certain percentages of revenues be allocated for education and urban services. Although in the 1990s there has been a trend to decentralize the public sector, many policymakers complain that there has not been an effective decentralization of responsibilities to accompany increased financial transfers from federal to lower level of governments. To strengthen democracy, it is crucial that state and municipal governments be made accountable to their electorates. To ensure this accountability, municipal and state governments need a transparent budgetary process. The electorate not only should have access to audits of their own local government but also should be able to compare municipal performance.

Conclusion

Although civilian rule was restored in Brazil in 1985, free local elections were not held until 1988. Prior to that time there were no real contests in major municipalities defined as important to national security. The 1988 and 1992 local elections, as well as the 1989 and 1994 presidential contests, were true in the sense that the military did not interfere in any way with the electoral process or its outcome. There have been constant transfers of power from incumbent to opposition parties at all government levels, and numerous parties of all sizes and ideologies participated in the electoral process. To quote a leading Brazilian scholar:

> Instability, fragility, fragmentation, non-differentiation, lack of cohesiveness and representativeness, are the words constantly used to depict Brazilian political parties. In fact, Brazil is one of the rare cases of democratic transition where the party framework which emerged with the end of the military rule retained little trace of the previous democratic party system. What has prevailed is an unsettled and unstable situation marked by party dissensions, often leading to splits and the creation of new parties (Kinzo, 1993:139).

Is it possible to draw any general conclusions from the three instances of local elections in Brazil? Before answering this question it is important to point out that only electoral results of state capitals, and not provincial towns, have been discussed in this chapter. If we look at party loyalties and durable party affiliation in six of the largest cities—São Paulo, Rio de Janeiro, Belo Horizonte, Recife, Salvador, and Pôrto Alegre—we see that some parties had more staying power than others. For example, in Rio de Janeiro the PDT won the local election both in 1985 and 1988 but lost in 1992; in Salvador the PMDB won both in 1985 and 1988 but lost in 1992; and in São Paulo no party had staying power (the rightist PTB won in 1985, the leftist PT in 1988, and PDS, a right-wing party, in 1992). In Belo Horizonte and Recife no party won more than once in the three elections analyzed here. In Pôrto Alegre the PDT won in 1985, while the PT won both in the 1988 and 1992 elections. To summarize the electoral results of Brazil's six largest cities, in 1985 as well as in 1988 the left won in three, the center in two, and the right in only one. In 1992 the center won in three of the six, while the left won in two and the right in one.

Geographically, Brazil is divided into five regions: north, northeast, southeast, south, and center west. But politically the diversity of regional interests and the internal dynamics of party competition among the states works naturally against the development of cohesive national parties (Kinzo, 1993:153). Thus, no political party has strong support or staying power in any one region partly because of the need for parties to be organized nationally according to the constitution. However, looking at Brazil as a whole, the PMDB remained throughout the three local elections the single largest party, controlling one-third of the towns.

Do local contests follow the national elections? In 1985 the PMDB's presidential candidate, Tancredo Neves, who had wide public support, died before his inauguration. At the local level the PMDB emerged as the dominant party. In 1988 local elections were held one year before the presidential elections. Many references to national political issues being raised during the campaign for mayors by the political parties that had presidential candidates. A record number of voters turned out, many for the first time. The presidential candidates supported the candidates for local office, and the results clearly indicated a shift of the axis to the center-left. One of the candidates for president who helped his party generate support at the local level was the PT's Lula. The PT won in thirty-one cities, among them three state capitals and three large cities. The local elections of 1992 were not supposed to be influenced by the presidential elections (they were held in 1994), but Collor's impeachment had a negative effect, and many voters opted to vote in blank or abstain. They also decided not to elect someone who had Collor's support.

The 1970s saw a proliferation of new urban social movements, which provided resistance to the military regime and in 1979 formed the basis for a new political party, the PT, as well as for labor unions. Leftist parties such as the PT and Brizola's PDT gave the most support to the new urban social movements; and, once in office, both parties promoted popular participation programs. A recent study tried to assess political parties' connections with grass-roots associations and found that even in the case of the PT, it is not so extensive as expected. Although 30 percent of PT state deputies were linked to trade unions and 15 percent to neighborhood associations, 51.5 percent had no link at all with civil society. Less can be said when we look at other parties: 71.5 percent of the PMDB's state representatives have no connection with grass-roots associations, and neither do 74.5 percent of those of the PDT and 67.9 percent of those of the PSDB (Kinzo, 1993). In general, participation by Brazilians in neighborhood associations seems to be at a low level, with only 4 percent affiliated with the latter (Kinzo, 1993:150). Thus, while under the military new urban social movements played an important role in opposing the regime and formed the basis for new parties and leaders, their role under democratic government is much more difficult to assess.

References

Alvarez, Sonia. 1990. *Engendering Democracy in Brazil: Women's Movements in Transition Politics*. Princeton: Princeton University Press.

Alves, Maria Helena Moreira. 1985. *The State and Opposition in Military Brazil*. Austin: University of Texas Press.

Ames, Barry. 1994. "The Reverse Coattails Effect: Local Party Organization in the 1989 Presidential Election." *American Political Science Review* 88, no. 1 (March):95–112.

———. 1992. "Disparately Seeking Politicians: Strategies and Outcomes in Brazilian Legislative Elections." Paper presented at the meeting of the Latin American Studies Association, Los Angeles.

———. 1987. *Political Survival: Politicians and Public Policy in Latin America*. Berkley: University of California Press.

———, and David Nixon. 1993. *Understanding New Legislatures? Observations and Evidence from the Brazilian Congress*. St. Louis, MO: Washington University, Department of Political Science, Paper No. 215.

Assies, Willem. 1993. "Urban Social Movements and Local Democracy in Brazil." *European Review of Latin American and Caribbean Studies* no. 55 (December):39–58.

Boran, Anne. 1989. "Popular Movements in Brazil: A Case Study of the Movement for the Defense of Favelados in São Paulo." *Bulletin of Latin American Research* 8, no. 1 (March):83–109.

Burdick, John. 1992. "Rethinking the Study of Social Movements: The Case of Christian Base Communities in Urban Brazil." In Arturo Escobar and Sonia Alvarez, eds., *The Making of Social Movements in Latin America: Identity, Strategy, and Democracy*, 171–84. Boulder, CO: Westview Press.

Caldeira, Teresa. 1986–87. "Electoral Struggles in a Neighborhood on the Periphery of São Paulo." *Politics and Society* 15, no. 1 (March):43–66.

Cardoso, Ruth Correa Leite. 1992. "Popular Movements in the Context of the Consolidation of Democracy in Brazil." In Arturo Escobar and Sonia Alvarez, eds., *The Making of Social Movements in Latin America: Identity, Strategy, and Democracy*, 291–302. Boulder, CO: Westview Press.

Corcoran-Nantes, Yvonne. 1990. "Women and Popular Urban Social Movements in São Paulo, Brazil." *Bulletin of Latin American Research* 9, no. 2 (June): 249–64.

Davidovich, Fany. 1993. "Poder local e municipio, algumas consideracoes." *Revista de Administração Publica* 27 (January-March): 5–14.

Dietz, Henry. 1987. "Electoral Politics in Peru, 1978–1986." *Journal of Inter-American Studies and World Affairs* 28, no. 4 (Winter 1986–87):139–63.

———. 1985. "Political Participation in the Barriadas: An Extension and Reexamination." *Comparative Political Studies* 18, no. 3 (October):323–55.

Dillinger, William. 1994. *Decentralization and Its Implications for Urban Service Delivery*. Washington, DC: World Bank, Urban Management Programme No. 16.

Diniz Eli. 1982. *Voto e máquina política: Patronagem e clientelismo no Rio de Janeiro*. Rio de Janeiro: Paz e Terra.

Escobar, Arturo, and Sonia Alvarez. 1992. *The Making of Social Movements in Latin America: Identity, Strategy, and Democracy*. Boulder, CO: Westview Press.

Ferreira, Pinto. 1992. *As eleicoes municipais e o municipio na constituição de 1988*. São Paulo: Editora Saraiva.

Ferreira, Wolgran Junqueira. 1993. *O municipio a luz da constituição federal de 1988*. São Paulo: EDIPRO.

Fleischer, David. 1989. "The Impact of the 1988 Municipal Elections on Brazil's 1989 Presidential Elections." Miami, FL: University of Miami, Institute of Interamerican Studies.

———. 1986. "Brazil at the Crossroads: The Elections of 1982 and 1985." In Paul W. Drake and Eduardo Silva, eds., *Elections and Democratization in Latin America, 1980–85*, 299–328. San Diego: University of California, San Diego.

———. 1984. "Constitutional and Electoral Engineering in Brazil: A Double-Edge Sword." *Inter-American Economic Affairs* 37, no. 1 (Summer):3–36.

Gay, Robert. 1994. *Popular Organizations and Democracy in Rio de Janeiro: A Tale of Two Favelas*. Philadelphia: Temple University Press.

Geddes, Barbara, and Arturo Ribeiro Neto. 1992. "Institutional Sources of Corruption in Brazil." *Third World Quarterly* 13, no. 4: 641–61.

ISTOE. 9/30/1992, 28.

ISTOE. 14/10/1992.

Jaquette, Jane, ed. 1989. _The Women's Movement in Latin America: Feminism and the Transition to Democracy._ Boston: Unwin and Hyman.

Keck, Margaret. 1992. _The Workers' Party and Democratization in Brazil._ New Haven, CT: Yale University Press.

Kinzo, Maria D'Alva, ed. 1993. _Brazil: The Challenge of the 1990s._ London: Institute of Latin American Studies and British Academic Press.

————. 1988. _Legal Opposition Politics under Authoritarian Rule in Brazil: The Case of the MDB, 1966–1979._ New York: St. Martin's Press.

Lamounier, Bolívar. 1986. _1985: O voto em São Paulo._ São Paulo: IDESP.

————, and Judith Muszynski. 1986. _A eleição de Janio Quadros._ São Paulo: IDESP, Working Paper No. 16.

Leal, Victor Nunes. 1977. _Coronelismo: The Municipality and Representative Government in Brazil._ New York: Cambridge University Press.

Maduro, Lidice Aparecida Pontes. 1990. "Eleicoes municipais: a virada das urnas." _Revista de Ciência Política_ (Rio de Janeiro) 33, no. 1 (November 1989-January 1990):91–101.

Mainwaring, Scott. 1991. "Politicians, Parties, and Electoral Systems: Brazil in Comparative Perspective." _Comparative Politics_ 24, no. 1 (October):21–43.

————. 1987. "Urban Social Movements: Identity and Democratization in Brazil." _Comparative Political Studies_ 20, no. 2 (July): 131–59.

————. 1986. _The Catholic Church and Politics in Brazil, 1916–1985._ Stanford, CA: Stanford University Press.

————, and Eduardo Viola. 1984. "New Social Movements, Political Culture, and Democracy: Brazil and Argentina in the 1980s." _Telos_ 61 (Fall): 17–52.

McDonald, Ronald, and J. Mark Ruhl. 1989. _Party Politics and Elections in Latin America._ Boulder, CO: Westview Press.

Medeiros, Antonio Carlos. 1986. _Politics and Intergovernmental Relations in Brazil, 1964–1982._ New York: Garland.

Moises, José Alavaro. 1993. "Elections, Political Parties, and Political Culture in Brazil: Changes and Continuities." _Journal of Latin American Studies_ 25, pt. 3 (October):575–611.

Roett, Riordan. 1984. _Brazil: Politics in a Patrimonial Society._ 3d ed. New York: Praeger.

Rosenblatt, David, and Gil Shidlo. 1997. "Quem tem mais recursos para governar? Uma comparação das receitas per capita dos estados e municipios brasileiros." _Revista de Economia Polítca_ 16, no. 1 (January-March):101–6.

Sarles, Margaret. 1982. "Maintaining Political Control through Parties: The Brazilian Strategy." *Comparative Politics* 15, no. 1 (October):41–72.

Selcher, Wayne, ed. 1986. *Political Liberalization in Brazil.* Boulder, CO: Westview Press.

Share, D., and Scott Mainwaring. 1986. "Transitions through Transaction: Democratization in Brazil and Spain." In Wayne Selcher, ed. *Political Liberalization in Brazil,* 175–216. Boulder, CO: Westview Press.

Shidlo, Gil. 1990a. *Social Policy in a Non-Democratic Regime: The Case of Public Housing in Brazil.* Boulder, CO: Westview Press.

———. 1990b. "The Brazilian Elections of 1989." *Electoral Studies* 9, no. 3 (September):251–56.

Skidmore, Thomas. 1989. "Brazil's Slow Road to Democratization, 1974–1985." In Alfred Stepan, ed., *Democratizing Brazil: Problems of Transition and Consolidation,* 5–42. New York: Oxford University Press.

———, ed. 1989. *Democratizing Brazil: Problems of Transition and Consolidation.* New York: Oxford University Press.

Soares, Glaucioary, Dillon. 1986. "Elections and the Redemocratization of Brazil," In Paul W. Drake and Eduardo Silva, eds., *Elections and Democratization in Latin America, 1980–85,* 273–298. San Diego: University of California, San Diego.

Verucci, Florisa. 1991. "Women and the New Brazilian Constitution." *Feminist Studies* 17, no. 3 (Fall):551–67.

Wesson, Robert, and David Fleischer, eds. 1983. *Brazil in Transition.* New York: Praeger.

Notes

1. The revision of the electoral system in 1966 (Institutional Act No. 3) abolished direct elections for the mayors of 202 municipalities, including twenty-five state capitals and cities in other areas considered vital for national security. About one-quarter of the Brazilian population was not allowed to vote for municipal executives, who were appointed by indirectly "elected" state governors. The position of the mayor was strengthened when in 1969 he was granted the right to submit legislative proposals and veto laws approved by the municipal council. Furthermore, the 1967 constitution and the constitutional amendment of 1969 gave the mayor authority over the budget without allowing the municipal council to amend it (Assies, 1993).

2. The so-called right to vote in Brazil is in fact an obligation. Only citizens older than seventy and between ages sixteen and eighteen or illiterates may choose not to vote. Anyone who does not vote cannot obtain a new passport, receive loans from banks, enroll in state schools and universities, take state employment exams, or get any job that requires a certificate from the military service or from the revenue service. State

employees who do not vote are not paid their salaries. Illiterates gained the right to vote only in 1988, together with those between ages sixteen and eighteen.

3. The first generation of neighborhood associations arose in the 1945–1964 period and were initially subordinated to populist politicians. They were known as SABs (Friends of the Neighborhood Societies).

4

Urban Electoral Behavior in Colombia

Gary Hoskin

A democratic system, however restricted and distorted at times, has prevailed in Colombia during most of the twentieth century, a record unsurpassed in Latin America. The durability of Colombian democracy can be explained in large part by the existence of a two-party system, consisting of the Liberal and Conservative parties, that traces its roots to the midnineteenth century and gradually became institutionalized by the turn of the century, if not before. Reflecting formidable regional differences, the traditional parties were highly decentralized confederations of local and regional notables, who generally sought to maximize their power through the forging of linkages with national party bosses, or *jefes naturales*. The traditional parties monopolized the vote and dominated the political system. Historical interparty feuds, propelled largely by the struggle for governmental hegemony and, to a lesser extent, ideological cleavages, have subsided, and interparty competition has become more tranquil, to some extent because of the conscious efforts of party leaders to depoliticize the society during the National Front (1958–1974), along with dramatic societal transformations during this period (Dix, 1967, 1987; Hartlyn, 1988; Hoskin, 1989a, 1990; Leal Buitrago, 1984; Leal Buitrago and Zamosc, 1990; Martz, 1992).

However, one prominent trait of Colombian parties—for the new as well as the old (González, 1993:15)—remains forceful, namely, the pervasive factionalism within them. Anchored in regional and local cleavages, personalism, clientelism, and generally weak ideological and programmatic differences, factionalism rather than interparty competition frequently constitutes the locus of political conflict. Although based upon multiple factions, the Liberal Party presently is "unified," while the Conservative Party is divided into four major factions: the Social Conservatives, the National Salvation Party, the National Conservative Movement, and the Independent Conservatives.[1]

The electoral system reflects the decentralized, faction-laden party structures and certainly contributes to their perpetuation. Elections for legislative bodies at every level are based upon proportional representation. As Matthew Shugart points out, "The most salient feature of the Colombian electoral system is that the seat allocation procedure was applied to lists and not to parties" (1992:24). Obviously, this procedure promoted factionalism and list proliferation, in many cases with the blessing of party directorates for reasons of vote maximization. Party leaders tended to be more interested in enhancing their vote totals than in attempting to impose party discipline through tighter control of electoral lists.

Selection of delegates for the 1991 Constituent Assembly represented a major innovation, in the sense that they were elected on a nationwide basis rather than by department, as was traditionally the case for congressional elections. This arrangement was inscribed in the 1991 constitution for the Senate, although the old system was retained for House elections. Finally, the electoral process generally has involved interparty competition as well as pronounced internal party contests. Moreover, with a few exceptions, elections have been regarded as legitimate, even though distortions result occasionally from fraud (Deas, 1993:334) and, more commonly, from buying votes, especially in rural areas and on the Atlantic coast.[2]

The highly decentralized structure of Colombian parties does not conform to the structure of governmental institutions, which has been highly centralized at the national level since the promulgation of the 1886 constitution. The president of the Republic appointed departmental governors who, in turn, designated city mayors. Departments and municipalities elected legislative bodies, but the national government, which tended to monopolize resources and power, overshadowed them. Moreover, the centralizing tendencies were compounded by the concentration of power in the presidency, particularly after the 1968 constitutional reforms. Not until the 1980s were there any major initiatives toward political decentralization—the first being the popular election of mayors in 1988, followed by the election of governors in 1991.

The National Front arrangement throttled extensive violence and improved interparty relations, but it contributed to a legitimacy crisis that manifested itself through mounting discontent with traditional *políticos* and the government's perceived inability to resolve societal problems, along with the pervasive violence linked to guerrilla movements, drug mafias, paramilitary groups, and common criminals.[3] Dramatic transformations in Colombian society supposedly were not accompanied by responsive and innovative political initiatives, thereby widening the distance between the government and civil society. Politicians from both traditional parties responded slowly to the crisis, partly because of their hegemonic grip on the electoral process and partly because of the absence of political movements perceived as viable alternatives.

After several aborted efforts to restructure the political system during the post-National Front period, reform efforts gained momentum during the Betancur administration (1982–1986) and peaked with the convocation of the Constituent Assembly in 1991. The new constitution was designed to reflect mounting pressures for a more participatory, equitable, and responsive political system. Expectations were high with respect to the ability of political reforms to transform Colombian society, thus almost inevitably resulting in disillusionment in the absence of expected change—traditional politicians have not vanished, new political groups remain fragile, moderate economic growth continues, pervasive poverty persists, and the violence does not abate.

This chapter focuses upon urban electoral behavior in Colombia. After a brief discussion of national electoral patterns, the next section examines electoral behavior in urban areas, which is to say cities with over 50,000 in population, along with the four major metropolitan areas of Bogotá, Medellín, Cali, and Barranquilla. Electoral data are for the lower house of Congress, the Cámara, primarily for the period between 1982 and 1990, although some aspects of the 1991 and 1994 elections will be analyzed. In the final section some generalizations are made about local elections for mayors from 1988 to 1994. The following questions will orient the analysis: How do electoral patterns at the local level deviate from national ones? Have any trends emerged since the 1980s that suggest a restructuring of political forces? In what ways, if any, have political reforms affected electoral behavior? Do the 1991 congressional elections represent a watershed? And finally, to what extent do local elections contribute to the consolidation of a more participatory democracy?

Electoral behavior in urban areas differs along several dimensions from national patterns, reflecting more pointedly the transformations in Colombian society. However, the impact of urban electoral behavior upon post-*constituyente* democracy remains mixed at this juncture. Although continued high urban abstention rates persist, proliferation of new electoral alternatives in urban areas suggests that the political spectrum may well become more reflective of civil society. Moreover, nontraditional mayoral candidates have enjoyed increasing success, particularly in intermediate-sized cities; and they won in two major metropolitan areas, Bogotá and Barranquilla, in the October 1994 elections. Consequently, political reforms aimed at fortifying local democracy are having the anticipated impact of weakening traditional party hegemonies, although it is too early to suggest that this trend signifies the demise of the two-party system, which may well assert its ascendancy after undergoing a period of realignment.[4]

National Electoral Patterns

The two major parties have dominated Colombian elections, a generalization that retained its validity until the December 1990 contest for the Constituent Assembly and the subsequent October 1991 congressional elections, for which they tallied 62.5 and 66.5 percent, respectively (their combined percentage rose to 70 percent in 1994). The Liberal and Conservative parties received an average of

Table 1. Electoral Returns for the Cámara, 1958–1994

Year	Liberal	Conservative	Other	Total Votes	Abstention Rate
1958	57.7%	42.1%	—	3,693,939	31%
1960	58.1	41.7	—	2,542,651	42
1962	54.5	41.7	3.7[a]	3,090,203	42
1964	50.5	35.5	13.7[a]	2,261,190	63
1966	52.1	29.8	17.8[a]	2,939,222	56
1968	49.9	33.7	16.1[a]	2,496,455	63
1970	37.0	27.2	35.5[a]	3,980,201	48
1974	55.6	32.0	9.5[a]	5,100,099	43
1978	55.1	39.4	—	4,180,121	63
1982	56.3	40.3	—	5,584,037	59
1986	47.6	37.0	6.6[a]	6,912,341	56

1990	59.0	32.1	—	7,631,694	45
1991	44.2	22.3[b]	8.8[a]	5,486,636	65
1994	47.0	23.2[b]	29.8[a]	5,576,174	67

Source: All the electoral data are taken from the 1990, 1991, and 1994 publications of the Registraduría Nacional del Estado Civil.

[a]From 1964 through 1974 this vote is for ANAPO, which used both traditional party labels through the 1970 elections. For the 1986 elections, this vote is for the New Liberal Party, headed by Luis Carlos Galán. To be consistent with previous years, this vote probably should be added to that of the Liberal Party, particularly since the New Liberals joined the Liberal Party in 1989. For the 1991 elections, this vote is for AD-M-19. The 1994 vote in the "other" category consists of all those votes not cast for either major party (5.8 percent for those classified as "other," 2.8 percent for AD-M-19, .8 percent for coalitions, .7 percent for Unión Patriótica, and 19.7 percent for nineteen distinct minor parties on the ballot).

[b]The Conservative vote consists of four factions: the Social Conservatives, the National Salvation Party, the National Conservative Movement, and Independent Conservatives.

87 percent of the total vote for the fourteen Cámara elections shown in Table 1. (This percentage includes the ANAPO (Alianza Nacional Popular) vote from 1962 through 1970, when it utilized both traditional party labels, and the New Liberal Party vote in 1986 is counted with the Liberal Party.) If the 1991 and 1994 election results are excluded, the two-party vote increases to 93 percent. The two-party proportion of the total vote ranged from a high of 99.9 percent in 1962 to 66.5 percent in 1991. Clearly, the traditional parties have monopolized the Colombian electoral arena, based to a considerable extent upon one-party hegemonies at the municipal level (Pinzón, 1989).

Bipartisan domination of the electoral arena reflects as well as promotes two salient aspects of the Colombian party system: 1) the ephemeral nature of third-party movements; and 2) the debility of the left. ANAPO largely disappeared from the electoral map after the 1974 elections, and the New Liberal Party followed suit when it rejoined the Liberal Party after the 1988 municipal elections. With its spectacular showing in the contest for the 1990 Constituent Assembly, receiving 27.2 percent of the vote, AD-M-19 (Alianza Democrática-M-19) seemingly represented a serious challenger to traditional party hegemony. However, its drive toward institutionalization stalled in the 1991 elections when its share fell to 8.8 percent and then plummeted to 2.8 percent in 1994. As a result of internal schisms and its relations with other parties, the future of AD-M-19 does not appear promising at this time, with one faction possibly uniting with the Liberals and others joining a restructured left.[5]

Even though displaying a higher degree of intraparty unity than the traditional parties, as reflected in the number of party lists presented at the polls, the Colombian left has not fared well electorally, lacking both a high degree of continuity and a respectable share of the votes. The leftist front, Unión Nacional de Oposición (UNO), received 3.1 percent of the vote in 1974; the left (UNO plus FUP, or Frente Unido del Pueblo) obtained 4.3 percent in 1978; and the left tallied 2.5 percent in 1982. The Unión Patriótica (UP) received 2 percent of the 1986 Cámara votes, .3 percent in 1990, 1.7 percent in 1991, and .7 percent in 1994.[6] The unusually low vote for the UP understates its support because the party also has participated in electoral coalitions and has suffered immensely from violence and persecution. However, the UP lost its leading role on the left to AD-M-19 in 1990, and its future depends not only upon the viability of AD-M-19 but also upon the peace negotiations. Considering its linkages with Colombia's largest guerrilla group (FARC, or Fuerzas Armadas Revolucionarias de Colombia), the UP is not likely to bolster its electoral strength significantly as long as leftist violence continues.

Since the 1930s the Liberal Party has dominated Colombian elections, averaging 52 percent of the Cámara votes between 1958 and 1994, as revealed in Table 1. The Conservative Party averaged 33.6 percent during the same period, once again including ANAPO Conservative votes through the 1970 election. If ANAPO Liberal votes and those cast for the New Liberals are included in its totals, the Liberal Party registered an absolute majority of the votes cast in every election shown in Table 1, with the exceptions of 1991 and 1994. The proportion of the Liberal Party's vote ranged between 59 percent in 1990 and 37.0 percent in 1970; for the Conservatives the figures fell between 42.1 and 22.3 percent in 1958 and 1991, respectively. The data shown in Table 1 indicate that the Liberal Party is the majority party, at least until 1991. This generalization also holds for presidential elections as well; even with Belisario Betancur's victory in 1982, the combined Liberal vote for Galán and for Alfonso López Michelsen exceeded 50 percent.

The December 1991 elections possibly marked a watershed in Colombian electoral behavior in two respects: 1) the combined bipartisan vote dropped from 90.9 percent in 1990 to 66.5 percent; and 2) the abstention rate increased from 45 to 65 percent. What prompted these results, and what are their implications for the future? The 1991 electoral outcome reflected the impact of the political reform process that began during the Betancur administration and culminated in the 1991 Constituent Assembly. Elections to the Assembly represented a preview of the 1991 contest, in the sense that the abstention rate escalated to 74 percent and the two parties garnered only 50 percent of the vote. A reform-oriented coalition, under the tripartite leadership of Horacio Serpa Uribe (Liberal Party), Alvaro Gómez (National Salvation Party), and Antonio Navarro Wolff (AD-M-19) dominated the Assembly. Ultimately, with support from President Julio César Gaviria, the convention voted to close Congress, in part because they were afraid that traditional party bosses would undermine the new constitution, a decision that alienated a large proportion of the *clase política*. New elections for Congress and governorships were scheduled for October 1991. High abstention rates for the Assembly and the 1991 elections may well represent voter fatigue; Colombians had been asked to cast ballots in five elections between 1988 and 1991.[7] Moreover, considering their opposition to major political reform, many traditional politicians did not mount sustained campaigns to turn out their constituents for the Assembly election. A similar lack of effort may have resulted from the decision of many politicians not to run for Congress in 1991, thereby making themselves eligible for executive posts. In the 1994 elections the two-party vote rose slightly (4.7 percent) in relation to 1991, and the abstention rate increased 2 percent, reaching an all-time high of 67 percent for Cámara elections.

An electoral outcome even more significant than the abstention rate is the relatively low two-party vote in the 1991 congressional elections, which resulted from an extension of the political spectrum—8.8 percent for AD-M-19 and 11.9 percent for other parties or movements—and a dramatic rise in the number of blank and null ballots, at 9.9 and 2.8 percent respectively. The escalation in the blank and null vote—both totaled .4 percent for the 1990 Cámara election—probably reflected the difficulties encountered by some voters with the ballot; this was the first time that the Registraduría Nacional printed congressional ballots. As for the blank ballots, they may well represent disillusionment with Congress, although survey data are required to pinpoint what prompted such voting. Turning to the nontraditional groups, AD-M-19 won 13 Cámara seats, the UP 3, and "other" groups 16 (out of 161 posts).

The 16 "other" seats were divided among fifteen lists. Nonetheless, dispersal of the nontraditional vote among several groups, along with several politicians abandoning their traditional party label for tactical reasons, suggests that it is premature to conclude that the "new" politics in Colombia has ended bipartisan domination. Discarding the blank and null votes in the 1991 election, the traditional parties obtained 76 percent of the votes cast for lists.

Urban Voting Patterns

Colombian society is becoming increasingly citified, with 70.5 percent of the population residing in urban areas in 1991 (Inter-American Development Bank, 1992:64). This trend is not likely to be halted in the near future as the bulk of Colombia's population growth is concentrated in urban areas. Electoral contests will be determined more and more by the urban vote, which in this analysis will be operationalized as those cities over 50,000 (sixty-nine municipalities). Thus, of those eligible to participate in the 1990 Cámara elections, 55.4 percent were urban (depositing one-half of the total votes cast). The four major metropolitan areas—Bogotá, Medellín, Cali, and Barranquilla—represented 75 percent of the potential urban vote (35.6 percent nationally) and deposited 71 percent of the urban votes (20.9 percent of the nation's). Finally, those living in Bogotá constituted 14 percent of the national electorate (25.6 percent of the urban potential), casting 16.7 percent of the national votes (33.5 percent of the urban votes).

The Liberal Party has dominated the urban vote to an even greater extent than its national pattern. During the National Front period, the Liberals derived 19.5 percent of their votes from departmental capitals (Cepeda and Lecaros, 1976:10); for the three elections after the expiration of the National Front (1974–1982), the figure was 20.3 percent.[8] As Table 2 reveals, in 1986 the Liberals received 25.3 percent of the total national vote from urban areas, and in 1990 the percentage increased to 31.4 percent (columns 2 and 3). Not unexpectedly, its proportion of the national vote was concentrated in those departments containing the four major metropolitan areas: Antioquia, Atlántico, Cundinamarca, and Valle. A majority of the Liberal vote came from urban areas (columns 4–6). Finally, the Liberals received around 60 percent of the urban vote (columns 7–9), with the exception of 1986, when its percentage fell to 49.7 as a consequence of the large urban vote for the New Liberal Party (if that vote is included in Liberal totals, its proportion of the urban vote increases to 59.4 percent). The Liberal Party received a majority of the urban vote in sixteen of the twenty-three departments in 1986, with the number rising to twenty in 1990. In summary, Liberals fared better in urban areas than nationally; in 1986 the party obtained 49.7 percent of the urban vote in comparison to 47.6 nationwide (the gap widened to 5.2 percent if the New Liberal vote is included). The difference mounted to 11.8 percent in 1990.

Table 2. Average Proportion of Liberal Vote Derived from Urban Areas*

Department	Liberal % of National Vote			Urban % of Liberal Vote			Liberal % of Urban Vote		
	1974–1982	1986	1990	1974–1982	1986	1990	1974–1982	1986	1990
Antioquia	1.7%	1.8%	2.7%	3.1%	3.7%	4.6%	5.1%	3.5%	5.4%
Atlántico	1.6	2.5	3.6	2.9	5.1	6.1	4.8	4.8	7.2
Bolívar	.8	1.1	1.3	1.5	2.4	2.3	2.4	2.2	1.2
Boyacá	.2	.5	.6	.3	1.0	1.0	.5	.9	1.2
Caldas	.5	.6	.9	.9	1.4	1.5	1.5	1.3	1.7
Caquetá	.1	.1	.0	.2	.2	.0	.4	.2	.0
Cauca	.2	.4	.3	.4	.8	.5	.7	.8	.6
César	.4	.4	.4	.7	.8	.7	1.2	.8	.8
Córdoba	.4	.8	1.3	.7	1.7	2.2	1.2	1.6	2.6
Cundinamarca	6.4	5.6	7.5	11.5	11.8	12.7	19.0	11.0	15.0
Chocó	.2	.2	.2	.4	.3	.3	.7	.3	.3
Huila	.4	.1	.4	.7	.2	.7	1.1	.2	.9
La Guajira	.2	.4	.4	.3	.8	.6	.5	.8	.7
Magdalena	.5	1.2	1.1	.9	2.5	1.9	1.5	2.3	2.3
Meta	.2	.4	.5	.4	.8	.8	.7	.7	1.0
Nariño	.4	.8	.7	.7	1.6	1.2	1.1	1.5	1.4
Norte de Santander	.7	1.3	.8	1.3	2.7	1.3	2.1	2.5	1.5
Quindío	.5	.7	.6	.8	1.4	.1	1.3	1.3	1.3
Risaralda	.7	.8	1.3	1.2	1.8	2.2	2.0	1.6	2.5
Santander	1.0	1.4	1.8	1.7	3.0	3.0	2.9	2.8	3.6
Sucre	.4	.4	.4	.6	.8	.7	.9	.8	.9
Tolima	.8	.6	.6	1.4	1.2	1.0	2.3	1.1	1.2
Valle	2.1	3.3	4.0	3.8	7.0	4.6	6.2	6.5	8.1
Totals	18.4%	25.4%	31.4%	36.4%	53.0%	50.0%	60.1%	49.5%	61.4%

Source: Registraduría Nacional del Estado Civil, 1990, 1991, and 1994.
*The averages for 1974–1982 are for capital cities of the departments, and the percentages for both 1986 and 1990 are for cities with over 50,000 inhabitants.

In sharp contrast to the Liberal Party, the Conservatives draw less of their electoral support from urban areas, as indicated in

Table 3. The Conservative urban vote represents around 15 percent of the national total, with approximately 42 percent of their strength in 1986 and 1990 associated with urban areas (columns 5–6), around 11 percent less than for the Liberals. More important, the Conservatives tallied only around 30 percent of the urban vote, in contrast to approximately 60 percent for the Liberals. In both the 1986 and 1990 elections, the Conservatives failed to obtain a majority of the urban votes in a single department. Their urban strength in those departments where 40 percent of the urban vote went to the Conservatives was concentrated in Antioquia, Bolívar, Caldas, and Córdoba for the 1986 elections, and in Antioquia, Boyacá, Caldas, and Norte de Santander for 1990.

Table 3. Average Proportion of Conservative Vote Derived from Urban Areas*

Department	Conservative % of National Vote			Urban % of Conservative Vote			Conservative % of Urban Vote		
	1974–1982	1986	1990	1974–1982	1986	1990	1974–1982	1986	1990
Antioquia	1.3%	1.8%	1.9%	3.5%	4.8%	5.6%	3.8%	3.5%	3.9%
Atlántico	.7	1.6	.9	1.8	4.4	2.7	2.0	3.2	1.8
Bolívar	.4	.9	.8	1.2	2.4	2.4	1.3	1.7	1.6
Boyacá	.1	.3	.2	.3	.8	.7	.4	.9	.5
Caldas	.5	.6	.6	1.3	1.5	1.9	1.4	1.1	1.2
Caquetá	.1	.1	.0	.2	.2	.0	.2	.2	.0
Cauca	.2	.2	.2	.5	.6	.5	.6	.5	.3
César	.2	.3	.2	.4	.7	.7	.5	.5	.4
Córdoba	.3	.7	.4	.7	1.9	1.3	.8	1.4	.9
Cundinamarca	2.6	2.5	3.4	6.9	6.9	10.2	7.6	5.0	6.8
Chocó	.1	.1	.0	.2	.2	.1	.2	.2	.1
Huila	.1	.3	.3	.3	.7	.8	.4	.5	.5
La Guajira	.1	.2	.2	.3	.6	.4	.3	.5	.3
Magdelena	.3	.5	.5	.8	1.3	1.6	.9	.9	.1
Meta	.2	.2	.2	.5	.5	.7	.5	.4	.5
Nariño	.4	.4	.3	1.1	1.0	.9	1.2	.8	.6
Norte de Santander	.4	.7	.5	.9	2.0	1.5	1.0	1.4	1.0
Quindío	.2	.2	.0	.6	.6	.2	.7	.5	.1
Risaralda	.3	.6	.4	.8	1.6	1.3	.9	1.2	.9
Santander	.4	.8	.6	.9	2.2	1.8	1.0	1.6	1.1
Sucre	.1	.2	.2	.3	.6	.5	.4	.4	.3
Tolima	.3	.4	.4	.8	1.2	1.1	.8	.9	.8
Valle	1.0	2.1	1.9	2.6	5.6	5.8	2.9	4.0	3.8
Totals	10.3%	15.7%	14.1%	26.9%	42.3%	42.6%	29.8%	31.3%	27.5%

Source: Registraduría Nacional del Estado Civil, 1990, 1991, and 1994.
*The averages for 1974–1982 are for capital cities of the departments, and the percentages for both 1986 and 1990 are for cities with over 50,000 inhabitants.

Table 4 shows the impact of urbanization upon the traditional parties' hegemony and each one's proportion of the vote from 1974 to 1990. Data for the elections between 1974 and 1986 conform to expectations, in the sense that the magnitude of hegemony diminishes as urbanization increases. Thus, for those years, hegemony decreases in the following order: rural, national, urban, metropolitan, and Bogotá. The order changes as follows for the 1990 election: rural, metro, urban, national, and Bogotá (see columns 3, 6, and 9). Thus, in a relatively high turn-out election (45% abstention in 1990), the traditional parties, especially the Liberals, are capable of mobilizing urban voters.

Table 4. Urbanization and the Traditional Party Vote[a]

	1974–1982			1986[b]			1990		
	Liberals	Conser-vatives	Total	Liberals	Conser-vatives	Total	Liberals	Conser-vatives	Total
National	55.7%	37.2%	92.9%	54.2%	37.0%	91.2%	59.0%	31.2%	90.2%
Urban[c]	59.7	29.4	89.1	59.6	30.7	90.3	62.8	28.3	91.1
Rural	53.2	41.4	94.6	48.8	43.8	92.6	55.2	38.0	93.2
Metro	58.7	29.3	88.0	57.7	32.5	90.2	62.3	30.1	92.4
Bogotá	61.7	24.8	86.5	60.3	19.2	79.5	59.7	29.3	89.0

Source: Registraduría Nacional del Estado Civil, 1990, 1991, and 1994.
[a]The averages for 1974–1982 are for capital cities of the departments, and the percentages for both 1986 and 1990 are for cities with over 50,000 inhabitants.
[b]The Liberal vote for 1986 includes that of the New Liberal Party.
[c]The urban vote includes that of the four metropolitan areas.

Looking at the magnitude of the two-party vote between 1974 and 1990, Table 4 reveals a relatively high degree of stability across the units of analysis. Their proportion decreases slightly at the national level and in rural areas, while it increases modestly in urban and metropolitan areas as well as in Bogotá. But these trends may well be random and reflect characteristics of specific campaigns. Thus, even though the two parties enjoy their greatest support in rural areas, these data suggest that their urban vote has not decreased. Clearly, the 1991 congressional elections reversed this trend—the Liberals and Conservatives received 66.5 percent of the national vote—but that election may well represent a blip rather than an electoral realignment. However, as will be discussed below, the two-party domination of the electoral arena is considerably less pronounced at the local level than in national elections.

With respect to the Liberal Party, the figures in Table 4 suggest that between 1974 and 1986 its strength decreased in the following order: Bogotá, urban, metro, national, rural. This pattern underscores the Liberals' stranglehold on Bogotá and their greater strength in urban compared to metropolitan areas. Considering that Bogotá and Barranquilla (traditionally a solid Liberal constituency) are included in the metro vote, it is obvious that the Liberal Party tends to dominate the smaller urban areas. The 1990 pattern is mixed: urban, metro, Bogotá, national, rural. The Liberal Party vote in each of the five constituencies across time is relatively stable, allowing for a slight increase in the 1990 election, except for Bogotá.

The Conservative Party's votes correspond to expectations for the 1974–1982 period; its strength descends in the following order: rural, national, urban, metro, Bogotá. In 1986 the party received more metro than urban votes; and in 1990, more support in Bogotá than in urban areas. The 1986 deviation from the perfect relationship between urbanization and the Conservative vote undoubtedly reflects its increased support in Medellín and Cali, along with a surge in Liberal voting in the smaller urban areas. The increase in Conservative voting in Bogotá for the 1990 election probably reflects the political impact of a Conservative mayor, Andrés Pastrana, during the previous two years. Looking at the trends across time, the Conservative Party's strength has been relatively stable in each constituency, allowing for the atypical margin of the 1990 Liberal victory.

Voter Turnout and Third-party Support in Urban Areas

One of the most distinctive features of urban electoral behavior consists of the high rates of abstention, compared to either national or rural voting patterns. As Table 5 suggests, the abstention rate was higher in urban areas than for the nation in 1986 and 1990, but about the same for the 1982 election. However, the number of those abstaining in the four metropolitan areas escalates in relation to the nation and cities over 50,000, (the metro rate averages 9.9 percent higher than the national rate and 6.2 percent higher than the urban rate). The correlation between urbanization and abstention is strengthened further by the higher abstention rates for Bogotá than for the other metropolitan areas. Finally, note the much lower rates of rural abstention.

Why do urban voters stay away from the polls more frequently than their rural counterparts? Probably the most convincing, though by no means exhaustive, explanation rests with the decline in traditional partisan attachments in urban areas (Pinzón and Rothlisberger, 1991:142–44), coupled with the often weakly financed, poorly organized, and transient nature of the opposition in urban areas. The rise in the number of weak partisans and independents complicates the task of mobilizing these potential voters. However, this is not an insurmountable endeavor, especially for presidential elections in which a candidate projects an image of change (which occurred for each election between 1970 and 1994, with the exception of 1978). The growth in the number of unattached, floating voters in urban areas complicates the task of electoral mobilization for traditional parties and, at the same time, enhances the opportunities for new political movements and minor parties to erode further the traditional bipartisan hegemony.

Table 5. Urbanization and Abstention, 1982–1990

	1982	*1986*[a]	*1990*
National	59.3%	27.0%	44.7%
Urban[b]	59.2	32.4	50.4
Rural	51.3	21.1	38.6
Metro	68.3	36.6	55.4
Bogotá	73.0	39.1	58.0

Source: Registraduría Nacional del Estado Civil, 1990, 1991, and 1994.
[a]The 1986 abstention rates are lower because they are based on an electoral census rather than on an estimated potential electorate. Consequently, the rates are valid internally but not very meaningful between elections.
[b]The urban vote includes that of the four metropolitan areas.

Urban electoral behavior in Colombia is more volatile than national patterns in terms not only of wide fluctuations in turnout but also in the magnitude of voting for dissident parties or movements (Cepeda, 1987:135). This behavior is expressed in the presidential vote for María Eugenia Rojas (ANAPO) in 1974; Galán (New Liberal Party) in 1982; and Navarro Wolff (AD-M-19) in 1990. Looking at these electoral returns in the four major metropolitan areas, the nontraditional party challengers received a larger vote share than their national averages, excepting Medellín in 1982 and 1990.

In 1974, María Eugenia obtained 9.4 percent of the national vote and 14.6 percent of the metropolitan vote, Galán tallied 10.9 percent nationally and 16.1 percent in metropolitan areas, and Navarro Wolff received 12.8 percent nationally and 18.9 percent of the metro vote. Perhaps because of its historical conservatism and a higher degree of interparty competition than its sister cities, Medellín was the least supportive of these dissident candidates. In contrast, Barranquilla expressed its volatility in a leftist direction, giving María Eugenia 21.1 percent of its vote and Navarro Wolff a remarkable 41.1 percent, along with a more tepid response to Galán of 3.5 percent. Galán's Bogotá vote (31.1 percent) represented a middle-class reaction against the *clase política*. Urban voting behavior reflects social class divisions through a combination of voter turnout, a tendency for lower-class voters to support dissident left-leaning candidates, and the traditional class differences between Liberals and Conservatives—Liberals have more strength among the lower class and Conservatives within the upper-middle and upper classes.

Local Reforms since 1986

Colombian local elections traditionally were virtually meaningless because mayors were appointed and municipal councils enjoyed limited autonomy as a consequence of severe administrative and fiscal constraints. However, this scenario underwent significant change when President Betancur introduced an extensive reform package in conjunction with his peace plan. While only a portion of the reform proposals was adopted (Santamaría and Silva, 1984), the Acto Legislativo Número 1 de 1986, passed by two consecutive sessions of Congress in 1984 and 1985, comprised what one analyst labeled the most significant constitutional reform in fifty years (Gaitán, 1988:94). That reform, along with implementing legislation passed during the Betancur and Barco governments, was directed toward administrative, fiscal, and political decentralization of the political system. It included: 1) popular election of mayors for two-year terms, delayed until March 1988; 2) transfer of funds generated by the national sales tax (IVA) to municipalities, reaching 50 percent by 1992; 3) local referenda, or *consultas populares*, at the municipal level; and 4) the creation of local administrative boards and consumer leagues with input into the delivery of municipal services. However, these reforms increased the responsibilities for delivering governmental services at the local level that the national government had formerly discharged (Dugas et al., 1992; Santamaría and Silva, 1984; Hoskin, 1989b).

A mystique surrounding the reforms evolved which implied that they would lead toward a reequilibrium of the political system, opening new channels of participation to groups operating outside the system, reducing the gap between the state and society by placing responsibility and resources for the delivery of public services at the local level, and making locally elected officials more accountable to their constituents. In addition, others viewed these reforms as a means of promoting ideological and programmatic behavior of the traditional parties, undermining their clientelistic practices. Assuming that local politicians would be held accountable by their constituents, then they would be forced to develop coherent programs and respond to citizens' demands, together with abandoning the pronounced tendency toward internal party factionalism, which would undermine their ability to compete successfully with other parties and civic groups. In short, the municipal reforms were portrayed as a major means of rejuvenating, from the bottom up, the democratic process in Colombia.

Previous administrative, fiscal, and political reforms were not only institutionalized in the 1991 constitution but were also extended considerably. The allotment of IVA funds to local governments was abandoned in favor of transferring a specified portion of the national government's current income to municipalities—14 percent in 1993, increasing annually until reaching 22 percent in 2002 (Dugas, 1994:34). As a consequence of these reforms, municipal government investment has mushroomed, increasing from 2.1 percent in the 1967–68 period to over 30 percent in 1994 (Santana Rodríguez, 1994:106).

With respect to political reforms, the 1991 constitution was designed to maximize opportunities for the expression of the popular will, creating a participatory democracy with the following channels through which the people might exercise their sovereignty: the vote, plebiscite, referendum, popular consultation, open meeting (*cabildo abierto*), legislative initiative, and recall (Sachica, 1991:43). With the implementing legislation now in place, mayoral candidates elected in 1994 will serve three-year terms and will be subject to recall after January 1, 1996, if they fail to implement their campaign program, which they were required to file with the Registraduría Nacional in order to appear on the ballot (referred to in the 1991 constitution as the *voto programático*).

Local Electoral Behavior since 1988

What has been the impact of political reforms upon urban electoral behavior since the popular election of mayors was instituted in 1988? Have participation rates increased? Do voters have a wider array of candidates from which to choose? Has the domination of the two traditional parties continued? To what extent do voting patterns in the four metropolitan areas deviate from smaller urban areas and the nation? In short, is there any evidence to suggest that democracy in Colombia is being reformulated from the bottom up?

Turning first to citizen participation in mayoral elections, the data are encouraging: 33 percent abstained in 1988, 42 percent in 1990, 58 percent in 1992, and 52.5 percent in 1994 (Santana Rodrí-guez, 1994:107). While an upward trend in abstention is evident, we should point out that the turnout in mayoral elections is con-siderably higher than for all other contests—presidential, congres-sional, assembly, and municipal council.[9] Thus, in 1990, the only case in which mayoral elections coincided with congressional elec-tions, the turnout for the mayoral races was 58 percent in compari-son to 55 percent for the Cámara, an unusually high turnout for that body. In 1994 the participation rate in mayoral elections was 47.5 percent, while decreasing to 33 percent for the Cámara and 43 percent for the second round of the presidential elections (34 per-cent in the first round).

However, the abstention rates in the four major metropolitan areas exceeded the national average considerably, averaging 41.3 percent in 1988, 48.9 percent in 1990, and 66 percent in 1992. Bogotá and Medellín registered the highest abstention rates in 1992, at 73.7 and 71.2 percent, respectively, followed by Barranquilla and Cali with around 60 percent. In summary, participation rates in may-oral races aggregated at the national as well as in the metropolitan areas are higher than for all other types of elections, an indication that political decentralization is exerting a positive impact upon eliciting citizens' involvement in politics.

Another dimension of political reform at the local level relates to its impact upon the party system. The innovations of the 1980s and in the 1991 constitution clearly represented an assault upon the traditional party hegemonies in the electoral arena. Has that been reflected in voting patterns for mayoral elections? As shown in Table 6, the two traditional parties still retain their supremacy, though to a lesser extent than in national elections: 85.8 percent in 1988, 89.3 percent in 1990, 68.1 percent in 1992, and 82.9 percent in 1994. However, this two-party percentage of the vote is understated because a number of traditional politicians ran under different party labels in order to maximize their electoral chances in view of the rather pervasive antitraditional party sentiments, especially in the metropolitan areas. The Liberal Party received about 45, 52, 40, and 48 percent of the *alcaldías,* with the 1990 resurgence clearly reflecting the impact of simultaneous elections. The Conservative factions won a smaller percentage of the *alcaldías* (about 41, 37, 29, and 35, respectively), but they exceeded their averages for recent congressional elections.

Table 6. Mayoral Elections by Political Party Affiliation, 1988–1994

	1988	*1990*	*1992*	*1994*
Liberal	44.5%	52.4%	39.5%	47.8%
Conservative	41.3	36.9	28.6	35.1
Other	10.2	7.2	28.4[a]	13.6[b]
Coalition	2.5	2.4	2.4	2.7
Unión Patriótica	1.6	1.1	1.2	.9
Total	100.1%	100.0%	100.1%	100.1%
Total Elected	1,001	1,005	1,012	1,026

Source: Registraduría Nacional del Estado Civil, *La democracia regional y local,* vol. 1, 1992, p. 288, and Santana Rodríguez, p. 108.
[a]The other category in 1992 includes one AD-M-19 mayor.
[b]The other category in 1994 includes three AD-M-19 mayors and the AD-M-19 coalition mayor of Pasto, Antonio Navarro Wolff.

The most dramatic electoral change associated with the popular election of mayors consists of the "other" vote (about 10, 7, 28, and 14 percent), most often associated with civic candidates, of which there are three types. First, there are those Liberal and Conservative candidates who seek to broaden their electoral base by skirting the negative sentiments associated with the *clase política* (they usually are nominated by their respective party directorates). A second group consists of those candidates representing civic movements that are a product of coalitions among base-level social movements and political factions of the traditional variety or of the left. The third type of civic candidates consists of those directly nominated by civic-popular movements without any support from political parties (Santana Rodríguez, 1994:112–13).

Most of the civic candidates generally were elected in the smaller and medium-sized urban areas. In 1994 thirteen civic or coalition candidates were elected mayors in large cities (seven in 1992). Four Catholic priests, with no partisan attachments, won in Cúcuta, Sogamoso, Montería, and La Dorada. Metropolitan mayors retained their traditional party labels until 1992, when a civic candidate, Padre Bernardo Hoyos, won the mayor's race in Barranquilla. His successor in 1994, Edgard George, likewise was a civic candidate, and the new Cali mayor ran on a coalition ticket, although he was listed as a Liberal on the ballot.

Perhaps the most phenomenal mayoral election in 1994 took place in Bogotá, where another civic candidate, Antanas Mockus, handily defeated (with 64 percent of the vote) the Liberal Party nominee, Enrique Peñalosa. Mockus, the former rector of the National University, scorned traditional campaign techniques—he did not open a large headquarters, raised virtually no money, distributed little campaign literature, made few public appearances, paid for no radio or television commercials, received little support from the media, and, significantly, offered neither his supporters nor the electorate any promises regarding bureaucratic posts or public works projects. "Neither the candidate nor the campaign was viewed as an end in itself. Rather, the candidate presented himself as an instrument and the campaign as a process that should be placed at the service of a project for the city, committed to the defense of the collectivity and the development of a culture of citizenship" (Lucía Peña, 1995:30). One of his principal campaign themes was *Todos ponen, todos toman* (Everyone contributes, everyone reaps the benefits). In short, he orchestrated a civic campaign, under the label *ciudadanía en formación*, designed to elicit widespread citizen participation in local government and improve governmental efficiency. Mockus emerged triumphant because of his independent stature,[10] widespread disillusionment with traditional politicians, and an unorthodox, albeit effective, campaign.

Postscript

The uncertainties preceding the local and regional elections of 1997 were unprecedented in Colombian electoral behavior for a variety of reasons. Clearly, the major source of anxiety surrounded the impact upon the conduct of elections related to intense guerrilla violence and intimidation of candidates, electoral officials, and voters in major portions of the nation. Whereas insurrectional activity traditionally has heightened during the year before presidential elections, the guerrillas, principally the Fuerzas Armadas Revolucionarias de Colombia (FARC) and the Ejercito de Liberación Nacional (ELN), shifted their strategy from pursuing local power through the electoral process to boycotting the 1997 elections in many municipalities. As a consequence of this strategy, 110 political leaders were assassinated and another 244 kidnapped in 1997, 359 mayoral candidates resigned, 1,520 lists for municipal councils were withdrawn, and electoral officials and voters were declared military targets in these areas.[11] Three days before the elections the ELN kidnapped two OAS electoral observers; they subsequently were released after nine days of captivity. The municipalities most affected by guerrilla activity were located in rural areas, with medium-sized cities and major metropolitan areas hardly affected.

Another source of uncertainty about the electoral process revolved around the complex political and economic situation of the country. Societal polarization resulting from the unsuccessful impeachment attempt of President Samper for his alleged knowledge of drug-related financial contributions to his campaign, the 8000 Process (judicial investigations of political leaders for ties with drug cartels), the government's mounting governability and legitimacy crises, the growing balkanization of the traditional political parties, and an economic recession all raised questions as to their combined impact upon electoral participation and the choice of candidates. The Samper government sought to enhance its credibility by offering eligible voters new incentives to participate in the elections.[12]

Another wild card inserted in the electoral process consisted of the Mandato para la Paz, a proposal emanating from civil society that asked voters to reject all forms of violence and demanded that actors involved in the armed conflict resolve their differences peacefully and respect humanitarian international law that forbids recruiting minors for armed combat and assassination of civilians. The peace theme intensified before the elections when Juan Manuel Santos's peace proposal was rejected outright by the government that labeled it a conspiracy because it supposedly called for

Samper's temporary exiting the presidency (a reflection of the guerrillas' refusal to negotiate with the weak and discredited Samper government).

When the polls opened at 8 A.M. on October 26, Colombians were asked to elect 32 governors (125 candidates), 1,004 mayors (3,416 candidates), 502 departmental assembly persons (1,895 candidates), 11,815 municipal council persons (28,643 candidates), and 5,927 local *ediles* (8,490 candidates). Voters also were offered an opportunity to vote for the Mandato por la Paz.[13] Election officials predicted a high turnout for the reasons mentioned above, as well as a huge increase in voter registration, which more than doubled in relation to the 1994 elections (2.63 million versus 5.3 million). In contrast to the 1994 local elections, President Samper refused to cancel elections in any of the country's 1,077 municipalities. To the surprise of many observers, the elections were conducted peacefully throughout most of the nation, probably with no more election day disruptions than in 1990 or 1994.

Preliminary returns suggest that the turnout was high, especially in metropolitan areas.[14] Projected participation rates were 42.6 percent for governors' races, 47 percent for mayors', and 48.9 percent for the Mandato. Participation rates in mayoral elections had been declining progressively since their inception, going from 66.8 percent in 1988 to 57.7 in 1990, 43.8 in 1992, and 45.5 in 1994, for an average of 53.5 percent.[15] Although the 1997 national participation rate in mayoral races was below the average for the previous four elections, it slightly exceeded the 1994 rate. However, preliminary data indicate that metropolitan voters turned out in record numbers, obviously suggesting that guerrilla intimidation diminished voting in many rural areas. A 43 percent turnout of eligible voters in Bogotá was unprecedented in a local election. In the previous four Bogotá mayoral races, participation rates were 30 percent in 1988, 26 percent in 1990, 15 percent in 1992, and 18 percent in 1994.

Why was there such a large turnout, especially in the large cities? Pending final returns and survey analyses, the answer seems to point toward an opportunity for voters to express their desire for a peaceful solution to the armed conflict as manifested in a vote of almost ten million for the Mandato. Additionally, the guerrilla boycott was implemented selectively; in those areas where either the guerrillas or paramilitaries had consolidated their territorial control, elections were conducted largely without incident. However, that was not the case in areas of territorial dispute. Also, guerrilla intimidation and disruption occurred in a few regions under their control, which demonstrated the political and military muscle of insurrectionary movements to Colombians as well as a debilitated Samper government, perhaps in hopes of enhancing their bargaining power in a future peace process.

Who were the winners in these elections? Answers to that question are complex and elusive, particularly with respect to the Mandato. Clearly, results of that vote suggest that Colombians are seeking a peaceful solution to the pervasive violence, yet translating that mandate into reality is another matter. The media tend to interpret the mandate as a defeat for the guerrillas, which may well sanitize the insurrectionary movement, further complicating the peace process.

Because of the decentralized and chaotic organization of the traditional parties and the often bizarre electoral alliances at the local and regional levels, interpreting electoral data along party lines is hazardous and often meaningless. For example, the former guerrilla movement, Esperanza, Paz y Libertad, now incorporated into the political system, won three mayoral races in Urabá, an area controlled by paramilitary forces. Moreover, several civic, independent, and coalition candidates were supported by factions of the traditional parties, which raises questions about which political forces predominated.

In the governors' races the Liberal Party won in twenty departments (a loss of two in relation to 1994); the Conservative Party elected four governors (a loss of three); and coalition and independent slates prevailed in eight races (a gain of five). Coalition or independent gubernatorial candidates won in important departments of Atlántico, Bolívar, Norte de Santander, Santander, Tolima, and Valle. The coalition candidate in Valle, Gustavo Alvarez Gardeazábal, defeated the Conservative candidate, Carlos Holguín, who was supported by the local political establishment. A leader of an indigenous movement in Guainía, Arnaldo Rojas, won in that department. The Conservative Party consolidated its electoral control in Antioquia, winning both the offices of governor and mayor of Medellín.

With respect to the mayoral races, preliminary data for twenty-nine of the principal contests reveal that the Liberals won in thirteen cities (45 percent), Conservatives in six (20.7 percent), and civic, coalition, and independents in ten (34.5 percent). Two Catholic priests, running as civic candidates, won in Barranquilla and Neiva;

coalition candidates prevailed in Bucaramunga, Cúcuta, and Pasto; and an independent, Enrique Peñalosa, was elected mayor of Bogotá. Although he ran twice previously for mayor on the Liberal ticket, Peñalosa discarded the party label and overwhelmingly defeated the Conservative-endorsed candidate, Carlos Moreno de Caro. The official candidate of the Liberal Party, Enrique Vargas Lleras, tallied around 2.5 percent of the Bogotá vote, a reflection of the weak leadership and disorganization of the Liberal Party.

Local and regional elections traditionally constitute an arena for politicians to demonstrate their political clout in anticipation of national elections, as well as for the guerrilla, paramilitary, and security forces to manifest their control of territory. In this regard, traditional political bosses won in some areas and lost in others. Political forces, aligned with Liberal presidential hopeful Horacio Serpa, lost mayoral races in Barrancabarmeja and Bucaramunga, Liberal electoral barons were overwhelmed in Antioquia by Conservative forces led by Fabio Valencia Cossio, and the traditional political class of El Valle suffered a tremendous blow in the governor's race. Finally, the political outcome of the struggle for territorial hegemony remains unanswered at this point, pending the magnitude of postelectoral violence and a possible peace accord. The large voter turnout undoubtedly will be utilized by the Samper government to bolster its fragile legitimacy, although it is not likely to have such an effect.

References

Bell Lemus, Gustavo. 1995. "La decentralización en Colombia: ¿Un reto administrativo o político?" Paper prepared for a conference entitled "The Colombian Process of Reform: A New Role for the State?" at the Institute for Latin American Studies, University of London, April 24–25.

Bergquist, Charles, Ricardo Peñaranda, and Gonzalo Sánchez, eds. 1992. *Violence in Colombia: The Contemporary Crisis in Historical Perspective*. Wilmington, DE: Scholarly Resources Inc.

Cepeda Ulloa, Fernando. 1987. "Las elecciones de 1986," pp. 115–38 in Monica Lanzetta et al., *Colombia en las urnas: ¿Qué pasó en 1986?* Bogotá: Carlos Valencia Editores.

———. 1976. *Ensayos políticos*. Bogotá: Universidad de los Andes.

———, and Claudia González de Lecaros. 1976. *Comportamiento del voto urbano en Colombia: Una aproximación*. Bogotá: Universidad de los Andes.

Deas, Malcolm. 1993. *Del poder y la gramática*. Bogotá: Tercer Mundo Editores.

Dix, Robert. 1967. *Colombia: The Political Dimensions of Change*. New Haven, CT: Yale University Press.

———. 1987. *The Politics of Colombia*. New York: Praeger Publishers.

Dugas, John. 1994. "The Economic Imperative of Decentralization in Colombia: An Inquiry into the Motives for Intergovernmental Reform." Unpublished paper presented at the Latin American Studies Association, March 10–12, Atlanta, Georgia.

———, Angelica Ocampo, Luis Javier Orjuela, and Germán Ruíz. 1992. *Los caminos de la decentralización*. Bogotá: Tercer Mundo Editores.

Gaitán, Pilar. 1988. "La elección popular de alcaldes: Un desafío para la democracia." *Análisis Político* 3 (January–April): 63–83.

———, and Carlos Moreno Ospina. 1992. *Poder local: Realidad y utopia de la decentralización en Colombia*. Bogotá: Tercer Mundo Editores.

Gilhodés, Pierre. 1993. "Sistema de partidos y partidos políticos en Colombia," pp. 69–114 in Oscar Delgado, ed., *Modernidad, democracia y partidos políticos*. Bogotá: FESCOL and FIDEC.

González, Fernán E. 1993. "Tradición y modernidad en la política colombiana," pp. 15–67 in Oscar Delgado, ed., *Modernidad, democracia y partidos políticos*. Bogotá: FESCOL and FIDEC.

Hartlyn, Jonathan. 1988. *The Politics of Coalition Rule in Colombia*. New York: Cambridge University Press.

Hoskin, Gary. 1990. "Los partidos tradicionales: ¿Hasta donde son responsables de la crisis política?" pp. 145–74 in Francisco Leal Buitrago and Leon Zamosc, eds., *Al filo del caos: Crisis política en la Colombia de los años 80*. Bogotá: Tercer Mundo Editores.

———. 1989a. "Los partidos políticos colombianos y la crisis coyuntural," pp. 199–226 in Patricia Vásquez de Urrutia, ed., *La democracia en blanco y negro: Colombia en los años ochenta*. Bogotá: Ediciones Uniandes.

———. 1989b. "Colombian Democracy: Political Reform, Elections, and Violence." Unpublished paper presented at the Latin American Studies Association, December 6–8, 1989, Miami, Florida.

Inter-American Development Bank. 1992. *Economic and Social Progress in Latin America*. Baltimore, MD: Johns Hopkins University Press.

Leal Buitrago, Francisco. 1984. *Estado y política en Colombia*. Bogotá: Editorial Siglo XXI.

———, and Leon Zamosc, eds. 1990. *Al filo del caos: Crisis política en la Colombia de los años 80*. Bogotá: Tercer Mundo Editores.

Lucía Peña, Sonia. 1995. "Rito y símbolo en la campaña electoral para la alcaldía de Bogotá." *Análisis Político* 24 (January–April): 22–35.

Martz, John D. 1992. "Party Elites and Leadership in Colombia and Venezuela." *Journal of Latin American Studies* 24 (February): 87–121.

Pinzón de Lewin, Patricia. 1989. *Pueblos, regiones y partidos: La regionalización electoral colombiano.* Bogotá: Ediciones Uniandes.

———, and Dora Rothlisberger. 1991. "La participación electoral en 1990: ¿Un nuevo tipo de votante?" pp. 116–32 in Rubén Sánchez David, ed., *Los Nuevos retos electorales.* Bogotá: Fondo Editorial CEREC.

Registraduría Nacional del Estado Civil. 1990. *Estadísticas electorales 1990.* Bogotá: Publicaciones de la Registraduría Nacional.

———. 1991. *Elecciones: Senadores, representantes, gobernadores.* Vol. 1. Bogotá: Publicaciones de la Registraduría Nacional.

———. 1992. *La democracia regional y local.* Vol. 1. Bogotá: Publicaciones de la Registraduría Nacional.

———. 1994. *Elecciones de Congreso 1994.* Vol. 1. Bogotá: Publicaciones de la Registraduría Nacional.

Sachica, Luis Carlos. 1991. *Constitución política de la República de Colombia 1991.* Medellín: Biblioteca Jurídica Diké.

Santamaría, Ricardo, and Gabriel Silva Luhan. 1984. *Proceso político en Colombia: Del frente nacional a la apertura democrática.* Bogotá: Fondo Editorial CEREC.

Santana Rodríguez, Pedro. 1994. "Las elecciones locales en 1994: La tercería cívica en las alcaldías." *Revista Foro* 25 (December): 105–16.

Shugart, Matthew Soberg. 1992. "Leaders, Rank and File, and Constituents: Electoral Reform in Colombia and Venezuela." *Electoral Studies* 11 (March): 21–45.

Notes

1. It is somewhat misleading to talk about a Conservative Party at the time of this writing (1995), for there are at least four factions, along with a couple of personalist groups that include conservative in their title, that are recognized by the National Electoral Council. In addition, the former mayor of Bogotá, Andrés Pastrana, heads what is called the Nueva Fuerza Democrática (NFD, or New Democratic Force), a supposedly nonpartisan movement that is composed mostly of Conservatives. Each of these factions or movements supported Pastrana's 1994 presidential candidacy. The degree of factionalism among the Conservatives is no more pronounced than in the Liberal Party, and I believe that their coalition tendencies and legislative behavior justify aggregating their votes. Pierre Gilhodés captures this organizational disunity: "Today there is no longer a conservative organization, only three groupings without a national structure" (1993:91).

2. Undoubtedly the one-party hegemonies in many muncipalities have been sustained to some extent through electoral fraud (Pinzón, 1989).

Comments of a late Liberal Party elder statesman, Darío Echandía, sustain this assertion. He argued that the parties had counted the ballots correctly for the first time in the 1974 elections (Cepeda, 1976:4). The most disputed contest during recent years was the 1970 presidential election. However, since then, most analysts consider Colombian elections to be relatively fraud free.

3. For an excellent analysis of the historical roots and contemporary violence in Colombia, see Charles Bergquist, Ricardo Peñaranda, and Gonzalo Sánchez, eds., *Violence in Colombia*.

4. The deeply embedded clientelistic and patronage patterns of the traditional parties continue to undermine the participatory and efficiency norms outlined in the new constitution. For an analysis of these practices on the Atlantic coast, see Gustavo Bell Lemus, "La decentralización en Colombia: ¿Un reto administrativo o político?"

5. For those readers not familiar with Colombian politics, ANAPO was the political movement of the former dictator, General Gustavo Rojas Pinilla. It emerged in the 1962 elections, using the traditional party labels as prescribed by the National Front agreement. After ANAPO became an independent party, it gradually disappeared as a major political force. Luis Carlos Galán's New Liberal Party splintered from the Liberal Party in the early 1980s and was reabsorbed into its parent after the 1988 municipal elections. It represented a revolt against the *clase política*, drawing its support largely from middle-class voters in metropolitan areas. AD-M-19 emerged from President Virgilio Barco's peace plan, in which it ran a candidate in the 1990 presidential election (guerrilla leader Carlos Pizarro was assassinated and Antonio Navarro Wolff replaced him on the ballot). As noted in the text, the AD-M-19 consistently has been losing its electoral appeal since its initial success in 1990.

6. Similar to the AD-M-19, the UP was a product of the effort to reincorporate the guerrilla movement into Colombian politics. It was created during the Betancur administration and first nominated candidates in the 1986 elections.

7. This fatigue may have been prompted by the following demands placed upon voters: Colombians cast ballots for mayors in March 1988; for legislative bodies, mayors, Liberal presidential candidates, and for a constitutional convention in March 1990; for president and, once again in May 1990, for or against holding a constitutional convention; for delegates to the Constituent Assembly in December 1990; and finally, for Congress and governors in 1991. Races for mayors, municipal councils, and departmental assemblies were held in March 1992. In 1994 voters went to the polls to elect congressmen and a Liberal presidential candidate in March, a president in May and June, and, finally, mayors, municipal councils, and assemblymen in October. Thus, Colombians may well be suffering from what one observer called "electionitis."

8. The 1991 and 1994 electoral data are not amenable to the same analysis as are previous elections because the Registraduría Nacional printed the results by list without designating party affiliation, other than by winning lists.

9. In 1986 the Registraduría Nacional instituted a system of voter registration that understates the potential electorate, if measured by the size of the population age eighteen years or older. For example, in the 1988

and 1990 mayoral elections, the voting-age population that cast ballots was 43 and 47 percent, respectively, in comparison to the Registraduría's figures of 67 and 58 percent (Gaitán and Moreno, 1992:89).

10. When he was rector of the National University, Mockus generated considerable media coverage and controversy throughout the country as a result of his unorthodox response to student questions at a rally—he dropped his pants and "mooned" the audience. For an excellent analysis of the Bogotá mayoral campaign, see Sonia Lucía Peña, "Rito y símbolo en la campaña electoral."

11. *El Tiempo*, October 26, 1997.

12. The incentives consisted of a 10 percent reduction in tuition at public universities, along with an increase of ten points in the ICFES examination (an SAT equivalent); a reduction in military service of one to two months; and, in cases of equal qualifications of applicants, preference for those who voted in the allocation of public-sector employment, scholarships, rural land titles, subsidized housing, and, with employer approval, half-day vacations.

13. The number of mayoral elections was less than the total number of municipalities (1,077) because some candidates withdrew before the August 14 deadline, and other were elected after the 1994 elections, thereby enabling them to complete their three-year term in accordance with a constitutional court decision.

14. The electoral returns utilized here are not from the Registraduría Nacional but from *El Tiempo*, November 2, 1997.

15. Lleana Kure, María Fernanda Sánchez, Cristina Querbin, "Cuantos elegimos a nuestros gobernantes?" (Unpublished manuscript, Departamento Nacional de Planeación, Bogotá, 1997), 2.

5

Urban Elections in the Dominican Republic, 1962–1994

Christopher Mitchell

In purely electoral terms the Dominican Republic has made considerable strides toward a democratic political system since 1962. In that year the foundation of a durable national system of political parties was laid, and the nation carried out its first fair election under universal suffrage. Since 1966, when U.S. occupation troops withdrew in the wake of a 1965 military intervention, Dominicans have conducted an unbroken series of national elections every four years. In the years since 1978, a relatively vigorous multiparty system has developed, sheltered by more consistent respect, on the part of the state, for individuals' civil liberties and the rights of opposition groups. The presidency has been yielded up by losing political parties following the 1978 and 1986 elections. In short, a long-standing national pattern, one of pendulum swings between authoritarian rule and periods of severe political instability, has been substantially modified.

However, it would be an overstatement to say that an ample democracy has been firmly established, even in the electoral arena. The system of elections and political parties in the Dominican Republic often leaves a wide gap between the most pressing concerns of the public and the use of governmental authority. Serious irregularities marred the voting in 1978, 1990, and 1994, and the outcomes of the first and last of these three contests were "pacted" by political elites, not determined by votes alone. Both national and local elected officials are often relatively unresponsive to voters and inactive in addressing issues of public policy. These practices, in turn, tend to prompt the electorate to apathy, interrupted occasionally by vigorous protest movements.

This essay will focus on these processes and problems as evidenced in significant cities and towns of the Dominican Republic. It will examine changes over time in voters' support for competing parties, assessing the influence of regional and class factors on those changes. It will also describe the links between national politics and urban elections and examine the relations between municipal politics and the growth of new social movements.

This analysis may remind us of the dialectical relationship between competitive elections and other significant aspects of democratic practice in Latin America and the Caribbean. Elections (along with a minimal respect for individual rights) are often established early in a process of democratization. Periodic voting tends to create a demand, both from the public and from elites, for such other elements of democracy as effective constitutionalism and public policies committed to social justice. Experience with elections often contributes to the growth of a national civic culture. All these developments have taken place, to a greater or lesser degree, over the past thirty years in the Dominican Republic. At the same time, the electoral system was partially reformed between 1992 and 1994. Additional efforts now under way to revamp both elections and the Dominican state budget may further affect local as well as national politics

National Elections and Their Linkage to Municipal Voting

The first modern election in the Dominican Republic was held in 1962, eighteen months after the assassination of Generalíssimo Rafael Trujillo, who had ruled the nation tyrannically for thirty-one years. In many ways the 1962 contest set the parameters for contemporary politics, including a high level of political participation, a strong role for national parties, and a focus on the presidency as the key electoral stake. The Partido Revolucionario Dominicano (PRD, or Dominican Revolutionary Party) emerged in 1962 as the first modern national party, with a populist structure and a reformist program. It won an overwhelming presidential victory with 58.7 percent of the votes cast. The PRD's sweeping triumph paradoxically weakened its overall political position, however. More conservative elites despaired of winning at the ballot box and allied with the military to overthrow President Juan Bosch of the PRD in September 1963.

A rebellion in April 1965 calling for a constitutionalist restoration of Bosch drew the United States to send in troops to prevent a "second Cuba." Conservative Dominican political forces benefited in three ways following the U.S. occupation. First, Bosch was prevented from retaking office, and instead an interim government, headed by Héctor García Godoy, was instituted. Second, notice was served in the plainest possible way that Washington would not tolerate a regime in Santo Domingo that it perceived as radical. Finally, former president Joaquín Balaguer, who had served as the last "puppet president" under the Trujillo dictatorship, recognized an opening in which to organize a mass-based conservative party. The new Partido Reformista (PR, or Reformist Party), founded by Balaguer in New York in 1964, united the interests of many peasants with those of business elites and a rising middle class. Balaguer led the PR to victory in national voting in 1966. That election was regarded by many non-Dominican observers as fair, although the PRD vehemently protested what it viewed as intimidation from military and political opponents during a foreign military occupation (Hillman and D'Agostino, 1992:111).

The 1970 and 1974 national elections, in which Balaguer was reelected, were not effectively competitive. The PRD and most other opposition parties abstained from both, protesting an atmosphere of intimidation which included "unofficial" political killings, open electioneering by the military, and other abuses.[1] The PRD and other challengers to the PR reentered national politics in 1978 , and the following five national elections have been very actively contested (see Tables 1 and 2). A three-party system has emerged during these years. The major political forces are the conservative PR (renamed in 1985 the Partido Reformista Social Cristiano, or PRSC), the centrist PRD, and the more left-wing Partido de la Liberación Dominicana (PLD, or Dominican Liberation Party), organized by Bosch after he resigned from the PRD in 1973. Personalism plays at least as strong a role in Dominican politics as does ideology; until the mid-1990s the PRSC and the PLD were dominated by Balaguer and Bosch, respectively, while the PRD has been an arena for rivalry among three or four major personalities. In 1978 and 1982 the PRD won the presidency but lost it in 1986 to Balaguer, who was reelected in 1990 and 1994.

Table 1. Votes, by Party, in Selected Elections at the National Level and in Six *Municipios*, 1962–1994

	1962	1966	1978	1982	1986	1990	1994[c]
NATIONAL							
PRD	619,491	494,570	855,765	854,868	819,205[a]	444,006	1,188,394
PRI						135,659	68,910
UCN	317,327						
PR/PRSC		759,887	698,183	669,176	855,565	678,065[b]	1,263,341
PLD				179,849	387,881	653,278	395,653
MUNICIPAL							
Santo Domingo							
PRD	139,557	147,087	262,301	236,428	224,513[a]	114,267	386,531
PRI						35,412	21,343
UCN	33,764						
PR/PRSC		91,128	125,405	117,957	195,243	178,553	274,939
PLD				56,809	128,053	153,746	195,319
Santiago							
PRD	27,436	28,539	63,516	48,989	37,638[a]	23,563	73,925
PRI						5,077	4,393
UCN	40,895						
PR/PRSC		60,206	42,067	40,441	47,063	34,850	87,948
PLD				25,765	47,436	59,748	51,461
La Vega							
PRD	18,266	20,505	32,371	24,925	25,834[a]	11,939	31,440
PRI						3,324	2,780
UCN	21,782						
PR/PRSC		33,363	24,484	24,372	27,013	17,393	38,955
PLD				7,593	15,642	30,565	24,297

San Pedro de Marcorís							
PRD	14,565	15,793	19,335	18,564	13,508[a]	6,168	28,887
PRI	3,517					1,196	1,348
UCN							
PR/PRSC		6,528	8,146	5,397	8,538	8,436	27,079
PLD				6,049	13,368	14,909	11,101
San Juan de la Maguana							
PRD	3,664	7,776	12,447	16,269	15,254[a]	4,868	15,777
PRI						3,468	3,095
UCN	2,727						
PR/PRSC		22,952	23,978	18,472	21,743	11,683	20,177
PLD				3,086	6,474	14,637	8,517
San Cristóbal							
PRD	37,250	15,276	29,358	19,860	22,174[a]	9,621	27,917
PRI	1,639					3,371	1,870
UCN							
PR/PRSC		33,427	31,233	22,360	29,149	19,188	36,425
PLD				2,820	7,978	12,613	7,690

Sources: For 1962 results: *Gaceta Oficial* No. 8749 (Santo Domingo, March 31, 1963); 1962 tallies within *municipios* show votes for municipal rather than national lists. For 1966, 1978, and 1982 results: Darío Contreras, *Comportamiento electoral dominicano: Elecciones dominicanas 1962–1982: Datos y análisis* (Santo Domingo: N.p., 1986). For 1986 results: Flavio Monción D., *Estadísticas electorales de 1986* (Santo Domingo: N.p., n.d.). For 1990 national results: Oficina Nacional de Estadística, *Boletín de estadísticas político-electorales* No. 1 (Santo Domingo, January 1992); for 1990 municipal results: *Gaceta Oficial* No. 9795-bis (Santo Domingo, 1990). For 1994 results: *Gaceta Oficial* No. 9901 (Santo Domingo, 1995).

[a]Includes votes for the 1986 PRD faction, "La Estructura."

[b]Includes 30,439 votes from four minor parties, giving Balaguer his winning margin.

[c]"National" totals for 1994 report numbers of votes in the presidential contest; "municipal" totals for 1994 report numbers of votes in municipal contests. All figures are for parties, not for multiparty alliances.

Table 2. Percentage of the Total Vote, by Party, in Selected Elections at the National Level and in Six *Municipios*, 1962–1994

	1962	1966	1978	1982	1986	1990	1994[c]
NATIONAL							
PRD	58.7%	36.8%	51.7%	46.7%	38.8%[a]	23.0%	39.4%
PRI						7.0	2.2
UCN	30.0						
PR/PRSC		56.5	42.2	36.6	40.5	35.1[a]	41.8
PLD				9.8	18.4	33.8	13.1
MUNICIPAL							
Santo Domingo							
PRD	74.2%	56.0%	63.2%	53.8%	40.1%[a]	23.0%	42.5%
PRI						7.1	2.4
UCN	18.0						
PR/PRSC		34.8	30.2	26.8	34.9	36.0	30.3
PLD				12.9	22.9	31.0	21.5
Santiago							
PRD	35.8%	39.0%	56.0%	39.0%	27.7%[a]	18.6%	32.4%
PRI						4.0	1.9
UCN	53.3						
PR/PRSC		63.0	37.1	32.2	34.7	27.5	38.6
PLD				20.5	35.0	47.2	22.5
La Vega							
PRD	36.1%	34.5%	53.3%	39.5%	36.7%[a]	18.7%	31.0%
PRI						5.2	2.7
UCN	43.1						
PR/PRSC		56.1	40.4	38.6	38.3	27.7	38.5
PLD				12.0	22.2	47.9	24.0
San Pedro de Macorís							
PRD	75.3%	65.3%	64.9%	58.9%	36.9%[a]	19.2%	52.2%

PRI							
UCN	18.2	27.0	27.3	17.1	23.3	26.3	38.0
PR/PRSC				19.2	36.5	46.5	15.6
PLD						3.7	1.9
San Juan de la Maguana							
PRD	17.2%[d]	23.4%	31.5%	40.0%	34.2%[a]	12.8%	31.6%
PRI							
UCN	12.8	69.2	60.7	45.4	48.8	30.7	40.4
PR/PRSC				7.6	14.5	38.4	17.0
PLD						9.1	6.2
San Cristóbal							
PRD	90.0%	29.0%	45.3%	41.0%	36.5%[a]	20.5%	35.8%
PRI	4.0						
UCN		63.6	48.2	46.0	48.0	40.9	46.7
PR/PRSC				5.8	13.0	26.9	9.9
PLD						7.2	2.4

Sources: For 1962 results: *Gaceta Oficial* No. 8749 (Santo Domingo, March 31, 1963); 1962 tallies within *municipios* show votes for municipal rather than national lists. For 1966, 1978, and 1982 results: Darío Contreras, *Comportamiento electoral dominicano: Elecciones dominicanas 1962–1982: Datos y análisis* (Santo Domingo: N.p., 1986). For 1986 results: Flavio Monción D., *Estadísticas electorales de 1986* (Santo Domingo: N.p., n.d.). For 1990 national results: Oficina Nacional de Estadística. *Boletín de estadísticas político-electorales* No. 1 (Santo Domingo, January 1992); for 1990 municipal results: *Gaceta Oficial* No. 9795-bis (Santo Domingo, 1990). For 1994 results: *Gaceta Oficial* No. 9901 (Santo Domingo, 1995).

aIncludes votes for the 1986 PRD faction, "La Estructura."

bIncludes 30,439 votes from four minor parties, giving Balaguer his winning margin.

c"National" percentages for 1994 report votes in the presidential contest; "municipal" percentages for 1994 report votes in municipal contests.

dThe major party vote was low in San Juan in 1962 because the Partido Nacionalista Revolucionario Democrático (PNRD), a short-lived minor party, polled 13,724 votes (64.5 percent) in the *municipio*. Those votes were more than one-third of the party's total backing nationwide.

Under the Dominican constitution and electoral laws from 1962 until 1992–1994, local elections were closely tied to national voting. Balloting for presidential, congressional, and municipal candidates took place simultaneously and on a single ballot, which always emphasized a voter's choice among parties rather than among candidates. In four of the six national elections between 1962 and 1990, it was technically possible to vote for different parties at the national and municipal levels.[2] However, a relatively small number of voters apparently took advantage of that opportunity.[3]

In 1992 the electoral law was changed, providing each voter in 1994 with three distinct ballots: one each for presidential, congressional, and municipal contests. Each category of ballot was collected and tallied separately; considerably more ticket-splitting took place, as is evident in Table 3. In 1994 the constitution was amended to bar immediate presidential reelection and to call for presidential elections in 1996. This second change means that unless further amendments are made, congressional and municipal elections will be held separately in the future, two years after each presidential contest.[4]

Table 3. Ticket-splitting in the 1994 National Election: Votes Received by Major Parties

	Presidential Votes	Municipal Votes
PRD	39.4%	38.8%
PRSC	41.8	37.3
PLD	13.1	16.8

Source: Calculated from data in *Gaceta Oficial* No. 9901 (Santo Domingo, 1995).

A system of proportional representation is used to select winning candidates for the national Chamber of Deputies and for the local post of *regidor*, as members of municipal councils are known. The size of each town's council is proportional to its population;[5] the capital city, Santo Domingo, presently elects sixty-two *regidores*, while second-ranking Santiago has twenty-one. Senators are elected by plurality (one for each of the nation's thirty provinces), while mayors (*síndicos*) are chosen by plurality within *municipios*.

The Dominican Republic is a nation with two major cities and about a dozen important regional towns. To assess urban elections, this analysis will discuss six *municipios*, chosen on criteria of population size and regional distribution (see Table 4). Santo Domingo, known legally as the Distrito Nacional, is in effect a *municipio* that is coterminous with a province. It has grown rapidly since the death of Trujillo, experiencing both extensive aggregate economic growth and immiseration for the very poor, as the capital has attracted migrants from throughout the nation. Santiago is the nation's second largest city, situated in the relatively well-endowed Cibao region, whose economy depends on diversified agriculture and mining. La Vega is a smaller Cibao city focused primarily on agriculture. San Juan de la Maguana lies in the poorest region, the Southwest, where scarce rainfall has contributed to low per capita income. San Pedro de Macorís, by contrast, is located in the East, which became dominated by sugarcane growing in the late nineteenth century. (Sugar, though in significant decline over the past fifteen years, is still the nation's leading commodity export.) Finally, San Cristóbal is a midsized city just west of Santo Domingo that is experiencing some suburban growth as that great metropolis expands; one significant political fact about San Cristóbal is that it was Generalíssimo Trujillo's hometown. As one may note from examining Table 4, the Southeast region (including Santo Domingo, San Pedro, and San Cristóbal) is systematically more affluent than the

Table 4. Population of Six Selected *Municipios* and Socioeconomic Characteristics of Their Regions

	Estimated Population (1990)	Median Yearly Family Income (1976–77)	Private Houses with Electricity (1981)	Illiterates among Those >10 Years Old (1981)
Southeast Region		RD$ 3,596	75.3%	21.1%
Santo Domingo	2,411,895			
San Pedro de Macorís	144,319			
San Cristóbal	137,494			
Cibao Region		RD$ 2,517	48%	27.8%
Santiago	489,522			
La Vega	303,047			
Southwest Region		RD$ 1,786	35.5%	38.3%
San Juan de la Maguana	129,688			

Sources: Population estimates: Oficina Nacional de Estadística, Secretariado Técnico de la Presidencia, *República Dominicana en cifras 1986*, Table 211-04. Socioeconomic characteristics: United Nations, *República Dominicana: Población y desarrollo 1950–1985*, Tables II.24, III.9, III.12. Median incomes for the late 1970s were probably as high in real terms as they are sixteen years later, and easier for North American readers to interpret. In 1976 the Dominican peso (RD$) was worth only slightly less than the U.S. dollar, while in 1995 it was worth 7.5 cents.

Cibao, which in turn enjoys a clear developmental advantage over the Southwest.

The Electoral Experience at the Local Level

Intraurban politics. Since 1978 there have been three major trends in competition among Dominican parties at the national level, some of whose effects may be observed best in Table 2. First, the PRD revived dramatically in the 1978 election after fifteen years out of office, becoming a vigorous if internally diverse political coalition. Second, the Reformist Party staged a notable recovery during eight years in opposition (1978–1986), modernizing some of its internal procedures, creating ties with the Christian Democratic International, and reversing the decline in its voting segment in the key cities of Santo Domingo and Santiago. Finally, the elections between 1982 and 1994 charted the national rise and relative decline of the PLD, from less than 10 percent of the vote to voting parity with its national rivals, and back to drawing less than 15 percent of the national totals.

Voting in Dominican cities has basically paralleled these developments in national party competition, with significant local variations. Three patterns emerge in voting trends in these six *municipios* since 1978:

1. In PRD strongholds, Santo Domingo and San Pedro de Macorís, the populist party was able to dominate the *sindicatura* in every election after 1978, with the exception of 1990 when two presidential candidates identified with the PRD were offered: José Francisco Peña Gómez for the main body of the party and Jacobo Majluta for the breakaway Independent Revolutionary Party (PRI).

2. San Cristóbal and San Juan de la Maguana are PRSC strongholds. The *reformistas* have never lost control of San Cristóbal's town government and were displaced in San Juan only by the PLD in 1990–1994.

3. Volatility has marked municipal voting in Santiago and its near neighbor La Vega. The PRD displaced the PR as the local winning party in 1978 and 1982; the PLD won both *sindicaturas* by 1990, only to lose them to the PRSC in 1994.

Limited data are available on the influence of social class upon voting in urban areas (see Table 5). Examining stratified groups of Santo Domingo neighborhoods in the 1978 and 1982 elections, José

Del Castillo and fellow researchers found a nearly monotonic relationship between ascending class status and support for the Partido Reformista, and between descending status and PRD voting.[6] The PRD also had notable support in 1978 even in "upper class" sections of the capital. By 1982 the same basic relationships held, except that at every class level the PLD had made inroads in the backing for both the PR and PRD.

Table 5. Support for Major Parties, as Percentage of Total Vote, in Class-stratified Barrios in Santo Domingo, 1978 and 1982

Barrios *Characterized by Dominant Social Class (% of All Voters in These Barrios)*	1978		1982		
	PR	PRD	PR	PRD	PLD
Upper class (5%)	47%	45%	43%	37%	8%
Middle class (23%)	34	57	30	48	11
Popular (45%)	26	67	20	53	14
Marginal (27%)	29	65	22	50	13

Source: José Del Castillo, "Cómo votan las clases en Santo Domingo," *Ultima Hora* (Santo Domingo), March 10, 1986:16.

Urban-national politics. The traditional straight-ticket ballot used in Dominican elections prior to 1990 was nicknamed the *boleta de arrastre*, literally the "dragging ballot." As one experienced national politician described this ballot's effect on local elections (and indeed on politics in general), "the presidential candidate was the locomotive, and we were the cars of the train" (Interview 103). The metaphor remains a helpful one, even though ticket-splitting increased under the new ballot system introduced for the 1994 contest. Dominican national parties have ultimate control over municipal nominations and list positions, and their influence (especially in larger cities) is strengthened by the absence of subdistricts within *municipios*. In preparation for the 1990 voting, for example, "the closed nature of candidate selection by top party leaders, particularly within the PRSC, had been such that after the filing date potential candidates appeared at Junta Central Electoral (National Election Board) sites around the country to inquire whether and where on the list they had been registered" (Hartlyn, 1990:97–98).

Yet central party leaders have typically needed to strike a balance between exercising central discretion and naming candidates who are popular with local party activists and perhaps with voters. To reward political services, cultivate local clients, or punish disloyalty, the locomotive has had to decide which cars to pull, but it has been important that those cars not be too heavy, that they have some electoral momentum of their own.

Each of the three major parties has struck this balance in a different way. The PRSC usually has the most centralized nomination method, with little weight given to suggestions from local party cadres (Interviews 103, 104, 106). The PLD tends to give the greatest voice to party leaders at the grass-roots level, while the PRD follows a kind of corporatist strategy in naming candidates for *regidor*: "List positions are given out to members of key constituent groups: lawyers, labor leaders, teachers, and so forth; of course, some attention is given to candidates' identification with *barrios* as well" (Interview 106).

Whenever possible, parties seek to maximize both the goals of patronage and municipal vote-getting. The PRD, for example, has recently begun including respected national notables—former cabinet ministers and the like—on municipal lists for the relatively lowly position of *regidor* in order to build up local vote tallies. The PRSC led the major parties in nominating women for legislative and municipal office in the 1980s, a trend that has grown in the succeeding ten years. From 1986 to 1994 the PRSC nominated a well-known television personality, Rafael Corporán de los Santos ("the Johnny Carson of the Dominican Republic") (Interview 103) for mayor of the capital. In 1986, Corporán's appeal probably contributed to the PRS's gain of nearly 80,000 votes from its 1982 showing in Santo Domingo, and in 1990 he was elected, polling 4.6 percent more votes than Balaguer in the Distrito Nacional.

There is some evidence to suggest that holding primaries (or local party conventions) to nominate municipal candidates helps to build social support for a political party in the long run. The revival in the PRS's urban fortunes at the polls in 1986 was preceded by a series of 102 municipal conventions at which candidates for síndico were chosen in open deliberations.[7] The notable growth in PLD voting after 1982 may have been based in part on its orientation toward the rank-and-file's preferences. To choose a presidential candidate for the elections scheduled for 1996, the PRSC held a national primary in October 1995 that decisively nominated Vice President Jacinto Peynado. However, most national leaders outside the PLD have tended to shy away from primaries, and the Dominican Republic does not have on its books a statute governing candidate choice and other procedures of political parties.

With local elections placed on a different calendar from presidential voting beginning in 1996, specific municipal concerns may exert greater influence on voters' choices in local races. On the other hand, national issues may still intrude. For example, a party holding the presidency might lose in prestige and power if voting in localities is used as an opportunity to lodge protests against a national administration at midterm. The one Dominican "test case" on this point in the post-Trujillo era is inconclusive. In May 1968 municipal elections were held throughout the country, midway between presidential contests. The PRD boycotted the voting, but the centrist Partido Revolucionario Social Cristiano nominated candidates, as did many local ad hoc "groups" and "movements" (see Table 6). Turnout in the six selected *municipios* was down by only 8 percent in comparison with 1966. The Reformist Party improved its relative vote in Santo Domingo, San Juan, and San Cristóbal and, in the only change of municipal control among the six cities in 1968, won the Santo Domingo mayoralty. The PR's tally declined in the two volatile Cibao towns and in the PRD stronghold of San Pedro; in those three areas local miniparties appear to have served as proxies for the absent PRD.

The Dominican national government exerts extensive budgetary control over municipalities, and this weapon is used with vigor in municipal politics and campaigns. Forms of taxes that in other nations frequently serve as local revenue sources, such as real estate taxes, are paid directly to the national government, leaving cities such as Santo Domingo with control over only minor imposts. In 1986 the Dominican state received nearly twenty-eight times as much direct revenue as all six selected cities combined (Oficina Nacional de Estadística 1986, Tables 343-01 and 343-05). Urgently needed national funds are provided to municipalities in two ways. Twenty percent of the money collected by the national tax agency, Rentas Internas, is returned to municipalities as the *subsidio ordinario* (Helena Rodríguez, 1992:56; Interview 106). The president also directly controls a *subsidio extraordinario*, which is usually vital to fund routine functions of local government but which may be turned on or off depending on the political interests of the National Palace. "Both Balaguer and the PRD adopted the same stance: to choke off payments to municipalities held by the other party, making it difficult for them to get funds" (Interview 103). Implicit in this practice is a strong message to local voters: Support the party that seems to have the best chance of winning the presidency.

Table 6. Votes and Percentage of the Total Vote, by Party, in Six *Municipios*, 1968

	Votes	Percentage
Santo Domingo		
Partido Reformista	151,707	64.8%
Partido Revolucionario Social Cristiano	50,084	21.4
Agrupación Independiente "Movimiento Republicano Democrático"	12,308	5.3
Agrupación "Movimiento de Acción Capitaleña Independiente"	13,125	5.6
Agrupación "Movimiento Independiente Candidatura Municipal"	6,908	2.9
Santiago		
Partido Reformista	40,109	47.8%
Partido Revolucionario Social Cristiano	2,167	2.6
Agrupación "Movimiento Independiente Conciliatorio"	22,951	27.3
Agrupación Municipal Independiente "Todo por Santiago"	18,740	22.3
La Vega		
Partido Reformista	20,501	51.4%
Partido Revolucionario Social Cristiano	2,720	6.8
Agrupación "Progresista Vegana Independiente"	16,650	41.7
San Pedro de Macorís		
Partido Reformista	5,348	24.9%
Partido Revolucionario Social Cristiano	1,088	5.1
Agrupación "Movimiento Macorisano Independiente"	15,011	69.9
San Juan de la Maguana		
Partido Reformista	21,840	79.0%
Partido Revolucionario Social Cristiano	5,800	21.0
San Cristóbal		
Partido Reformista	29,135	78.6%
Partido Revolucionario Social Cristiano	7,940	21.4

Source: Gaceta Oficial No. 9094 (Santo Domingo, August 15, 1968).

A challenge to this centralized and politicized financial system was launched in 1995 by the leadership of the Liga Municipal Dominicana (Dominican Municipal League). Founded in 1938, the League's function is to distribute the *subsidio ordinario* to the nation's *municipios*. An enterprising group of PRD politicians achieved leadership in the League in 1994 through a coalition with local officials elected by the PLD. The League has presented a series of draft bills to Congress, aimed at better training and preparation for local officials, guarantees of stable and unbiased financial backing from the central government, greater local autonomy to impose minor taxes, and other measures (Interview 111; Fundación Siglo 21, 1995). As the League's secretary general, Julio Maríñez, told a gathering of municipal officials in 1995, "Although decentralization may dispense with democracy, under today's circumstances modern democracy can hardly be said to exist without adequate decentralization" (Maríñez, 1995:1).

A political career at the municipal level is seldom a stepping-stone to national parliamentary or executive office; it is much more common for mayors and council members to remain in exclusively municipal political pursuits (Interview 101). The *síndico* of Santo Domingo, however, is indisputably a national figure, the executive official whose work is salient to more voters than anyone except the president (Interview 109). The capital's mayor may well enter office with presidential ambitions, or come to entertain them within a short time. PRD Mayor Pedro Franco Badía (1978–1982) hoped to succeed President Antonio Guzmán, and the next mayor, José Francisco Peña Gómez, ran hard for the PRD's presidential nomination in 1986.[8] Nominees for *síndico* in Santo Domingo conduct campaigns that are somewhat separate from those of the national ticket. According to a politician with experience in the capital's campaigns for the Senate, "A candidate in Santo Domingo needs to distinguish himself by actually *doing* something, responding to people's needs and not just going around with a sound truck and appearing on television two or three times" (Interview 108). This campaign environment gives some advantage to candidates who are independently wealthy, or who have other means to provide patronage. Corporán's television show, for example, offered small donations to meet the needs of petitioners who appeared on the program.

The ambitions of some Santo Domingo mayors have been well known to Dominican presidents, who have responded with the familiar "choking-off" strategy, even if the *síndico* represented the president's own party. When Franco Badía declared his presidential ambitions after two years in office, the *subsidio extraordinario* was cut off by President Guzmán, "and all sorts of municipal services declined because there was no money" (Interview 106; see also Interview 109). In early 1993 relations were reportedly cool between the flamboyant Corporán and President Balaguer, although the chief executive persuaded the mayor not to resign under fire for the terms of a privatization contract for trash removal. On the other hand, good working relations may exist across party lines between Santo Domingo's City Hall (the *ayuntamiento*) and the presidency. Between 1986 and 1990, PRD Mayor Rafael Suberví had generally cordial dealings with Balaguer, apparently because the mayor realized that he needed assistance from the state to perform well and Balaguer may have hoped to create yet another faction within a rival party (Interview 106).

Urban Politics, Public Needs, and New Social Movements

As we have seen, Dominican elected officials in cities and towns are dominated fiscally by the national government and electorally by the national political parties. Their budgets are meager and subject to naked political manipulation by the president. Except in the capital their efforts have been largely ignored by the mass media, which stress partisan conflict affecting the central government, not the many problems of urban management. Local politicians have been obliged to run in elections where (with rare exceptions, as in the case of the Santo Domingo *síndico*) their individual candidacies may be little known to the average voter. Since the size of city councils is proportionate to municipal population but no urban subdistricts exist, the larger the city, the more anonymous the candidates for *regidor* are likely to be.

An important new constraint is now coming to affect Dominican local government as well. The national state is exerting influence to place traditional local administrative functions in the hands of autonomous agencies or private contractors. In Santo Domingo, for example, the task of supplying water has been transferred from the *ayuntamiento* to the autonomous Santo Domingo Water and Sewer Corporation (CAASD), administration of urban transport is no longer in the hands of municipal authorities, and garbage collection is gradually being privatized *barrio* by *barrio*.[9] As one experienced PRD political leader in the capital laments, "The municipal government has been left with providing fire-fighting service, some cultural tasks, and the administration of cemeteries! It is increasingly a hollow shell in terms of real functions, with a consequent running-down of political significance, efficacy, and morale" (Interview 109; Navarro, 1995:7–13).[10]

Under these circumstances, too often municipal politics proceeds on two levels. On the one hand, there is an ideological struggle among *regidores* along party lines, marked at times by city council resolutions deploring alleged missteps by the national government. On the other hand, patronage politics is very active, with mayors and council members seeking to advance their own interests and those of their backers in the distribution of jobs, contracts, and preferments (Interviews 108, 109).[11] Neither of these patterns of behavior among elected officials is closely linked with urban public needs, and the public is understandably cynical. In a survey conducted in three poor neighborhoods of Santo Domingo during the 1980s, residents were asked what would be the best means to resolve problems of the *barrio*. Fifty-nine percent responded that unity among residents would serve best, while 37 percent looked to "aid from the government." Only 6 percent had confidence in "aid from political parties" (Pérez and Artiles, 1992:148).

In the years after 1978, especially between 1984 and 1990, Dominican cities and towns experienced a wave of grass-roots organization and protest. This growth of new popular organizations was stimulated largely by the increasing cost of living and the cutbacks in public services resulting from austerity policies urged on the state by the International Monetary Fund. In April 1984 violent popular protests in the capital were met by army repression; more than seventy people were killed in the clashes (Mañón, 1985:37–59; Moya Pons, 1992:562). Elected urban officials responded only spasmodically to pressure from these new social movements, which bore varied names such as "Committees for Popular Struggle" and "Committees for the Defense of Neighborhood Rights." As one politician in Santo Domingo related, "Okay, when there was pressure, the approach was: 'send to pick up the garbage in such-and-such a *barrio*, vaccinate against disease somewhere else, but don't do anything fundamental about any of the issues'" (Interview 108).[12]

The neighborhood organizations for their part, were poorly structured and weakly coordinated, and some (such as the Comunidades Eclesiales de Base related to the Catholic Church) deliberately avoided involvement with political parties so as not to divide their politically heterogeneous memberships. For these reasons, most of the new social movements had little effect on urban party organizations even during a decade that saw a rising protest vote for the PLD and a startling decline in electoral backing for the PRD in the cities of Santo Domingo and Santiago (Pérez and Artiles, 1992:94–112).

At times, to be sure, urban politicians have shown themselves capable of creating links with neighborhood groups. Some of these alliances have led to demonstrable improvements in conditions and services in urban *barrios*. Between 1978 and 1982, *síndico* Franco Badía's administration encouraged the creation of *juntas de vecinos* in neighborhoods of the capital, "to serve as grass-roots organizations to help in carrying out a program for the common good, and to strengthen the activities of the *ayuntamiento*" (Pérez and Artiles, 1992:139; Interview 108). These committees sometimes became vigorous local pressure groups, often under the leadership of women and frequently steering clear of any affiliation with political parties (Interview 106). Franco Badía took considerable criticism for fomenting the juntas to further his national political ambitions. Yet the aspirations of city politicians to perform well on a national stage constitute one of the few mechanisms that occasionally render local government somewhat responsive to voters and conscientious in tackling pressing urban needs. That motive, however, can seldom make headway against the formidable political, fiscal, and legal obstacles that hamstring municipal administrations. As one politician observed of the Santo Domingo *sindicatura*, "The office has few resources and one cannot deliver much of what is expected. It wears politicians down and they tend to decline politically after holding it" (Interview 109).

Conclusion

Rosario Espinal has observed that the field of political reform is one of the few areas where Caribbean governments now have some latitude to effect structural change in the ways that power is distributed and used, at a time of severe international economic and financial constraints (Espinal, 1992). This perception applies clearly in the case of Dominican urban elections and politics. In their highly dependent existence under the electoral system in existence until 1994, urban elections (and the resulting political leadership in cities and towns) have represented an important missed opportunity to help consolidate Dominican democracy. Municipal governments have seldom been able to work effectively for their constituents' interests, and their inability to do so in the settings that are most familiar to most citizens may well have tarnished democracy's image. One can easily surmise that the low expectations of what government will do, reflected in urban surveys in the 1980s, contributed to the abstention rate of 40 percent in the 1990 national election. President Balaguer's implicit message in attending nearly one hundred municipal PRSC nominating conventions in 1986—"local politics are important, they're closer to the people"—puts the matter succinctly, although he too soon ignored his own insight.

Among the numerous projects for political reform currently under consideration in the Dominican Republic, increasing attention is being paid to revisions needed at the municipal level (Fundación Siglo 21, 1994 and 1995). Four important reforms might invigorate urban elections, making popularly chosen city officials more responsive and efficacious. First, in the larger cities, districts should be created to subdivide the present huge electorates. In such subdivisions, candidates for *regidor* might become better known by those whom they hope to represent. Because of the longtime Dominican affinity for proportional representation, it does not seem wise to create single-member districts, but such representation could easily be retained within subunits of fewer than 100,000 persons. Second, party primaries or conventions to choose municipal candidates appear desirable indeed, to limit the now-sweeping influence of national party authorities over nominations. (Party leaders at the national level may be marginally less concerned about the choice of local candidates now that they do not have to face the voters on the same party list at the same election.) Third, municipalities should be given greater authority over services that are primarily local in character, while periodic administrative reviews are set up to place some limits on clientelism in urban administration. And finally, consideration should be given to reforming Dominican public finance, to share revenue more evenly between municipalities and the state. Effective, popular urban leaders chosen in a more open democratic process will not be able to perform significantly better if they cannot look to more ample and stable resources than are now doled out by the state authorities in the capital.

References

Published Sources

Brea Franco, Julio. 1986. *El sistema constitucional dominicano.* 2 vols. Santo Domingo: Editorial CENAPEC.

———. 1987. *Administración y elecciones: La experiencia dominicana de 1986.* San José, Costa Rica: Centro Interamericano de Asesoría y Promoción Electoral (CAPEL).

———. 1989. "Reforma electoral y representación política en el sistema electoral dominicana." *UNIBE: Revista de Ciencia y Cultura* 1, no. 1 (January-April 1989): 67–79.

Butten Varona, Nelson. 1983. *Temas electorales, 1980–1982.* Santo Domingo: Editores Asociados.

Campillo Pérez, Julio G. 1986. *Historia electoral dominicana 1948–1986.* Santo Domingo: Junta Central Electoral.

Del Castillo, José. 1985. "Partidos y electores." Series of five articles in *Ultima Hora* (Santo Domingo daily newspaper), August 13–17.

———. 1986. "Elecciones '86." Series of ten articles in *Ultima Hora* (Santo Domingo), February 5-March 14.

———. 1992. "Elecciones y democracia." Series of eight articles in *Hoy* (Santo Domingo daily newspaper), April 6–16.

Espinal, Rosario. 1992. Presentation at conference on "Current Issues in Caribbean Politics and Policy," Bildner Center for Western Hemisphere Studies, City University of New York, New York City, December 11.

Ferguson, James. 1992. *Dominican Republic: Beyond the Lighthouse.* London: Latin America Bureau.

Fundación Siglo 21. 1994. *Proyectos para la reforma del sistema de representación.* Santo Domingo.

———. 1995. *Acuerdos sobre la reforma municipal.* Santo Domingo.

Hartlyn, Jonathan. 1990. "The Dominican Republic's Disputed Elections." *Journal of Democracy* 1, no. 4 (Fall):92–103.

Helena Rodríguez, Miguel A. 1992. "La Liga Municipal Dominicana hacia el desarrollo integral." *Ambito Municipal* (Santo Domingo) 1, no. 4:55–56.

Hillman, Richard S., and Thomas J. D'Agostino. 1992. *Distant Neighbors in the Caribbean: The Dominican Republic and Jamaica in Comparative Perspective.* New York: Praeger.

International Foundation for Electoral Systems. 1994. *Dominican Republic: International Election Observation Final Report—May 1994.* Washington, DC.

Mañón, Melvin. 1985. *Cambio de mandos*. Santo Domingo: privately printed.

Maríñez Rosario, Julio. 1995. "Palabras de clausura del X Congreso Nacional de Municipios." Santo Domingo: Liga Municipal Dominicana.

Moya Pons, Frank. 1992. *Manual de historia dominicana*. Santo Domingo: Caribbean Publishers.

National Democratic Institute for International Affairs. 1994. *Interim Report on the May 16, 1994, Elections in the Dominican Republic*. Washington, DC.

Navarro, Josefina. 1995. "Ahogados por la gula presidencial." *Rumbo* (Santo Domingo), August 9–15.

Nelson, William Javier, and Diómedes Perez. 1992. "Dominican Republic." In Charles D. Ameringer, ed., *Political Parties of the Americas, 1980s to 1990s*, 243–66. Westport, CT: Greenwood Press.

Oficina Nacional de Estadística, Secretariado Técnico de la Presidencia, Dominican Republic. 1986. *República Dominicana en cifras 1986*. Santo Domingo.

Pérez, César, and Leopoldo Artiles. 1992. *Movimientos sociales dominicanos: Identidad y dilemas*. Santo Domingo: Instituto Tecnológico de Santo Domingo (INTEC).

United Nations. 1988. Economic Commission for Latin America and the Caribbean. *República Dominicana: Población y desarrollo 1950–1985*. San José, Costa Rica: Centro Latinoamericano de Demografía.

Wiarda, Howard J., and Michael J. Kryzanek. 1992. *The Dominican Republic: A Caribbean Crucible*. Boulder, CO: Westview Press.

Interviews

Interview 101—Dominican social scientist; Los Angeles, California, September 27, 1992.

Interview 102—Political aide to experienced Dominican national politician; Santo Domingo, March 16, 1993.

Interview 103—Experienced Dominican national politician; Santo Domingo, March 16, 1993.

Interview 104—Dominican social scientist; Santo Domingo, March 16, 1993.

Interview 105—Dominican historian; Santo Domingo, March 17, 1993.

Interview 106—Former elected official (PRD) in the Santo Domingo municipal government; Santo Domingo, March 17, 1993.

Interview 107—Official at the Dominican Junta Central Electoral; Santo Domingo, March 18, 1993.

Interview 108—Politician (PRSC) experienced in elections in the Distrito Nacional; Santo Domingo, March 19, 1993.

Interview 109—Politician (PRD) experienced in elections in the Distrito Nacional; Santo Domingo, March 19, 1993.

Interview 110—Experienced Dominican lawyer and another seasoned political observer; Santo Domingo, August 15, 1995.

Interview 111—Administrator at the Liga Municipal Dominicana; Santo Domingo, August 18, 1995.

Notes

1. Former President Bosch, an effective communicator and phrasemaker via radio broadcasts, dubbed Balaguer's governing style in the mid-1970s as *medàlaganismo* (roughly translated: "because I feel like it"). Because of the limited competitiveness of the national elections of 1970 and 1974, their results are not displayed in Tables 1 and 2.

2. Ticket-splitting was possible in 1962, 1978, 1982, and 1990, in the first three instances by literally dividing party ballots along perforated lines, and in the last case by checking different boxes on a single multiparty ballot. See Campillo Pérez, 1986:356; Brea Franco, 1986, 1:395–97.

3. The extent of ticket-splitting before 1994 is difficult to establish unequivocally without survey data. However, Dominican voting statistics suggest that few voters divided their ballots (although occasionally urban candidates, especially aspirants for *regidor* in the larger cities, probably won as a result of ticket-splitting). In 1962 the PRD tallied 8.4 percent fewer votes for its municipal slate in Santo Domingo than for the national ticket headed by Juan Bosch but still overwhelmingly gained control of City Hall. Nationally that year, municipal slates garnered only 0.6 percent fewer votes than did national tickets. In 1990 the PLD municipal candidates in Santo Domingo won 6 percent fewer votes than did their presidential candidate (again Bosch) but lost by a wider margin. Overall in 1990, 1.8 percent fewer votes were cast for municipal tickets than for presidential candidates.

4. The 1994 constitutional amendments resulted from a "Pact for Democracy" concluded by Balaguer and José Francisco Peña Gómez in August of that year. This bargain sought to resolve a political confrontation stemming from the disenfranchisement of at least 45,000 voters in 1994, most of whom would probably have voted for the PRD in an election that Balaguer was proclaimed as winning by fewer than half that number of votes. International observers had raised pointed questions about these clear irregularities (International Foundation for Electoral Systems, 1994; National Democratic Institute, 1994). Two aspects of the complex 1994 controversy are relevant here. First, the new alternating schedule for congressional and municipal elections resulted from bargaining over the presidency and was not planned as an electoral reform. And second, the official 1994 election returns should be read with considerable caution, since many thousands of legitimate voters were turned away from the polls.

5. In most *municipios*, one *regidor* is elected for each 14,000 inhabitants (or fraction larger than 7,000), with a minimum of five *concejales* (councilmen) per municipality. However, 25,000 residents of Santo Domingo are required to elect a council member, and 17,000 are needed in Santiago.

These rules were instituted in the Trujillo era to limit the size of councils in the big cities (Brea Franco, 1986, 1:319).

6. The only exception is the slight tendency for marginal neighborhoods to support the PR more than did the better-off "popular" *barrios*. Probably both patronage politics and Balaguer's appeal as a *caudillo* help account for this pattern.

7. Balaguer himself attended most of these meetings. "His message was that 'local politics are important—they're closer to the people' " (Interview 104).

8. Peña Gómez was already a major national political figure by the late 1960s, and he was widely expected to try for the presidency at some point. One important motive for him to serve as mayor of the capital was to acquire demonstrable executive experience.

9. In a vivid illustration of the transnational forces at work in Latin America's current wave of privatizations, garbage is currently collected in nearly half of Santo Domingo by a British-based contractor, Attwoods Dominicana.

10. The Liga Municipal is currently pressing for constitutional changes that would place responsibility for varied functions now held by the central government in *municipios*. Those areas of activity include sports, community development, local streets, orphanages, and community centers (Fundación Siglo 21, 1995:17–18). Experienced Dominican political observers do not believe that these reforms will readily be adopted, since they involve the dispersion of power from (and by) those who now hold it (Interview 110).

11. Political influence is pervasive in the distribution of public-sector jobs in the Dominican Republic, where the state may employ as many as 300,000 persons. There is no functioning civil service system (Ferguson, 1992:45–46). Further research would be needed to establish precisely how patronage posts—that is, virtually all jobs— in municipal government are distributed. Most influence probably lies with the *síndico*, but some positions may be distributed by municipal council members.

12. Although this description came from a PRSC leader criticizing a past PRD administration in Santo Domingo, there is little partisan disagreement on how the *ayuntamiento* responded to the 1980s protest movements.

6

National and Local Elections in El Salvador, 1982–1994

Ricardo Córdova Macías and Andrew J. Stein

The "elections of the century," held in March and April 1994, promised to be the most inclusive and democratic of the multiple contests held in El Salvador during the process of the transition to a civilian, democratically controlled government. In contrast to previous elections, the 1994 vote was the first to be held in peacetime and to include the full spectrum of political actors within El Salvador, including also for the first time the former combatants of the Farabundo Martí National Liberation Front (FMLN) guerrillas. Within Central America, El Salvador was held by American policymakers to be the model example of a successful transition to democracy among the violent, exclusionary, and authoritarian political systems of the Isthmus. For others, however, the elections were nothing more than a facade and an extension of the counterinsurgency war being waged. The extent to which national and local elections have been characterized over the twelve-year period from 1982 to 1994 by increased competitiveness among parties and access for citizen participation will be addressed here. The party competition and shifts in electoral results cannot be understood outside of the context of the country's changing electoral legislation and institutions, nor can their impact on democratization be understood without an examination of politics on the municipal level. While Salvadoran elections have continued to suffer from low voter turnout (40 percent abstention, nearly twice that of every country in the region except Guatemala) and from charges of procedural irregularities, the electoral process has gone from being historically fraudulent to one that has become semicompetitive to competitive (Baylora, 1995).

There are still problems in the system in terms of voter registration, campaign finance, and media access, and it may indeed be the case that elections alone cannot address the inequities of Salvadoran society or bring full implementation of and compliance with the peace accords.[1] However, it is undeniable that certain aspects of Salvadoran politics are qualitatively different from what they were in the 1980s. These changes merit careful examination to explore the implications for further democratization of the country.

El Salvador: Elections, Civil War, and Democracy

The coup d'état of October 15, 1979, is an event that is crucial for understanding Salvadoran politics during the past fifteen years. It marked the breakdown of the authoritarian regime that had ruled in prior decades and is the origin of the political transition, the final outcome of which remains unclear.[2] The civil war began in 1980 (Benítez Manaut, 1989), and in this context two political phenomena with an opposite logic emerged: elections in the midst of war; or, if one prefers, war with elections. The press described this situation in El Salvador as one in which the country lived between bullets and ballots. Academic and journalistic debate revolved around the relationship of elections to democracy and counterinsurgency, but analysis of the political parties, the party system, and electoral behavior received little attention. What little attention was given to the study of electoral processes that took place had strongly ideological and polarized perspectives. On the one hand, there were those who considered the elections as "demonstration elections" (Herman and Brodhead, 1984), while, on the other hand, others argued that these elections marked the evolution of El Salvador into a political democracy, though one with imperfections remaining in the political system.[3]

In the face of the impossibility of a military solution to the conflict, after 1990 the path toward a negotiated settlement to the war was advanced. After twenty-three working meetings in slightly less than two years of negotiations, and with the mediation of the United Nations, an accord put an end to twelve years of civil war (Córdova Macías, 1993). The historic signing of the peace accords on January 16, 1992, between the government and the FMLN is without doubt the most important event in modern Salvadoran political history.

Whatever limitations the elections held in recent decades may have had in terms of the lack of guarantees and violations of human rights, significant numbers of the population went to the polls in the midst of high levels of political violence to elect chief executives, legislators, and mayors. Nearly one million Salvadorans have gone to the voting booth to exercise their right of suffrage.

With the signing of the peace agreement, the former guerrilla groups have been transformed into a political party. They participated for the first time in elections of March and April 1994, and they now control a substantial minority bloc of seats in the Legislative Assembly. In addition to being the first Salvadoran elections to be held in peacetime and to include all actors, the 1994 vote also was the first time that presidential, legislative, and municipal contests were held simultaneously with those for the Central American Parliament.

The Electoral Process: The Salvadoran Setting

Scholars who have analyzed Salvadoran elections have tended to focus on the context in which they were held and their consequences for the establishment of a democratic regime in the country. However, most have considered each election separately, seeking explanations of who won and why. These attempts to write the history of winners and losers (Goodman, LeoGrande, and Mendelssohn-Forman, 1992; Booth and Seligson, 1989; Dunkerley, 1988) mean that research with a focus on the electoral system, contending forces, their programs, campaign strategies, and advertising has not yet been done. Voting behavior, for example, simply has not been dealt with. How and why Salvadorans have voted as they have is a question that has not been addressed systematically in academic studies (for exceptions see Bowdler, 1974; McDonald, 1969; Seligson et al., 1995). To begin to fill this gap, we will start with the elections held between 1982 and 1988 and then analyze those of 1989 to 1994.

There has been an evolution of political parties active in the elections for the period 1979–1994. In those held between 1982 and 1988, a total of ten parties participated, although not all of them did so in each one. Only five parties took part in all of the elections. In the 1982 contests there were six, eight in 1984, nine in 1985, and eight in 1988. These parties tended to cluster around the center and the right. Due to the fact that political polarization is one of the traits that has characterized the Salvadoran political process, and that the left remained excluded from elections between 1982 and 1988, the polarity manifested itself at the extremes of the space allowed for electoral competition, which is to say between the reformist center-right (Partido Demócrata Cristiano, or PDC) and the extreme right (Alianza Republicana Nacionalista, or ARENA).

In 1989 the novelty in the electoral process was the decision by the nonarmed forces of the left to participate for the first time in a coalition known as the Convergencia Democrática (CD, or Democratic Convergence),[4] thus widening the spectrum of political competition. The democratic left did poorly, however, for two reasons: because of structural limitations of the political system that did not generate peaceful conditions for the realization of competitive elections, and because of limited public support for the new leftist coalition.

For the legislative and municipal elections of 1991, the peace negotiations between the government and the FMLN achieved a truce that improved the political conditions for competitive elections. These were the first elections without military harassment (given a unilateral cease-fire by both sides), although voting still took place in the context of the militarization and polarization of the war. Moreover, a leftist party, the Nationalist Democratic Union (UDN), participated for the first time in elections. This contest saw an increase of the vote for the left.

As a consequence of the electoral outcomes of 1989 and 1991, only eight parties remained in the electoral register: the UDN, MNR, PSD, MPSC, PDC, PCN, MAC, and ARENA. The competing parties in the March 1994 presidential election were ARENA, MAC, PCN, PDC, MSN, MU, and the leftist coalition (MNR, CD, FMLN). The changing fortunes of the parties, such as the decline of the Christian Democrats after 1988 and the ascent of ARENA and the parties on the left, can be observed in Table 1.

The 1994 elections reflect a high degree of polarization between ARENA and the FMLN, especially in the legislative contests. While ARENA retained its thirty-nine seats, the rest of the political parties and factions experienced a decrease in their representation in the Legislative Assembly (see Table 2). Only the FMLN, in this its first election, gained twenty-one seats and proved to be an exception to this trend. In the distribution of votes, small and centrist parties suffered the most from this polarization.

Table 1. El Salvador: Electoral Results by Party, 1982–1994

Type of Election	PCN	PDC	ARENA	FMLN	CD	Total Valid Votes
1982 (Constituent Assembly)	261,153 (19.16)[a]	546,218 (40.09)	402,304 (29.53)	NP	NP[b]	1,362,339
1984 (Presidential)[c]	244,556 (19.31)	549,727 (43.41)	376,917 (29.76)	NP	NP	1,266,276
1985 (Legislative)	80,730 (8.36)	505,338 (52.35)	286,665 (29.69)	NP	NP	965,231
1988 (Legislative)	79,713 (8.50)	330,324 (35.22)	450,100 (47.99)	NP	NP	937,946
1989 (Presidential)[d]	38,212 (4.07)	338,369 (36.03)	505,370 (53.82)	NP	35,642 (3.80)	939,078
1991 (Legislative)	94,531 (8.99)	294,029 (27.96)	466,091 (44.33)	NP	127,855 (12.16)	1,051,481
1994 (Presidential)	70,854 (5.34)	215,936 (16.27)	651,632 (49.11)	331,629[e] (24.99)	[f]	1,326,836
1994 (Legislative)	83,520 (6.21)	240,451 (17.87)	605,775 (45.03)	287,811 (21.39)	59,843 (4.45)	1,345,277

Source: Córdova Macías (1994b).
[a]Figures in parentheses refer to percentage of total valid votes obtained. Only parties that had a 4 percent or greater vote share in all elections are included.
[b]NP: did not participate.
[c]Results are from first round.
[d]The parties of the center-left (MNR, PSD, and MPSC) participated for the first time in the 1989 presidential election as the Democratic Convergence (CD) coalition.
[e]Based on first round, March election. The FMLN, CD, and MNR ran together on one ballot for the presidential race.
[f]The leftist parties (FMLN, CD, MNR) participated as a coalition in the presidential election.

Votes, Seats, and Municipal Councils

The share of the vote obtained by the parties in the different elections does not necessarily reflect their strength in the Legislative Assembly or in the municipal councils, given the structure of the Salvadoran electoral system.[5] In this sense, the pattern in El Salvador corresponds to a standard finding in the electoral systems literature—namely, that in districts where the magnitude is small (that is, where there are few seats per district), seat allocation rules under proportional representation penalize the smaller parties. The number of seats rarely corresponds 1:1 to the share of the total vote obtained.

Table 2. Number of Seats and Percentage of Votes by Party, 1991 and 1994

	Number of Seats		Percentage of Votes	
Party	1991	1994	1991	1994
ARENA	39	39	44.33	45.03
PDC	26	18	27.96	17.87
PCN	9	4	8.99	6.21
CD	8	1	12.16	4.45
FMLN	NP[a]	21	NP	21.39
MU	NP	1	NP	2.49
UDN	1	C[b]	2.68	C
MAC	1	0	3.23	0.9
Totals	84	84	100	100[c]

Source: Córdova Macías (1994b); Tribunal Supremo Electoral (1994).
[a]NP: did not participate.
[b]C: member of the CD coalition.
[c]Does not include votes for parties (MNR and MSN) that did not obtain the 1 percent minimum required by law.

The total number of seats remained at sixty between 1982 and 1989. With the constitutional reforms agreed to by the government and the FMLN within the framework of the peace process, the number of deputies increased to eighty-four in the following way: sixty-four continued to be elected on the basis of proportional representation in each of the fourteen territorial districts (or departments), while twenty were elected on a national list, also by means of the proportional representation system.[6] The national district with its twenty new seats increased the district magnitude and proportionality in that district only.

Between 1982 and 1988, the electoral system and the political process tended to strengthen three dominant parties: ARENA, the PCN, and the PDC. Following the elections of 1989 and 1991, with the expansion of the political spectrum, the parliament became more diversified, as was the case with the parliament elected in 1991 and 1994. Because of the discrepancy between votes and deputies in the March 1991 elections, the CD with 12.16 percent of the vote obtained eight seats, while the PCN with 8.99 percent was awarded nine seats (see Table 2). This difference highlights the need to include the distribution of seat by party, distinguishing between those elected by quotient or by remainder.

Table 3 reveals three important patterns. First, in the 1991 elections, combining the legislators selected by quota and by remainder, only two parties elected deputies from all departments (ARENA and the PDC). Second, fifty-one of the eighty-four deputies elected were chosen by means of the quota, while thirty-three (less than 40 percent of the total deputies) were selected by remainder. However, the remainder system has benefited the opposition parties somewhat more, particularly those with a small share of the vote. The UDN and the MAC had their sole representatives selected by remainder. In contrast, the PDC won eleven of its twenty-six seats by remainder. Third, the system of the national list tended to favor the participation of smaller opposition parties. Of the twenty seats on the national list, the governing party gained nine; the remaining eleven seats went to the opposition in the following manner: six for the PDC, two for the PCN, one for the MAC (its only seat), and two for the CD.

Table 3. Distribution of Seats by Party in the 1991 Elections, Controlling by Means of Selection

Department	ARENA		PDC		PCN		MAC		CD		UDN	
	Quo	Rem	Quo	Rem	Quo	Rem	Quo	Rem	Quo	Rem	Quo	Rem
San Salvador	7	–	3	1	–	1	–	–	3	–	–	1
Santa Ana	2	1	1	1	–	–	–	–	–	1	–	–
San Miguel	2	–	1	1	–	1	–	–	–	1	–	–
La Libertad	2	1	1	–	–	–	–	–	–	–	–	–
Usulután	1	1	1	–	–	1	–	–	–	–	–	–
Sonsonate	1	1	1	–	–	1	–	–	–	–	–	–
La Unión	1	–	1	1	–	–	–	–	–	–	–	–
La Paz	1	1	1	–	–	–	–	–	–	1	–	–
Chalatenango	1	–	–	1	–	–	–	–	–	–	–	–
Cuscatlán	1	1	–	1	–	–	–	–	–	–	–	–
Ahuachapán	1	–	–	1	–	1	–	–	–	–	–	–
Morazán	–	1	–	1	–	1	–	–	–	–	–	–
San Vicente	1	1	–	1	–	–	–	–	–	–	–	–
Cabañas	1	–	–	1	–	1	–	–	–	–	–	–
National list	8	1	5	1	1	1	–	1	2	–	–	–
Totals	30	9	15	11	1	8	0	1	5	3	0	1

Source: Córdova Macías (1994b).
Quo = Quota, Rem = Remainder.

With respect to the 1994 votes to seats distribution, four important elements need to be mentioned. First, the only party to have deputies from all departments was ARENA (see Table 4). The FMLN did not have deputies from La Unión or Cabañas, and the PDC failed to get a seat in Cuscatlán. Second, in the 1994 elections, forty-nine of the eighty-four deputies were selected by means of the quota, while thirty-five (42.6 percent) were chosen by remainder. Third, the present system worked to the advantage of opposition parties. For instance, the FMLN had eleven of its twenty-one deputies allocated by remainder (the pattern is more accentuated if we momentarily eliminate their seats gained in San Salvador and on the national list). The FMLN gained only two deputies by quota.

Table 4. Distribution of Seats by Party in the 1994 Elections, Controlling by Means of Selection

Department	ARENA		PDC		PCN		MU		CD		UDN	
	Quo	Rem	Quo	Rem	Quo	Rem	Quo	Rem	Quo	Rem	Quo	Rem
San Salvador	7	–	1	1	–	1	–	–	–	1	4	1
Santa Ana	2	1	1	–	–	1	–	–	–	–	1	–
San Miguel	2	–	1	–	–	1	–	–	–	–	–	1
La Libertad	2	1	–	1	–	–	–	–	–	–	1	–
Usulután	1	1	–	1	–	–	–	–	–	–	–	1
Sonsonate	1	1	–	1	–	–	–	–	–	–	–	1
La Unión	1	1	–	1	–	–	–	–	–	–	–	–
La Paz	1	–	–	1	–	–	–	–	–	–	–	1
Chalatenango	1	–	–	1	–	–	–	–	–	–	–	1
Cuscatlán	1	1	–	–	–	–	–	–	–	–	–	1
Ahuachapán	1	–	–	1	–	–	–	–	–	–	–	1
Morazán	1	–	–	1	–	–	–	–	–	–	–	1
San Vicente	1	–	–	1	–	–	–	–	–	–	–	1
Cabañas	1	1	–	1	–	–	–	–	–	–	–	–
National List	9	–	3	1	1	–	–	1	–	–	4	1
Totals	32	7	6	12	1	3	0	1	–	1	10	11

Source: Córdova Macías (1994b).
Quo = Quota, Rem = Remainder.

Finally, a discrepancy exists between votes and the distribution of municipal councils as a consequence of the electoral system. According to the Electoral Code, the party or coalition that wins a simple plurality of the vote wins all the seats on the municipal council. Because of the two different electoral systems governing elections for the Legislative Assembly on the national level and for municipalities on the local level, the distribution of council seats among the different political parties is even more skewed toward the larger parties than it is in the legislative elections. The psychological effect of this electoral system is to discourage voters from selecting a minority or small party in local elections because a vote for a party with no chance of winning a plurality by itself may be considered wasted.

Table 5 shows that ARENA and the PDC dominated local government between 1985 and 1994, with the PCN occupying a very distant third place. The results for the FMLN at the local level (March 1994) were poor, since it won only fifteen municipalities. In large part, the explanation for the domination of local government by ARENA and the PDC can be found in the electoral system.

Table 5. Number of Municipal Councils by Party in the Elections of 1985, 1988, 1991, and 1994

Party	1985	1988	1991	1994
ARENA	107[a]	178[b]	176	207
Liberación	—	1	—	—
MAC	—	—	1	1
PAISA	1	—	—	—
PCN	—	4	14	10
PDC	154	79	70	29
CD	—	—	1	—
FMLN	—	—	—	15[c]
Total	262	262	262	262

Source: Córdova Macias (1994b); Tribunal Supremo Electoral (1994).
[a]In 1985, ARENA was in coalition with the PCN.
[b]In 1988, for the mayoralty of San Salvador, a coalition formed among ARENA, PPS, PAISA, and Liberación.
[c]Mayoralties won in coalition between the FMLN and CD.

The gap between votes and municipal council seats is more pronounced than in the case of the Legislative Assembly. Two examples demonstrate the consequences of this dual electoral system. The FMLN won 20.3 percent of the vote in 1994 on the municipal level, and yet it gained control of only fifteen municipal councils. In contrast, ARENA, with 44.8 percent of the vote, obtained control of 78.6 percent (207) of the municipal councils.

In addition, it is important to highlight a curious situation. In several municipalities the winning party received fewer votes than those of all other parties combined. In some cases they won by less than three hundred votes. Those parties that were defeated, though by as few as a hundred votes, remain totally excluded from local government for three years. Given the manner in which this simple plurality system is biased in favor of the majority parties such as ARENA, and in the 1980s the PDC, it is surprising that the dual allocation rules were not changed as part of the peace accords. In fact, the accords contain only a one-paragraph chapter on electoral legislation with vague promises of a general reform of the system.

The other important political phenomenon is the tendency for one party to win the majority of local and national elections, thus remaining in control of a substantial part of the municipal politico-administrative apparatus. The party that wins the majority of the municipal councils usually also gains control of the majority of department capitals. In 1985 the PDC won 154 municipal councils and controlled all of the department capitals except Cuscatlán, Ahuachapán, and Cabañas (see also Table 5). In 1988, ARENA obtained 178 municipal councils and controlled all department capitals except La Unión. In 1991, ARENA obtained 176 municipal councils and controlled all department capitals except Usulután, La Unión, and Morazán. The pattern was repeated in 1994 with ARENA sweeping all provincial capitals except La Unión.

Local Elections

A review of various publications about Salvadoran elections that took place between 1982 and 1994 reveals an almost exclusive attention to voting at the national level. Local contests receive virtually none. In addition, in those few works that examine legislative or municipal elections, the local characteristics are not dealt with (Montes, 1985, 1988). For the purposes of this chapter, legislative and presidential elections are considered to be national, while municipal elections are local. In exploring the political dynamics at work in local elections, we focus on four factors.

The first is the geographical distribution of the vote. In early 1993 the preliminary results of the Fifth Population Census were published (República de El Salvador, 1993). This census clearly reflects the increasingly urban concentration of the national population. The Department of San Salvador alone represents 29.2 percent of the total population. San Salvador, along with the departments of La Libertad, Santa Ana, and San Miguel, makes up 56.1 percent. One-half of the country's fourteen departments contains 74.6 percent. This high population concentration in a few departments and the urban profile of the country are expressed in electoral terms. In the 1994 elections, the Department of San Salvador represented 30.1 percent of the vote, La Libertad 11.3 percent, Santa Ana 9.9 percent, and San Miguel 6.3 percent. In other words, these four departments account for 57.6 percent of all valid votes.

Second, in terms of the total number of voters, local elections show approximately the same level of turnout as national ones (see

Table 6). There is overlap between the quantity of valid votes for legislators and municipal councils for all departments in the 1991 elections. Only in the case of La Libertad does the pattern differ; in this instance there were 13,000 more votes for seats in the Legislative Assembly.

Table 6. Difference in Votes between Legislative and Municipal Elections, 1985–1994

Year of Election	Total Valid Votes in Legislative Elections	Total Valid Votes in Municipal Elections	Difference in Votes (Municipal minus Legislative)
1985	965,231	982,766	17,535
1988	937,946	942,554	4,608
1991	1,051,481	1,036,326	-15,155
1994	1,345,277	1,345,454	177

Source: Tribunal Supremo Electoral (1994).

In the 1991 vote, ARENA received more votes in one-half of the local elections than it did in the national contests; the opposite occurred in the other half of the departments. For the remainder, with the exceptions of San Salvador and Chalatenango, the differences were minimal. On average, nationally ARENA gained about 1 percent more votes in local elections, which means that there was no significant variation in the quantity of votes obtained by ARENA as a function of the type of election. In the 1994 elections, there was minimal variation in the local and national vote share, with a slightly higher total in San Salvador and Chalatenango. In the case of the PDC, in 1991 and 1994, in all departments local elections brought fewer votes than did national ones. The most dramatic shift for the PDC was its fall from mid-1980s dominance on the local level, from its peak of 154 municipal councils to only twenty-nine in 1994.

Third, because of its recent electoral participation, technical limitations, and association with the left, in all departments the Democratic Convergence received more votes nationally than at the local level. Here there is a significant difference in the vote for the CD by type of election in both 1991 and 1994. By the time of the 1994 vote, the CD had become a much less important factor, receiving one-third the vote share that it had obtained three years earlier. Much of this vote shifted to the newly legalized FMLN party. The FMLN's vote share did not vary substantially between local and national elections except in former war zones like Morazán and Chalatenango (Tribunal Supremo Electoral, 1994).

Fourth, voter abstention has remained an important problem. Voting levels peaked in the midst of war in the 1980s, but since 1988 nonvoting has remained at around 40 percent, despite repeated surveys where 80 to 85 percent of respondents express an intention to vote (Baloyra, 1995). A study of urban Salvadorans found that 63 percent of eligible voters turned out in elections, the lowest of any of the countries of Central America.[7] As in the experience of the United States and other Western industrial democracies, sociodemographic factors such as education, sex, and age help predict voter turnout in El Salvador. Citizens with lower levels of education, females, and the youngest and oldest age cohorts exhibited lower voter turnout. Another important relationship was that between abstention and the failure to register to vote. In addition, factors such as public trust and support for the political system were important predictors in addition to the demographic factors. Individuals with higher levels of support for the political system were more apt to register to vote.

Grass-roots Democracy: Municipal Autonomy, Decentralization, and Popular Participation

During the political transition following twelve years of civil war, local level or grass-roots democracy can be an important factor for consolidating peace and democracy. This section focuses on the themes of municipal autonomy, decentralization, and popular participation as three central aspects of local level democracy. Local government is a key component because it is the first and closest contact that many citizens have with government. It takes on added importance in the present moment in El Salvador, where levels of citizen support for the political system are low. (Seligson and Córdova, 1992, 1995; Blair et al., 1995).

According to survey results, Salvadorean citizens as a rule have a greater knowledge of local than of national government.[8] Of the respondents in one survey (CID-Gallup, 1991), 47 percent knew the name of their mayor, while only 14 percent could identify their department representative in the Legislative Assembly. This gap is hardly surprising, since local level officials are the ones with whom citizens are most likely to have contact. Salvadorans are not only far more aware of local government, but they also display a more positive evaluation of its functioning than they do for national government. A total of 20.2 percent were of the opinion that there was no corruption in the municipalities, while only 11.6 percent said the same of national government. The survey suggests higher levels of trust in the integrity of local government than in the national administration. In terms of electoral choice, 71 percent justified their vote on the basis of party, while 20 percent did so by candidate.

It is necessary to comment on the prospects for strengthening democracy on the local level. First, the Constitution of 1983 opened the way for municipal autonomy. Article 202 recognizes that the municipalities are autonomous in economic, technical, and political terms. The next advance was the promulgation of the Municipal Code in 1986, in which the limits of municipal competence and powers are spelled out precisely (República de El Salvador, 1995). From a formal point of view, much has been achieved with respect to municipal autonomy. However, it is important to be familiar with the cities' problems in order to understand the contemporary limitations of Salvadoran local government. The critical variable for understanding the municipal reality of the country is the size of local budgets in relation to the size of the urban population.

In Table 7 various key elements stand out. First, small municipalities (those with less than 20,000 in population) number 201 (category A). In terms of size, 76.7 percent of all municipalities are classified as small. Second, of these, 161 have a population of less than 10,000. Third, in most cases, these small municipalities do not have the financial means to provide their residents with the basic services for which they are responsible. The 201 municipalities generated only 8.1 percent of their total resources from local income. In addition, local income sources are minimal, and wide disparity exists between the per capita tax revenue in poor, rural, and smaller municipalities versus larger urban areas. A recent study found examples of 8:1 or 9:1 differences in taxes raised per capita. This inequality is compounded by two more factors: the small rural municipalities were the areas most damaged by the civil war (with the least prospect of funds for reconstruction), and a government program of subsidies for poorer municipalities reinforces the inequality since it is based on population size (Blair et al., 1995). Fourth, the other sixty municipalities (categories B, C, and D), together with San Salvador, make up 70 percent of El Salvador's total population and account for over 90 percent of locally generated municipal revenue.

Table 7. Population and Municipal Revenues, 1992

Category	Population Range	Number of Municipalities	Local Revenue as % of Total Revenue
A	less than 20,000	201	8.1%
B	20 to 40,000	35	29.0
C	40 to 80,000	16	56.3
D	more than 80,000	9	76.9
San Salvador	422,570	1	98.4
Total		262	40.8

Sources: República de El Salvador, Ministerio de Economía (1993).

As Table 8 shows, 117 municipalities have five or fewer employees; only eleven have one hundred or more employees. Thus, the question arises of whether municipal governments have a sufficient and capable base of human and financial resources.[9]

Table 8. Number of Employees Hired by Municipality

Number of Municipal Employees	Number of Municipalities
1 to 5	117
6 to 10	74
11 to 20	24
21 to 50	27
51 to 100	9
over 100	11

Source: U.S. Agency for International Development, San Salvador (1993).

From the previous description, two basic measures for strengthening municipal autonomy stand out: increasing fees and charges on municipal services, which has not been done in decades; and undertaking tax reform. A property tax as the principal source of local revenue does not exist in El Salvador. Until a few years ago, a "wealth tax" (*impuesto patrimonial*) included property, but it was collected and retained by the central government. This potential revenue was unavailable to municipal governments; and because of this, some form of local property taxes becomes all the more important as a means of increasing financial capability. Municipalities cannot achieve full autonomy unless they have their own source of funding, not only for operational expenses but also for investment in infrastructure and equipment.

Finally, citizen participation at the local level is another key aspect of grass-roots democratization. The Municipal Code of 1986 required the convening of open town meetings (*cabildos abiertos*) as a consultative mechanism for citizen opinions, and the Code also provides for a form of popular consent (*consulta popular*). The institutionalization of *cabildos abiertos* in recent years seems to be a positive step toward greater citizen involvement. However, in practice they have functioned more as a mechanism for making requests for assistance from the central government than as an exercise in community decision making. Two measures are key for the development of more democratic forums: the introduction of proportional representation in municipal council elections, so the losers are not fully excluded from office for three years; and the opening of council sessions to the public to ensure the honest and efficient functioning of local government.

Conclusion

The pattern of El Salvador in the period covered is one of electoral domination of the ARENA and PDC on the national and local levels. This dominance is related to the existing electoral system and the lack of proportionality between votes obtained and seats allocated. While the FMLN has become the second most important political force in the country's elections, close examination of the 1994 results on the local scene shows that the PDC still retains substantial vote-getting capacity on the regional and local level. In the years since the 1983 Constitution was passed, substantial gains have been made in the competitiveness of national and local elections, and in the area of popular input to municipal government. However, without the inauguration of a proportional representation system, losing parties will continue to be excluded totally from local affairs at three-year intervals.

Elections in El Salvador have been much more than a facade for counterinsurgency. Nonetheless, two disturbing factors in Salvadoran elections persist: nonparticipation by more than one-third of all eligible citizens (based on fear, indifference, and distrust of the political system); and the procedural complexity and questionable integrity of the reformed Tribunal Supremo Electoral, which was charged with mishandling voter registration and consequently excluding thousand of voters from the lists. These institutional and participation weaknesses must be addressed in concert with any discussion of reforming the electoral system.

Postscript

The March 1997 municipal and legislative elections that were held in El Salvador were marked by much continuity, and some historic changes. On the one hand, several of the problems that we pointed to for the period from 1982 to 1994 persisted—low voter turnout, citizen distrust of government institutions (particularly the courts and the Tribunal Supremo Electoral) and apathy toward politics, public doubt about the government's and parties' ability (or interest) to solve major issues of the day such as crime and economic inequality. In addition, the media portion of the campaign was characterized by allegations of FMLN financing through sales of leftover arms caches to leftist rebels in Peru and elsewhere, right-wing assassinations of FMLN activists in the days leading up to the vote, and allegations of misconduct by the Tribunal and irregularities on election day.

Much to the contrary of the previous nine years in which ARENA had become the unquestioned dominant party in the system, the March 1997 vote gave a historic victory to the FMLN at the municipal level (according to Tribunal figures, the left—the FMLN, CD, and two factions that split off—won fifty-four municipalities, more than double their 1994 figure), in the three most important urban centers including San Salvador, and in the Legislative Assembly, where ARENA and the FMLN had the identical number of seats of the sixty-four apportioned by department (twenty-one), and were close in their share of the remaining twenty seats decided by national list. As remains to be seen, what the 1997 elections could come to mean is the first real opportunity for the left in Latin America since the end of the Cold War to govern (certainly, this is the case without equal within Central America). This experience of governing may give the FMLN key credibility with the private sector, ARENA legislators, and other essential members of society whose cooperation is necessary if the country is to continue evolving toward a more fully democratic and competitive party and electoral system.

The supposed realignment after the 1988 and 1989 elections that had ushered in a period of ARENA dominance was not sustained. The public gave a vote of no confidence to the performance of the Calderón Sol administration. What has happened is the total collapse of the PDC, now the fourth party in importance after the PCN. If we consider the regional strengths of the parties in light of past patterns discussed in this chapter, it is clear that the FMLN legislative strongholds are San Salvador, Santa Ana, and La Libertad. Similarly, most of ARENA's territorially apportioned seats in the Legislative Assembly are from San Salvador, Santa Ana, San Miguel, and La Libertad. No other party has more than one seat per department of the sixty-four territorially determined seats in the Legislative Assembly.

References

Baloyra, Enrique. 1985. "Dilemmas of Political Transition in El Salvador." *Journal of International Affairs* 38 (Winter):2, pp. 221–42.
———. 1987. "Democratic Transition in Comparative Perspective." In Enrique Baloyra, ed., *Comparing New Democracies: Transition and Consolidation in Mediterranean Europe and the Southern Cone*, pp. 9–52. Boulder, CO: Westview Press.
———. 1995. "Elections, Civil War, and Transition in El Salvador, 1982–1994: A Preliminary Evaluation." In Mitchell A. Seligson and John A. Booth, eds., *Elections and Democracy in Central America Revisited*. Chapel Hill: University of North Carolina Press.
Benítez Manaut, Raúl. 1989. *La teoría militar y la guerra civil en El Salvador*. San Salvador: UCA Editores.
Blair, Harry, et al. 1995. "Civil Society and Democratic Development in El Salvador." Mimeo. U.S. Agency for International Development, February.
Booth, John A., and Mitchell A. Seligson, eds. 1989. *Elections and Democracy in Central America*. Chapel Hill: University of North Carolina Press.
Bowdler, George A. 1974. "Political Participation in El Salvador: A Statistical Analysis of Spatial, Historico-Temporal, and Socio-Economic Relationships to Voter Registration and Total Votes Cast, 1964–1972." Ph.D. diss., Department of Political Science, University of South Carolina.
Butler, David, et al. 1981. "Introduction: Democratic and Nondemocratic Elections." In *Democracy at the Polls: A Comparative Study of Competitive National Elections*, 1–6. Washington, DC: American Enterprise Institute.
CID-Gallup Survey. 1991. San Salvador. Agency for International Development, internal document.
Close, David. 1991. "Central American Elections, 1989–90: Costa Rica, El Salvador, Honduras, Nicaragua, Panama." *Electoral Studies* 10 (January):1, pp. 60–76.
Córdova Macías, Ricardo. 1990. "El Salvador: Análisis de las elecciones presidenciales y perspectivas políticas." *Polémica* 11 (May–August):2–18.

————. 1992. "Procesos electorales y sistema de partidos en El Salvador, 1982–1989." *Foro Internacional* 32 (April–September):128–29, 519–59.

————. 1993. *El Salvador: Las negociaciones de paz y los retos de la postguerra.* San Salvador: Instituto de Estudios Latinoamericanos.

————. 1994a. *El Salvador en transición: El proceso de paz, las elecciones generales de 1994 y los retos de la gobernabilidad democrática.* San Salvador: FUNDAUNGO, Documentos de Trabajo, Serie Análisis de la Realidad Nacional 94-4, July.

————. 1994b. "Las elecciones de marzo de 1994: Un balance preliminar." San Salvador: mimeo.

Cruz, José Miguel. 1997. "Las encuestas de opinión pública y las elecciones de 1997." In Félix Ulloa, Carlos Guillermo Ramos, and José Miguel Cruz, eds., *El Salvador: Elecciones 1997.* San Salvador: Fundación Dr. Guillermo Manuel Ungo/Friedrich Ebert Stiftung.

Dunkerley, James. 1988. *Power in the Isthmus: A Political History of Modern Central America.* New York: Verso.

Goodman, Louis W., William M. LeoGrande, and Johanna Mendelssohn-Forman, eds. 1992. *Political Parties and Democracy in Central America.* Boulder, CO: Westview Press.

Herman, Edward S., and Frank Brodhead. 1984. *Demonstration Elections.* Boston: South End Press.

Hernandez, Oscar. 1990. "Análisis del abstencionismo en las elecciones presidenciales de Costa Rica en el período 1953–1986." *Anuario de Estudios Centroamericanos* 16, no. 2, 117–37.

Karl, Terry Lynn. 1986. "Imposing Consent? Electoralism vs. Democratization in El Salvador." In Paul Drake and Eduardo Silva, eds., *Elections and Democratization in Latin America, 1980–1985,* pp. 9–36. San Diego: University of California, Center for U.S.-Mexican Studies and Institute of the Americas.

————. 1988. "Exporting Democracy: The Unanticipated Effects of U.S. Electoral Policy in El Salvador." In Nora Hamilton et al., eds., *Crisis in Central America: Regional Dynamics and U.S. Policy in the 1980s,* pp. 173–91. Boulder, CO: Westview Press.

Lijphart, Arend. 1994. *Electoral Systems and Party Systems.* New York: Oxford University Press.

Mainwaring, Scott. 1990. "Presidentialism in Latin America." *Latin American Research Review* 25, no. 1, 157–79.

Malloy, James M., and Mitchell A. Seligson, eds. 1987. *Authoritarians and Democrats: Regime Transition in Latin America.* Pittsburgh: University of Pittsburgh Press.

McDonald, Ronald H. 1969. "Electoral Behavior and Political Development in El Salvador." *Journal of Politics* 31, no. 2, 397–419.

————, and J. Mark Ruhl. 1989. *Party Politics and Elections in Latin America*. Boulder, CO: Westview Press.

Montes, Segundo. 1985. "Las elecciones del 31 de marzo." *ECA* 438 (April): 215–28.

————. 1988. "Las elecciones del 20 de marzo de 1988." *ECA* 473–74 (April): 175–89.

Montgomery, Tommy Sue. 1995. *Revolution in El Salvador: From Civil Strife to Civil Peace*. Boulder, CO: Westview Press.

————. "El Salvador's Extraordinary Elections." *LASA Forum* 28, no. 1 (Spring 1997): 4–8.

O'Donnell, Guillermo, and Philippe Schmitter. 1986. *Transitions from Authoritarian Rule: Tentative Conclusions about Uncertain Democracies*. Baltimore: Johns Hopkins University Press.

República de El Salvador. 1995. *Código Municipal de 1986 y sus reformas*. San Salvador: Fundación Dr. Guillermo Manuel Ungo / Friedrich Ebert Stiftung.

————. Ministerio de economía. 1993. "Censos Nacionales V de Población y IV de Vivienda, resultados preliminares." San Salvador.

Samayoa, Mario. 1986. "Legislación y procesos electorales en El Salvador." In Augusto Hernandez Becerra, et al. eds., *Legislación electoral comparada: Colombia, México, Panamá, Venezuela y Centroamérica*, 109–32. San José: Centro de Asesoría y Promoción Electoral.

Seligson, Mitchell A., and Ricardo Córdova Macías. 1992. *Perspectivas para una democracia estable en El Salvador*. San Salvador: Instituto de Estudios Latinoamericanos.

————. 1995. *El Salvador: De la guerra a la paz: Una cultura política en transición*. San Salvador: FUNDAUNGO-IDELA/University of Pittsburgh.

Seligson, Mitchell, et al. 1995. "Who Votes in Central America? A Comparative Analysis." In Mitchell Seligson and John Booth, eds., *Elections and Democracy in Central America Revisited*, 151–82. Chapel Hill: University of North Carolina Press.

Taagepera, Rein, and Matthew Shugart. 1989. *Seats and Votes: The Effects and Determinants of Electoral Systems*. New Haven, CT: Yale University Press.

Tribunal Supremo Electoral, 1994. "Memoria de labores de las elecciones de 1994." San Salvador.

Ulloa, Félix. 1993. *El sistema electoral salvadoreño*. San Salvador: Instituto de Estudios Jurídicos de El Salvador. Cuadernos Electorales 3.

U.S. Agency for International Development, San Salvador. 1993. *Municipal Development Strategy*. Mimeo.

U.S. Department of State. 1988. "El Salvador: The Battle for Democracy." Washington, DC: Public Information Series.

Notes

1. There were technical irregularities that limited citizen participation and also had an impact on the counting stage of the elections. However, there is not sufficient evidence to question the overall legitimacy of the electoral results. One has to accept the judgement of the Secretary General of the United Nations, who remarked with regard to competitiveness and personal liberty and security of the 1994 elections that "the electoral results can be considered acceptable." See Report of the Secretary General of the United Nations, 31 March 1994 (mimeo): 7.

2. The literature on the topic of "transitions" tends to define political transition in general terms as the path from one authoritarian regime toward an uncertain "something else," with this "something" being the establishment of political democracy or the reestablishment of a new form of authoritarian rule. This conceptualization of transitions focuses on the interval between one political regime and its successor, which often means the process between the breakdown of the original authoritarian regime and the creation of a new type (whether it is democratic or another form of authoritarianism). Of the numerous publications on regime transition, see Baylora (1985, 1987); O'Donnell and Schmitter (1986); and Malloy and Seligson (1987).

3. U.S. Department of State, "El Salvador: The Battle for Democracy" (1988). For more on this debate over "electoralism" and "democratization" in the case of El Salvador, see Karl (1986, 1988).

4. Created in 1987, the CD was comprised of the National Revolutionary Movement (MNR), the Social Democratic Party (PSD), and the Popular Social Christian Movement (MPSC).

5. Legislators are elected by means of the proportional representation system known as the Hare or simple quota and largest remainders system (Taagepera and Shugart, 1989; Lijphart, 1994). Seats are allocated as follows: the total number of valid votes that legislators receive in each department is divided by the number of deputies that corresponds to the same department (total seats in each of the fourteen territorial districts), thus arriving at the electoral quota. Once this is determined, the parties and coalitions obtain seats as often as the electoral quota determined by votes received by each party or coalition in the district under consideration. If there is a seat yet to be assigned, the party or coalition with the largest remainder will receive it. If two are vacant, the second will go to the party or coalition with the largest remainder and thus subsequently until the total number of deputies for a given department has been allocated. From 1982 to 1989 there were fourteen districts (coinciding with departmental divisions). Since that time (including the 1991 and 1994 elections) a fifteenth (national) district was added, comprised of twenty seats and also selected by the same proportional representation method. The electoral system is designed so that votes obtained in the fourteen districts are added to arrive at the votes for the national list.

6. For further discussion, see Samayoa (1986) and Ulloa (1993). Instability has been constant, with numerous constitutions and electoral laws in force, including four codes in the past ten years. The most significant is the present law passed on December 14, 1993, implemented following the 1992 peace accords.

7. A multistage stratified sample of 910 voting-age adults was conducted in El Salvador during 1991. The sample included metropolitan San Salvador and its eight surrounding satellites and municipalities: Soyapango, Cuscatancingo, Ciudad Delgado, Mejicanos, Nueva San Salvador (Santa Tecla), San Marcos, Ilopango, and Antiguo Cuscatlán. For a more detailed description of the data, see Seligson et al. (1995:152–53).

8. CID-Gallup Survey, San Salvador, September 1991, in which 1,240 adults were interviewed.

9. The total number of municipalities in El Salvador is unusually large in the context of Central America. The country has three times as many as Costa Rica and twice as many as Nicaragua (Blair et al., 1995).

7

Opening the Electoral Space in Mexico

The Rise of the Opposition at the State and Local Levels

Victoria E. Rodríguez

The sometimes grudging admiration for Mexico's political system and its stability was best expressed by Peru's Mario Vargas Llosa, when he referred to it as "the perfect dictatorship." His Mexican literary counterpart and rival, Carlos Fuentes, lost no time in formulating a reply, as he defended his country by saying that it was, rather, an "imperfect democracy." There may be much substance to Vargas Llosa's phrase, as undoubtedly there are many clearly authoritarian elements in Mexico's political system. By many standards Mexico may still be far from being a democracy. Nevertheless, significant progress has been made. Sometimes in fits and starts, and sometimes even reversing moves that would otherwise clearly point to democratization, Mexico has taken important steps toward the institutionalization of democracy in the past ten years.

The presence of new political openings is best expressed by the fact that, for the first time in over sixty years of one-party dominance, the opposition has gained significant access to power at both the state and local levels throughout the country. While many analysts argue that such victories are little more than the mechanism whereby the dominant PRI (Partido Revolucionario Institucional) seeks to maintain its hold on power, the recognition of these victories has to be measured as important for a party that has ruled virtually unchallenged for most of this century. In this view, the democratization process is likely to advance in Mexico only as far as the national power of the PRI is not threatened. As long as the PRI retains control of the presidency, there appears to be a genuine willingness to accommodate at least some of the opposition at the local and even at the state levels. In this fashion the transition toward democracy can proceed while political stability is maintained. Although most of the move toward democratization initially occurred within the context of President Carlos Salinas's program of economic and political liberalization (1988–1994), other events in the past decade have also had a lasting effect. Of these, the birth of a new civic culture, rooted in the demands of the citizenry for a more transparent electoral process, and the demands of the opposition for increased representation represent a sea change in the fortunes of the ruling PRI and have altered drastically Mexico's electoral landscape. Thus, an overview of the national level provides the context for a better assessment of the impact of local urban elections on the country's democratization project.

The first section of this chapter provides a summary of the major advances toward democratization that have occurred during the 1980s and early 1990s. There follows an analysis of the impact of the electoral reforms upon the national legislature's more pluralistic representation, seeking to assess the divergent patterns of national versus local elections. While it is clear that the ruling PRI has thus far steadfastly held on to power at the federal level, the opposition has made significant progress at the state and local ones. Finally, an assessment is provided of the importance of state and local urban elections to the country's democratization efforts. To anticipate the conclusion, the argument developed below is that local elections and local politics play a critical role in the country's democratic transition. Moreover, they have already begun to deliver on their promise to have a more lasting effect by forcing all parties in government to perform better if they aspire to win the next election.

Mexico's Centralist, One-Party Tradition

The rich scholarly literature on Mexico's political system offers a variety of interpretations on the degree of authoritarianism and the nature of its democracy. Nevertheless, certain elements of the system elicit little disagreement: it is highly centralist, with enormous power vested in the presidency, and the level of pluralism has been extremely limited. Since its emergence in the 1930s, and until the historic 1988 election, the PRI ensured that almost all of its presidential candidates regularly won 85 percent of the total vote. Although in 1988 the PRI's candidate, Carlos Salinas de Gortari, won with a highly questionable 51 percent of the vote and in 1994 the margin of victory of Ernesto Zedillo was 20 percent, Mexico's PRIísta presidents have ruled virtually unchallenged in regular but nonrenewable six-year cycles, or *sexenios*. Also, until 1988, the transition of power from one administration to the next occurred relatively smoothly, something worth noting in a continent where coups and countercoups have taken place with great regularity.

The centralization of power in the figure of the president is symbolic of the high degree of centralization that permeates the entire system and that dictates the country's social, political, and economic activities. While the last decade has seen major efforts and some significant advances toward decentralization, by and large centralization has persisted. Indeed, a variety of policies designed to decentralize fiscally, politically, and administratively have in effect led to more centralization. This paradox is particularly notable in the patterns of intergovernmental relations among the federal, state, and municipal levels of government. In spite of all the constitutional and legal provisions for municipal autonomy, local governments have remained subordinate to their state and federal hierarchs. As argued elsewhere, decentralization in Mexico, for all practical purposes, has been designed to centralize more effectively (Rodríguez, 1992, 1997; Bailey, 1994).

A direct outcome of such centralization was that, in the past, authoritarianism could sometimes occur unchallenged. Indeed, many observers believe that political repression and intimidation were widespread and systemic (Schers, 1972; Bartra et al., 1975; Cockroft, 1982; Harvey, 1989). Periodically, however, there were upwellings of dissent, such as erupted in the student disturbances in 1968, the rural guerrilla movements during the early 1970s, and other urban social movement disturbances. Some of the labor unions in Mexico, too, occasionally set themselves against the official union structure; and, particularly from the 1970s onward, there have been strong pressures within several of these organizations to break away and form others with more independent, democratic, and representative structures (Middlebrook, 1991). Community groups have asserted themselves as well through coordinated urban social movements (Ramírez Saiz, 1986; Foweraker and Craig, 1990); and since the early 1980s local leaders have tended to be far more representative of their followers than formerly (Montaño, 1976; Ward, 1993; Harvey, 1989; Paas et al., 1991). In the past, dissent also manifested itself in the occasional municipal victory of an opposition party, but prior to the 1980s this was only likely to occur if popular dissatisfaction with the PRI or with a local power elite had become intolerable (see Bezdek, 1995, for example, for the case of San Luis Potosí).

By the late 1960s there were widespread pressures toward change that went beyond these surges of unrest. Most significant, within the PRI itself, some senior leaders recognized the need for internal democratic reform. They found a vehicle for voicing their discontent through Carlos Madrazo, who, for a short period until his untimely death in an airplane accident, was president of the PRI during the 1960s. A large part of the discontent of these PRIístas stemmed from their recognition that the system had to become more pluralistic. Up until then only one party, the Partido Acción Nacional (PAN), at the right of the political spectrum, had provided any significant electoral opposition to the PRI, although its share of the national vote never exceeded 20 percent. Other parties, especially those to the left of the spectrum, were either outlawed altogether or their existence and fortunes were stage-managed by the PRI in order to ensure the semblance of electoral competition (González Casanova, 1970; Molinar, 1991). Until 1979, elections were often rigged, not so much to prevent opposition parties from winning but to reduce abstentionism to a level that would not undermine the legitimacy of the regime and of PRIísta victories (Hansen, 1974; Smith, 1979; Camp, 1993).[1]

By the 1980s the facade of Mexican democracy had become so badly tarnished that the entire political system was in dire need of revitalization. Juan Molinar (1986, 1991) has characterized the changes that have occurred since the early stages of the political crisis as a shift from PRI monopoly to hegemony to one of limited competition. While some significant advances were made in the elections of 1983, when several important victories of the opposition were recognized in some critical cities (including five state capitals), these trends were reversed in the state and local elections of 1986. The de la Madrid government gave in to pressure from certain powerful sections of the PRI's inner ranks, which refused to yield space to the opposition, and once again the PRI resorted to any and all measures to secure victory. There is little doubt that widespread fraud took place in the 1985 and 1986 elections (Aziz,

1987; Guadarrama, 1987; Bezdek, 1995). These events, coupled with stringent economic austerity measures, led to great disillusionment among many PRIístas, especially the young, who recognized that the need for reform of the system had to come from within the PRI's own ranks.

Such was the background for the creation of the *corriente democrática* (democratic current), the movement formed within the PRI under the direction of several senior and influential party members, that was to mark the beginning of the sea change that occurred as a result of the presidential election of 1988. A group of PRIístas, strongly dissatisfied with the internal system of candidate designation (perhaps because it stifled their own political ambitions) and seeking internal democratic reform, banded together behind the leadership of three prominent party members, Porfirio Muñoz Ledo, Cuauhtémoc Cárdenas, and Ifigenia Martínez, all of whom had occupied senior elected and appointed positions within the party and/or the government. Supported by other left-wing parties, the *corriente* hastily formed the Frente Democrático Nacional (FDN) to contest the presidential election and proposed Cárdenas as its candidate to run against the PRI's Salinas and the PAN's Manuel Clouthier.[2]

The 1988 election has been extensively documented and analyzed (Cornelius, Gentleman, and Smith, 1989; Barberán et al., 1988; Molinar, 1991). In short, Cárdenas did so well that some analysts even insist that he won. Certainly the evidence seems to indicate that the results were "adjusted" in order to ensure a majority for Salinas, as the officially declared vote gave him a bare 51 percent majority. Cárdenas received 31 percent of the vote, and Clouthier 17 percent, the typical percentage for the PAN in a presidential election (Camp, 1993:152). But even though some analysts also suggest that Salinas did actually win, albeit perhaps with a smaller percentage than was declared, the point to emphasize is that this election marked the beginning of a new era in Mexico's electoral politics. For the first time the PRI's candidate was genuinely challenged, as voters expressed their dissatisfaction with government performance and sought to exercise their vote for change. Perhaps the votes that went to Cárdenas and Clouthier were much more against the PRI than supportive of the PAN or the FDN, but what matters is that, as Salinas himself acknowledged the day after the election, "The era of a virtual one-party system has ended, giving way to a period of intense political competition" (Cornelius and Craig, 1991:1).

In the aftermath of the 1988 election, electoral politics has gained center stage. No longer are electoral results easily predicted in advance, particularly as the opposition has learned to intervene by actively monitoring elections, conducting quick counts, and contesting results, often having them reversed in its favor. Indeed, although in most cases relatively peaceful acts of civil disobedience are sufficient to overturn the results, in other instances there has been violence and even death. Sometimes protest is unnecessary, as the victories of the opposition are recognized outright. While several examples of all these cases are discussed in more detail below, the point emphasized here is that, as a result of 1988, the PRI was obliged to undertake a series of internal reforms in order to gain credibility when electoral results were announced. The reforms paid off soon; in the 1991 and 1992 elections the PRI did relatively well, especially in certain regions of the country where it had done poorly and had sometimes been defeated by both the PAN and the PRD (Partido de la Revolución Democrática). The 1991 congressional election, in particular, showed a major swing back to the PRI. Whether by means fair or foul, by late 1993 both the PRI and the government appeared to have regained much of their lost legitimacy.

There has also been an opening up of the civic culture and process since 1988. Clientelistic relations between community and labor groups with PRI politicians and government officials have declined and been replaced by more systematic and routinized patterns of interaction (Ward, 1986), although some would argue that Salinas's Solidarity program turned the clock back, toward populism and clientelism (Dresser, 1991, but see Cornelius, Craig, and Fox, 1994). Powerful bosses in principal labor unions, such as PEMEX (petroleum workers) and the SNTE (teachers), were either removed or undermined. Generally speaking, unions today seem to offer more democratic representation for their members (Cook, 1990; Foweraker, 1993). Residents' associations and community organizations are also more likely to be led by democratically elected leaders or individuals (Foweraker and Craig, 1990). There has also been an opening up of the press, particularly in the realm of national weekly or monthly publications, such as *Este País* and *Voz y Voto*, and through more independent dailies, such as *Reforma*. Also, since 1988, the media have been much more open in publicizing the results of opinion polls conducted by a growing number of partisan and nonpartisan organizations. Indeed, public opinion polls became one of the major focuses of attention in the 1994 presidential election and have continued to play an important role in subsequent elections.

Most important, several national movements have emerged with the purpose of monitoring and protecting the vote at elections, defending the democratic advances that have been won and denouncing any attempt to interfere with these advances. Such nongovernmental organizations include Alianza Cívica, the Convergencia para la Democracia, and the Movimiento Ciudadano Democrático, which was born in San Luis Potosí and now extends to the national level.[3] An important feature of this rapid growth of NGOs and informal associations is that they rarely have overt ties to a political party, although most tend to be broadly supportive of the opposition because they do not wish to lose credibility by being linked to a party whose fortunes may fluctuate. Nor do they wish to be co-opted by a partisan orthodoxy that would drive them away from civic-oriented processes and goals (see Hernández and Fox, 1994; Moguel, 1994). Finally, there has been a growing concern over the protection of civil rights. In 1989, President Salinas created the Comisión Nacional de Derechos Humanos, which appeared to make some progress in reducing civil rights abuses nationwide. Although allegations of abuse continue to persist, at the very least today almost every state has its own statewide commission, the first of which was created by a government of the opposition (the PAN in Baja California).

The August 1994 presidential election, however, provided the acid test of the extent of democratization in Mexico. The credibility regained by late 1993 has undeniably been affected by a string of events that badly shook the nation, particularly the uprising in Chiapas in January 1994; the assassination of the PRI's presidential candidate, Luis Donaldo Colosio, in March 1994; and then the assassination of the PRI's general secretary, José Francisco Ruiz Massieu, in September of the same year. These events, and a whole series of others unprecedented in Mexico—kidnappings, car bombings, open drug-ring wars, allegations of PRI involvement in drug cartels, and politically motivated assassinations—have shattered the confidence of the Mexican people in the system that claimed to be leading them out of the worst political and economic crisis that has afflicted the nation in modern times. All of these events, followed by the December 1994 economic crisis at the start of the current *sexenio*, present President Zedillo and his party with a major (and also unprecedented) challenge of how to maintain his party in control of the government.

The Institutionalization of Political Reforms:
Cambiar todo para que nada cambie
(Changing everything so that nothing changes)

The political background delineated above has been both a cause and an effect of electoral politics. In order to revitalize and to sustain the credibility and legitimacy of the PRI and of prospective PRIísta governments, a series of electoral reform initiatives was undertaken beginning in 1963, extended in 1973 and 1977, again in 1986, and most recently in 1993 and 1994.[4] Significantly, this process is always referred to as *apertura política* but never as *apertura democrática*—perhaps unwittingly, because although there may have been a willingness to make space for the opposition, the intention was never to allow it to become too powerful.[5]

From the mid-1960s to the mid-1970s the opposition averaged about 17 percent of the seats in the Chamber of Deputies (Camp, 1993:147).[6] The 1973 reform allowed for the existence of a wider range of political parties, particularly those on the left (including the Communist Party). Most important of all was the 1977 Federal Law of Political Organizations and Electoral Processes (LOPPE), which set aside one quarter of all seats in the Chamber to be divided among the opposition parties on the basis of proportional representation.[7] Thus, although their legislative power remained highly constrained, especially since the PRI never let its own internal divisions carry over into splits in the vote, opposition parties now had their foot in the door.[8] Both the activity and the quality of debate in the Chamber improved, and was no longer blindly supportive of legislation initiated by the PRI or the president.

The important point to recognize is that the fundamental purpose of the reform was not to weaken the authority and the role of the PRI, but rather to enhance and sustain them. In essence, the political reforms of 1977 were introduced as a needed change in the political system. As Kevin Middlebrook (1986, 1991) and others argue, these reforms were a regime-sponsored effort to retain stability and to head off declining support for the system. The reduction of regime support and political legitimacy, which was openly exposed by the Tlatelolco student massacre in 1968, became steadily evident in public opinion polls and in the decline of voter participation as well as in the emergence of several new opposition parties. Perhaps more important, it was clear that the decline in the fortunes of the PRI meant a rising incapacity to fulfill its primary functions of delivering the vote and achieving social control over the poorest segments of the population (Hansen, 1974). Briefly, the clear objective of the reforms was to strengthen the PRI by encouraging a more credible (but carefully constrained) opposition. Indeed, although the initiation of a *plurinominal* deputy system gave encouragement to opposition parties, their representation between 1979 and 1985 remained roughly stable, suggesting that, in the Congress at least, there was little evidence of growth (Camp, 1993:148). Moreover, the reforms turned out to be problematic because they not only failed to give the opposition a real opportunity to participate, but because they also were opposed by state governors and local political bosses who believed that their own power depended on the PRI's continued total domination of state and local governments.

President Miguel de la Madrid introduced a further reform in 1986 that sought to enhance the opposition parties' opportunities for adequate representation (Craig and Cornelius, 1995:295–96). Through this reform, the winning or majority party could never obtain more than 70 percent of the seats in the Chamber of Deputies; the total size of the legislature was increased to 500 seats, split into 300 for those elected by relative majority in their congressional districts and 200 for proportional representation. The party obtaining the greatest number of the 300 majority seats was allowed to receive additional seats through the proportional representation mode, which permitted one given political party to obtain an overall majority within the Congress. Thus, while the opposition's representation was raised to a minimum 30 percent of the now-enlarged legislature (that is, 150 of the 500 seats), the PRI managed virtually to guarantee its own hold on the legislature by extending *plurinominal* (proportional) seats to any party receiving less than 50 percent of the legislative seats. Once again, the points to underscore here are that the increased opposition party presence was one allocated by the government rather than one earned by those parties, and that the PRI was willing to make space for the opposition only to the extent that its own majority position in the Chamber was not threatened.

The 1988 elections were historic not only because the victory of the PRI's presidential candidate was dubious but also because for the first time opposition parties acquired sufficient strength in the Chamber of Deputies to shape the policy process, particularly when a two-thirds majority vote to change the Constitution was required. By 1989 opposition parties had acquired close to 50 percent of the Chamber seats, thus suggesting the first true alteration in the PRI's power. With its dominance dropping to well below the 66 percent majority required for Constitutional changes, the PRI had to seek coalition partners for any such amendments.

However, opposition parties were not satisfied with their gains, especially in light of the PRI's significant electoral success in 1991. Since 1989 the opposition has pressed hard for major Constitutional changes and for improvements in the conduct of electoral processes through the Código Federal de Instituciones y Procedimientos Electorales (COFIPE).[9] In 1989, also, the Instituto Federal Electoral (IFE) was created as an independent entity to organize and monitor the electoral process in a manner above suspicion. The predecessor to the IFE was the Federal Electoral Commission, whose credibility, at best, was suspect. Since its creation, the IFE has spared no effort in making for itself a reputation as an autonomous and transparent institution, bending over backwards to accommodate the demands of all political parties, but particularly of the opposition. In preparation for the 1994 presidential election, the IFE boasted of having one of the more accurate voter registration lists (*padrón electoral*) in the world (47.5 million registered out of 50 million qualified to vote) and released it to be audited and inspected by both national and international organizations. Also in preparation for this election, the IFE spent over U.S.$730 million in updating and revising the *padrón* and producing a voter identification card that has more antitampering devices in it than, as an IFE official put it, "the ID of a NASA engineer wishing to board a space shuttle."

In spite of all the expenditure and effort put into the 1994 election, there were still allegations of fraud and complaints about the electoral procedures. In the aftermath, the final verdict was that the election, overall, was clean but not fair.[10] The fraud, many observers contended, was committed by the PRI *before* the actual election, through unfair access to campaign finance resources and virtually unlimited access to the media. Also, irregularities were reported throughout the country, such as running out of ballots during the early hours of voting. Other cases of reported irregularities led to an overturn of results. For example, in the election for the municipal presidency of Monterrey, the PRIísta victory was annulled in favor of the PAN (Rodríguez and Ward, 1996).

Congressional debate on electoral reform had reached a stalemate by 1993; and although the PRI could have easily built the necessary two-thirds majority to push through some innocuous reforms, it was reluctant to do so. President Salinas wanted the COFIPE passed with at least the support of the PAN, in order to provide greater legitimacy for the 1994 elections. In effect, this meant that the COFIPE had to pass through the Congress by August 1993. At the last minute, in order to win PANista support, the PRI offered major concessions. The most important is that, after 1994, each state will have four senators, three of which will be by direct election and the fourth allocated to the party coming in second.[11] Other concessions obtained relate to greater equity in access to the media during election campaigns; the imposition of some limits upon financial contributions to parties; the removal of the so-called "governability clause," which since 1987 had ensured a working majority in the Congress for the PRI;[12] and passing to the local electoral councils and to the IFE the process whereby incoming congresses voted to approve their own election (*autocalificación*). Also, the *padrón* will be verified by an independent body. The opposition was unsuccessful in two other significant areas that they had fought for: first, that there be limits on the direct participation of public functionaries in electoral campaigning; and second, that no party be allowed to make use of the colors of the national flag as its own.[13]

It seems certain that the process of amplifying and bolstering an opposition party presence in both houses of the Congress will continue beyond the 1994 reforms, and it is likely to be a contentious issue in the 1997 midterm election. Indeed, as the data in Table 1 show, the 1994 election expanded the presence of the opposition in both the Senate and the Chamber of Deputies, albeit without giving them even a combined majority. Thus, the reforms of the past thirty years underscore the fact that while the precedent was one of creating a plurality, it was also one that was heavily constrained and aimed at assuring the PRI's dominance in the legislature, although on terms that were less favorable from its point of view than in the past. These rules under which legislatures were constructed provided the framework for state congresses, and even municipal governments, to begin thinking about proportional representation at the local level.[14]

Table 1. Composition of the Congress, 1994–1997

	Won by Majority Vote	Awarded by Proportional Representation	Total	Percent
Chamber of Deputies				
PRI	274	27[a]	301	60.8%
PAN	19	99	118	23.9
PRD	5	64	69	12.9
PT	0	10	10	2.0
Annulled elections[b]	2	1	2	0.4
Total	300	200	500	100.0%
Senate[c]				
PRI	95	0	95	74.2%
PAN	1	24	25	19.5
PRD	0	8	8	6.3
Total	96	32	128	100.0%

Source: Instituto Federal Electoral, *1994: Tu elección—Memoria del proceso electoral federal* (México, D.F.: Instituto Federal Electoral, 1995), tables 8.1 and 8.2, pp. 367–68. Cited in Cornelius, 1996, p. 28.
[a]Includes two seats provisionally assigned to the PRI, pending the results of special elections to be held in districts where results of the August 1994 elections were annulled.
[b]Seats corresponding to congressional districts in which the results of the August 1994 elections were annulled.
[c]Includes 32 senators serving terms running from 1991 to 1997 as well as those elected to serve from 1994 to 2000.

The Local in the National: The Rise of the Opposition at the State and Local Levels

It is not only within the Congress that there has been an expansion of pluralist representation. From 1982 onward, a significant number of city governments were also won by opposition parties. The de la Madrid administration took the first steps in exercising the principles embodied in the political reform when in 1983 it recognized several outright victories of opposition parties at the municipal level, including some in major cities. No less than five of these were state capitals (Chihuahua, Durango, Hermosillo, Guanajuato, and San Luis Potosí); another was a large border city (Ciudad Juárez). The idea was that this political opening would help to alleviate some of the frustrations of the economic crisis of the 1980s. But for many, giving in to the opposition seemed too high a price to pay, and the moves toward greater pluralism were subsequently reversed, often through electoral fraud. In southern Mexico, for instance, the left won in the municipality of Juchitán but was never allowed to take power. The case was heavily publicized and brought seriously into question the administration's true intentions of political liberalization.

Indeed, some of the victories of the opposition, such as the PDM (Partido Demócrata Mexicano) in Guanajuato and the PST (Partido Socialista de los Trabajadores) in Ensenada, both in 1983, appear to have been orchestrated by the PRI itself in order to promote a semblance of democracy (Rodríguez and Ward, 1995). Others occurred when splits within the PRI led to such a level of disagreement over candidate selection that the door was left open for an opposition party to win. Also in 1983, in cities such as Durango, Ciudad Juárez, and Chihuahua, the PRI seems to have been caught off guard by the massive swing to the PAN.

This ambivalence between liberalization, on the one hand, and retaining absolute political control, on the other, resurfaced with a vengeance in the midterm elections of 1986. There seems little doubt that the opposition, specifically the PAN, won major victories in many municipalities within the country and particularly in the north, where it had been so successful in 1983. However, the PRI resorted to its time-worn practices of intimidation, vote rigging, and ballot stuffing in order to contrive victories in these electoral districts (see Cornelius, Gentleman, and Smith, 1989), in spite of the fact that these irregularites were widely condemned at home and abroad, especially in the United States. In retrospect, it seems almost certain that de la Madrid was obliged to sacrifice his willingness to move toward political liberalization in order to sustain his hard-nosed monetarist policies of austerity and economic control.

Since the presidential election of 1988, and in every other subsequent election, opposition victories have multiplied. At the state level, the first major breakthrough was the PAN's victory in the gubernatorial elections of Baja California in 1989, followed by Chihuahua in 1992 and then by Jalisco, Guanajuato, and Baja California (again) in 1995. Indeed, when in the 1989 elections in Baja California the PAN became the first opposition party to win a state governorship, it was suggested that Salinas may have deliberately let the opposition win (or at least let the PRI lose) as part of his own political project. The 1992 elections in Chihuahua appeared to be less suspect. However, while not wishing to discredit in any way this PANista victory, many analysts believe that the 1992 victory was one negotiated at the higher levels.[15] How and when and between whom these negotiations take place is difficult to ascertain, but it does seem clear that negotiations over electoral results have become a crucial factor in today's electoral process. However, the process does not apply equally to all parties. While it has evidently worked well for the PAN, that is certainly not the case with the PRD, given that not all of the opposition is treated equally (even though the protests of the PRD tend to be more vociferous than those of the PAN).[16] To a large extent President Salinas's democratization project has been equated with negotiation, but because of the origins of the PRD (the party born from the *corriente democrática* and the FDN that caused the debacle of 1988) it is virtually impossible for there to be any negotiation between the PRD and the government. Once again the 1992 election serves as illustration. While the PAN's gubernatorial win was readily recognized in Chihuahua, the PRI claimed victory in the state of Michoacán and held tough on it, even though the case was widely publicized as the electoral results were hotly contested by the PRD. Although in the end Salinas was obliged to give in, he did so only partially; the sworn-in PRIísta governor was obliged to take a "leave of absence" and was replaced by an interim governor—but one from the PRI, not the PRD. When the 1994 presidential election came around, Baja California and Chihuahua remained as the only two states in the history of contemporary Mexico to have been won by the opposition.[17] However, a major wave of opposition victories at the state level in 1995 brought the PAN to hold the governorships of Jalisco and Guanajuato and, perhaps even more significant, to win that of Baja California for the second time.

At the municipal level the wins of the opposition have not stopped; indeed, in some cases (San Luis Potosí, Zamora, León, San Pedro Garza García, Ensenada, and Tijuana) the same municipality has been won consecutively by an opposition party. As the data in Table 2 indicate, the number of municipal governments controlled by the opposition has grown considerably. As of 1994, over 230 municipalities in the country were governed by the opposition; and although this number may be considered relatively small (at the time there were 2,392 municipalities in Mexico, a number that has increased to 2,412), what is relevant is that many of these are critically important cities, not small rural communities. Moreover, this number has increased further as a result of the widespread opposition victories of both the PAN and the PRD in the states of Veracruz and Tabasco late in 1994, and scores of others in 1995, including

Table 2. Municipal Governments, by Party and State, 1996

State	No. of Municipalities	Controlled by PRI	Controlled by PAN	Controlled by PRD	Controlled by Others*
Aguascalientes	11	7	4	0	0
Baja California	5	3	2	0	0
Baja California Sur	5	5	0	0	0
Campeche	9	9	0	0	0
Coahuila	38	35	1	1	1
Colima	10	9	1	0	0
Chiapas	111	84	5	18	4
Chihuahua	67	55	10	1	1
Durango	39	21	12	2	4
Guanajuato	46	37	5	2	2
Guerrero	76	68	0	6	2
Hidalgo	84	83	0	1	0
Jalisco	124	63	53	6	2
México	122	108	6	4	4
Michoacán	113	43	14	54	2
Morelos	33	32	0	1	0
Nayarit	20	19	1	0	0
Nuevo León	51	45	6	0	0
Oaxaca	570	111	11	35	413
Puebla	217	186	23	7	1
Querétaro	18	17	1	0	0
Quintana Roo	8	8	0	0	0
San Luis Potosí	58	49	6	0	3
Sinaloa	18	12	5	1	0
Sonora	70	62	6	1	1
Tabasco	17	13	0	4	0
Tamaulipas	43	34	6	3	0
Tlaxcala	60	50	5	4	1
Veracruz	207	148	19	27	13
Yucatán	106	93	12	1	0
Zacatecas	56	42	11	2	1
Total	**2,412**	**1,551**	**225**	**181**	**455**

Source: Based on information from the Centro de Servicios Municipales "Heriberto Jara," Mexico City.
*"Others" includes the PT, PFCRN, PPS, PARM, PDM, and CM. The 413 municipalities of Oaxaca in this column were elected by *usos y costumbres*, the goverance structure whereby indigenous groups of a given community elect their civic leaders according to traditional practices and criteria (*usos y costumbres*). These leaders are recognized as municipal government officials by the state electoral authorities.

Aguascalientes and Guadalajara, while holding on to large cities such as Tijuana, León, and Ciudad Juárez. Altogether, in the 1994 and 1995 elections, the opposition extended its victories to some of the largest cities and several state capitals, including such traditional PRIísta strongholds as Oaxaca, Puebla, and Aguascalientes, all of which were gained by the PAN. Thus, in addition to those mentioned above, key cities such as Guadalajara, Monterrey, Ciudad Juárez, Chihuahua, Mérida, Durango, León, Morelia, and many others have at various times been governed by the opposition in the past ten years. Indeed, in the election of 1988, had Mexico City had a constitution that allowed for the election of its local officers, the opposition parties (especially the Frente) would have swept the board (Ward, 1990).

The relative closeness of the 1988 election results, together with the major advances of opposition parties and the heated contention for the 1994 presidential election, have raised for the first time the possibility of non-PRI or coalition governments. Indeed, the PAN's Ernesto Ruffo is likely to run for the presidency in the year 2000 under the same campaign slogan—*Sí se puede* (Yes, it can be done)—that attracted considerable attention from the media and won him the governorship, and there is widespread opinion that he may do very well. A first critical move in the direction of a non-PRI (or mixed) federal government can be interpreted in the presidential appointment of a PANista to a key position, that of Antonio Lozano as attorney general. But while not wishing to undermine the significance of this appointment, the most serious sign of change may well be victories of the opposition at the state level, not the least because they took place in critically important states: Guanajuato, Jalisco, and Baja California. Guanajuato, the cradle of Mexican independence and a conservative stalwart of the PAN, is now governed by the controversial and charismatic Vicente Fox who, having "lost" in 1991, obtained an easy victory after a successful campaign led by the smashing slogan *Ahora sí* (Now, yes). In Jalisco, the other principal conservative state with strong traditions of Sinarquismo, the PAN swept the board, taking not only the governorship but also the state congress and most municipalities, including the second most important metropolitan region in the country, Guadalajara. In Baja California, in what many observers anticipated would be an extremely close election on the basis of the results of the 1994 presidential contest, the PAN also managed by a considerable margin to retain the governorship and control of the state congress and the city of Tijuana and to win, for the first time, the capital of the state, Mexicali. All of these victories add up to the fact that as of 1995, approximately one-fourth of Mexico's population was governed by "the opposition."

Changing Electoral Traditions: Some Intraurban Experiences

Various reasons account for the increased success of the opposition in urban local elections. Two in particular are critical. First, as a new civic culture has emerged in Mexico with a citizenry that demands electoral transparency, the entire electoral process at the national and local levels has been subject to a renewed set of revisions and controls. During the last decade the conduct of local elections has changed to the extent that it has become the arena in which much of the civic process operates today. The second crucial issue for many victories of the opposition relates to leadership, and indeed some critical victories of the opposition have hinged upon individual personalities. Much of their appeal emanates from their own political trajectories and from their ability to mount a real challenge to the PRI. Yet here again, until recently, the PRI insisted on retaining control; from the president and the PRI's perspective, some leaders of the opposition were more acceptable than others, especially when it came to having their victories actually recognized.

The critical turnaround in urban local elections began in the 1980s. Prior to that time, the PRI's principal enemy nationally was abstentionism, rather than any opposition party. In those states where the opposition parties had carried no real force, dissatisfaction with the regime was such that abstentions often reached over 60 percent (Molinar, 1991:132). Whether to defeat the opposition locally or to raise voting to acceptable levels, the PRI's traditional recourses included ballot box stuffing, intimidation, mobilizing support through its corporatist organizations, and repression. In the early and mid-1980s, as opposition parties became more active and more successful in elections, they also became more sophisticated and adept at detecting fraud. But despite this progress, it remained difficult for them to prove conclusively that fraud or electoral irregularities had significantly affected the result. More recently, postelection protest has often been effective not only in having more of their victories recognized (sometimes, as described earlier, having electoral results overturned in their favor) but also in obliging the PRI to put on a better show of vote counting.[18] In recent elections, voter roll inflation, waiting hours in line to cast a ballot, and manipulation of computerized results have proven to be more effective.

The 1986 and 1992 elections in Chihuahua serve as good examples of the changes that have occurred in Mexico's local electoral traditions as the country advances toward democratization. The 1986 contest has gone down in history as one of widespread fraud. Several national and international groups (including the Organization of American States) have concurred. In addition to the traditional types of fraud discussed above, 1986 included false voter registration, the late release of registered voter lists, and the jailing of observers (in theory, the presence of observers is legally permitted in each district). Juan Molinar (1986, 1991) has suggested that although it is not unusual for the PRI to inflate the numbers on the electoral list by 200 to 300 percent, in 1986 in Chihuahua the party inflated the list by about 600 percent, thereby allowing the opposition to detect the fraud more easily.

The postelectoral reaction in Chihuahua in 1986 consolidated an earlier practice that has become increasingly effective in recent years: civil disobedience. It took the form of hunger strikes, demonstrations, public denunciations by Church leaders, appeals to international agencies, and the boycott of supermarkets. While major upwellings of civil unrest were to prove highly successful in the states of San Luis Potosí and Guanajuato in 1991, that was not the case in 1986 in Chihuahua. The government did not make any concessions to the protesting PANistas, who declared that they would go on a hunger strike to the death, if necessary. The strike ended after forty days without any changes in the declared electoral results. However, the impact of the 1986 postelection protest had its real impact six years later, in the elections of 1992. As in 1986, once again Francisco Barrio ran for the governorship on the PAN's ticket. The campaign was a tough one, as the PRI picked a popular *chihuahuense*, Jesús Macías, as its candidate. But this time all went smoothly; the voting results declared Barrio to be the outright winner; and although the PRIístas protested faintly, the results remained.

To a large extent, the PAN's 1992 victory in Chihuahua was due to Barrio's popularity, and the same can be said for the PAN's success in Baja California's election of Ernesto Ruffo in 1989, the first two governorships ever won by an opposition party. The dramatic PANista victories in Baja California and Chihuahua were almost certainly attributable to the party's candidate selection. Both of them enjoyed widespread support locally, while the PRI fielded relatively weak candidates. That Ruffo was able to break the sixty-year logjam of PRIísta governorships and become the first governor of the opposition may be explained by several factors: first, the appalling record of his predecessors had lost all credibility for the PRI; and second, his record as mayor of Ensenada was especially successful. Ruffo's personality and track record are crucial for explaining the fact that the state voted overwhelmingly for Cárdenas in the 1988 elections, yet scarcely a year later voted in Ruffo as the first PANista governor (rather than the candidate from the PRD). While much of the vote for Ruffo may have been anti-PRI, nonetheless his positive record and the PRI's negative one was crucial for the PAN's winning the election, rather than the PAN per se. A similar story unfolded in Chihuahua, where Barrio was widely believed to have been robbed of the election in 1986. In the intervening six years he matured considerably as a politician, and his strategy in 1992 was far less antagonistic toward the central government. His appeal was best put by a prospective voter: "I'm a PRIísta and will always be one, but I'm going to vote for Pancho Barrio." In the 1992 August elections, Barrio won with a significant majority, though not a large one. Nonetheless, it is difficult to envisage any other PANista candidate winning that election.

In addition to the leadership of both Barrio and Ruffo, a key factor in explaining the victory of both men was the political space created by President Salinas and his willingness to accept and respect these particular election results. This recognition was not always forthcoming. No one knows, for example, whether Fox won the Guanajuato gubernatorial elections in 1991. He certainly had a strong personal following within the state, as demonstrated by the wide margin with which he won when he ran again for the governorship in 1995. Like Barrio before him, Fox maintained a loyal following in the period between elections and took the time to become more circumspect and politically mature. However, back in 1991, his bombastic and uncompromising style made him unsuitable for office in the president's view; when Salinas was searching for a PANista to serve as interim governor, Fox was promptly overlooked (indeed, vetoed by the PRI) and replaced by Carlos Medina Plascencia, who posed a lesser threat.

Thus, the rise of opposition parties to power via the electoral system is conditioned by factors that go beyond voting returns. In addition to being sanctioned by the president and other party higher-ups, the fortunes of opposition parties are tied to a myriad of elements, including the leaders whom they choose. Even a cursory assessment of the most significant successes of the opposition shows that individual personalities matter a great deal. Although party electoral politics is paramount, the difference between an opposition party winning or losing a local election (or being a significant force) often relates to the individual candidate. In addition to the cases mentioned above, one cannot begin to understand San Luis Potosí politics or election results without fully recognizing the following and respect for that state's independent leader, the late Dr. Salvador Nava Martínez (Bezdek, 1995). Alienated from the PRI, Nava ran in the 1950s as an independent candidate and went on to win the mayorship of the state capital; he is also widely thought to have won the governorship in 1959, although his victory was not recognized. His dramatic return to the electoral arena in the 1991 gubernatorial elections, a contest he is thought to have won, led President Salinas to request the resignation of the "victorious" PRI governor only weeks after his inauguration. This turnabout was prompted by civic unrest throughout the state and by Dr. Nava's three-hundred-mile march from San Luis to Mexico City, which aroused international attention. After Nava's death in 1992, his widow sought to step into his shoes in the new gubernatorial elections called in April 1993. Although widely respected, she did not carry the following of her husband and made a disappointing showing in the elections.

Other women have fared better than Sra. Nava, although the representation of women in Mexican politics remains critically low. In spite of the fact that women hold approximately 15 percent of the seats in the Congress (a relatively high percentage by some Latin American standards), they have been able only marginally to influence policy design and implementation. Moreover, the few women appointed to Cabinet positions within the last administrations have never held the critically important posts (Interior, Treasury, or even Health and Education), but instead have been relegated to secondary ministries (Fisheries, Tourism). To date, there have been only three female state governors, and all have been from the PRI. At the local level, women have gained access to an even smaller percentage of municipalities than the opposition, although, interestingly, two women of the opposition (PAN) currently hold the mayorships of the two largest municipalities governed by women. They have not been notably successful in making a good show in local urban elections, although it is at the local level where women have been able to directly affect policymaking. However, in spite of their low numbers in government, the presence of women in diverse arenas of political life is growing rapidly as they participate more actively through means other than appointed or elected office, including NGOs, labor unions, and feminist organizations (Rodríguez, 1997).

In assessing local elections in Mexico, therefore, the individual personalities (and gender) of candidates matter, often decisively. All political parties, including the PRI, have begun to understand this lesson and now take more care in the selection of candidates. As more competent ones are chosen to run for office, their victories are increasingly translated into more effective modes of governance. A more competitive electoral system thus means not only that urban electoral traditions have begun to change in Mexico, but also that its impact can be felt in the creation of a new civic culture that demands a more transparent government.

The Intraurban Consolidation of Democracy: More Pluralism, Better Governance

The extension of proportional representation to the state and municipal levels came as part of the 1977 and 1986 reforms described earlier. Individual state-level formulas, however, vary. Each state congress determines the specific distribution of party representation in state and municipal government. These formulas generally set minimum percentages of the popular vote which must be obtained, and may exclude parties that win single-district elections. In some cases all parties are included in the distribution of *plurinominal* seats. The appointed and elected positions that comprise the basic administrative structure at the municipal level are laid down in each state's municipal code.

Each state in Mexico is governed by a legislature elected every three years and by an executive led by the governor, who is elected for a six-year term. The governor presides over the state legislature; with his six-year term, he works with two different bodies. In the election for municipal government, citizens vote for a mayor of a particular party and for a slate of *regidores* (aldermen). Thus, although they vote only for the mayor, at the same time they also vote for a team of council members. In some cases the allotment of council members is based on the principle of proportional representation for the vote after the election; in others, the winning party takes all of the council seats, except for those allocated on a nominal representation basis to the other parties that participated in the election (that is, one seat for each party).[19]

In addition to the elected *regidores* from his or her own party, the mayor also appoints the officials who hold the most influential positions in local government, such as the treasurer, the secretary, and, in some cases, the director of public works. Together, all appointed and elected officials make up the *ayuntamiento*, or city hall. In conjunction with the mayor, these appointed officers constitute the executive power of the *ayuntamiento*, while elected council members constitute, in effect, the legislative branch. Along with the mayor, the *regidores* have voting rights and must meet regularly in order to approve policy and budgets; other appointed officials also attend, but they do not have a vote. These council meetings form the *cabildo*, which is the highest authority of the local government. Given that the *cabildo* is made up of elected officials, its purpose is to act as a balance against the mayor and his appointed officers, so not unnaturally he seeks to ensure that he has a working majority in his council. This majority usually tends to be the case, since the composition of the *cabildo* follows closely the proportion of the victory of the mayor's party. Therefore, although they will be in the minority, opposition parties may usually expect to be represented.

The composition and structure of municipal government clearly suggest that although opposition members have gained access to local councils, their impact on policymaking is minimized by the large majority that is provided to the party of the incoming mayor.[20] But however minimal their impact on setting the policy agenda may be, the point that must be underscored is that their mere presence has brought a new style of governance to the local level. City hall meetings have increasingly become arenas of intense debate, where council members argue vehemently not only along party lines but also along those formed by factions within the same party. Not infrequently a *regidor* may turn against the mayor or be critical of a policy area, and in these circumstances local government may become extremely divisive and conflictual. As a result, even the PRI has been forced to embrace this new form of local governance. No longer can PRI candidates expect to win an election with an unquestioned majority; they must also learn to negotiate their policies with their council members. It is in this regard, perhaps, where the most significant impact of opposition parties can be seen: while minority parties may still encounter difficulties in having their victories recognized, by offering a real option to the electorate they have forced the PRI and prospective PRIísta governments to be more democratic and to govern better.

This case is particularly true in certain areas of the country where local politics have developed along party preferences. For example, the northern part, including the relatively progressive states of Baja California Norte and Chihuahua, has clearly come to reflect a loyalty to the PAN. The northern industrial state of Nuevo León, though under a PRIísta governor, also has a large PANista constituency, including the municipalities of Monterrey and San Pedro Garza García, two of the wealthiest areas in Mexico. The same PANista pattern applies to the opposite tip of the country, Yucatán, which is also a PANista stronghold. The PRD holds as its most important regional base the state of Michoacán, the home of Cuauhtémoc Cárdenas, where he served as a former PRIísta governor from 1980 to 1986. His appeal in that state was clearly reflected in the 64 percent share of the presidential vote that the Frente received in the 1988 election, in addition to both federal Senate seats and 11 of the 13 *uninominal* seats in the national Congress (Bruhn and Yanner, 1995). However, this appeal seems to be sliding, partly because the enthusiasm of 1988 has worn down, partly because the PRI has made major efforts to win back the vote, and partly because the PAN has gained increased strength. Thus, while in the 1989 election the PRD won fifty-two municipalities, that number was halved in 1992. In 1995 the PAN came in second for the governorship, behind the winning PRI, but won the mayorship of the capital city, Morelia, for the first time. Mexico City presents a continuing and fascinating dilemma for the PRI: how to win back its appeal, after it massively voted for the PRD in the 1988 presidential election. Moreover, after the reforms addressing the issue of elected government in the Federal District, and the vociferous opposition to how the provisions addressed perpetuated the city's nondemocratic form of government, it is evident that the PRI has not regained its strength.[21] This issue is critical for the city that is the central seat of the government.

Thus, while clearly regional loyalites along party lines have developed, the country's capital has not served as a role model. By and large, local elections in Mexico appear to follow either regional partisan loyalties or the appeal of a particular candidate, as the cases of Nava in San Luis Potosí, Ruffo in Baja California, Barrio in Chihuahua, and Fox in Guanajuato clearly demonstrate. In every election held in the early 1990s, including the 1994 presidential election, each party has gained or lost votes based primarily on its own record. Contrary to earlier electoral patterns in Mexico, where the PRI could be expected to sweep the board in federal, state, and local contests, individual regions are now voting along patterns that in no way mirror federal results.

Conclusion

All of the processes described above—political liberalization, growing pluralism, greater civic involvement—indicate an important opening in the political space, but they do not necessarily add up to democratization. The period from 1968 onward has been characterized by many authors as one of "transition," as Mexico moves away from the traditional political and social order built around Revolutionary principles (Aguilar Camín and Meyer, 1993; Barros et al., 1991). But does this political transition also constitute a democratic one? While recognizing that it is not feasible to respond definitively to this question, the progress in opening the electoral space to recognize more victories of the opposition at the state and local levels seems to indicate that at least as far as local elections and access to political office are concerned, Mexico may well be on its way to consolidating its democratization. The test, naturally, will be whether this urban electoral pattern can be transferred to the national level. As some analysts have argued, the consolidation of democracy in Mexico will only become evident when a candidate of the opposition wins the presidency of the Republic. That seems, indeed, a rather ambitious yardstick by which to measure a democratic transition.

Since the early 1980s, often in a hesitant manner, successive presidential administrations have increasingly experimented with reallocating power in an effort to sustain the political base of the PRI and as a measure to regain the government's credibility, not the least by giving more autonomy to local governments and by recognizing election victories of opposition parties at both the state and local levels. But at least in its early stages, the reallocation of power in no way signaled an intention to loosen central control.

Indeed, as Bailey (1994) argues, instead of a decentralization process Mexico has witnessed an increase in centralized power and presidential control, particularly under the Salinas administration. Smith (1979) emphasized earlier that the question was one of limited pluralism and the need to extend this limitation, but without sacrificing control over legitimacy. Under Zedillo, however, the situation may take a different twist. Having assumed the presidency in the midst of the worst political and economic crisis that the country has experienced in modern times, Zedillo has had little choice but to effectively make an effort to redistribute political power. Paradoxically, by doing so, he has weakened the institution of the presidency and loosened the grip from the center.

However, even Zedillo's open and conciliatory attitude conceals a reluctance to let go. The process of political opening seems to have stopped short of allowing for the possibility of the PRI's losing overall control at the federal level. Several factors suggest that the political space for democratic opening is more fertile in the outer reaches of the country; in both Baja California and Chihuahua, and in other areas far enough away from Mexico City, such as Yucatán and even Monterrey and Guadalajara, the government seems prepared to concede territory to the PAN. But not the center; that remains, undisputedly, under the firm control of the PRI. These decisions not only reinforce centralization but also pose major question marks over the entire democratization process. While Zedillo has made a commitment to separate the PRI from the government and has refrained from dictating party politics, the decision to respect electoral results has unequivocally come from the president's office. Evidently, there are major problems associated with this construction of a plurality from above. It demonstrates that presidentialism and centralism continue to be entrenched within the political system and, ultimately, that the consolidation of democracy will advance only as far as the president is prepared to let it go.

While recognizing, therefore, that the electoral process and the conduct of elections have changed in Mexico, there are several important lessons to be learned. The first is that electoral victories are most likely to occur where the PRI grossly miscalculates the strength of the opposition and the level of discontent with the government and the PRI. The second is that winning will continue to be more likely in those places where a political space has been created in which the strength of opposition parties may be openly expressed and registered. The third lesson must be learned by opposition parties themselves. As the political process opens up and a new political culture emerges, they must also learn to mature politically; and they must learn as well to accept electoral results that do not declare them the victors. It does the transition to democracy no good if electoral results have to be reversed in order to accommodate the demands of a political party that is a sore loser and is prepared to show its discontent in often dangerous ways. In this context, it becomes most difficult to assert unequivocally that democratization has been consolidated in Mexico. But at least it has started. As demonstrated in this chapter, urban elections contribute to democratization by offering the voting public a genuine choice and by obliging all political parties in power to govern better.

Postscript

As this book is being prepared to go to press, there has been an important midterm election in Mexico that requires brief discussion. At stake in the July 1997 election were the entire national Congress, six governorships, and, for the first time ever, the post for governor of the Departamento del Distrito Federal (DDF) in Mexico City (this position was formerly a presidential appointee called the *regente*). As is widely known, since the electoral results have been amply reported and discussed in the national and international media, the ruling PRI suffered the greatest loss since the party was created in 1929. The 1997 elections have been widely hailed as "historic" and cited as evidence of Mexico's transition to democracy.

For the first time in seventy years of almost unchallenged one-party rule, the PRI has lost its majority in Congress. In the congressional vote the PRI won 39 percent, the PAN 27 percent, the PRD 26 percent, and the remainder distributed among several small parties, of which the most significant has become the Partido Verde Ecologista Mexicano (PVEM, the Green Party). In terms of seats, of the total 500 (300 allocated on the basis of direct election and 200 on the basis of proportional representation), the breakdown converts to 239 for the PRI, 125 for the PRD, 122 for the PAN, 8 to the PVEM, and 6 to the PT. There are no longer any independents. In addition, in the Representative Assembly of the Federal District, the PRD swept the board, winning 38 of the 40 direct election seats (the PAN took the other 2). Therefore, they will have a large majority in the 60-seat Assembly. Indeed, within the metropolitan area as a whole, the PRD dominated in almost all congressional district and Assembly elections.

This loss of overall majority in the Congress is certainly a huge blow to the PRI. What will be most interesting to observe in the coming months and years will be the building of coalitions among the PRIísta deputies and those of the PAN and the PRD. As has been the case in the past, when it was necessary, the more likely alliances of the PRI will be with the PAN on economic issues and with the PRD on social and political issues. The change, nonetheless, will be that these alliances will more likely than not be forged on the basis of issues, rather than on political and personal loyalties.

On the state level of government there also have been some notable outcomes. Of the six governorships that were up for grabs, the PAN won two outright and the PRI won four. Only in one state, Campeche, was there any significant period of postelectoral contestation, with the PRD candidate (a former PRI senator who left the party in December 1996) contesting the PRI's 8-percentage point victory. It is important to note that PAN's two victories occurred in critically important states, Nuevo León and Querétaro, and that this extends considerably its governing domain. The PAN now governs six states, not to mention countless municipalities. But out of these six states, two are the wealthiest and most developed states in the country, Nuevo León and Jalisco. In addition, the vast majority of state capitals are now in the hands of the PAN. Even in those states where the PRI won the governorship in 1997, the capital city often went to the PAN, as did a large number of municipalities. The PRD also managed to capture an important number of municipalities, but at the local level no election was more important than that of Mexico City. With the stunning victory of Cuauhtémoc Cárdenas, the PRD has placed itself in a key position to continue being a major player in electoral contests to come, and most certainly in the presidential election in the year 2000. Overall, after these elections, just over 50 percent of the total population is governed by the opposition.

The question more frequently asked in the aftermath of the election is: Who won? In this case, there were many victors. First, the Mexican people were the most victorious. The 1997 election demonstrated unequivocally that the Mexican public has effectively reached a stage of maturity in its newly developed political culture, one that is in tune with a truly democratic and participatory system. The people know that their vote counts; electoral procedures and institutions are considered as respectable and trustworthy; and political parties have learned that all of them must now play by the rules. Second, among the political parties the PRD emerged as a suprisingly strong party, both in terms of its landslide victory in Mexico City and in winning a slightly larger number of seats in Congress than the PAN, which had traditionally come in second (in congressional and all other major elections). Third, in some ways the PRI is also a winner in two important respects. First, because this election will force the PRI to recast and reinvent itself in a way that is reflective of this new political culture and this new electoral scenario. The PRI must now learn to behave and proceed as a political party if it is to continue to win any elections in the future. And, second, because even though the PRI suffered important losses, it still holds a majority grip on the government: 25 states, the largest majority in Congress, and, most important, the federal executive. In no respect should the PRI be discarded as the loser of the 1997 election; if anything, it will most likely demonstrate, once again, its resilience and resurface reformed and invigorated in electoral contests to come.

References

Aguilar Camín, Héctor, and Lorenzo Meyer. 1993. *In the Shadow of the Mexican Revolution: Contemporary Mexican History, 1910–1989.* Austin: University of Texas Press.

Aziz Nassif, Alberto. 1987. *Prácticas electorales y democracia en Chihuahua.* Mexico: Centro de Investigación y Estudios Superiores de Antropología Social, Cuadernos de la Casa Chata, No. 151.

Bailey, John. 1994. "Centralism and Political Change in Mexico: The Case of National Solidarity." In Wayne Cornelius, Ann L. Craig, and Jonathan Fox, eds., *Transforming State-Society Relations in Mexico: The National Solidarity Strategy,* pp. 97–119. La Jolla: University of California at San Diego, Center for U.S.-Mexican Studies.

Barberán, José, et al. 1988. *Radiografía del fraude: Análisis de los datos oficiales del 6 de Julio.* Mexico: Nuestro Tiempo.

Barros Horcasitas, José Luis, Javier Hurtado, and Germán Pérez Fernández, eds. 1991. *Transición a la democracia y reforma del estado en México.* Mexico: Miguel Angel Porrúa/FLACSO.

Bartra, Roger, et al. 1975. *Caciquismo y poder político en el México rural.* Mexico: Siglo XXI.

Bezdek, Robert. 1995. "Democratic Changes in an Authoritarian System: *Navismo* and Opposition Development in San Luis Potosí." In Victoria E. Rodríguez and Peter M. Ward, eds., *Opposition Government in Mexico*, 31–61. Albuquerque: University of New Mexico Press.

Bruhn, Kathleen, and Keith Yanner. 1995. "Governing under the Enemy: The PRD in Michoacán." In Victoria E. Rodríguez and Peter M. Ward, eds., *Opposition Government in Mexico*, 113–31. Albuquerque: University of New Mexico Press.

Camp, Roderic. 1993. *Politics in Mexico*. New York: Oxford University Press.

Cockroft, James. 1982. *Mexico: Class Formation, Capital Accumulation, and the State*. New York: Monthly Review Press.

Cook, Maria Lorena. 1990. "Organizing Opposition in the Teachers' Movement in Oaxaca." In Joe Foweraker and Ann Craig, eds., *Popular Movements and Political Change in Mexico*, 199–212. Boulder, CO: Lynne Rienner Publishers.

Cornelius, Wayne A. 1996. *Mexican Politics in Transition: The Breakdown of a One-Party Dominant Regime*. La Jolla: University of California at San Diego, Center for U.S.-Mexican Studies, Monograph Series No. 41

———, Judith Gentleman, and Peter Smith, eds. 1989. *Mexico's Alternative Political Futures*. La Jolla: University of California at San Diego, Center for U.S.-Mexican Studies, Monograph Series No. 30.

———, and Ann L. Craig. 1991. *The Mexican Political System in Transition*. La Jolla: University of California at San Diego, Center for U.S.-Mexican Studies, Monograph Series No. 35.

———, Ann L. Craig, and Jonathan Fox, eds. 1994. *Transforming State-Society Relations in Mexico: The National Solidarity Strategy*. La Jolla: University of California at San Diego, Center for U.S.-Mexican Studies, U.S.-Mexico Contemporary Perspectives Series No. 6.

Craig, Ann L., and Wayne A. Cornelius. 1995. "Houses Divided: Parties and Political Reform in Mexico." In Scott Mainwaring and Timothy R. Scully, eds., *Building Democratic Institutions: Party Systems in Latin America*, pp. 249–84. Stanford, CA: Stanford University Press.

Dresser, Denise. 1991. "Neopopulist Solutions to Neoliberal Problems: Mexico's National Solidarity Program." La Jolla: University of California at San Diego, Center for U.S.-Mexican Studies, Current Issues Brief No. 3

Favela, Alejandro. 1992. "El gobierno salinista y la reforma del estado." *Estudios Políticos* 3:9, pp. 55–73.

Foweraker, Joe. 1993. *Popular Mobilization in Mexico: The Teachers' Movement, 1977–1987*. New York: Cambridge University Press.

————. 1995. *Theorizing Social Movements*. London: Pluto Press.

————, and Ann L. Craig, eds. 1990. *Popular Movements and Political Change in Mexico*. Boulder, CO: Lynne Rienner Publishers.

González Casanova, Pablo. 1970. *Democracy in Mexico*. New York: Oxford University Press.

Guadarrama, Graciela. 1987. "Entrepreneurs and Politics: Businessmen in Electoral Contest in Sonora and Nuevo León, July 1985." In A. Alvarado Mendoza, ed., *Electoral Patterns and Perspectives in Mexico*, pp. 81–110. La Jolla: University of California at San Diego, Center for U.S.-Mexican Studies.

Guillén López, Tonatiuh. 1993. *Baja California, 1989–92: Balance de la transición democrática*. Tijuana: El Colegio de la Frontera Norte.

Hansen, Roger D. 1974. *The Politics of Mexican Development*. Baltimore, MD: Johns Hopkins University Press.

Harvey, Neil. 1989. "Personal Networks and Strategic Choices in the Formation of an Independent Peasant Organization: The OCEZ of Chiapas, Mexico." *Bulletin of Latin American Research* 7:2, pp. 299–312.

Hernández, Luis, and Jonathan Fox. 1994. "La difícil democracia de México: Las ONG y el gobierno local." In Charles A. Reilly, ed., *Nuevas políticas urbanas: Las ONG y los gobiernos municipales en la democratización latinoamericana*, pp. 211–46. Arlington, VA: Interamerican Foundation.

Klessner, Joseph. 1991. "Challenges for Mexico's Opposition in the Coming *Sexenio*." In E. Butler and J. Bustamente, eds., *Sucesión presidencial*, pp. 149–75. Boulder, CO: Westview Press.

Mabry, Donald J. 1974. "Mexico's Party Deputy System: The First Decade." *World Affairs* 16, no. 2:221–33.

Middlebrook, Kevin. 1986. "Political Liberalization in an Authoritarian Regime: The Case of Mexico." In Paul W. Drake and E. Silva, eds., *Elections and Democratization in Latin America, 1980–1985*, pp. 73–104. La Jolla: Joint publication of the Center for Iberian and Latin American Studies, Center for U.S.-Mexican Studies, and Institute of the Americas, University of California at San Diego.

————, ed. 1991. *Unions, Workers, and the State in Mexico*. La Jolla: University of California at San Diego, Center for U.S.-Mexican Studies.

Moguel, Julio. 1994. "Poder local y alternativas de desarrollo: La experiencia del movimiento urbano popular en el norte de México." In Charles A. Reilly, ed., *Nuevas políticas urbanas: Las ONG y los gobiernos municipales en la democratización latinoamericana*, pp. 247–68. Arlington, VA: Interamerican Foundation.

Molinar Horcasitas, Juan. 1986. "The Mexican Electoral System: Continuity by Change." In Paul W. Drake and E. Silva, eds., *Elections and Democratization in Latin America, 1980–1985*, pp. 105–14.

La Jolla: Joint publication of the Center for Iberian and Latin American Studies, Center for U.S.-Mexican Studies, and Institute of the Americas, University of California at San Diego.

————. 1991. *El tiempo de la legitimidad: Elecciones, autoritarismo y democracia en México.* Mexico: Cal y Arena.

Montaño, Jorge. 1976. *Los pobres de la ciudad de México en los asentamientos espontáneos.* Mexico: Siglo XXI.

Paas, D., et al., eds. 1991. *Municipio y democracia: Participación de las organizaciones de la sociedad civil en la política municipal.* Mexico: Fundación Friedrich Naumann.

Ramírez Saiz, Juan Manuel. 1986. *El movimiento popular en México.* Mexico: Siglo XXI.

Rodríguez, Victoria E. 1992. "Mexico's Decentralization in the 1980s: Promises, Promises, Promises. . . ." In Arthur Morris and Stella Lowder, eds., *Decentralization in Latin America,* pp. 127–43. New York: Praeger.

————. 1993. "The Politics of Decentralization in Mexico: From *Municipio Libre* to *Solidaridad.*" *Bulletin of Latin American Research* 12:2, pp. 133–45.

————. 1997. *Decentralization in Mexico: From Reforma Municipal to Solidaridad to Nuevo Federalismo.* Boulder, CO: Westview Press.

————, and Peter M. Ward. 1992. *Policymaking, Politics, and Urban Governance in Chihuahua: The Experience of Recent Panista Governments.* Austin, TX: Lyndon B. Johnson School of Public Affairs, University of Texas at Austin.

———— and ————. 1994. *Political Change in Baja California: Democracy in the Making?* La Jolla: University of California at San Diego, Center for U.S.-Mexican Studies, Monograph Series No. 40.

———— and ————. 1994a. "Disentangling the PRI from the Government in Mexico." *Mexican Studies/Estudios Mexicanos* 10:1, pp. 163–86.

———— and ————, eds. 1995. *Opposition Government in Mexico.* Albuquerque: University of New Mexico Press.

———— and ————. 1996. "The New PRI: Recasting Its Identity." In Rob Aitken et al., eds., *Dismantling the Mexican State,* 92–112. London: Macmillan.

Schers, D. 1972. "The Popular Sector of the PRI in Mexico." Ph.D. diss. University of New Mexico, Department of Political Science.

SPP (Secretaría de Programación y Presupuesto). 1988. *México: Desarrollo regional y descentralización de la vida nacional: Experiencias de cambio estructural 1983–1988.* México.

Smith, Peter H. 1979. *Labyrinths of Power: Political Recruitment in Twentieth-Century Mexico.* Princeton, NJ: Princeton University Press.

Ward, Peter. 1986. *Welfare Politics in Mexico: Papering over the Cracks.* London: Allen and Unwin.

————. 1990. *Mexico City: The Production and Reproduction of an Urban Environment*. London: Belhaven Press.

————. 1993. "Social Policy and Political Opening in Mexico." *Journal of Latin American Research* 25:613–28.

————, et al. 1994. *Memoria of the Bi-National Conference: Mexico's Electoral Aftermath and Political Future*. Austin: Mexican Center of the Institute of Latin American Studies, University of Texas at Austin.

Notes

1. There have also been occasions for suspecting the use of fraud to prevent opposition candidates from winning office. Specifically, many Mexicans believe that the opposition candidate won the presidential election in 1929, 1940, and 1988 (Camp, 1993:62). Similarly, others have argued that at various times in the recent past, opposition candidates were denied the governorships of the states of San Luis Potosí, Chihuahua, and Baja California Norte (see Bezdek, 1995; Aziz, 1987; Guillén López, 1993). There are many more examples when it comes to municipal elections.

2. Cuauhtémoc Cárdenas, a former governor of Michoacán, is the son of President Lázaro Cárdenas (1934–1940), who was enormously popular. Indeed, it has been argued that one of the major reasons why Cárdenas did so well in 1988 was name recognition, especially in the rural areas of the country where his father is still a beloved figure. Clouthier was a well-known businessman from the state of Sinaloa who provided the PAN with charismatic leadership. Eventually the Frente disappeared and served as the foundation for the creation of a new political party, the Partido de la Revolución Democrática (PRD).

3. The latter two organizations overlap somewhat; each incorporates a host of NGOs whose concern is to develop and protect citizens' rights, safeguard the vote, and encourage awareness of political and electoral rights.

4. The most important achievement of the reforms of the 1960s was the establishment of a system of proportional representation. The 1963 reforms allowed for the representation of parties obtaining a minimum of 2.5 percent of the national vote. Five congressional seats were to be assigned for the first 2.5 percent of the national vote obtained, and an additional seat for every additional half percent obtained. However, a 20-seat cap was placed upon the opposition's representation, which demonstrates the limited reach of the reform. In fact, seats were also given to the PARM and the PPS (both parties closely associated with the PRI), even though neither one of them obtained the required 2.5 percent of the national vote. This system effectively inflated the congressional representation of these parties vis-à-vis their electoral proportions and, more significantly, gave the PRI an unquestioned majority (Molinar, 1986; Klessner, 1991; Favela, 1992). The constrained nature of the reform was especially relevant for the PAN; although it continued to increase its vote at the national level, the 20-seat cap on any non-PRI party kept its representation within the Chamber of Deputies to below 10 percent (Marbry, 1974). The 1972 re-

forms lowered the total vote threshold from 2.5 to 1.5 percent, and the 20-seat cap for opposition parties was raised to 25.

5. For a thorough description of the major changes in Mexico's electoral laws since 1918, see the Appendix in Craig and Cornelius (1995:290–97).

6. In Mexico, as in the United States, federal legislative power is divided into two separate houses, the Chamber of Deputies and the Senate. Elections are held at staggered intervals for all three levels of government: federal, state, and municipal. State and federal representatives (*diputados*) serve for three-year terms, and senators for six.

7. The principle of *representación mayoritaria* (majority representation) formed the basis for the election of representatives to the so-called *uninominal* offices, such as the president, governors, senators, the three hundred federal deputies, and a number of state deputies that is determined in each state's constitution. In some municipalities the same principle applies to the election of the mayor, *síndicos* (trustees), and *regidores*. Proportional representation was designed to enable more members of the opposition to hold public office, thereby making possible the election of representatives to positions referred to as *plurinominales*, comprising one hundred federal deputies, a number of state deputies (again determined by each state's constitution), and a proportion of *regidores* in each *ayuntamiento*. In 1988 there were 1,314 *regidores* from opposition parties sitting on local governments (SPP, 1988).

8. The reforms of 1977 meant that opposition parties now had 100 of the then 400 seats. These *plurinominal* seats were to be distributed on the basis of proportional representation to the qualifying minority parties. The remaining 75 percent of the congressional seats would be determined on the basis of the official electoral returns from the single-member districts, the *uninominal* seats. A second outcome of the reforms was to facilitate the formation of new (but small) parties at the regional or national level, thus potentially fragmenting further the political opposition.

9. The series of reforms for increased representation of the opposition described above clearly illustrate that the PRI has not been willing to make changes that would imply its losing overall control of the electoral process. It had a majority on both the Electoral Commission and the Electoral Tribunal.

10. For an in-depth analysis of the 1994 election from various perspectives, see Ward et al. (1994).

11. The PRI wanted a proviso that the opposition had to receive "a respectable proportion of the vote" and suggested a threshold of 25 percent, but it will eventually be reduced to 0 percent (that is, no threshold). Tactically this is very clever, since it reduces the likelihood of PAN-PRD coalition candidates. Each party will want to compete for the fourth senatorial spot. Even where the PRI loses the direct elections in a state, it could always expect to come in second, and thus it is almost certain to enjoy a large majority in the Senate.

12. No party now will be able to obtain more than 63 percent of the seats in the Congress. Therefore, any party wishing to propose constitutional changes will have to build an agreement with another party.

13. This latter is obviously aimed at the PRI, whose party symbol uses the same colors as the national flag, and at government programs like

Solidarity, which also incorporate them into their logo. For more on this conflation of PRI-government nationalism see Rodríguez and Ward (1994a). It seems likely that in the long term this will also be conceded by the PRI, but only after it has been able to educate and cajole its traditional followership into recognizing a new set of colors. Obviously this task was not one that it felt able to undertake within twelve months.

14. The extension of proportional representation to the state and municipal levels came as part of the 1977 and 1986 reforms. Individual state-level formulas, however, vary from state to state. Each state legislature determines the specific distribution of party representation in state and municipal government. These formulas generally set minimum percentages of the popular vote that must be obtained and may exclude parties that win single-district elections. In some cases all parties are included in the distribution of proportional (*plurinominal*) seats.

15. Although all these negotiations are secret, the general interpretation is that the PRI and the PAN have reached a modus operandi whereby the PRI is willing to let electoral results stand in some places in exchange for social tranquility in other elections and in other places. Only in this way can one explain cases that seem rather bizarre. In the 1993 election in Baja California Sur, for example, the PAN won a majority in the congressional elections and took several of the leading cities, yet lost the governorship. The losing gubernatorial candidate, outraged, declared openly that his defeat had been traded by the PAN party leadership against victories elsewhere; thus, he affirmed, the PAN was allowed to keep the congressional seats and the municipal governments in exchange for the PRI's keeping the governorship.

16. While the PRI and the government have evidently found a more or less workable arrangement with the PAN, this is not the case with the PRD. The PAN has been allowed to win outright numerous municipalities and even four states, whereas the PRD has had to fight hard for recognition at the local level. Also, while the municipalities governed by the PAN have not, as the norm, been starved of the resources coming from the federal and state PRIísta governments, this has not been the case with PRD municipalities (Bruhn and Yanner, 1995). For a detailed analysis of how and why this interparty pattern of intergovernmental relations has functioned in various localities, see Rodríguez and Ward (1992, 1994, 1995).

17. A third state, Guanajuato, was also governed by a PANista, but he was an interim governor placed in office by President Salinas. Carlos Medina Plascencia was not even a candidate in the 1991 gubernatorial elections in that state; he came into the position only because the PRI candidate's electoral conduct had been discredited and the president wished to make a conciliatory gesture to the PAN. Even among PANistas his governorship was seen as lacking in legitimacy. Elsewhere, doubts over the conduct of elections or postelection civil disturbance obliged President Salinas to remove or withdraw successful candidates, in spite of the fact that under state constitutions, theoretically, only the local congress can remove a governor and designate an interim in his stead. In this way the PAN was given its third governorship, Guanajuato. In other notable cases, such as Tabasco, San Luis Potosí, and Michoacán, interim PRI governors were installed.

18. As an article in the *Dallas Morning News* covering the 1992 election put it, "It is as important, or more important, to have 50,000 people in the streets the day after the election as it is to have 300,000 voters the day of the election" (2/11/1992).

19. Thus, in some municipalities where the PRI will have no electoral opposition, all the *regidores* will be from the PRI. If other parties compete in the election, they will receive at least one council seat. By and large, these *regidores* will be charged with the less important assignments (for example, oversight of sports and recreation, as opposed to finances or public works).

20. For a detailed account of municipal-level government structures, see Rodríguez (1996). For an analysis of a variety of fascinating state and municipal government experiences where members from the so-called New PRI and from opposing parties govern, see Rodríguez and Ward (1992, 1994, 1995, 1996).

21. For a detailed analysis of voting patterns in Mexico City in 1988, and for the city's "government without democracy," see Ward (1990).

8

Urban Elections in Peru, 1980–1995

Henry A. Dietz

The analysis of local urban elections offers a chance to address several questions about electoral behavior and political party systems that may be obscured on the national level or in presidential elections. For example, what sorts of relationships can develop between urban social movements and electoral politics? Under what conditions (if any) does a city's urban informal sector engage in bloc voting? Do electoral results reflect social class differences? When and how and why will individuals in a large primate capital vote differently from their counterparts in provincial cities? And can a minor party develop support in one city and not another, or in several cities but not in the countryside?

Since 1980, Peru and its capital of Lima have witnessed some of Latin America's most difficult and tumultuous economic, social, and political times, including the emergence of the Sendero Luminoso (Shining Path) as the Western Hemisphere's most brutal insurgency, the collapse of the country's economy in the late 1980s, the seeming inability of any party or candidate to govern successfully, and the emergence of a highly unpredictable electoral situation and highly fluid party system. But Peru and Lima have also seen three presidential and six municipal open, clean, and contested elections take place since 1980, a fact with no precedent in Peru since its independence in the 1820s.

Historically, local elections and anything approaching home rule in Peru have either been infrequent or missing altogether. For most of its colonial and postcolonial history—that is, since 1824—local mayors and other officials were all appointed by the viceroy or by the president. Peru experimented briefly with electing mayors in the World War I period, but this trial was soon aborted, and the nation had to wait until the 1960s before local elections became an accepted element in the electoral landscape. All elections were suspended from 1968 to 1978, when the military ruled, but since that time local elections have been held regularly and have been vigorously contested by political parties and candidates representing all shades of the ideological spectrum.

The Background and Context of Local Elections

National politics and elections reflect and are reflected by what happens in Lima, which is a classic Latin American primate city. Not only is it some eight times larger than the country's second largest city (Arequipa), but Lima in the mid-1990s also contains about 30 percent of Peru's total population and about one-third of its voters and has for centuries been its economic, social, political, and cultural capital. But since World War II, Lima has gradually shed its image as a white European enclave. Hundreds of thousands of rural-origin migrants have moved to Lima so that, as the end of the twentieth century approaches, the city for the first time in its history can be said to be "Peruvian" in that its populace has finally come to represent the nation as a whole (Matos Mar, 1986). Peru's elites still live in Lima, and while they still play a dominant role, this "peruvianization" has come to mean that traditional parties and elites can no longer dictate who runs for office or who wins in the capital. Indeed, the results in Lima of the presidential elections of 1990 and the municipal races of 1989 and 1993 indicate that a true sea change may have occurred in Peru and especially in Lima, and that through the weight of sheer numbers, Lima *chicha* (that is, mestizo, informal, working-class migrant-origin Lima) has finally managed, in still inchoate and unformed ways, to throw off the domination of Lima *pituco* (formal, Western, white, wealthy Lima) and to elect, if not one of its own, at least someone not controlled by the city's ruling elites.

Lima's physical and demographic expansion has been paralleled by similar migrant-driven growth in the provincial cities. In 1940, Lima had a population of about 600,000, about one-tenth of the entire country. Peru was then still very much a rural country, with only one-third of its populace living in urban areas. By 1980, when civilian rule was restored, these proportions were reversed: two-thirds of the country lived in urban settings, and Lima had grown to close to six million people, which was Peru's total population in 1940.

Especially during the 1960s, Lima and its provincial counterparts grew because these rural-origin migrants came looking for employment, education, and opportunity that they could not find in the countryside. The repercussions of such rapid and massive growth included most crucially the creation of a labor force that was unprepared for skilled urban work and that overwhelmed the local economy's ability either to employ or house them. The result was the creation of what came to be, by the 1980s, arguably the world's largest (in terms of national population) and perhaps best studied urban informal sector (de Soto, 1987; Carbonetto et al., 1988). The contribution of the *informales* to Lima's manufacturing, commercial, transportation, and housing sectors has for decades been crucial to the city's survival and growth. The most obvious facet of informal housing has been the creation and growth of low-income districts composed almost entirely of self-help dwellings. These *barriadas* or *pueblos jóvenes* grew from a 1961 population of about 110,000 people, or about 10 percent of Lima's total, to close to three million, or about one-half of Lima's six million in 1980.

All of these changes manifested themselves politically first during the period from 1956 to 1966, when national elections were held, and then again much more noticeably (due to the size of the informal sector) beginning in 1980, when a reformist but ultimately failed military government stepped down and allowed the restoration of civilian rule. The new constitution that had been approved in 1979 lowered the voting age to eighteen and allowed illiterates to vote. It also mandated nonconcurrent nationwide local elections for mayors and city councils to be held every three years in November, starting in 1980. The first such elections came six months after presidential and legislative elections in May 1980 and were held thereafter as scheduled in 1983, 1986, and 1989. In 1992, however, and as discussed later, they were postponed until January 1993.

Formally, all Peruvian citizens eighteen years of age or older, literate or not, are obliged to vote. In 1980, when they first received the franchise, illiterates accounted for about 13 percent of the total popular vote. If a citizen does not vote, a fine is imposed; and, more important, aggravating bureaucratic paperwork is required to restore an individual's *carnet electoral*. Yet, the abstention rate is still relatively high, especially in rural areas and especially in municipal elections. For instance, abstention reached about 16 percent in the 1978 Constituent Assembly elections, and 19 percent in the 1980 presidential race, but it rose to 30 percent in the local elections of the same year. Throughout the decade of the 1980s abstention in presidential races generally ran between 10 and 20 percent, but it averaged well over 20 percent on the municipal level (Pareja Pflucker and Gatti Murriel, 1993; Tuesta, 1994).

Other rules of the game have importance, both for being elected as well as governing. For example, and as opposed to the president, who is constitutionally required to win a simple majority or to compete in a run-off election, mayors are elected by a simple plurality. Thus, parties in local races do not necessarily attempt to create coalitions quite as readily as they might under simple majority rules. The division of seats for city councils is done through straight proportional representation, but with one unique twist: the winning party automatically occupies the smallest simple majority of council seats, while the remaining parties divide the rest proportionally to the popular vote that they receive.[1]

The several meanings attached to the delimiter "Lima" should also be made clear. Lima refers to one of eleven regions[2] and one of twenty-four departments (states) of the entire country. It is also the name given to one province (county) of the department of Lima, as well as a name given to one district of that province. The department of Lima includes considerable rural territory as well as the city itself, and it is composed of ten provinces plus Callao, Lima's port city; the province of Lima is in turn composed (in 1995) of forty-three districts. The mayor of metropolitan Lima is simultaneously mayor of all of the city's districts as well as of the district of Lima (generally referred to as Cercado de Lima), but each of the remaining forty-two districts also elects its own mayor and city council by the same rules that govern the election of the city's mayor. Local mayors and city councils have traditionally had very little real power, especially in regard to taxation and other fiscal matters; the same is true for provincial and departmental authorities, although the creation of regions in the late 1980s was accompanied by much discussion of the need for local autonomy.

The following account discusses the municipal elections in Peru that occurred in 1980, 1983, 1986, 1989, 1992, and 1995. While results from the provinces are included and noted, Lima receives a good deal of attention, for two reasons. First, the Lima data are much more complete—that is, fully disaggregated to the provincial level—and much more reliable. Until recently the only data reported for municipal elections are departmental or, at best, provincial. Second, given Lima's overwhelming hegemony, what goes on there has much more of an impact on the nation than what happens in any other city. Nevertheless, provincial results identify particular party strengths and weaknesses and also are discussed.

Political Parties in Peru and Lima, 1980–1995

Across its history, Peru has never had well-institutionalized parties such as, for example, the Liberals and Conservatives in Colombia or Acción Democrática in Venezuela. Rather, most parties in reality have been largely personalist movements that have depended more on the strength of their leaders than on their ideological coherence or their institutional strength and integrity. In addition, many parties and movements (especially on the left) have been highly fluid, frequently splintering and coalescing due to personality differences and struggles for power. Given these tendencies, it is remarkable that the same four major political parties dominated Peruvian politics on both the national and local levels throughout the 1980s. Even so, these four parties all experienced difficulties of various descriptions by the beginning of the 1990s.

The left. Peru has had a formal leftist party for decades (the Peruvian Communist Party goes back to the 1930s), but it was not until the Constituent Assembly elections in 1978 that the left showed any electoral strength. A coalition of leftist movements took slightly less than one-third of the seats in the Assembly, leading its proponents to announce the arrival of leftist strength nationally. But the coalition collapsed shortly thereafter; five separate candidates combined took less than 15 percent of the popular vote in the 1980 presidential elections. This defeat forced the left into a coalition called IU (Izquierda Unida, or United Left) under the leadership of Alfonso Barrantes. Six months later, Barrantes showed some strength in Lima as IU's mayoral candidate; and three years later, in 1983, he won the race outright. IU district-level candidates in Lima also won all of their races in the city's *barrios populares* (lower-class districts). But 1983 was IU's apogee. Barrantes ran as IU's presidential candidate in 1985 and was beaten by a 2:1 margin by APRA. He then ran for reelection in 1986 against an APRA candidate and lost by a slender margin. These losses reawakened all of IU's self-destructive tendencies of internal power struggles based on personalities and esoteric ideological arguments, and by 1990 the left took less than 5 percent of the popular presidential vote.

APRA. The oldest and best-organized (though not necessarily the most successful) of Peru's major parties has for decades been APRA (Alianza Popular Revolucionaria Americana, or American Popular Revolutionary Alliance), founded in 1924 by Victor Raúl Haya de la Torre. He was the party's presidential candidate several times, but Haya de la Torre and the party never won, largely because of a bitter enmity between it and the military, which more than once either outlawed APRA, annulled elections that it might have won (for instance, in 1962), or called out a coup prior to an election that it could have won (for instance, in 1968). In the 1978 constituent elections, however, the then aged Haya de la Torre was elected head of the Constituent Assembly and was able to guide a new constitution to approval. He died shortly thereafter, precipitating a power struggle within the party that lasted well into the early 1980s. Alan García emerged as the next generation of APRA leadership in time for the 1985 elections, which he won by a wide margin. Locally, APRA has historically had trouble in Lima; its strength regionally lies in Peru's north, where in cities such as Trujillo and states such as La Libertad and Lambayeque it has been unbeatable.

The APRA was from its founding until the 1950s Peru's radical, though non-Communist, party. Beginning in the 1950s, it became increasingly centrist and by the 1980s bore a strong ideological resemblance to West European social democratic parties. It has been notable for its strong internal cohesion, the fierce loyalty of its adherents, and its sometimes bitter "we-they" mentality.

AP. Acción Popular or AP (Popular Action) was founded in the 1950s by Fernando Belaúnde Terry, for whom it has been a vehicle ever since, a fact that is simultaneously its strength and its weakness. Belaúnde was twice elected president (1963–1968, when he was overthrown by a military coup, and 1980–1985); he ran both times as a moderate reformist who appealed to the urban and rural middle classes. Both terms of office were characterized by considerable personal popularity but relatively weak leadership, administrative inefficiency, and hints of scandal and corruption among those surrounding him. The AP represents the center-right in Peruvian politics; Belaúnde's economic policies have been mildly neoliberal in nature, and each of his terms has ended with worsening economic conditions. In 1990, AP formed a critical part of the FREDEMO alliance that supported Mario Vargas Llosa and that lost to Alberto Fujimori.

PPC. In 1966, Luis Bedoya Reyes, a well-liked former mayor of Lima, founded the PPC (Partido Popular Cristiano, or Popular Christian Party) both to serve as his own party and to represent the Peruvian business community. Bedoya has always been popular in Lima, especially in its upper-class districts. He ran for the presidency in both 1980 and 1985 but was never able to transfer his popularity to the provinces. In 1990, PPC was another key component of the FREDEMO alliance, but its electoral strength was confined to some upper-class districts in Lima.

For the decade of the 1990s, what is more noteworthy, perhaps, is the apparently successful reestablishment of electoral rule in Peru. From World War I to 1980 the country had only once (1945) seen an elected civilian president turn power over to an elected successor, a history that did not give grounds for optimism regarding democratic procedures in 1980. Yet since 1980 (and up until April 1992), all elections, presidential as well as local, went off as scheduled; all parties that wished to participate could do so (and did so); transfers of power to opposition parties occurred in each presidential and in most local contests; and at no time was there any effort by the military to disrupt or influence the electoral process. These are not trivial accomplishments in any country under the best of circumstances, and even less so in Peru during the 1980s, when economic and social difficulties of the most severe kind could have easily derailed elections and undermined the whole process.

Peru from 1987 through 1991 suffered through its worst economic crisis of the twentieth century: inflation reached 7500 percent in 1990, real income dropped dramatically, the gap between the wealthy and the poor widened, and poverty, both rural and urban, became more widespread than ever (Crabtree, 1992). Rates of communicable diseases and infant mortality rose to unprecedented levels. At the same time, the Shining Path began its campaign of terrorism in 1980. One of its principal goals was to subvert and delegitimize the whole electoral process (in which it refused to participate), which meant concerted attacks on candidates and the widespread intimidation of voters. Given such conditions, the ability of Peru and its citizenry to sustain electoral politics during the 1980s has been truly remarkable.

As Peru entered the 1990s, however, electoral democracy seemed threatened, ironically enough by one of its major beneficiaries. Fujimori, a complete political outsider who was elected by a substantial majority in a run-off election in 1990, seized power unconstitutionally in an *autogolpe* (literally a "self-coup") in April 1992. In so doing, he dismissed the Congress, purged the judicial system, suspended constitutional guarantees, and ordered the writing of a new constitution that, upon approval, gave him the right to run for direct reelection. Fujimori held legislative elections in November 1992, which most major opposition parties boycotted, thereby giving him a working majority in the Congress. Local elections, which were to have been held in November 1992, were finally run in early 1993, but the degree to which politicians and citizens alike will put much trust in the electoral process after such transgressions is very much an open question. In spite of such misgivings, Peruvians reelected Fujimori in 1995 by a huge margin.

Fujimori made some significant progress in lowering inflation from its catastrophic 1990 levels and in passing a multitude of neoliberal laws to facilitate foreign investment and to encourage the privatization of much of the public sector. Nevertheless, investment remained elusive and insufficient for the country's needs, especially in light of the magnitude of the problem. By 1990 only 11 percent of Greater Lima's labor force was adequately employed, while 8 percent were unemployed, meaning that more than eight in every ten members of the labor force was underemployed (Crabtree, 1992:143). While it cannot be concluded that all underemployed workers belong to the informal sector, the economic crisis of the late 1980s and early 1990s forced many individuals to search for informal employment solutions. The numbers of workers who moved into this "independent" sector grew by more than 11 percent per year from 1987 to 1989 (Crabtree, 1992:142), strongly suggesting that Lima's urban informal sector was more swollen than ever. Once again, whether such economic dislocation will lead to electoral disaffection or to tendencies to support populist or authoritarian figures remains a troubling and unclear question.

The Local Urban Electoral Experience, 1980–1995[3]

As noted, Peru returned to civilian rule in 1980 through presidential and legislative elections. Fernando Belaúnde Terry and his AP party, who had been overthrown twelve years earlier by the military, returned to power handily in May of that year, taking 45 percent of the vote to APRA's 27 percent and PPC's 9.5 percent. The combined left gathered in a total of about 12 percent, and the rest was divided among various minor parties.

November 1980. These elections were followed in November with national local contests to elect mayors and city council members throughout Peru. Belaúnde's coattails were still a factor; AP took 35.9 percent of the total popular vote, and AP candidates won Lima, Callao, and several other major provincial cities as well, including Cuzco, Ica, Huancayo, Piura, and Puno. Within metropolitan Lima, AP candidates took more than one-half of all of the city's district races (twenty-three of thirty-nine). Yet AP's total popular vote decreased across the board, compared with its showing in the presidential race just a few months earlier.

The left had only recently coalesced under the leadership of Alfonso Barrantes into the IU. Yet IU finished second overall, edging out APRA, and showed substantial strength despite winning few races outright. Its most surprising victory occurred in Arequipa, Belaúnde's hometown. Barrantes himself finished a close second in metropolitan Lima, and IU candidates won four district-level mayoral races in the capital, all in lower-class neighborhoods.

The APRA finished third in the popular vote; it managed to hold onto its strongholds in northern Peru, taking Cajamarca, Trujillo, and Chiclayo, but its internal power struggles following the death of Haya de la Torre weakened its overall performance, which fell well below its previous totals and its hopes. For example, APRA had taken 25 percent of the total popular vote in metropolitan Lima in the 1978 Constituent Assembly race, when Haya de la Torre was still alive. However, in the 1980 presidential elections, this total fell off slightly to 22.7 percent and then more precipitously to 16.3 percent in November 1980.

Finally, PPC finished last overall. The party did not run candidates in many provincial areas; indeed, almost three-quarters of its national vote total were cast in metropolitan Lima. The PPC won no provincial mayoral races and only two district-level races within Lima. Its national vote total in 1978 (24 percent) had been artificially inflated by the absence of AP, which did not participate, for by 1980 it took only one-tenth of the total popular vote in both the presidential and local races.

Regionally, IU showed its strength to be in those southern parts of Peru that were urban, involved with mining, and largely peasant. It also ran well in Lima's lower-class districts, but it had little support in the north. The APRA, on the other hand, was just the opposite: strong in its traditional northern homeland, it dropped off dramatically in the south. The AP had no special strengths or weaknesses; it competed with all of the other parties wherever they were strong and won more or less evenly throughout the nation. The PPC was the most extreme, depending almost entirely on Lima for whatever votes it received. Yet, within Lima, PPC did not do well in 1980, winning only two district-level races (the same as APRA), despite that fact that PPC won 311,000 popular votes and APRA only 248,000.

Overall, local results in 1980 more or less mirrored those from the presidential elections six months earlier. There were indications, however, that Belaúnde's personal attractiveness did not necessarily adhere to all of his party's candidates; and while AP clearly dominated local results, IU's showing in a few of Lima's lower-class neighborhoods was a portent of things to come. Lima's poor had shown themselves capable of mobilizing and of being mobilized in the late 1970s, when they participated in a series of general strikes that led to the military's decision to step down. Just how this particular segment of the capital (which was a majority of the city's population) would act in future elections, local or national, was unknown. In addition, APRA, though very much in internal disarray and therefore not viable in many instances, had shown great resiliency in its long history and could not be counted as down and out.

November 1983. The municipal elections of 1983 represented somewhat of a watershed in Peruvian voting history. In the first place, an organized leftist coalition showed substantial electoral strength, winning the mayoralty of Lima; second, with presidential elections only eighteen months away, the military showed no signs of intervening in the electoral process or of finding such results unacceptable; and third, APRA showed that it was on the path to renewed health. Each of these developments deserves examination.

The 1983 elections were widely viewed as a referendum on Belaúnde's terms in office. By late 1983 his administration was in trouble. Economically, conditions were starting to deteriorate; inflation was a stubborn problem as was diminishing purchasing power. Politically, Belaúnde was widely seen as having squandered his opportunity to govern; despite the fact that AP had won a majority in both houses of the Congress in 1980, Belaúnde's policy initiatives were timid and uncertain. At the same time, IU had become better organized; Barrantes was viewed as a viable, nonextremist candidate for mayor of Lima, and much neighborhood campaigning had generated a certain amount of grass-roots support in lower-class neighborhoods. The APRA had also managed to regroup itself around Alan García and to at least paper over its major internal power struggles.

The 1983 elections were a clear rejection of Belaúnde and his party and policies. The AP, which had taken about 36 percent of the total popular vote in 1980, reached only 17 percent three years later. The PPC rose only slightly from 11 percent to 14 percent. Thus, the major victors were obviously IU and APRA, and each had something to exult over when the votes were counted.

The APRA showed what has to be seen as a most impressive resurgence. It took 33 percent of the total vote throughout the country and won individual races in many of the major cities, including Trujillo, Callao, Chiclayo, Arequipa, Cajamarca, and Ica. Its strength was also revealed in the fact that in virtually all races across the country it took at least 20 percent of the popular vote in a four-way contest. Its candidate, Alfredo Barnechea, finished a strong second to Barrantes in Lima.

The IU took a total of 29 percent of the vote; outside of Lima, IU won the mayoral races in (among others) Cuzco, Huanayo, Puno, Abancay, and all of the states in the Amazonian region. It lost its bid to recapture Arequipa, however. By and large, IU maintained its strength in the central and southern parts of the country and in Lima; it offered no challenge to APRA's "solid north." The IU's major victory was, of course, in Lima. Barrantes took 36 percent of the city's vote and won the mayoral race by some nine percentile points over APRA. The IU also won one-half (twenty-one of forty-one) of Lima's district-level races, taking all of the city's *barrios populares*. This last datum was especially significant. It indicated (or seemed to indicate at the time) that the left had established itself with Lima's lower classes as their ideological representative, and the IU made much of what it proclaimed to be an alliance with labor, the urban working class, the city's *informales*, and the urban proletariat and dispossessed in general.

Indeed, the ideological center of Peru in general and AP in particular must have viewed the results of the 1983 municipal elections with alarm and despair. The two major opposition parties (IU and APRA) took a total of 62 percent of the popular vote, while AP's own total fell short of its 1980 total by half. But a careful observer of the elections who had sympathies for the left also might have felt some misgivings. The IU took more than one-half of its popular vote in Lima, indicating that it had some distance to go to develop truly national strength. Its nature as a coalition of ideologically fissiparous individuals and parties also added to its problems. The party that emerged in strong shape for the future was APRA. Its new, young, and energetic leadership under García not only attracted many new or unattached voters but also injected new life into the party faithful.

November 1986. The municipal elections of 1986 were enormously influenced by the presidential contests of the previous year. In 1985, APRA and García won a sweeping victory, taking the presidency by a 2:1 margin over IU and Barrantes. The APRA won convincingly throughout the nation, finishing second to IU in only two of twenty-six departments. The APRA also won simple majorities in both the Senate and the Chamber of Deputies. The IU finished second overall, but well back, in the presidential and legislative races, while AP virtually disappeared, finishing last with 7 percent of the total vote. The PPC, renamed CODE (Convergencia Democrática, or Democratic Convergence) because of alliances made with small minor parties, took its predictable tenth of the popular vote.

With such resounding strength, APRA had two final targets for 1986: winning the mayoralty of Lima, and making a strong showing on the municipal level nationally. For the first, it nominated Jorge del Castillo, a young lawyer, who ran against Barrantes, whom IU put up for reelection. This race was closely watched to see if IU had developed a true following in Lima or if the 1983 vote had been more a protest against AP and Belaúnde than anything else. The APRA and García went all out for del Castillo, to the extent that many newspapers commented on the entry of the president into a local election.

García's coattails proved to be barely long enough: del Castillo won, with 37.5 percent of the total popular vote to 34.7 percent for Barrantes across the city. In district-level races, the three major parties contending (AP's defeat in 1985 had been such that the party did not enter any municipal races) split the city more or less evenly. The APRA led with seventeen victories, followed by PPC with thirteen and IU with eleven. But this apparently even distribution was in fact a defeat for IU, since it meant that IU lost not only the metropolitan mayoral race but also several of the districts that it had won three years earlier. These results all meant that IU had not been able to create a solid and predictable base among its putative constituency. The PPC's higher-than-average total was due not only to its always solid support in Lima's upper-income areas but also to AP's absence.

Barrantes's defeat for reelection came as a major blow to IU in several ways. In the first place, the Lima results showed that IU did not have a lock on the lower-class vote. As a rule, a plurality of people in the *barrios populares* voted for IU, but there was enough desertion from IU to APRA to give del Castillo the mayoral race and to break IU's brief grip on the city's lower-class districts. By 1986, Barrantes was a known quantity who, despite being universally seen as an earnest and reasonably successful mayor had not been able to deliver on all of his campaign promises. In addition, the populist charisma of García and the strength of a recharged APRA were too much for both IU and Barrantes. The fragile coalition that had been IU soon fractured once again; Barrantes quit (or was ousted, depending on whom one listened to), and the left, blaming itself as well as everyone else, rapidly declined as a major electoral force in Lima and throughout the country.

Nationally, APRA simply left all of the other contenders behind. It finished first in the popular vote in every one of the country's twenty-four departments and won virtually every one of the major mayoral races, showing strength not only in its traditional northern settings but also in the central and southern parts of the country. By the end of 1986, therefore, APRA had, after more than fifty years of disappointment, won the presidency, the Congress, and the great majority of mayoral positions around the country. It only remained to be seen how García and his party would govern.

November 1989. The impact of the García period on Peruvian history will be examined for some time, but there can be no doubt that the late 1980s were the worst years that Peru has experienced since it was defeated in the War of the Pacific in the 1880s. Inflation soared to unheard-of levels, reaching 7500 percent in 1990; unemployment, and especially underemployment, included more than 80 percent of Lima's labor force; Peru became persona non grata internationally when it failed to make any pretense of meeting its debt obligations; the Shining Path became more and more threatening and intimidating, especially as it began to move into Lima;

and a litany of social ills moved to Peru into the company of the poorest and worst-off of all Latin American nations.

The 1989 municipal elections, however, must not be seen exclusively as a referendum on the García administration. Polls indicated that the populace, regardless of social class, had lost faith not only with García but also with the nation's political system, regardless of party or ideological persuasion. The 1989 elections thus occurred at an especially critical time; and, given the overall level of disenchantment with the status quo (however defined), the traditional political parties found themselves facing strong, new, and independent opposition.

The first such group to emerge was FREDEMO (Frente Democrático, or Democratic Front), a coalition that arose following a widely attended rally protesting the García administration's attempt to nationalize the banking and financial sector in Peru in mid-1987. Principal among the speakers at this rally was Mario Vargas Llosa, Peru's preeminent living novelist and a relatively recent convert to neoliberal economic policies. Vargas Llosa was at that time a close confederate of Hernando de Soto, whose work on Lima's informal sector had received international attention. The FREDEMO appeared some months later as a political movement dedicated to neoliberal economic policies and to recovering the centrist-right segment of the ideological spectrum. By the time of the 1989 municipal races, FREDEMO had formed an alliance made up of AP and PPC as well as other groups and individuals who supported neoliberal policy lines along those recommended by the International Monetary Fund, the World Bank, and other multilateral lending organizations.

The second new face in politics was Ricardo Belmont, a popular television personality in Lima who had first been mentioned as a mayoral candidate in 1983 by AP (Tuesta, 1985:61). Belmont entered the 1989 mayoral race as no party's candidate, running instead independently under the Obras ("Works" as in public works) label. He was also a solitary candidate in that he had no running mates on the district level.

Both the Lima and the national results showed that these new faces and alliances could tap into deep discontent. In Lima, Belmont won easily, taking 45 percent of the popular vote, followed by FREDEMO with 27 percent. These two nontraditional candidates thus took over 70 percent of the capital's vote. Insofar as district-level voting was concerned, FREDEMO showed significant support, winning twenty-seven of the city's forty-one districts. The IU managed to hang onto six districts, but this total was far from its previous victories in 1983 and 1986 and indicated that the left had lost much of its appeal to its supposedly "natural" constituency. The most disastrous performance came from APRA, which ran mayoral candidates in the metropolitan mayoral race as well as in every district but lost every one—and this from the party that had won the citywide as well as seventeen district races three years earlier. Overall, APRA and IU took slightly more than one-tenth of the Lima vote apiece, grim evidence that an economic crisis would and could utterly destroy prior allegiances and electoral support.

Nationally, FREDEMO was a notable victor. The party took 26 percent of the popular vote, while one-third of its candidates won their individual races. Independent candidates running under a wide variety of party and movement names placed second, taking 30 percent of the vote and one-quarter of the races. Such successes could only mean that IU and APRA were left well behind, which was indeed the case: the two of them together took only 30 percent of the popular vote. Each party had its own particular triumphs, but departmental results by and large reflected overall tendencies. The FREDEMO won the popular vote in sixteen departments; IU placed a distant second with seven such victories, while APRA managed only one, in its northern stronghold of La Libertad. Independents won in Lima, as noted, and in Tacna. Further, the abstention rate in 1989 was the highest (at 36.2 percent) in any of the municipal races, implying a considerable disenchantment with the candidates and perhaps with the whole process.

January 1993. All nations go through occasional intense periods when a great deal of history seems to be compressed into a few moments. Peru did so from 1989 to 1993, a period which saw a number of critical events transpire over a very short time. In the first place, Alberto Fujimori, a complete outsider in national politics, came out of nowhere in March 1990 to finish a strong second to Vargas Llosa in the first round of voting and then to defeat him by a 3:2 margin in a run-off election in June. Fujimori, who had run on a vague platform that stressed work, honesty, and technology immediately implemented a series of draconian neoliberal economic policies. These policies caused instant escalations in prices and an abrupt recession, but the prevailing nightmarish 7500 percent inflation rate also fell precipitously. Meanwhile, an unprecedented wave of violence by the Shining Path that focused especially on Lima (as well as on assassinations of political incumbents and candidates) caused enormous damage and intimidation before its leader, Abimael Guzmán, was finally captured.

Finally, Fujimori declared an *autogolpe* in early 1992. As noted earlier, he dismissed the Congress, purged the judiciary, and suspended constitutional guarantees. He then called for congressional elections in November 1992, postponed the municipal contests scheduled for that time, and charged the new Congress with the job of producing a new constitution. Most major parties boycotted these contests, but they were held regardless, and Fujimori's Cambio '90 ("Change '90"), the movement that swept him into the presidency, won a majority of the seats, thus assuring him of a constitution to his liking—that is, one that would permit direct reelection to the presidency, which had not been permitted for decades in Peru.

The postponed municipal elections of January 1993 thus took place within a tumultuous context. Despite the authoritarian nature of Fujimori's actions and the considerable international outcry against them, most of the major parties participated in these elections. But the most striking development was the emergence of dozens, if not hundreds, of independent candidates, parties, and movements throughout the country that operated on all levels (APOYO, 1993). Such a change had been foreseen in the 1989 election of Belmont in Lima and in the Fujimori victory itself. But by early 1993 independents had proliferated, often down to the level of a specific Lima district, where they ran under names such as the Independent Lurín Alliance or the Popular Leftist Front of New Comas, both of which won.

These independent movements and the overall public attitude that encouraged them flourished throughout Peru and in Lima. Within the capital, Belmont was easily reelected, taking 45 percent of the popular vote. His total, combined with that for Lima 2000, another independent movement, came to almost three-quarters (73 percent) of the total vote. The most astonishing aspect of the election came from the failure of the traditional parties (APRA, AP, IU, and PPC), which took a combined total of only 15 percent of the vote. Across Lima's districts, the results were much the same. Obras candidates won one-half of the district races; AP and PPC each took five, while other independents (all of whom operated only on the level of their district) won eleven. The APRA won none; the IU won none.

Nationally, results were equally mixed and opaque. Excluding Lima, independent candidates won mayoral races in twelve provincial capitals, while the traditional parties won five apiece. In terms of the popular vote, independents took slightly more than three-fifths of the total national vote; the four parties of the 1980s (AP, APRA, IU, and PPC) combined for about 35 percent, but the highest single total for any one of these (APRA) was only 12.6 percent. As IU had failed in Lima, so too did it fail nationally. Once again and analogous to Lima, independent candidates were department-specific, as witnessed by names such as Reconstruction Front of Pasco, the Independent Movement of Abancay, and the Independent Movement toward Progress of Sullana (APOYO, 1993).

This proliferation of parties and movements throughout Lima and Peru indicated that the citizenry viewed the traditional parties of any and all ideological stripes with great suspicion and distrust. The AP, IU, and above all APRA, all of whom had enjoyed some significant success either in Lima or nationally (or both, especially in the case of APRA), fell to new depths. The APRA historically had always been able to count on one-third of the popular vote at any time in any presidential election, and to count as well on winning every provincial mayoral race on the northern coast of Peru. Its collapse was almost total: its failure to win any district-level race in Lima, to take only 3 percent of the city's popular vote, to manage only four provincial mayoral victories, and to win only one in eight national voters—all paint a gloomy picture, but one that is attributable almost entirely to García's tragic governance.

In addition, the splitting of the vote presaged difficulties for governing. Although Peruvian law stipulates that the winning party on a mayoral race automatically receives a simple majority (50 percent plus one) on his or her city council, the fragility and fluidity of the party system came to mean (at least in the 1993 and 1995 elections) that many mayors took office with small pluralities indeed. For example, in 1993 the independent candidate who won in Huamanga (the capital of Ayacucho) took only 15 percent of the popular vote. He ran against nine other major candidates who took a combined 64 percent, not to mention other smaller movements and candidates who took another 21 percent (APOYO, 1993). Such splintering and fragmentation implies a need for coalition politics and for consummate politicking that may be extremely hard to come by. It also implies (at least as important) that anything approaching consensus in the Peruvian political arena may be a goal that is in retreat rather than being attained.

November 1995. The local elections in 1995 were preceded by a presidential race in April, which (thanks to the 1993 Constitution) allowed Fujimori, the incumbent, to run for direct reelection. Most observers and pollsters agreed that he would win; the only uncertainty was whether he would be able to win outright and avoid a runoff, and whether his party would gain an absolute majority in the unicameral legislature. In the event, both questions were resolved in Fujimori's favor. He won a stunning victory, taking about 64 percent of the popular vote; Javier Pérez de Cuellar, his nearest opponent, finished with about 22 percent, while thirteen additional candidates took the remaining 14 percent. His triumph was national in scope; he took an absolute majority in all but one department and more than 60 percent in all but four, while taking over 70 percent in four. The collapse of the nation's traditional parties was thus complete; those who competed (APRA, AP, IU, and PPC) took a total of less than 10 percent.[4] Fujimori thus won an extraordinary victory. Yet as the November municipal elections approached, the question arose of whether he could transfer his popularity six months later in the municipal race to Jaime Yoshiyama, his hand-picked candidate.

Yoshiyama first came into public life as Fujimori's minister of energy in 1992. He then was elected president of the Congress in 1993, where he played a major role in passing the new constitution. He stepped down in 1995 to run as the Cambio '90 candidate for mayor of Lima. His major opponent was Alberto Andrade, an independent (though formerly associated with PPC) and highly popular incumbent mayor of Miraflores, an upper-class commercial and residential district of the capital.

Although Andrade started the race with a considerable lead, Fujimori threw all of the weight of his office behind Yoshiyama, and three weeks or so prior to the election the polls showed a race too close to call. But two weeks beforehand, Andrade and Yoshiyama squared off in a televised debate. Virtually all observers agreed that Andrade won the debate by a substantial margin, and polls from that date onward showed him pulling ahead. The final results gave Andrade a 53 percent to 47 percent victory.

Insofar as district races within Lima were concerned, Andrade's movement, Somos Lima ("We Are Lima"), won twenty of the city's forty-three districts; Cambio '90, Fujimori's party, won nineteen.[5] As might be expected, Somos Lima candidates won in virtually all of Lima's upper- and middle-class districts, while Cambio '90 saw victory in all but one lower-class district.

What occurred in Lima also occurred in the provinces. Nationally, independents won all but four mayoral races in departmental capitals (AP won in Huancayo and Chiclayo, Obras in Piura, and Frente Nacional de Trabajadores y Campesinos (FRENETRACA) in Arequipa). Otherwise, independent candidates won races that were based almost exclusively on local issues. Given the weakness of national parties, most provincial races had numerous candidates running for office, and as a result many candidates won with pluralities that were sometimes very small. Governance may become difficult, since anything resembling party discipline appears to be nonexistent.

The fact that the two major candidates in the Lima mayoral race were independents, and that the traditional parties of the 1980s were nowhere to be seen, provide further evidence of the lack of institutionalization in the party system. In the Lima race in particular, personalities, along with past records, assumed great importance; ideological arguments (certainly in any left-right sense) played no role. But the election also demonstrated an intractable shortcoming of personalist rule, in that Fujimori could not transfer his undoubted personal appeal to Yoshiyama, a candidate intimately associated with him. Thus, the long-term question of how a stable party system might be constructed seemed in 1995 further away than ever.

Conclusion

The case of Peru since its return to civilian rule in 1980 is fascinating and not a little curious. On the whole, its electoral experience has been unprecedented: elections on both the national and local levels have been held as scheduled (except for 1992-93), incumbent parties have transferred power to opposition parties on all levels, all parties that wished to participate could do so (none was proscribed), and the military did not interfere in any way with the electoral process or with its results. Indeed, in Peru the military is charged with conducting the elections insofar as guaranteeing security and collecting ballots are concerned, and Lima newspapers make a point after each contest of recognizing the military's role in safeguarding the electoral process.

What general conclusions can be drawn from the six instances of local elections in Peru recounted here? Several suggest themselves: these concern local elections as indicators of future trends, of party loyalties, of voter dissatisfaction, and of regional strengths.

Peru's municipal elections throughout the decade have often been a reflection of presidential elections and of national issues, but they also have been a bellwether for the subsequent presidential election, especially when local results have been perceived as a referendum on or evaluation of an incumbent regime. The local elections of 1983 (halfway through the Belaúnde period) and of 1989 (at the end of the García administration) are the two most notable examples of such referenda-like elections. [6] The discontent manifest in these local contests was not only clear, but also each time the party in danger was unable to do anything about its defeat, despite the warning of the local vote. It is worth noting that the highest abstention levels occurred in the 1983 (35.5 percent) and the 1989 (36.2 percent) municipal races—that is, in the races that took place when economic conditions were deteriorating and toward the end of an incumbent's term.

Closely related is the matter of party loyalties and durable party affiliation. Peru's local elections demonstrated all too clearly that no party could assume a loyal constituency over any length of time, whether on the national or the local level. In general terms, no party showed staying power or an ability to develop a loyal Lima constituency, whether it was (in the case of Lima) AP in 1983 or IU in 1986 or APRA in 1989 or even Fujimori's Cambio '90 in 1995. The first three won substantial presidential victories in Lima, only to lose badly three years later. Whether Yoshiyama's 1995 loss presages trouble for Fujimori and Cambio '90 in 1998 cannot at this time be predicted.

This rejection of a candidate or of a party or of a movement or of an ideology (as the case may be) held true, regardless of the candidate or party or movement or ideology. One by one, all of the major parties (AP, APRA, and IU) won victories over one another, only to lose in the next election. But losers soon outnumbered winners, and by 1989 all had lost, none had been reelected, and the result was the rise of the independent candidate and movement, first in Lima and then throughout the nation on both local and presidential levels. This process of elimination of what by Peruvian standards were its best institutional parties was doubtless due to one overwhelming factor: the inability of any of them to create and sustain economic improvements that made people's lives better. The 1995 elections are from this perspective more puzzling. Fujimori's success during his first term obviously propelled him to his extraordinary reelection in 1995, but this same success was not enough to let Yoshiyama win the Lima race.

The issue of economic betterment might normally be thought of as a national concern for presidential politics, but given the high degree of centralized power in Peru and the salience of Lima in national politics, dissatisfaction with an incumbent president traditionally translates into a low vote for his party's mayoral candidate in Lima and support for an opposition figure. This connection, in addition to the fact that governing Lima is universally seen as the second most difficult job in Peru (if not the most difficult, given the very limited ability of any city or town or village to raise funds autonomously), meant an intimate and always mutually suspicious relationship between the capital and the nation.

The local elections also clearly demonstrated, especially to the left, that the urban masses in the nation's *barrios populares* did not constitute a predictable voting bloc. The urban poor showed themselves to be, in the aggregate, considerable vote switchers, moving (in the case of Lima) from the center-right of AP (1980) to the left of IU (1983) to the center-left of APRA (1986) to the populist nonideology of Ricardo Belmont (1989, 1993). Such movement was doubtless due to the lack of success of any administration in creating jobs in Lima or in bringing order out of its chaotic transportation system or in maintaining its streets or in doing any of the myriad of things that a Third World city and its populace requires, demands, needs, hopes for, or dreams about. Lima's *informales* did not vote consistently as a bloc, nor did they vote election after election for the same party or candidate (much to the left's dismay).

Yet the 1989 and 1993 municipal elections, as well as the 1990 and 1995 presidential ones, were crucially important in that they showed for the first time that the Lima-based elites could no longer assume that their parties and their candidates will or can win. Belmont, the television personality and political novice, won significant margins where APRA and the left had won previously, largely because he was able to claim that he represented no party.

Similarly, Fujimori won by a wide margin in Lima's *barrios populares* by campaigning on a platform that he was *un presidente como Ustedes* ("a president like you"). Belmont and Fujimori both were twice able to ride the enormous, if still inchoate, wave of discontent and dissatisfaction with the social and political status quo and the opinion of a great number of the Peruvian *masas populares* that traditional elites and parties did not speak for them, and that new figures independent of these traditional institutions and parties deserved their votes and support. Yet, here again, Fujimori, the quintessential maverick and independent, could not persuade Lima's voters to support his candidate in the 1995 mayoral race.

Within Lima since 1980, two separate issues deserve some discussion. The first is women in municipal politics. Women have played a relatively minor role in formal political life in Peru. Lima has never elected a female metropolitan mayor, parties have not usually nominated many women, and there are no rules (as there are in Argentina) requiring parties to nominate a certain percentage of them for all electoral posts. Yet all parties since 1980 have run women in various district-level races; seventeen were elected as district mayors from 1981 through 1995 (Tuesta, 1994). No party dominated in these races, however; APRA, AP, IU, FREDEMO, Obras, PPC, and independent candidates all won. Overall, from 1963 to 1993, less than 5 percent of all provincial mayors were women, whereas the figure in Lima was about 8 percent. Under Fujimori in the 1990s women did come to occupy major posts in the Congress. More important, perhaps, women have for decades played key roles in the multitude of informal neighborhood associations and nongovernmental organizations in Lima's lower-class districts.

Second, as the post–World War II decades have passed, the mass media have played an increasingly important role in the electoral process. Such developments have been especially important in Lima, where the media, electronic and otherwise, are traditionally highly partisan. Radios and televisions have become virtually ubiquitous in Lima households regardless of socioeconomic status. The 1993 census reported that over 90 percent of all households in metropolitan Lima had a radio; 62 percent had a black-and white television set, while almost one-half (47 percent) had color (INEI, 1994). All major parties used radio and especially television in the weeks preceding elections, and debates between major candidates became increasingly common.[7] Precisely how much effect political advertising had on electoral behavior remains, as it does in most countries around the world, uncertain and a matter of much discussion. That Lima's mass media openly and blatantly took sides in all of the elections and attempted to influence voters, however, was absolutely clear.

Away from Lima, municipal elections showed that few cities or regions of the nation were predictable. Only APRA could demonstrate any claim to regional loyalty in its northern strongholds, but even there its core vote showed signs of weakness in the 1990s. In the rest of the country as in Lima, party loyalties were evanescent, with one party first winning, only to lose to another the next time around.

There can be little doubt that local elections in Peru have allowed what would be minor parties on a national scale to achieve power. The left is one good example; IU's moment of glory, Barrantes's 1983 mayoral victory, permitted the left to demonstrate that it could (or at least Barrantes could) govern rationally and without setting off ideological warfare. The APRA's regional strength in the north allowed that party to recover in the early 1980s without completely disappearing from the electoral map. And in the late 1980s and early 1990s local races allowed all manner of independents to emerge and to try their luck at campaigning and governing in something less than a national arena—a circumstance that could, under the right conditions, encourage both a new generation of provincial-origin politicians and parties to learn their trade.

Each of these potentially optimistic interpretations, however, has its downside. It is apparent that Peruvian politics, divided as it is between Lima and the provinces, makes it difficult for one party to succeed in both arenas. Occasionally, this success has occurred: AP enjoyed local dominance in both for a short period, as did APRA and (to some extent) Cambio '90. Yet the sheer magnitude of coping with Lima often contrasts sharply with the isolated nature of Peru's provincial cities and their own problems. Moreover, if and when decentralization and regionalization policies implanted in the late 1980s take hold, candidates and parties that focus on the problems of a specific department or region may well hold the upper hand electorally over parties that attempt to be national in scope.

The successes of many independent candidates and movements in the 1993 and 1995 municipal elections may signal a new period of pluralism (or perhaps fragmentation) in Peruvian politics; and

222 *Urban Elections in Democratic Latin America*

the new parties, after some inevitable shaking down, may emerge as competition for or successors to the country's traditional ones. Similarly, the new parties may serve to reinvigorate the older ones by forcing them to adopt new policy ideas and perspectives. Adam Przeworski (1991) has argued that a democratization can be defined as the "institutionalization of uncertainty," meaning that all sides in an election must be willing to accept an outcome that is, until the election itself, unclear or uncertain. But democracy depends in part upon stable institutions, whether of the state or not, including political parties, bureaucracies, a judiciary, and the like. To claim that for a democracy to take hold and thrive, uncertainty may well have to be institutionalized, is no doubt true. But institutions themselves also have to become institutionalized for the process of uncertainty to be acceptable to all sides. Ironically, the appearance (and victory) of so many independent candidates since 1990 may indicate the extreme to which uncertainty has taken hold in the Peruvian electoral arena.

After assuming power in 1990, President Fujimori showed that one of his principal political strategies was to deinstitutionalize the country by fiat or by collecting power to himself. With Congress and the judiciary delegitimized, the constitution replaced by one written at Fujimori's behest that allowed direct reelection of the president, and traditional parties in disarray, the future of democracy in Peru as it confronted the twenty-first century is unclear at best.[8] Such a state of affairs can only be bitter recompense for a nation that has tried so hard to reestablish democracy under such trying circumstances.

References

APOYO. 1993. "Resultados de las elecciones municipales de 1993." Lima: APOYO.

Carbonetto, Daniel, et al. 1988. *Lima: Sector informal*. Lima: CEDEP.

Crabtree, John. 1992. *Peru under García: An Opportunity Lost*. Pittsburgh, PA: University of Pittsburgh Press.

De Soto, Hernando. 1987. *El otro sendero*. Lima: Instituto Libertad y Democracia.

INEI (Instituto Nacional de Estadísticas e Informaticas). 1994. *Censos Nacionales 1993: Resultados Definitivos a Nivel Provincial y Distrital: Departamento de Lima, Provincia Lima, No. 2*. Lima.

Matos Mar, José. 1986. *Desborde popular y crisis del estado*. Lima: Instituto de Estudios Peruanos.

Pareja Pflucker, Piedad, and Aldo Gatti Murriel. 1993. *Elecciones municipales en las provincias de Lima y Callao*. Lima: Fundación Friedrich Ebert.

Pease García, Henry. 1991. *Construyendo un gobierno metropolitano: políticas municipales 1984–1986*. Lima: Instituto para la Democracia Local.

Przeworski, Adam. 1991. *Democracy and the Market: Political and Economic Reforms in Eastern Europe and Latin America*. New York: Cambridge University Press.

Roncagliolo, Rafael. 1980. *¿Quién Ganó?* Lima: DESCO.

Schonwalder, Gerd. 1995. "Urban Popular Movements, Political Parties, and the State in Post-Authoritarian Peru: The Local Government Nexus." Ph.D. diss. Montreal: McGill University, Department of Political Science.

Tuesta, Fernando. 1983. *Elecciones municipales: Cifras y escenario político*. Lima: DESCO.

———. 1985. *El nuevo rostro electoral*. Lima: DESCO.

———. 1986. *Perú 1985: El derrotero de una nueva elección*. Lima: Universidad del Pacífico.

———. 1987. *Perú político en cifras*. Lima: Fundación Friedrich Ebert.

———. 1994. *Perú político en cifras (segunda edición)*. Lima: Fundación Friedrich Ebert.

Notes

1. As noted in the Introduction, neither this chapter nor the book as a whole tries to take on the topic of urban governance. Thus, laws and regulations concerning how a mayor governs, or accounts of specific mayoral administrations, are not included here. For an excellent example of such an account dealing with the Barrantes administration of 1984–1986 in Lima, see Pease (1991) and Schonwalder (1995).

2. Peru has legally been divided into regions only since the late 1980s, and while these regions exist on paper, their importance as functioning political and fiscal entities is uneven and in general not well established. As of this writing, people more commonly refer to (and identify with) departments than to regions.

3. Electoral statistics throughout are taken from Tuesta (1994), unless otherwise noted. Tuesta's collections and recalculations of official electoral results are of great use to anyone involved in analyzing electoral patterns in Peru. Other sources of electoral data include other works by Tuesta (1983, 1985, 1986, 1987) as well as Roncagliolo (1980).

4. Some of the totals were truly minuscule. The once-proud APRA party took 4 percent nationally, while AP (1.56 percent) and IU (.54 percent) virtually disappeared.

5. One candidate for AP won a district race; independent candidates won the other three. The data used here are unofficial and were reported in *Caretas* (30 November 1995): 76.

6. Whether the defeat of Yoshiyama in 1995M should be considered in this same light is questionable. Andrade was a highly popular district mayor with a reputation as a skilled administrator. While some of his support might well have come from Fujimori's opponents, it is equally likely that most of Andrade's votes were cast in his favor and not against Yoshiyama (or Fujimori). Moreover, there were probably a good number of voters who simply believed that the Yoshiyama candidacy was a too-blatant effort by Fujimori to gather even more power into his own hands.

7. The two most notable recent examples were the debates between Fujimori and Vargas Llosa prior to their run-off election in 1990, and between Alberto Andrade and Jaime Yoshiyama in the 1995 Lima mayoral race. Most opinion polls indicated that the first was largely a draw and that few voters changed their minds because of the debate. The second debate, however, held about ten days before the election, apparently brought about a significant shift toward Andrade.

8. During the 1995 presidential campaign, Fujimori was asked about the future of democracy in his country. His response—"How much more democracy do you want? There are fifteen candidates running for president"—did not address the problems of pluralism becoming fragmentation or of political parties becoming nothing more than personalistic followerships. Presumably these problems were very much to Fujimori's liking.

9

Why Are There No Local Politics in Uruguay?

Aidan Rankin

Even by the standards of Latin America, Uruguay is underreported in the English-speaking world. If it is mentioned at all, it is in terms of the Battle of the River Plate (the war movie, more often than the actual event), or the Tupamaros, an alliance of agrarian and middle-class rebels, whose strategy of urban guerrilla warfare brought their country close to a revolution in the late 1960s and, according to some cynics, "put Uruguay on the map."

Yet, it is in South America's smallest republic that the strongest resistance to the regionally dominant ideology of "market reforms" is taking place, and the left is the main beneficiary of this resistance to change. Uruguay is perhaps one of the only places where the left is making sustained electoral progress without either presenting itself in bland, media-friendly packaging or chasing after an elusive "rainbow" coalition of disparate minority interests. The strength of the Uruguayan left is indeed in its old-fashioned resilience, its refusal to accept what many regard as the inevitable trappings of modernity: privatization and the irreversible decline of the welfare state. And this strategy appears to be working. In November 1994 the candidate of the Encuentro Progresista, Tabaré Vázquez, gained 30.1 percent of the vote, the highest of any single candidate but (under electoral vagaries to be explained below) not enough for victory.[1] The winning Colorado candidate, former President Julio María Sanguinetti, spent most of the election campaign competing with the left for the vote against neoliberal "reform."

Uruguay's left, therefore, speaks the language of conservatism and stands in direct opposition to radical change. In so doing, it does not carve out new political territory but steps into the area once occupied by the Colorados and Blancos, the two "traditional" parties. At the same time, however, it is introducing Uruguayans to a different style of politics that is community based and decentralized. By any standards, Uruguay is an unusual country. It not only has the longest democratic record in Latin America but is also the most uncompromisingly unitary of states. It led the region, and indeed the world, in welfare and secularizing legislation, but today it is probably a more conservative *machista* society than Argentina or Brazil.[2] It has produced writers of the stature of Eduardo Galeano, and yet its people often display a remarkably defensive, parochial attitude toward matters of culture, deferring to Paris, London, and Buenos Aires.

For most of this century, Uruguay has been held up by academic observers and its own politicians as a democratic role model for Latin America. A succession of elected civilian governments since 1903, a literacy rate of over 90 percent, and a generous system of social benefits have combined to give the impression of a stable, integrated civil society. Politics was dominated by the two traditional parties, of which Lord Bryce, echoing Gilbert and Sullivan, observed that "a child is born a little Blanco or a little Colorado, and rarely deserts his color."[3] These were loose coalitions of interests, based on historical loyalties rather than on ideology. Even now, Uruguayans like to compare the Colorados and Blancos with the Democratic and Republican parties of the United States. Smaller movements, mostly of the left, participated freely and openly in the political structure, while a well-informed electorate opted repeatedly for moderation and compromise. Women won the right to vote in 1934 (two years before France), and in the same year homosexual relationships between consenting adults were discreetly decriminalized.[4] Unlike neighboring Argentina, there was no military conscription, and the rhetoric of militarism was refreshingly absent from political debate. The armed forces, recruited largely from the less-sophisticated regions of the interior, played a marginal role in national life. Again, unlike Argentina, the military (with the possible exception of the air force) was regarded as a low-status profession. In 1933, when a temporary constitutional crisis arose in Montevideo, the nation's capital, President Gabriel Terra appealed not to the army but to the police and the fire brigade.

This idealized impression of Uruguayan politics may appear surprising in the light of subsequent developments. The 1970s witnessed the transformation of a state known for its tolerance and political openness into "the torture chamber of South America." By 1975 the country that had once aimed to surpass Western Europe in advanced legislation had the world's largest proportion of political detainees.[5] Paradoxically, the qualities that had seemed to contribute most to democracy's success facilitated political repression. From 1973 to 1985 a self-styled *gobierno militar-civil* took advantage of Uruguay's small size, homogeneity, and urban centeredness to impose rigorous political censorship and social control. Citizens were classified A, B, or C according to their political correctness in the eyes of the regime. The abuse of psychiatry against political detainees rivaled that of the Soviet Union in the era of Leonid Brezhnev.[6] What the military regime lacked in headline-grabbing brutality, it compensated for in subtle ruthlessness and a tenacious hold on political power. Its economic policy, meanwhile, veered between a reactionary corporatism of the "classic fascist" model and a frenzied proto-Thatcherite agenda reminiscent of Augusto Pinochet's Chile.

To Romeo Pérez, one of Uruguay's most astute political commentators, the return to democratic government in the 1980s was characterized by "an attitude of looking back to the past."[7] This perception, widespread on the left, arose largely because Uruguay reverted to the constitution of 1967, which had been suspended by the military regime in 1973. The *constitución naranja*, as it is often scornfully referred to by the left, is described by Uruguayans as "semipresidential" because the powers of the executive are severely circumscribed by Congress.[8] It was these checks and balances that successfully prevented the disastrous former president, Luis Alberto Lacalle, from beginning a systematic assault on the welfare state.

Unlike their Argentine and Brazilian neighbors, Uruguayans were able to draw inspiration from a tradition of democratic, pluralist practice in their resistance to dictatorship. The pre-1968 generation, almost uniquely in the hemisphere, had been raised on the assumption that elected governments were not the exception but the rule. Nostalgia for *Uruguay feliz*, a golden age of stability, coupled with a popular desire to restore "normal" political conditions, helped to ensure the election of President Sanguinetti in

November 1984 (see Table 1). The quest for normality suspended debate over the country's political structure and electoral arrangements.

Table 1. National Election Results (Parties and Main Candidates), 1971, 1984, and 1989

1971		1984		1989	
Colorado Total	41.0%	Colorado Total	41.2%	Colorado Total	30.3%
Bordaberry	22.8	Sanguinetti	31.3	Batlle	15.5
Jorge Batlle	14.6	Pacheco	9.7	Pacheco	14.8
Vasconcellos	2.9	Blanco Total	35.0	Blanco Total	38.7
Blanco Total	40.2	Zumarán	29.4	Lacalle	16.6
Ferreira	26.4	Ortíz	4.4	Pereyra	11.1
Aguerrondo	13.7	Paysee	1.1	Aguirre	5.9
Frente Amplio		Frente Amplio		Frente Amplio	
Total	18.3	Total	18.3	Total	21.2
Seregni	18.3	Seregni	18.3	Seregni	21.2
				Nuevo Espacio	
				Total	9.0
				Batalla	9.0

Source: Office of Fuente Amplio.

Sanguinetti's election also represented the temporary restoration of the Colorados as the *partido del estado*—that is, the natural party of government. The 1984 results seem to bear out Charles Gillespie's contention that, despite its failure to adapt to economic and institutional crisis, the Colorado-Blanco duopoly "was relatively stable at the time of the 1973 coup (and remained so thereafter)."[9] The parties' share of the vote had not altered significantly since 1971, when the last relatively free elections were held. Even the left-wing Frente Amplio (Broad Front, or FA), which had hoped to profit from a reaction against the dictatorship, failed to capture Montevideo's *intendencia* (mayoralty). An uneasy alliance of Christian Democrats, Marxists, and left-wing defectors from the traditional parties, the Frente was nevertheless the only "third force" in Uruguayan politics to capture more than 10 percent of the vote. Its main problem was an inability to expand its electoral base beyond the white-collar unions and the intellectual middle class.

Such a cautious, consensus-based transition did not seem to provide a fertile ground for political realignment. The retreat into past certainties, however, was to prove short-lived. Uruguayans mobilized across party lines on such issues as the military amnesty law, while politicians responded to the end of the Cold War and the subsequent crisis of anticommunism. It became increasingly apparent that traditional political allegiances did not meet the requirements of the new democracy.

In 1989 the balance of power shifted in favor of the Blanco Party, whose main candidate, the aforementioned Luis Alberto Lacalle, won the presidency. The left, which now included the Nuevo Espacio coalition (NE) as well as the Frente, collected 30 percent of the vote, exactly even with the Colorado Party (PC).[10] More significantly, the Frente took control of Montevideo with 34.5 percent of the vote, while the urban-based Colorados were pushed into third place (see Table 2). This result, and the left's resounding triumph in the capital in 1994, confirms the fact that the primacy of the traditional parties has been brought to an end, but still no clear realignment has emerged in its wake.

Table 2. Political Parties: Distribution of Votes (Montevideo and the Interior), 1971, 1984, and 1989

	1971	1971	1984	1984	1989	1989
Colorado	39.5%	42.0%	36.0%	45.8%	25.0%	34.8%
Blanco	29.7	47.9	27.0	42.9	26.6	49.3
Frente Amplio	30.1	9.6	33.6	10.3	34.5	9.9
Nuevo Espacio	–	–	–	–	13.1	5.5

Source: Office of Fuente Amplio.

Historical Perspective

The fact that a nontraditional movement now controls Montevideo is in itself a minor political revolution. Nearly one-half of the population of three million lives in the capital, and the post of *intendente* of Montevideo is often described as the most prestigious after the presidency. The previous incumbent and presidential candidate, Dr. Vázquez, is not a conventional politician. He has often surprised colleagues in his own Socialist Party (PSU) with his independent, almost populist approach. As the Montevideo-based political scientist and Frenteamplista Olga Beltrand explains, "Tabaré was a PSU militant and a medical doctor. Our political class doesn't usually come from the social movements in the way that he did. He spent twenty years praticing medicine in La Teja [a poor working-class district], providing community health care and free meals. People are tired of traditional politicians with their corruption and their lies. Tabaré is seen as honest."[11]

In the past, social movements have played a minimal role in Uruguayan politics. The country has perhaps not only the longest tradition of civilian government in the region but also the most "professionalized" political elite, to which newcomers are not welcome. The welfare reforms and secularizing measures enacted in the early twentieth century by Colorado President José Batlle y Ordónez (1903–1907, 1911–1915) were the result of benevolent direction from above rather than mobilization from below. Batlle was a strong supporter of organized labor, "this enormous mass of men that until now believed that their duty lay in working in silence." But his main constituency was not the still predominantly anarcho-syndicalist workers' movement but a progressive urban bourgeoisie influenced by the best traditions of the Enlightenment. Historian and sociologist Germán Rama describes him as "the leader of an unequivocally middle-class movement. We must explain his action as leader in the identification of the middle class with the proletariat in a common program."[12]

Batllismo shared many of the characteristics of future "populist" movements in Latin American politics. It had a charismatic leader, a multiclass, largely urban following, strong centralizing tendencies, and a program of pragmatic social reforms. Unlike populist leaders such as Brazil's Getúlio Vargas or Argentina's Juan Peron, Batlle came from the country's political elite (he was the son of a former president, General Lorenzo Batlle). He was also committed to pluralist politics and to using the state as a mediating force between competing political and economic interests. By the 1930s successive Colorado-led governments had introduced the eight-hour day, safety regulations at work, and legal protection for trade unions. This emphasis on social reform was accompanied by a powerful strain of secular rationalism, including the legislation of divorce, the abolition of prayer in state schools, and, in 1917, the complete separation of religion from the state. The continued emphasis on secularism has become a distinguishing feature of Uruguayan politics. At one level, it has resulted in relative freedom from repressive moral legislation. A weak Church means, however, that an important component of grass-roots local organization in other Latin American states was missing in Uruguay. Although there is a lively tradition of Catholic radicalism, which includes the human rights activist and liberation theologian, Luis Pérez Aguirre, there has been no equivalent of the ecclesial base communities that have played such an important part in politicizing the Brazilian poor.

The concept of an activist state was the guiding force of public policy until the late 1960s and remains the dominant strand in Uruguayan public opinion. In a referendum of December 1992, 72 percent voted to overrun a law that would have permitted the privatization of the most important public utilities. This vote was in direct defiance of President Lacalle and all of the main Colorado and Blanco leaders except for the canny Sanguinetti. It also demonstrated a remarkably tenacious resistance to the neoliberal dogma, which since the end of the Cold War has swept the region with the implacable harshness of a new viral agent.

The Batllista search for a middle course between laissez-faire capitalism and revolutionary socialism now seems to many voters to be better reflected in the programs of the Frente Amplio and Nuevo Espacio than in the traditional parties. It is possible that the growing electoral strength of the left owes more to the Colorado and Blanco leaders' support for neoliberal economic policies than to an increasing radicalism among voters.

Batllismo sought to transform an unstable but prosperous republic into a "model country"—a unified, centralized state with a framework of advanced legislation. That moderate government and a remarkable degree of political openness survived until the crisis of the late 1960s is testimony to President Batlle's success. It is not within the scope of this chapter to examine the social and economic crisis of this period, or the rise of authoritarian politics and the well-publicized actions of the Tupamaro guerrillas. Martin Weinstein has described these years as Uruguay's "loss of innocence."[13] The significance of the collapse of democracy is that it has exposed the traditions of Uruguayan politics to critical scrutiny. Politicians of all parties are not only addressing questions of economic management but also the problem of *gobernabilidad*. In the era of redemocratization, two of the most fundamental aspects of the Batllista political settlement have been called into question: the system of "coparticipation" and the double simultaneous vote.

Coparticipation

The traditional parties began life as military factions that emerged after independence in 1828. They derive their names from the Battle of Carpintería of 1836, when the followers of General José Fructoso Rivera wore red hatbands and those of his rival, General Manuel Oribe, wore white. As Richard Moore has pointed out, the political life of Uruguay for much of the twentieth century was "fundamentally one with the military."[14] Military conflict gave way to competitive civilian politics through a series of treaties mapping out spheres of political and economic interests for the majority Colorado and the minority Blanco forces.

Independence came at the price of political instability and violence.[15] During the Guerra Grande (1838–1851), Oribe laid siege to Montevideo, which was defended by France, Brazil, and Italian followers of Giuseppe Garibaldi. Blanco support came largely from Argentina's caudillo, Juan Manuel de Rosas. The Paz de Abril of 1868 gave the Blancos control over four out of nineteen departments: Canelones, San José, Cerro Largo, and Florida. It was the first successful agreement between the two factions, and it formed the basis of coparticipation. This process of power-sharing between the traditional parties has subsequently dominated Uruguayan public life.

Coparticipation has evolved from a simple division of territory and spheres of influence to the sharing of public appointments and political leadership. In 1897, Blanco leader Aparicio Saravia led a revolt in which he demanded control of eight departments. The Pacto de la Cruz accorded him six. It contended that Saravia's revolt against Batlle in 1904 resulted in a military victory for Colorado forces and a political victory for the Batllista wing of the Colorado Party.

The politico-military history of nineteenth-century Uruguay remains directly relevant to today's constitutional debate. Aldo Solari, the sociologist, has rightly observed that the accords between Colorados and Blancos resemble treaties between enemy nations more than attempts to reconcile national political rivals.[16] Politics in Uruguay, therefore, was the continuation of war by other means. In the twentieth century, coparticipation developed into a sort of spoils system. Political offices, including managerial posts in public utilities, were apportioned in accordance with the two parties' share of the vote. As a political researcher who was not a supporter of the new parties explains, "In Uruguay, we have no administrative class, no 'civil service.' We have only political appointees."[17] This arrangement survived the military regime, since most officers had traditional party affiliations. The system of coparticipation played a critical role in the development of centralized institutions that stifled opportunities for local initiatives. Since 1989 it has been thrown into confusion by the breaking of the traditional parties' electoral stranglehold.

Electoral Reform and the Double Simultaneous Vote

The *doble voto simultaneo* (double simultaneous vote) is the product of the 1910 Ley de Lemas, which enables party tickets (*lemas*) to divide into competitive factions (*sublemas*). The votes for these factions are then accumulated according to a party ticket. Thus, the most-voted-for candidate of the most-voted-for party gains the presidency. Superficially, this arrangement resembles an election in the United States, with the primaries and presidential vote held at the same time. An important difference is that in the United States the primary is an internal party affair, whereas in Uruguay the double simultaneous vote means that inter- and intraparty competition takes place simultaneously. This system makes for a dynamic very different from U.S. politics because there is no pressure on the parties' various factions to agree on a common platform. Intraparty negotiation and compromise are more likely to take place after the election as part of the process of coalition formation.

The injustices that may arise from this system are best illustrated by two examples. In 1950 veteran Blanco leader Luis Alberto de Herrera was 92,000 votes ahead of his nearest rival, Luis Batlle Berres, who was elected president because the total Colorado vote outstripped the Blanco total. In 1971, a critical election year, Wilson Ferreira Aldunate, a Blanco and the most antiauthoritarian of the traditional party candidates, received 26.4 percent of the vote but lost to Colorado Juan María Bordaberry with 22.8 percent (see Table 1). The Colorado total of 41.0 percent, as against the Blanco share of 40.2 percent, was obtained through the presence of three fringe candidates.

In Uruguay, elections for president, Senate, House of Representatives, and departmental *intendencias* take place simultaneously. Voting is compulsory, and citizens are obliged to vote for an entire party list. There is no ticket-splitting, and it is impossible to delete the name of an unwanted candidate at the national or local level without invalidating the entire ballot. As the politics professor and Colorado former senator, Manuel Flores Silva, complained, "Even in the Soviet Union, it is possible to cross out the candidates you don't want."[18]

Since the 1989 election a consensus has emerged among the parties on the need to separate local and national ballots. Critics of Dr. Vázquez, for example, maintain that he won the *intendencia* largely through the popularity of the Frente's presidential candidate, General Liber Seregni, with Montevideo voters. For the traditional parties, the election of a leftist *intendente* in the largest department was a worrying symptom of the erosion of its power base. The Frente Amplio believes that the decentralization of government and the extension of proportional representation to the *juntas departamentales* (currently elected by the "first-past-the-post" system, which can allow one *sublema* to dominate the regional administration) would give the left a political space in the interior. The separation of votes for president and vice president as well as for senator and deputies is not yet on the agenda. It is hinted at in such differing quarters as Dr. Julio Batlle of the Colorado Party and the younger generation of Frente Amplio activists, such as Dr. Rodrigo Arocena of the Vertiente Artiguista.

Democratic Realignment and Local Politics

Uruguay's electoral laws have inhibited the development of local government. Historically, the departments have acted as pawns in the struggle between two rival factions vying for control over the centers of power. This situation is reflected today in the impossibility, for example, of voting for a Colorado *intendente* and a Frente Amplio presidential candidate. Local themes tend to be eclipsed at election time by national issues and personality contests. There are, nonetheless, many instances of individual loyalty toward local candidates. One elderly woman known to this author travels from Montevideo to her hometown of San José to cast a vote for a deputy from the Pachequista wing of the Colorado Party. As its name suggests, the Movimiento Nacional de Rocha, a section of the Blanco Party with a reformist program and a paternalistic, conservative social vision, has historical ties with Uruguay's easternmost department. The Movimiento's presidential candidate, Carlos Julio Pereyra, was nevertheless outpolled in Rocha by Lacalle and Jorge Batlle in the 1989 election.

Past analyses of Uruguayan politics have tended to contrast the urban-centered, secular character of the Colorados with the rural

Catholic allegiances of the Blanco Party. To an extent, this view reflects voting patterns during the twentieth century but ignores a strong urban-progressive Blanco tendency that accepted much of the Batllista social program and a conservative, Catholic wing of the Colorados exemplified by the authoritarian president, Jorge Pacheco Areco (1968–1971). The 1989 election witnessed a reversal of roles for the traditional parties. Colorado defectors (to the Blancos and the Nuevo Espacio) enabled the Blancos to extend their electoral base in Montevideo at the expense of their traditional rivals. The Frente Amplio's control of the capital has produced a combative opposition to President Lacalle's *coincidencia nacional* and its attempt to steer the country toward neoliberal economic "reforms." This example is the first in modern Uruguayan politics of an effective opposition orchestrated by a regional administration.

Political realignment has resulted in some curious ideological paradoxes. The most visible evidence of a growing informal economy in Montevideo has been the presence of *vendedores ambulantes* (street traders) on the main thoroughfare, the Avenida 18 de Julio. Given the reality of a strong and growing black market (the product of the military regime's economic liberalism), practical support for the traders has come from the more traditional business community, while the *ambulantes'* example of private initiative has little appeal for Colorado and Blanco supporters of privatization. In August 1991 a narrow congressional majority overruled city ordinances permitting the *ambulantes* to operate along the 18 de Julio. Voting patterns reflected a correlation between opposition to ambulantismo and enthusiasm for free-market radicalism. Meanwhile, the *ambulantes* have been allowed to remain on the 18 de Julio while the city and central governments negotiate over zoning regulations.[19] The role of Vázquez as their protector illustrates his administration's ability to seize upon popular issues even when they lie outside the conventional leftist agenda. In Uruguay, *vendedores ambulantes* and self-employed artisans are the usual constituency of the parternalist right.

Unlike other Southern Cone countries, Uruguay has not produced a successful populist movement since the defeat of Saravia in 1904. This failure is partly due to the catch-all nature of political allegiance, which has meant that no significant group of voters (such as Perón's *descamisados*, or organized labor, traditionally allied to the Colorado or Communist parties) has been left unrepresented. The personalist element of Uruguayan politics is usually expressed through party factions—for example, Batllismo or Wilsonismo; the system of accumulation discourages breakaway candidacies. Nonetheless, there have been political movements that contain many of the ingredients of populism. One of these, ruralismo, the brainchild of broadcaster and polemicist Benito Nardone, displayed populist and even fascistic tendencies in the postwar years. The movement's antiurbanism made it unable to acquire a substantial political following, and it lost its radical edge after incorporation in the Blanco-led government of 1958–1964. In the same way as Nardone appealed to the *botudos* (small rural producers), Pablo Millor's extreme right-wing Cruzada '94 currently seeks a political base among the urban poor. Millor's corporatist movement often emulates the language of social democracy and claims to be upholding "true" Batllista principles: "Today the Batllistas are surrounded [by] the two tendencies that do not work for Uruguay or for the rest of humanity; on one side totalitarian Marxism, and on the other that naked liberalism . . . which has been adopted by some sectors of the Partido Colorado."[20]

Neither movement has the multiclass component essential to populism. Vázquez, however, has shown that he is capable of putting together a wider coalition of those who are disaffected with conventional politics. In 1980 the Communist-led Democracia Avanzada gained 10.1 percent of the vote, or nearly one-half of the Frente Amplio's total. This support has declined substantially in response to events in Eastern Europe and the former Soviet Union. The Partido Comunista Uruguayo (PCU) is in terminal crisis, but former Communists have remained within the Frente, transferring their allegiances to the PSU and new movements such as the Vertiente Artiguista. The Frente's opposition to privatization is justified on pragmatic grounds rather than through a resort to traditional dogmas. It is the system of management and not the form of ownership, the left maintains, that ultimately determines economic viability. Both the Montevideo *intendencia* and the Frente Amplio's congressional leaders have signaled a willingness to reach an accord with private capital. This is a far cry from the confrontational tactics of the recent past. The left called for a decentralization of *entes autonomos* (public industries) and an end to political appointments and clientelistic practices. As Senator Danilo Astori (the Frente's vice presidential candidate in 1989) noted, "Very often the managers of state enterprises are members of the Colorado and Blanco parties who have failed to be elected as deputies and are given these jobs as compensation, as a reward for political support, or merely as a step in their political careers."[21]

The Montevideo *intendencia* represents the first attempt to move away from the politics of coparticipation. The extent of its success has helped to determine the electoral map in 1994. Already the Vázquez administration is viewed as a working model of nontraditional party government. General Seregni indicated in 1991 that he did not wish to run for office again, leaving the field open to Tabaré Vázquez, whose unconventional political career and strong regional base have aroused the suspicions of his political opponents. Some, including the leftish Colorado Flores Silva, have cited his rise as evidence of the *fujimorización* of Uruguayan politics. Vázquez, however, has political and social experience far beyond the Peruvian president, who lacked a party base and has used an *autogolpe* to force through controversial economic measures. As *intendente*, he has jettisoned many past dogmas, but his movement has a more concrete political program than Cambio '90. The most serious problem faced by the new Uruguayan left is that of attracting support outside the capital, of transforming itself from a regional to a national political movement.

Montevideo and the Interior

In the context of Uruguay, it is largely misleading to speak of an urban-rural divide because, despite the national economy's agrarian base, over 80 percent of the people live in cities and towns. The true social and cultural division is between the capital and the "interior," which includes the coastal departments and adjoining Montevideo. As previously mentioned, nearly one-half of the population of three million lives in the capital, where political life is still almost wholly concentrated. An atmosphere of mutual suspicion remains between the two population blocs, analogous to the dichotomy between Paris and the provinces under the French Third Republic. Beltrand observed that "in the interior, they still have caudillismo."[22] This ignores the fact that Pachequismo, the most caudillistic of Uruguayan political movements, came second in Montevideo in 1989. Conversely, there persists an antiurban form of conservatism based on adulation of the gaucho and "authentic" *criollo* values. This mentality, with a surprising resemblance to German Volkisch thought, is best exemplified in a florid quotation from the eccentric British-descended *estanciero*, Carlos Reyles: "The countryside enriches the nation morally and intellectually with the vital juices of its energy and the spiritual strengths that come from work itself."[23]

Political division between Montevideo and the interior are confirmed by the results of the 1989 election. This division is particularly apparent when we study the results in terms of votes per presidential candidate (see Table 3). Seregni, the leader in Monte-

Table 3. Presidential Elections, 1989: Votes per Candidate (National, Montevideo, and Interior Totals)

National	Montevideo		Interior	
1. Lacalle 444,119 (Blanco: conservative)	1. Seregni	312,778	1. Lacalle	310,946
2. Seregni 418,403 (Frente Amplio: broad left)	2. Pacheco	132,002	2. Batlle	203,243
3. Batlle 291,287 (Colorado: neoliberal)	3. Lacalle	124,000	3. Pacheco	156,856
4. Pacheco 288,858 (Colorado: right-wing authoritarian)	4. Batalla	118,977	4. Pereyra	125,856
5. Pereyra 218,355 (Blanco: moderate reformist)	5. Pereyra	92,919	5. Seregni	105,625
6. Batalla 177,435 (Nuevo Espacio: social democratic)	6. Batlle	87,934	6. Zumarán	87,006
7. Zumarán 100,757 (Blanco: centrist)	7. Zumarán	23,751	7. Batalla	51,476
8. Fernández 14,482 (Colorado: moderate reformist]	8. Talice	6,728	8. Fernández	9,574
9. Talice 10,835 (Partido Verde: ecologist)	9. Fernández	5,908	9. Talice	4,107

Source: Office of Fuente Amplio.

video by a margin of 280,776 votes, was in fifth place outside the capital. Jorge Batlle, whose new and "radical" interpretation of Batllismo encompasses privatized pension schemes, was second in the interior and sixth in Montevideo, where he alienated the powerful pensioners' lobby. Arguably, the election results represent the triumph of the interior over the capital. At the same time, the unprecedented change of government in Montevideo created an opposition movement with strong regional roots. The conflict between the Lacalle and Vázquez administrations has led to a reexamination of the role of local government in Uruguayan politics and society. It also gave Vázquez the opportunity to acquire a national base and launch himself as the left's first serious contender for the presidency.

Conclusion

The development of pluralist institutions in Uruguay has corresponded (some would say paradoxically) with the centralization of power. Compromise between two political cultures, from which the modern state emerged, was built on the surrender of local rights. Coparticipation, or the dispensation of political office between the traditional parties in proportion to their share of the vote, depended on a centralized distribution system. Uruguayan electoral law, with its requirement that voters select an entire factional list, has further reduced the significance of local government in national political life. Centralization also has meant that grass-roots movements (agricultural cooperatives, environmental campaigns, women's organizations, and Christian base communities) associated with democracy elsewhere in Latin America have been slow to acquire political influence in Uruguay.

One of the distinctive features of Uruguayan society is the relative weakness of autonomous institutions. Traditionally, the focus of political and cultural unity has been the state. This focus partially accounts for the continuing popularity of interventionist economic policies, and the strength of support for a centralized welfare state that has been readily exploited by the left. The Batllista welfare apparatus, the left contends, is part of the *patrimonio* of Uruguayan citizens. At one level, therefore, the left has broadened its popular base by appealing to the basic conservatism of the electorate. The vote against privatization in December 1992 was more a vote against change than an endorsement of an alternative vision of society.

In this sense, the movement away from the Colorado and Blanco parties represents a reactive conservatism rather than a public demand for reform. The end of the two-party system in Uruguay and the corresponding fall of communism abroad have given the left a new role in the debate over *reforma del estado*. Together with the recent memory of democratic breakdown, when authoritarian pressures on the centralized state became too strong, this debate has dramatically increased demands for a wider democratization of Uruguayan society. Since 1989, and more especially since 1994, a multiparty system has challenged the traditional relationship of the executive and the legislative powers. At the same time, a fiercely independent *intendencia* in Montevideo offers new hope for decentralization and local government.

Uruguay, then, remains a country of paradoxes. Its most traditional political forces advocate radical economic change and communicate with voters in an unfamiliar neoliberal tongue. The left, meanwhile, expands its electoral appeal through a mixture of "social movement" politics and the defense of traditional values. The 1994 election has produced a state of deadlock that most Uruguayans probably desired, despite their most vociferous claims to the contrary. Given this almost stridently nonideological atmosphere, it is ironic that two deputies from the Movimiento de Liberación Nacional (National Liberation Movement, or MLN), better known as the Tupamaros, have been elected to carry the banner of the Frente Amplio's far left. Their acceptance as a political party, and a fairly harmless one at that, represents for many Uruguayans the closing of a chapter of confusion.

President Sanguinetti, who succeeded the ill-fated Lacalle in March 1995, seems to personify the current nondogmatic mood of the electorate. He is, however, a somewhat protean political figure, a Uruguayan "Vicar of Bray" who has been associated with the authoritarian regimes of Pacheco and Bordaberry in the 1970s, the peaceful, well-ordered return to democracy in the mid-1980s, and, in 1989, a scare-mongering campaign against the opponents of the total amnesty for the armed forces. He now presents himself as the "caring" candidate of the center-left. Yet, perhaps it is this mixed political pedigree that has made him the most suitable candidate. His task, after all, will be to square the circle: to address the left's demands for decentralization and the preservation of the welfare state while appeasing the modernizing tendencies in the traditional parties. His success, or lack of it, will do much to determine the shape of Uruguayan democracy at the end of the twentieth century.

References

Alisky, Marvin. 1969. *Uruguay: A Contemporary Survey*. New York: Praeger.

Amnesty International French Medical Commission and Valerie Marange. 1991. *Doctors and Torture: Resistance or Collaboration?* London: Bellew.

Finch, Henry, ed. *Contemporary Uruguay: Problems and Prospects*. Liverpool: University of Liverpool, Working Paper No. 9.

Gillespie, Charles Guy. 1991. *Negotiating Democracy: Politicians and Generals in Uruguay.* New York: Cambridge University Press.

Moore, Richard K. 1978. "Soldiers, Politicians, and Reaction: The Etiology of Military Rule in Uruguay." Ph.D. diss. Tucson: University of Arizona.

Pearce, Jenny. 1980. *Uruguay: Generals Rule.* London: Latin American Bureau.

Pérez Anton, Romeo. 1989. "Political Developments and Electoral Prospects." In Henry Finch, ed., *Contemporary Uruguay: Problems and Prospects.* Liverpool: University of Liverpool, Working Paper No. 9.

Rankin, Aidan. 1991. "Religion and Safe Sex in Montevideo." *Times Literary Supplement* (London), January 24, 1991.

La República (Montevideo). Various issues.

Vanger, Milton I. 1963. *José Batlle y Ordoñez of Uruguay: The Creator of His Times.* Cambridge, MA: Harvard University Press.

———. 1980. *The Model Country: José Batlle y Ordoñez of Uruguay, 1907–1915.* Hanover, NH: Brandeis University Press.

Weinstein, Martin. 1975. *Uruguay: The Politics of Failure.* Westport, CT: Greenwood Press.

———. 1988. *Uruguay: Democracy at the Crossroads.* Boulder, CO: Westview Press.

Notes

1. The Encuentro Progresista (literally, "progressive meeting") was a broad-based coalition whose U.S. counterpart would encompass everything from the most liberal of Democrats to the Socialist Labor Party. It is an enlarged version of the Frente Amplio (Broad Front), the country's main left-wing coalition. Uruguay's unusual electoral arrangements will be discussed at some length in this paper. Tabaré Vázquez was the popular *intendente* (mayor) of Montevideo from 1989 to 1994. The current officeholder is Mariano Arana, former Frente Amplio senator and the country's best-known modernist architect.

2. Uruguayan women played an important role in the struggle against the military dictatorship, in particular through the *caceroleos* (pot-banging disturbances) in the working-class districts of Montevideo. Like their counterparts in Buenos Aires, the Mothers of the Disappeared, they were able to use their traditional gender roles as a highly effective political weapon. Despite a long secular tradition, the feminist movement has yet to make significant inroads in Uruguayan culture. The left is in many ways the least feminist sector of all, associating feminism with the neoliberal wing of the Colorado Party.

3. James Bryce, *South America: Observations and Impressions* (1912). At the time when Bryce was writing, civil war between the parties was still a distinct possibility. He even likens their red and white ensigns to the green and orange of his native Ireland. The complex power-sharing

arrangements of Uruguayan politics were remarkably successful in reducing this primal animosity.

4. Uruguay has remained free of the U.S.-derived urban gay life-style that has gathered momentum throughout Latin America since redemocratization in the 1980s. There is now a gay rights movement, Homosexuals Unidos, but it is occupied more with building and nurturing a community of interest than asserting a political agenda, and it shows no interest at all in carving out a commercial niche.

5. Jenny Pearce, *Uruguay: Generals Rule* (1980), 53. In the 1970s, Uruguay had five thousand political prisoners in a population of under three million.

6. See Amnesty International French Medical Commission and Valerie Marange, *Doctors and Torture: Resistance or Collaboration?* (1991), 61–72.

7. Romeo Pérez Anton, "Political Developments and Electoral Prospects," 27. Pérez is a leading member of CLAEH (Centro Latinoamericano de Economía Humana), a policy think tank associated with the Christian Democratic Party. In Uruguay the Christian Democrats are a center-left movement highly critical of both state-socialism and free-market dogma.

8. The term "semipresidential" is misleading because it is more usually applied to systems such as the French, the Finnish, and the Portuguese, in which political responsibilities are shared between an elected head of state and a prime minister answerable to the parliament. Some constitutional reformers in Uruguay, from Sanguinetti's wing of the Colorado Party in particular, look with favor on this form of government, which they refer to admiringly as "the French model."

9. Charles Guy Gillespie, *Negotiating Democracy: Politicians and Generals in Uruguay* (1991), 32.

10. The Nuevo Espacio, a small center-left coalition, broke away from the Frente Amplio in 1989 in an attempt to break the stranglehold of Marxism on the Uruguayan left. Its main components are the Partido por el Gobierno del Pueblo (PGP) and the Christian Democrats, who have played a leading role in the debate on constitutional reform. The Nuevo Espacio polled 9 percent of the vote (13 percent in Montevideo) in the November 1989 elections. Its candidate was Senator Hugo Batalla of the PGP.

11. Author's interview with Olga Bertrand, Montevideo, 1991.

12. Martin Weinstein, *Uruguay: The Politics of Failure* (1975), 32–24.

13. Martin Weinstein, *Uruguay: Democracy at the Crossroads* (1988), 35.

14. Richard K. Moore, "Soldiers, Politicians, and Reaction" (1978), 13.

15. For a highly readable account of Uruguayan history since 1800, see Marvin Alisky, *Uruguay: A Contemporary Survey* (1969).

16. Weinstein, *Politics*, 53.

17. Author's interview with confidential source, Montevideo, 1991.

18. Author's interview with Manuel Flores Silva, Montevideo, 1991.

19. See Aidan Rankin, "Religion and Safe Sex in Montevideo," January 24, 1991. The article also describes the unusual level of Catholic influence in President Lacalle's administration and the expansion of the Uruguayan left since 1989.

20. *La República* (Montevideo), August 27, 1991.

21. Author's interview with Danilo Astori, Montevideo, 1991.

22. Author's interview with Beltrand, Montevideo, 1991.

23. Weinstein, *Politics*, 45.

10

Venezuelan Local and National Elections, 1958–1995

Angel E. Alvarez*

Until the mid-1900s, Venezuela had held only two competitive presidential elections, once in 1846 and then in 1897 (Navas Blanco, 1993). In both cases the winners were fraudulently prevented from assuming office by the government in power. The first legitimate, direct, secret ballot and competitive general elections were held on December 14, 1947. This election occurred because of the emergence of independent political parties during the 1930s and 1940s that represented the rural masses and middle-class sectors as well as the small working class that was just beginning to develop within the oil industry.

These political parties first appeared in 1936 after the death of dictator Juan Vicente Gómez, who had ruled Venezuela for almost thirty years, and were led by the so-called Class of 1928 (Sosa and Lengrand, 1981). Both the Venezuelan Communist Party (PCV) and the Acción Democrática (AD), which perceived itself to be the democratic revolutionary alternative to PCV (Martz, 1966:120–25), were clandestinely founded during the regime of Gómez's successor, General Eleazar López Contreras. But it was not until the 1940s that they could legally participate, and then it was in conjunction with two other historically important parties, the Unión Republicana Democrática (URD) and the Comité de Organización Política Electoral Independiente (COPEI). The latter later became the Social Christian Party, which, although not organized by the Catholic Church, was and is of Christian inspiration (Herman, 1980; Combellas, 1985:57–72).

*Translated by Christina Helmerichs.

In 1945, after an unsuccessful attempt to select a candidate acceptable to both the government and the opposition, leaders of AD, along with young Army officers, toppled General Isaías Medina's government. The leaders of the October 18 Revolution justified their actions by arguing that the existing electoral system (which they saw as overrun by nepotism and embezzlement) had to be replaced with direct presidential elections, and by pointing out the need for a pay increase among the lower- and mid-rank officers (Velázquez, 1976:75–76). In 1946 a Constitutional Assembly was elected to draft a new constitution, followed in 1947 by general elections in accordance with that new document. In these elections AD candidate Rómulo Betancourt garnered 74 percent of the vote, followed by COPEI candidate Rafael Caldera with 23 percent, and by the PCV's Gustavo Machado with 3 percent.

In 1948 the Army that earlier had been aligned with AD in the "revolution" against Medina once again interrupted the democratization process. As a result, General Marcos Pérez Jiménez came to power and remained there for almost ten years. Although AD and PCV were outlawed, presidential elections were again held in 1952, with the URD's Jovito Villalba declared the unofficial winner. However, General Pérez Jiménez refused to recognize the results.

On January 23, 1957, Pérez Jiménez's regime was overthrown by a civilian-military coalition in which AD, PCV, and URD took part. General elections were then scheduled for December of that year. Although they could not agree upon a single compromise candidate, on October 31 three of the parties (AD, COPEI, and URD) signed the Punto Fijo Accords, wherein they committed themselves to assure the stability of the democracy by pledging to respect the election's results and agreeing to participate in a reform-oriented coalition government. On the day after the December elections, these same three parties signed the Joint Minimum Policy Statement, detailing the economic policies (import substitution industrialization) and social policies (income redistribution) to be implemented.

With Betancourt garnering 49.5 percent of the votes, AD became the first party to win a majority in a multiparty system. AD proceeded to form a government with the participation of the two other signatories of the Punto Fijo Accords. In 1961 the National Congress approved a new constitution that still remains in effect. During the 1960s and 1970s, Venezuelan democracy survived several military uprisings as well as the activities of an urban-rural guerrilla movement led by PCV and the Movimiento de Izquierda Revolucionaria (MIR), a radical offshoot of the AD party.

The Role of Caracas in Politics

Since the 1950s, Caracas, the nation's capital, has played a significant role. Besides being the seat of government and the headquarters of the three strongest political parties (AD, COPEI, and URD), Caracas is also the largest and most politicized city in Venezuela. Technically, Caracas consists only of the autonomous municipality of Libertador, which is located in the Federal District and has a population of 1.2 million. In reality, however, only the central and western portions of the Caracas metropolitan area are found within the Libertador municipality. The entire eastern half of the city encompasses four additional municipalities located in the state of Miranda: Chacao to the northeast, Sucre to the east, and Baruta and El Hatillo to the southeast. Another economically important part of the Caracas metropolitan area is the autonomous municipality of Vargas, which, though still a part of the Federal District, lies just on the other side of the mountain range now included in the El Avila National Park. If Caracas is defined as those individuals who live in Vargas, Baruta, Sucre, Chacao, and El Hatillo, the city's population is about three million. Including surrounding bedroom communities in Miranda that are directly involved in and influenced by the urban, political, and economic processes of the Caracas metropolitan area, the total population rises to about four million. This figure is not only 20 percent of the nation's total population but is also one-fifth of all those on the permanent voters' registration roll.

Caracas with its surrounding metropolitan area has been the center of all the important student movements, such as those of 1928, 1936, and 1958 as well as those of the 1960s and 1970s (Vivas, 1982). It has also been the epicenter of major political and military uprisings such as the 1945, 1948, and 1958 coups d'état; the urban upheavals of 1960 and 1961 that preceded the urban guerrilla warfare of the 1970s ; the violent civil uprisings of February 27 and 28, 1989, locally known as the *sacudones*, which initially started in the municipalities of Vargas and Guarenas and then spread throughout the entire metropolitan area and Valles del Tuy in Miranda;

and the two recent military coup attempts of February 4 and November 27, 1992, respectively known as the 4F and 27N revolts.

Caracas always has been and still is a highly politicized city, but today the capitals of the states of Aragua, Bolívar, Carabobo, and Zulia are also important centers of political activity. Each of these states plays a major part in the nation's economic industrial fabric. Aragua and Carabobo, and more specifically their capitals of Maracay and Valencia, are located in the nation's midsection about one hundred kilometers from Caracas and are home to most of the nation's manufacturing industry. They represent 7 percent and 8 percent of the national population, respectively. In the west, Zulia has 12 percent of the population and leads the nation in oil and cattle production. Its capital, Maracaibo, is the second largest city in Venezuela. For the last thirty-five years, the southern state of Bolívar has been the cradle of the nation's basic industries (steel, aluminum, and hydroelectricity). Although only 4.5 percent of the population resides there, much of the skilled and technically trained labor force lives in the cities of Puerto Ordaz and San Felipe, which are jointly known as Ciudad Guayana. Table 1 provides a comparative description of the states' population and electoral makeup.

Caracas and the nation's other major cities benefited the most from the protectionist economic growth programs and policies that the Venezuelan government started during the 1950s and continued up through 1989. But because of the progressive breakdown of the protectionist model throughout the 1990s, these cities have experienced severe recession, high levels of inflation, a lack of essential goods, extreme deterioration of all public services, an increase in unemployment, and the expansion of the informal sector. As a result, profound changes in political behavior have become more and more evident in the urban areas, as demonstrated by the 1992, 1993, and 1994 election results as well as by the attitudes toward the overall political system, its parties, and its principal institutions.

Having survived the period of guerrilla activity of the late 1960s, Venezuela's political system enjoyed almost twenty years of stability, which was based primarily on the period's economic abundance coupled with a national political elite with extensive leadership and negotiating abilities. Since 1989, however, Venezuela again has entered into a period of upheaval brought on by a combination of financial crisis with the corresponding imposition of several severe but inconclusive macroeconomic measures, and the open-

Table 1. Venezuelan Demographic and Electoral Data by State, 1995

	Population	Voters	No. of Deputies[a]	Mayors	Council Members[a]	Parish Board Members
Federal District	2,279,442	1,367,164	—[b]	2	60	233
Amazonas	94,285	43,146	17	7	63	0
Anzoátegui	1,028,926	494,338	29	21	245	132
Apure	378,727	148,324	20	7	93	80
Aragua	1,337,115	632,393	35	16	211	59
Barinas	516,014	244,262	23	11	134	122
Bolívar	1,134,239	462,472	32	10	131	138
Carabobo	1,819,190	779,334	35	14	202	136
Cojedes	226,083	115,918	17	9	90	49
Delta Amacuro	113,308	50,896	17	4	43	63
Falcón	696,631	371,078	23	25	258	464
Guárico	580,379	281,062	23	15	171	123
Lara	1,423,362	672,024	35	9	136	174
Mérida	677,391	329,345	23	23	248	198
Miranda	2,288,358	1,084,403	35	21	307	191
Monogas	553,380	285,404	23	13	150	267
Nueva Esparta	328,008	169,352	20	11	131	129
Portuguesa	715,573	308,226	26	14	172	66
Sucre	779,374	377,877	26	15	191	169
Táchira	942,570	430,616	29	28	304	123
Trujillo	561,308	303,835	23	20	221	281
Yaracuy	463,487	225,258	20	14	161	210
Zulia	2,801,404	1,175,466	35	21	302	354
Total	21,729,330	10,345,193	566	330	4,024	3, 761

Source: Consejo Supremo Electoral.

[a]Sum of elected and appointed.

[b]The Federal District has no Legislative Assembly.

ing up of new channels of direct political participation, both at the national and local levels. All of these changes have occurred within an environment of increasing public distrust of national political leadership.

From 1961 through 1995, Venezuela held eight national and five (separate) local elections. The first five national elections were general contests for the presidency, the National Congress, state representatives, and members of municipal councils. The first time that municipal elections were held separately was in 1979, one year after the 1978 general elections. At that time voters could only choose among specific slates of candidates presented by each party; all write-in and independent candidates were ineligible. Separate municipal elections were once again held in 1984, but due to important legal changes, more offices were subject to the popular vote. In 1989 the reforms legislated by the new Organic Law of Municipalities and the new Voter's Rights Law required that not only municipal councils but also, for the first time, mayors and state governors be elected by direct popular vote.

In December 1992 local elections were again held and this time included all mayors, the 279 municipal councils, and twenty-two state governors as well as 750 parish councils. Each municipality is divided into several parishes (roughly equivalent to precincts), and each parish is governed by a council composed of elected officials who serve three-year terms. The inclusion of these parish councils expanded the percentage of political positions now subject to direct election to two-thirds of all political offices. In December 1993 a new president as well as new national and state legislative bodies were elected. Finally, in 1995, the remaining positions, as listed in Table 1, were filled.

For many years, Venezuela's voting and verification systems remained unaltered. In 1979 some changes began to occur, so that by 1989 change had become the norm. Generally, these changes have sought to make the elections more personality- and less party-oriented as well as to increase citizen participation by allowing the direct election of additional regional and local officials, by increasing trust in the voting and verification procedures, and by creating more openness in campaign finances.

This process of opening up the voting process has been undertaken without modernizing the whole system. Venezuelans still vote and count their votes as they did in 1958. The only difference is that up until 1968 there were two ballots per party, one for the presidential candidate and the other for the party's slate for all the remaining positions, including the municipal councils, legislative assemblies, and the National Congress. This system not only limited the voters' ability to select among candidates, but it also facilitated their coercion because citizens could be required to show which party they voted for by showing which parts of the ballot remained in their possession. Since 1973 there has been only one ballot per election, the so-called *tarjetón electoral*. Voters select their candidate or party by marking the party's symbol or the candidate's picture. Once all the votes are in, the polling judges, who are party representatives designated by the Supreme Electoral Council, count them in a formal public ceremony in the presence of witnesses sent by each of the parties to verify the count. It is this tradition that has produced one of the practical principles of Venezuelan electoral competitions, the *acta mata voto*. In other words, what really matters is not the actual number of votes that each candidate receives but the number of votes officially counted by the party representatives who are acting as polling judges. This procedure, over the years, has forced the parties to expend a large portion of their organizational efforts on the creation of a highly trained election apparatus that is willing to defend, by any means necessary, their own votes while frequently trying to pilfer those of the other parties.

In practice, this principle has been not only used to alter actual results but also, by intentionally committing tallying errors and thus invalidating that site's results, to permit election officials to favor one candidate over another. The types of errors most commonly seen include failing to sign a tally sheet, faulty addition, and differences in the number of voters seen and the number of votes tallied. But regardless of the type of error, all of them cause a tally sheet to be declared null and void, excluding those votes from the official count. The intentional undermining of the official tallies does not render the document itself invalid, but it cancels out all the ballots cast for that specific candidate at that site. In certain local elections, formal complaints filed alleging these types of irregularities have forced new elections.

As a part of the effort to make the election process more transparent, voting procedures were modified in 1993 and 1995. First, tallying in most urban centers was upgraded by bringing in electronic equipment to read the still-in-use single ballot. Then the election law was amended to require the warehousing of all the marked ballots in certain military installations instead of allowing them to be destroyed, as had formerly been the case. Thus, for the first time, the official tallies could be verified. It should be noted that throughout Venezuela's democratic history, on Election Day the armed forces have been the guardians of the State. It is the responsibility of the military to deliver the uncounted ballots to each of the polling centers, control the public's access to these same sites, transfer the marked ballots to the tallying centers, and accompany the final count to the Supreme Electoral Council.

While controlling certain types of fraud, these procedural changes have not impeded the use of the nullification schemes that can alter the final results. For this reason in 1995, besides expanding the use of the automated readers, procedures once again were amended in order to allow up to a 3 percent inconsistency in the number of votes cast, as long as these inconsistencies did not alter the final results. These last changes caused a major uproar just prior to the 1995 elections. Some observers believed that the changes simply legitimized electoral fraud, while others saw them as a means of preventing partisan polling judges from using intentional errors as a way of canceling out votes. Just as in 1993, the 1995 automated readers failed to perform as expected, although they had functioned properly during the test runs. Whatever the specific results, it remains clear that the practice of "killing votes" is still alive and well in Venezuela.

Despite these weaknesses, during Venezuela's thirty-five years of democratic government, allegations of fraud have been quite sporadic—due, in part, to the negotiating skills of the nation's political elites, especially those associated with AD and COPEI, who have been obsessed with maintaining a stable democracy, which they believe to be an end in itself. The elites, through their participation in the Supreme Electoral Council, have managed to minimize conflict during each electoral process. When conflict has become unavoidable, they have known how to resolve it without violence. A salient example occurred in 1968 when, after a narrow vote which certain factions of AD might have contested, the party's leadership (specifically, former President Betancourt) ordered the AD candidate, Barrios, to recognize COPEI's election. This gesture established a tradition: if the party in power loses the election, its candidate will publicly recognize the opposition's triumph, even before receiving the official results.

The recent decentralization of the electoral process, the ability to elect local and regional officials, and the lack of support for the traditional parties have all transferred political power to inexperienced local party leaders, who are more concerned with winning elections than with the consequences of their decision on the overall system. As a result, at the regional and local level outside the control of the central party leadership, new leaders and organizers previously unable to participate in the internal negotiations of either of the major national parties have risen to power, resulting in a higher incidence of political conflict which the party elites have been unable to control. So, even before the results of the 1992 and 1995 gubernatorial and municipal council elections were announced, Venezuela experienced unprecedented massive and violent confrontations that required the intervention of both the National Guard and the Army. In 1992 these confrontations took place in the streets of Caracas, Cumaná (in Sucre), Barquisimeto (Lara), and Barinas (Barinas). In Caracas, the confrontations were primarily between La Causa Radical (LCR) and AD followers. In Barquisimeto and Cumaná, it was AD versus the Movimiento al Socialismo (MAS). In Barinas, it was AD versus COPEI. In Sucre and Barinas, the irregularities were such that the Supreme Court intervened and ordered new elections. As a result of these two court-ordered contests, the opposition parties won, defeating local AD candidates. In 1995 the Army was forced to intervene when members of LCR took on some of AD's more militant adherents in Zulia, Anzoátegui, and Bolívar. In Barinas, the confrontations again involved AD and MAS.

It should be noted that through the years some sectors have tried to resolve the main source of the conflict, the lack of public confidence in the tallying procedures, by creating informal non-governmental organizations such as the Escuela de Vecinos, Fiscales Electorales, and Queremos Elegir. These organizations have begun to assume watchdog positions for educating the electorate and for assuring the openness of the election procedures and the impartiality of the count. To date, these efforts have primarily been a short-term experiment by some members of the middle class.

On the other hand, since 1973, the ability to elect state and local government representatives directly seems to have produced changes that confirm the development of a stable, dual party structure throughout the country. But one must not forget that the results of the first three national elections (1958, 1963, and 1968) had a multiparty configuration (see Table 2). In 1958 the two primary political parties garnered 64.7 percent of the vote, with the third party only achieving a 15 percent showing. In 1963 and 1968 the two leading parties only garnered 53.5 and 49.7 percent respectively. The distribution and fragmentation of the vote seen from 1963 to 1968 was even greater than that registered during the 1973–1988 period (Rey, 1989).

During the period from 1958 to 1968 there existed as well marked regional differences (Myers, 1975; Bloom, 1980). COPEI enjoyed overwhelming support in the Andean region, while AD was favored in the rural east and in the Llano region, especially in the states of Monagas, Sucre, and Anzoátegui. Caracas voters were always atypical. In marked contrast with the rest of the country, in

all three elections, the winning candidates in the capital were ideologically and politically different from those favored throughout
the rest of the nation (Alvarez, 1990).

Table 2. Percentage of AD and COPEI Vote versus Other Parties, 1958–1993

	AD and COPEI	Others
1958	64.7	35.3
1963	53.5	46.5
1968	49.8	50.2
1973	74.6	25.4
1978	79.5	20.5
1983	78.6	21.4
1988	74.3	25.7
1993	45.9	54.1

Source: Consejo Supremo Electoral.

For example, in 1958, URD came in second at the national level
but won in Caracas. At that time, URD was a left-of-center party.
Its presidential candidate, retired Vice Admiral Wolfgang Larrazábal, while still active in the military, had held the office of provi-
sional president after the fall of the Pérez Jiménez dictatorship.
During the 1958 election, Larrazábal's candidacy also had the support of PCV. In 1963, IPFN's candidate, writer Arturo Uslar Pietri,
won the Caracas vote. His campaign focused on a series of economic reforms that sought to stimulate free competition in the
marketplace. Simultaneously, the AD-COPEI coalition government
was implementing a set of economic and social policies that called
for industrial protectionism and federal intervention in the marketplace. Also, Uslar Pietri had proposed a general amnesty for all
guerrilla leaders, who tended to be members of PCV and MIR. Thus,
he was perceived to be a radical alternative to the candidates of the
coalition government parties; and by the end of the campaign, notwithstanding his support for a free marketplace, COPEI had labeled him a communist (Alvarez, 1994:103–15). In 1968, Caracas
voted for Luis Beltrán Prieto, the candidate of the Movimiento Electoral del Pueblo (MEP), a center-left party that broke off from AD
and had the clandestine support of the outlawed PCV.

By 1973 a multiparty configuration, led by two strong political
forces, was once again in place. Although many parties participated,
AD and COPEI and their respective candidates won the majority
of the votes (see Tables 3 and 4). The remaining votes were scat-
tered among almost two dozen lesser parties, of which the most

important tended to be leftist: MEP, MAS (which broke off from PCV in 1970, and MIR. By 1988 the Nueva Generación Democrática (NGD) party appeared, taking 3.3 percent of the votes (fifth place). At first, NGD described itself as right of center and more recently as "liberal."

Table 3. Number of Candidates and Parties Participating in Presidential Elections, 1958–1993

	No. of Presidential Candidates	No. of Political Parties
1958	3	8
1963	7	11
1968	6	33
1973	12	37
1978	10	29
1979[a]	–	23
1983	12	52
1984[a]	–	26
1988	23	78
1989[b]	–	155
1992[b]	–	491
1993	18	274

Source: Consejo Supremo Electoral.
[a]Municipal council elections.
[b]Mayoral elections.

As Tables 2 and 4 show in 1973 the two primary political powers (AD and COPEI) controlled 74.6 percent of the vote, less than the 1958 AD-URD's 76.2 percent. In 1973, MEP obtained only 4.9 percent of the vote, while in 1958 third-place COPEI garnered slightly more than 15 percent. In 1978, AD-COPEI took 79.5 percent, while the third place party, MAS, obtained 6.2 percent. Again, in 1983, AD-COPEI came in with a combined total of 78.6 percent; MAS was third, with 5.7 percent. Also during the 1973 to 1988 period, regional differences seemed to dissipate slightly as AD's and COPEI's percentage of the gubernatorial and municipal votes, at least from a geographical perspective, became more homogeneous (Stambouli, 1980).

By 1988 these bipartisan tendencies weakened slightly, with the AD-COPEI parties managing 74.3 percent of the vote while MAS reached 10.2 percent, although by 1993 the total number of votes garnered by the two powerhouses fell below the total number won by all the other parties. More specifically, by 1993 the AD-COPEI total came to about 46 percent, while all the other parties garnered a total of 54 percent (LCR took 20.7 percent, Convergencia 13.1 percent, and MAS 11.8 percent).

Table 4. Percentage of Votes Obtained by Parties during
National Elections, 1958 to 1993

	1958	1963	1968	1973	1978	1983	1988	1993
AD	49.5	32.7	25.5	44.4	39.7	49.9	43.2	23.3
COPEI	15.2	20.8	24.3	30.2	39.8	28.7	31.1	22.6
URD	26.7	17.4	9.2	3.2	1.7	1.9	1.4	0.6
PCV	6.0	$-^a$	2.8^c	1.9	1.0	1.8	1.0	0.5
IPFN	–	13.3	2.6^d	0.3	–	–	–	–
FND	–	9.6	5.3	1.2	–	–	–	–
CCN^b	–	7.3	2.6	0.3	–	–	–	–
FDP	–	–	10.9	4.3	1.6	–	–	–
MEP	–	–	12.9	4.9	2.2	1.9	1.6	0.6
MAS	–	–	–	3.7	6.2	5.7	10.2	11.8
MIR	–	$-^e$	$-^e$	1.0	2.4	1.6	$-^f$	$-^f$
LCR	–	–	–	–	–	0.5	1.6	20.7
Convergencia	–	–	–	–	–	–	–	13.1
Others	2.6	6.2	6.5	4.9	5.4	8.0	9.8^g	7.4

Source: Consejo Supremo Electoral.
^{a}Party banned.
^{b}Cruzada Cívica Nacionalista, followers of the former dictator, Marcos Pérez Jiménez.
^{c}The PCV-legitimized UPA (Unión para Avanzar) participates in the congressional, legislative, and municipal council elections.
^{d}The IPFN became the FND.
^{e}Participation suspended due to joining the guerrillas.
^{f}MIR joined MAS in 1988.
^{g}Includes the Nueva Generación Democrática votes.

The weakening of Venezuela's dual party system came about within a framework of general dissatisfaction and lack of support for all political parties and, as will be discussed later, produced unsettling but important changes in local and regional voting patterns. The electorate's rejection of all parties was first shown when the public's overall opinion of them became more and more negative, when fewer and fewer people chose to formally join a party, and finally by ever-increasing voter absenteeism. This negative attitude toward political parties is not a new phenomenon. In a study done by John Martz and Enrique Baloyra (1979) during the 1970s, although 70 percent of the sample surveyed believed that overall the parties were an important part of the political process, an overwhelming 95 percent believed that there were too many parties, 81 percent thought that the parties were controlled by a powerful minority, and 70 percent said that parties were only concerned with winning elections.

According to more recent studies, public opinion of not only the parties but also the politicians has deteriorated even further. A survey published in *El Nacional* (1992) revealed that 65 percent of those polled believed that "this country's political parties are worthless," while only 26 percent replied that "they are the best tool we have available for solving Venezuela's problems." In the metropolitan areas, the rejection rate was 78 percent; three-quarters of the university students expressed the opinion that the parties were of no value. Thus, the electorate's perception of the political parties has been increasingly negative (see Table 5). In 1982, for example, 54 percent of those surveyed had a positive image of political parties, while only 30 percent viewed them in a negative light. In 1989

Table 5. Political Parties: The Evolution of Venezuelan Public Opinion, 1982–1992

	Favorable	*Not Favorable*
1982	54%	30%
1984	47	39
1985	52	48
1987	45	41
1989	55	37
1990	42	51
1991	35	59
1992	32	60

Source: Njaim et al., 1992.

the results were the same: 55 percent in favor and 37 percent against. Yet two years later, in March 1990, the figures were reversed: 51 percent considered parties to be of no value, while 42 percent believed that they were still a vehicle through which change could be achieved. Throughout 1991, polls showed that more than one-half of those surveyed had a negative opinion. Likewise, the public's image of politicians as managers was very negative. Of those polled, one-half believed that when it came to governing, politicians were highly or totally incompetent, while only 27 percent and 14 percent believed them to be either somewhat or very competent, respectively. Another national survey found that 60 percent of the population considered themselves to be against political parties, while only 14 percent viewed them favorably (Njaim et al., 1992).

This negative public opinion is consistent with the electorate's behavior during the 1993 presidential contests. In this election there were very clear distinctions among the four primary candidates. Three were young politicians who had held three of the most important positions available, yet the voters chose Rafael Caldera, an old leader who only five years earlier had presented himself as victim and opponent of the party machinery.

Although Caldera's 1993 campaign was the least party-oriented and most personalistic of the four, in many ways he represented the status quo. With a campaign platform that opposed the political changes and macroeconomic policies of the outgoing and disgraced government of Carlos Andrés Pérez, Caldera won the elections outright (see Table 6). Some of the political policies that he called into question included decentralization, competitive transfers, privatization of state-owned enterprises, and the liberalization of governmental economic controls. The results of the 1993 elections were labeled a "political earthquake" because for the first time since 1948, AD and COPEI lost a direct presidential vote. Prior to this time, these two parties had historically garnered the majority of the presidential votes. In 1993, together they took 45.3 percent.

Table 6. Percentage of Vote by Candidates in Presidential Elections, 1988 and 1993

1988 Candidates	Party	Vote	1993 Candidates	Party	Vote
Carlos Andrés Pérez	AD	52.9	Rafael Caldera	MAS-Convergencia	27.6
Eduardo Fernández	COPEI, MIN, FNP, ICC	40.4	Andrés Velázquez	LCR	21.3
Teodoro Petkoff	MAS	2.7	Oswaldo Alvarez Paz	COPEI	22.1
Godofredo Marín	ORA	0.9	Claudio Fermín	AD	23.2
Others		3.1	Others		5.8

Source: Consejo Supremo Electoral.

Although during his campaign Caldera berated the "topdogs" of the traditional parties, during this (his second presidency) he maintained the elite style of political negotiations which, up until 1988, had been the norm. In order to maintain control of the National Congress, Caldera was forced to make a pact with the conservative branch of AD. Lead by the party's Secretary General, Alfaro Ucero, this group opposed Pérez's leadership and policies.

Another tendency becoming more and more evident in Venezuela is the lack of party affiliation (see Table 7). Since 1973, when one-half of those polled indicated some type of party affiliation, all parties have seen their ranks shrink. In 1983 surveys showed that party affiliation had dropped to 38 percent; in 1990 and 1992 it was one-quarter.

Table 7. Percentage of Party Affiliation, 1973–1992

	Affiliated	*Not Affiliated*
1973	49.0	51.0
1983	38.4	61.6
1990	23.6	76.4
1992	26.1	72.9

Sources: For 1973, Martz and Baloyra (1979); for 1983, Torres (1985); for 1990, Molina and Pérez (1993); for 1992, Njaim et al. (1992).

A third example of how the electorate is distancing itself from the political party system is the increasing rate of absenteeism. Prior to 1973, absenteeism rates were consistently below 10 percent. Although this level rose somewhat during the 1983 and 1988 elections, rates seen during the 1993 election were truly alarming. Such changes are much more obvious at the national level than at the local and regional level, where abstention has always been much higher (see Table 8).

Table 8. Percentage of Absenteeism in National and Local Elections, 1958–1993

National Elections	*Absenteeism*	*Local Elections*	*Absenteeism*
1958	8	1979	27
1963	9	1984	40
1968	6	1989	53
1973	3	1992	45
1978	12	1995[a]	60
1983	12		
1988	18		
1993	40		

Source: Consejo Supremo Electoral.
[a]Unofficial figures.

Although absenteeism has always been higher in the local and regional elections than in the national ones, when compared to 1979 and 1984 the rates seen in 1989, 1992, and 1995 were markedly higher. And despite the fact that beginning in 1989 local elections have been held immediately after the implementation of major reforms in the political system, the absentee rate increased. To date, the decentralization of the political system as well as the direct election of local and state authorities have been the most profound changes made since 1958, when Venezuela embarked upon its democratic adventure. But the levels of absenteeism seem to indicate that, at least from the electorate's point of view, these changes have not generated the support that their proponents promised. The explanations given for this increase are varied but generally include the electorate's rejection of the existing political party system, the delegitimization of the national elites, and the perceived lack of usefulness of the electoral process (Sosa, 1993).

Throughout the twentieth century, after having survived the regional caudillos imposed upon them by Juan Vicente Gómez, Venezuela's political mind-set has been nationalistic and centralist. But, starting in 1958, partisanship also came into play. Venezuela has never seen a nonpartisan election like those that sometimes occur at the local level in the United States. National parties, with their centralist organizational style, have always played an important role in not only local parish elections but even in one such as those held within local unions and neighborhood associations. Some attribute this enormous presence of highly centralized and disciplined party politics to the organizational void that seems to exist in Venezuelan society (Levine, 1973). Others attribute it to the socialist or Christian democratic foundation of most of the major parties that caused them to emphasize the vote of the economically disadvantaged and to provide a State that seeks to provide solutions for the social and economic problems of its citizenry. Even during candidate-driven campaigns, the candidate is presented as a sensitive person who identifies with the problems of the poor and who will be able to satisfy their needs once in office. A highly accurate word to describe Venezuelan politics is "populist" (Brito García, 1988).

On the other hand, Venezuelan politics has always been predominately male oriented. Women were not able to vote until after the October 18 Revolution of 1945; and although each party has its women's caucus, such groups have generally been weak. Traditionally, women's participation both in the overall party organization as well as in government has been low. During the entire thirty-eight years of democracy, only twice have women run as candidates in the party primaries (once in AD and once in MAS). On both occasions, they were roundly defeated. Never has a woman aspired to be COPEI's presidential candidate. Women have only run twice for the presidency. Ismenia de Villalba, widow of URD party founder Jovito Villalba (who along with Caldera and Betancourt signed the Punto Fijo Accords), ran in 1989 but won only 0.9 percent of the votes. The other female candidate ran in 1993 and garnered less than 0.1 percent. Within the executive branch, one cabinet position, the Ministry of the Family, is reserved for women. All other cabinet posts are held almost exclusively by men.

Beginning in 1979, important changes in the democratic process began to revive independent and local activities within the nation's regions which, with time, have made themselves manifest in part by the increasing tendency toward personalist local and regional politics. These changes have also somewhat opened the process up to women. One of the most noticeable is the emergence of a new, locally based leadership that depends more directly on its immediate constituency and is not as strictly bound to the national leadership's policies. Although the majority of all the municipal councils, mayors, and governors are still members of either AD or COPEI, the separation of national and local elections in conjunction with the new direct election of the governors and mayors has opened up the possibility for the development of new types of leadership. First, it allows the smaller national minority parties, such as MAS and La Causa R, to elect candidates to the top executive offices in some states and municipalities (see Tables 9, 10, 11, and 12).

In the gubernatorial and mayoral elections of 1989, only two governors and thirteen mayors (10 percent and 4.7 percent respectively) were not members of either AP or COPEI. In 1992, seventeen (out of twenty-two, or 22.7 percent) governors were from AD/COPEI, yet this coalition took only slightly more than half of the country's mayoral races. Finally, in 1995, the number of non-AD/COPEI governors rose to seven (of twenty-one, or 31.8 percent), while in the mayoral contests in the country's twenty-seven largest cities, non-AD/COPEI mayors won eleven races.

A second significant development has been the success of specific local or regional organizations openly opposed to the national parties. A perfect example is the 1992 campaign of Angel Enrique Zambrano, the son of an old-time AD leader, who became the independent candidate of Decisión Ciudadana (Citizen's Decision), a political organization made up of neighborhood associations from the southeastern parts of Caracas. Zambrano was elected mayor of Baruta. By 1995, however, the voters' evaluation of his performance had soured. Although he ran for reelection, he was defeated by Ivonne Attas, who ran with COPEI's support. Another interesting example is Proyecto Carabobo, a regional offshoot of COPEI and a

Table 9. Election Results by Party of Gubernatorial Races, 1989, 1993, and 1995

	1989		1993		1995[a]
	Percentage of Vote	Number of Governors	Percentage of Vote	Number of Governors	Number of Governors
AD	39.7	11	32.5	8	10
COPEI	32.0	7	42.7	9[b]	4[c]
AD-COPEI	–	–	–	–	1
MAS	17.8	1	13.8	4	4[d]
LCR	2.5	1	6.1	1	1
Convergencia	–	–	–	–	1
Others	8.1	0	5.0	0	1
Total	100.1	20	100.1	22	21

Source: Consejo Supremo Electoral.
[a]Official figures for percentage of vote unavailable.
[b]Coalition with MAS in Carabobo, Falcón, and Miranda.
[c]Coalition with MAS in Nueva Esparta.
[d]Coalition with COPEI in Aragua, with Convergencia in Lara and with COPEI and Convergencia in Portuguesa and Sucre.

Table 10. Election Results by Party of Mayoral Races, 1989, 1992, and 1995

	1989*		1992*		1995**	
Party	Number of Mayors	Percentage	Number of Mayors	Percentage	Number of Mayors	Percentage
AD	152	56.5	124	25.7	11	40.7
COPEI	104	38.7	123	25.6	5	18.5
MAS	9	3.3	224	46.6	2	7.4
LCR	2	.7	5	1.0	2	7.4
Others	2	.7	5	1.0	7	25.9
Total	269		481		27	

Source: Consejo Supremo Electoral.
*Number of mayors elected nationwide.
**Number of mayors elected in 27 largest cities.

Table 11. Election Results by State of Gubernatorial Races, 1992 and 1995

	1992 Winner	Party	1995 Winner[a]	Party
Amazonas	Edgar Sayago M.	MAS	Bernabé Gutiérrez	AD
Anzoátegui	Ovidio González	COPEI-MAS	Denis Balza[b]	AD
Apure	Marcelo Oquendo	AD	José C. Montilla	AD
Aragua	Carlos Tablante	MAS	Didalco Bolívar	MAS-COPEI
Barinas	Rafael Rosales	AD	Gerhard Cartay	COPEI
Bolívar	Andrés Velázquez	LCR	José Carvajal[c]	AD
Carabobo	Henrique Salas R.	COPEI-MAS	Henrique Salas F.	Proyecto Carabobo
Cojedes	José F. Machado	COPEI	Alberto Galíndez	AD
Delta Amacuro	Emery Mata M.	COPEI	Emery Mata M.	COPEI-AD
Falcón	Aldo Cermeño	COPEI-MAS	José Curiel	COPEI
Guárico	José A. Malavé	COPEI	Rafael Silveira	AD
Lara	José M. Navarro	AD	Orlando Fernández	MAS-Convergencia
Mérida	José R. Nucete	COPEI	William Dávila	AD
Miranda	Arnaldo Arocha	COPEI-MAS	Enrique Mendoza	COPEI
Monagas	Guillermo Call	AD	Luis E. Martínez	AD
Nueva Esparta	Morel Rodríguez	AD	Rafael Tovar	COPEI-MAS
Portuguesa	Elías D'onghia	AD	Ivan Colmenaes	MAS-COPEI
Sucre	Ramón Martínez	MAS	Ramón Martínez	MAS-Convergencia
Táchira	José Ron Sandoval	AD	Ricardo Méndez[c]	AD
Trujillo	José Méndez Q.	AD	Luis E. González	AD
Yaracuy	Nelson Suárez	COPEI	Eduardo Lapi	Convergencia
Zulia	Oswaldo Alvarez[d]	COPEI	Francisco Arias	LCR

Source: Supreme Electoral Tribune.

[a]Unofficial results.

[b]Results impugned due to public uproar.

[c]Resigned to participate in 1993 campaign. Lolita Anillar was elected as MAS substitute.

Table 12. Election Results by City of Mayoral Races, 1992 and 1995

	1992 Winner	Party	1995 Winner[a]	Party
Acarigua	Pedro Zapata	AD	Dimas Salcedo	COPEI-MAS
Barcelona[b]	José Salazar	AD	José Salazar	AD
Barinas[b]	Miguel Rosales	PP	Rogelio Peña	AD
Barquisimeto[b]	Nelson Piña	COPEI	Macario González	MAS-Convergencia
Bolívar[b]	Leonel Jiménez	LCR	Leonel Jiménez	LCR
Guayana	Clemente Scoto	LCR	Pastora Medina	LCR
Coro[b]	Rodolfo Barráez	COPEI	Rodolfo Barráez	COPEI
Cumaná[b]	Eloy Gil	AD	Eloi Figuera	MAS
Guanare[b]	Juan C. Pérez O.	COPEI	Juan C. Pérez O.	COPEI-MAS
Los Teques[b]	Freddy Martínez	COPEI	Freddy Martínez	COPEI
Maracaibo[b]	F. Chumaceiro	COPEI	M. Rosales[c]	AD
Maracay[b]	William Querales	MAS	Estela de Asuaje	AD
Maturín[b]	José López	COPEI	Domingo Urbina	AD
Mérida[b]	Simón Valdés	COPEI	R. Colmenares	AD

	1992 Winner	Party	1995 Winner[a]	Party
Porlamar	Pedro Velázquez	COPEI	Carlos Rodríguez	AD
Pto. Ayacucho[b]	Nelson Silva	AD	Hugo Alencar	AD
Pto. Cabello	Ricardo J. Dao	AD	Alfredo Sabatino	MAS-Convergencia
Pto. La Cruz	José Brito	COPEI	José Brito	MAS
Punto Fijo	Rolando Mora	COPEI	Rolando Mora	COPEI
San Carlos[b]	Teófilo Rangel	COPEI	Teófilo Rangel	COPEI
San Cristóbal[b]	Sergio Calderón	COPEI	Sergio Calderón	COPEI
San Felipe[b]	Estelita de Rua	COPEI	Fhandor Quiroga	MAS-Convergencia
San Fernando[b]	Dario Barrientos	AD	Simón Navas	AD
San Juan[b]	Argenis Ranuárez	COPEI	Julio Torrealba	AD
Trujillo[b]	Antonio García	AD	Leonardo Torres	AD
Tucupita[b]	Ramón Yánez	MAS	Ramón Yánez	MAS
Valencia[b]	Argeris Escarri	COPEI	F. Cabrera	Proyecto Carabobo

Source: Supreme Electoral Tribunal.
[a] Unofficial results.
[b] State capital.
[c] Results impugned due to public uproar.

personalistic organization similar to what Angelo Panebianco calls a professional electorate party (Panebianco, 1982). This independent organization grew out of a split within COPEI when Henrique Salas Feo, the son of Governor Henrique Salas Römer, refused to accept the party's decision to back the mayor of Valencia, Argeris Escarri, for governor. Salas Feo broke ranks and campaigned for the office as an independent candidate, for which he was summarily expelled from the party. Interestingly, his father, who openly supported the campaign and the new organization, is still one of the venerated militants within the party. Taking on not only COPEI's but also AD's candidate, Proyecto Carabobo won both the governor's seat as well as the mayoral race in Valencia.

As can be seen from Tables 9–12, AD in 1995 won more elections than any of the other parties, taking ten gubernatorial seats and 162 of a possible 330 mayoral races. Of the smaller parties, MAS was the most successful. In fact, the party that has benefited the most from the increase in regional politics is MAS.

MAS. Founded in 1971, at the national level MAS has always attempted to portray itself as a valid option for those who are to the left of AD or COPEI. However, it was not until 1988 that MAS experienced any significant increase in its share of the votes cast either in the presidential or congressional elections. But, at the local and regional levels, the party has been more successful. Indeed, during the last three national elections MAS's share has always been between 4 and 6 percent. In response, many of the party's faithful coined the phrase, "the 5 percent glass ceiling." By softening its socialist stance and radical governmental programs along with the development of a "two front" campaign strategy that focused more on the positive personal images of its regional leaders and less on the traits of its presidential candidate, Teodoro Petkoff, MAS broke through the glass ceiling in 1988. Later in 1992, a combination of three other factors advanced MAS's position even more: 1) the successful campaigns waged by its candidates for governor in Zulia, Aragua, Sucre, and Amazonas; 2) the high regard that voters had for several of its candidates, who, although they did not win their respective races, had a very positive showing in Lara and Táchira; and 3) the enormous popularity of its presidential candidate, Rafael Caldera.

The MAS is no longer simply a large centralized party; instead, it has become the national umbrella organization for several strong regional leaders. Former leaders such as Teodoro Petkoff, Pompeyo Márquez (a member of Caldera's cabinet), and Freddy Múñoz (who left the party in 1995) no longer exercise the influence they once had. No longer is there just one party line, one program, or one clearly defined national image. Much of MAS's success at the regional level is due to the popularity of local leaders who are either relatively or completely unknown in the national arena.

LCR. Up through 1993, LCR also experienced substantial growth in its share of the electorate. Founded by former PCV leader Alfredo Maneiro, LCR does not have a clearly defined ideology or set of programs. Since 1983 the party has been under the quasi-Stalinist control of three different men: Andrés Velázquez, a leader in the workers' movement who began his political career at the state-owned foundry, Siderurgia del Orinoco (SIDOR); Aristóbulo Iztúriz, a former teacher and member of AD and MEP; and Pablo Medina, who during the 1960s was an activist and guerrilla. Since 1993 several retired military officers who were very critical of the existing political system have joined the LCR leadership. A prime example is retired Lt. Col. Francisco Arias Cárdenas, the 1995 candidate for governor of Zulia. In 1992, Colonel Arias was one of the primary organizers of the failed 4F military uprising. During the 1983 and 1988 elections, LCR's share of the national vote grew at a modest rate, but in 1989 its candidates for governor of the state of Bolívar (Andrés Velázquez) and mayor of that state's most important city (Clemente Scoto) won their races. Then, in 1992, not only were Velázquez and Scoto reelected, but Aristóbulo Iztúriz was elected mayor of Caracas. The following year, in the presidential election, LCR came in third, capturing 21 percent of the vote, right behind AD and COPEI, each of whom garnered about 23 percent. More important, LCR beat out both MAS and Convergencia.

At the national level LCR's growth between 1983 and 1993 can only be described as amazing. In 1983 only 5,917 votes (0.09 percent) were cast for its candidates, putting it in eighth place. Again, in 1988, LCR came in eighth (1.6 percent). But by 1989 the situation had changed radically. Velázquez took 40.3 percent of the vote and won the governor's race in Bolívar; he then was reelected in 1992 with 63.4 percent. In Caracas, Iztúriz took on two powerful opponents, Claudio Fermín, the incumbent mayor and 1993 AD presidential candidate, and Petkoff, MAS's 1993 presidential candidate. But Iztúriz drew 34.5 percent and won, making him the mayor of the seat of national government. This result is in sharp contrast to the prior national elections (1989) when the LCR candidates had only managed to win 1.4 percent of the vote.

This surge in public acceptance suffered a major setback during the 1995 campaign, when all three LCR leaders were either directly or indirectly defeated. The party's primary rival, AD, won the governorship in LCR's home state of Bolívar as well as the mayor's race in the Libertador municipality of Caracas. Pablo Medina, who on two prior occasions had run for governor of Miranda, came in fourth behind AD, COPEI, and Convergencia. Its only success was the election of Colonel Arias in Zulia, but even this result cannot be attributed to a growing acceptance of LCR in the region. Arias's election was more likely due to his personal charisma and the split in MAS, whereas former MAS members supported Arias instead of the party's candidate, Lolita Anillar.

At least in Caracas and Miranda, the LCR decline is due to the basic characteristics of the party's organization and the informal affiliation of its constituents. In analyzing LCR's organization, Gonzalo Barrios Ferrer (1995) predicted the existence of an upper limit to the party's ability to expand its constituency and support base. Barrios Ferrer argued: 1) that the party's ideology and political discourse were ambiguous and lacked specific responses to public issues; 2) that the party's organization not only did not have a permanent machinery but also lacked a pool of members to assume government positions; and 3) that it was extremely sectarian and nondemocratic.

Another factor is that LCR's internal structures have also been changing. A local leadership now exists that is directly linked to its constituents and that is not obligated to follow instructions blindly from national headquarters. Also, the relationship between the state and national governments has been changing because up until 1989, governors were appointed and served at the will of the president. The majority of these new regional leaders are in their forties and apparently are willing and able to replace those leaders who have been in control since 1958, when democracy became Venezuela's form of government. In fact, in the 1993 elections three of the four main candidates were local or regional officeholders: two were governors and one was a mayor. AD's candidate was Claudio Fermín, the relatively young mayor of Libertador; COPEI's was Oswaldo Alvarez Paz, the then governor of Zulia; LCR backed Andrés Velázquez, the governor of Bolívar and the youngest of all of the candidates. Even MAS, before selecting Rafael Caldera as its candidate, had debated the possibility of naming Carlos Tablante, the young two-term governor of Aragua.

Oswaldo Alvarez Paz's selection as the COPEI candidate set a precedent. He had been governor of Zulia, having been first elected in 1989 with one-third of the vote and then reelected in 1992 with two-thirds. In 1993 he ran in Venezuela's first experiment with direct party primary elections. Close to one-quarter of all registered voters participated in the COPEI primaries. The two other candidates were COPEI Secretary General Eduardo Fernández, who in 1987 had ousted Caldera as the leader of the party machinery and been the party's presidential candidate in 1988, and Humberto Calderón Bertí, a former Minister of Energy, Minister of Foreign Relations, and former president of OPEC. Alvarez Paz soundly defeated both of these competitors, taking 64.4 percent of the vote, while Fernández won 29.3 percent and Calderón Bertí 6.7 percent.

Another figure to watch in COPEI is the governor of Carabobo, Henrique Salas Römer. He was first elected governor in 1989, but in 1992, when he ran with the support of not only COPEI but also of MAS and twenty other political organizations, Salas Römer was reelected with the highest percentage of votes ever garnered by any candidate in Venezuela, 72.9 percent. An able politician, he managed to survive the rift that split his party in 1992. Alvarez Paz's people were pitted against Caldera's followers; Caldera finally left the party that he had helped found to establish the Convergencia. During the 1993 elections, Salas Römer was able tacitly to support Caldera without having to abandon COPEI. He is now being touted as a possible candidate for the 1998 presidential campaign, not only by COPEI but also by Convergencia, since its main leaders are both sons of Rafael Caldera and constitutionally cannot succeed him.

The regionalization and decentralization process of Venezuelan politics has not been easy, and it has unleashed an impressive struggle for power. As Daniel Levine (1973) pointed out more than two decades ago, the political system set in motion in 1958 has a set of clear and known "rules of the game" accepted by all of the parties. These rules, together with the society's great organizational vacuum and the extensive organizational capacities of the structurally centralized, highly disciplined, but internally undemocratic political parties, provided Venezuela with the means to manage conflict by reducing it to its smallest form. In other words, the

nation's process of minimizing conflict has presupposed the existence of Leninist-style political organizations. Yet these same organizations have been in crisis since the 1970s, given that most of
their constituents no longer feel represented and their effectiveness has been eroded by progressive regionalization. Thus, the
political conflicts that the Caracas-based national leadership used
to regulate and even prevent have become much more frequent.
One of the consequences of the decentralization process has been
the undermining of the elites' national political power, which has
increased the struggle for control at the local and regional level.

This growth in the electorate's support for new leaders such as
Velázquez, Iztúriz, Tablante, and other candidates of traditionally
small parties gives clear evidence of how regional and local politics is becoming more dynamic. The opening up of new channels
of voter participation due to the national decentralization policies
has renewed the political class, at least at the regional level. Although it is still unclear if these new leaders will be successful in
their efforts to replace the traditional political elites, what is known
is that given their rapid growth, parties such as La Causa Radical
are having difficulty in controlling and disciplining their new members and leaders.

The 1995 election confirms the continuation of this change.
During these elections not only the results but also the campaigns
themselves are evidence of how the local and regional leaders are
becoming more autonomous. A clear example is how parties that
at the national level are bitter rivals were able to enter into coalitions at the regional level. Table 11 shows how for the first time in
the history of Venezuela, AD and COPEI were able to work together
on behalf of one candidate, Emery Mata Millan, as governor of Delta
Amacuro. The same two parties also attempted to work jointly in
Lara, but failed when Orlando Fernández, a candidate supported
by MAS and Convergencia, won the governorship.

During 1995 other states saw the establishment of other local
coalitions as parties attempted to get their candidates elected. In
Aragua, MAS aligned itself with COPEI, although at the national
level these two opposed one another. Convergencia aligned itself
with its primary presidential opponent, AD. In Sucre the incumbent, Ramón Martínez, was reelected after brokering a coalition with
MAS, COPEI, and Convergencia. And finally, in the island state of
Nueva Esparta, COPEI's candidate Rafael Tovar, the owner of the

only maritime passenger and cargo service to the island, won after getting the support of MAS and COPEI.

While all the local and regional realignments were being negotiated, at the national level, again for the first time in Venezuelan history, AD, with the support of COPEI and LCR, voted to censure Carlos Walter, the Minister of Public Health, an act that constitutionally required him to resign. But this unprecedented move had no influence on coalitions at the regional and local level, thus indicating that the regions have acquired a high degree of political independence.

An important case of leadership that deserves special mention, because it is paradigmatic of the changes that seem to be occurring in the Venezuelan political system, concerns Irene Sáez. In her role as a mayor she exemplifies not only changes within the national political system but also redefinition of the role of women, the replacement of the old partisan leadership with a more personalist one, and the inauguration of a new style of political showmanship. In 1989, as a former Miss Universe who was the corporate representative of an important financial group, Sáez was elected mayor of Chacao with the support of a multiparty coalition that included AD and COPEI. When her term was up, again a coalition of parties that included everyone except LCR supported her; and although the absenteeism rate was 60 percent, she won 90 percent of the vote. During her term in office, however, Sáez has managed to remain an independent.

Chacao was created by the Miranda legislative assembly in 1989, separating it from the municipality of Sucre. Chacao consists of the most exclusive areas of Caracas and several important commercial areas and malls. It has the lowest poverty rate in the country as well as the lowest population density. In other words, Chacao is the richest and least problematic of all of Venezuela's municipalities. For Sucre, the separation of Chacao was a major economic blow. Sucre was left with a small upper-class residential area, some industrial and commercial areas, and Petare, which has more than one million extremely poor residents.

Taking advantage of the huge tax potential of the new Chacao municipality, Sáez established a political regime based upon an effective program of urban beautification and public safety. This agenda, coupled with an adroitness in handling the news media, has permitted the mayor to present herself as an efficient manager and as a real, politically viable option. The leading issues of her campaign have been the improvement of the administrative and traffic police forces. She recruits young students and professionals who tend to be taller than average and lighter skinned than most of the police in the city and supplies them with uniforms that are more up-to-date than in other areas.

This image is important because in Venezuela, and especially in Caracas, the police are looked down upon. They are regularly accused of being corrupt and of violating human rights. Their blue uniforms are generally disheveled. They are badly armed, badly paid, and tend to live in the poorest parts of town, next door to the very criminals and gang members whom they are supposed to control. The same can be said for the national highway police. Thus, when Sáez created the two new police forces, her popularity soared, not only within Chacao but also throughout the country. All of these accomplishments have made it likely that she will be a presidential nominee in 1998.

Irene Sáez's case is the end result of two important tendencies seen in Venezuela's urban political scene: showmanship and personalism. Sáez does not depend on the leadership of any of the parties. To the contrary, she manages to use their machinery to advance her agenda. She has no well-defined or articulated ideology, nor does she talk about specific plans or programs, instead limiting her speeches to underlining the importance of governing Chacao in an efficient and honest fashion. She is the favorite of the news media.

The importance of personality in Sáez's government is so overwhelming that in Chacao the emergency phone number is 800-IRENE, and the city's residents tend to call the area Ireneland. During her recent reelection campaign, she took advantage of the busy holiday season to introduce a Barbie-like doll bearing her name. Although these acts may seem anecdotal, they are key to understanding how Venezuela's political system has become trivialized, interested in the packaging rather than in the policies themselves, and dependent upon the constant use of and support from the news media.

Irene Sáez's political career has influenced campaigns throughout the nation. During the 1995 campaign season, many candidates promised their constituents a life like that in Chacao. An example occurred in Ivonne Attas's race in Baruta. A former vice president of the Chacao city council, Attas printed copies of a photograph of her with Sáez and emblazoned it with the slogan, "From Chacao to Baruta, one straight shot."

It must be pointed out that Irene Sáez is neither the first nor the only female to be mayor within Caracas. Gloria Capriles of COPEI governed Baruta from 1989 to 1992. From 1992 through 1995, El Hatillo, formerly a part of Baruta, was also governed by a woman. Notwithstanding all these examples, statistically women have not played an active role in Venezuelan municipal politics. In 1992, of a total of 1,365 mayoral positions, women only took part in 11 percent of the races. In the Caracas area, the female participation rate is only slightly higher (16 percent) during the 1995 elections, although such rates always tend to be higher in the urban areas.

Entertainers and television and radio personalities have also been cropping up at the local and regional level. The most famous of these may be Irene Sáez, but Ivonne Attas is a former soap opera star; and in one of the outlying bedroom communities in Miranda, Lila Morillo, a well-known singer, ran an exuberant race for mayor. On the gubernatorial level, Orlando Fernández, who in 1995 became governor of Lara after serving two terms in the National Congress (1988 and 1993), first became famous because of his radio show where he systematically attacked all the local officeholders. Another case is Alexis Rosas, a prominent political reporter, who in 1993 was elected to Congress for the LCR party and then in 1995 ran for governor of Anzoátegui, where he finished second.

In Venezuela the participation of such personalities is not new, since celebrities have always been active in campaigns, appearing in radio and television spots on behalf of the presidential candidates of AD, COPEI, and MAS. What is new, however, especially given the nationwide pattern of rejecting political parties, is the number of celebrities who are running for either municipal council or mayor.

Election Campaigns

Today's local leaders' communication styles with the voters differ from those previously employed by the national political elites. Since 1973, when political and ideological debates concerning the guerrilla problem were overcome, political debate in Venezuela has been characterized by a remarkable similarity in the platforms presented by all of the presidential candidates as well as in the positions taken on the most important campaign issues (Njaim, 1980).

Given the need that each candidate has to differentiate his platform from the other candidates' in the eyes of the voters, each campaign has emphasized the personality of its front-runner and the
personal flaws of the opponents (Alvarez, 1987).

Edelman (1988) has argued that the language used during these
campaigns by the media turns political reality into mass entertain-
ment. In Venezuela this phenomenon has taken the form of a populist show, where the candidates become individuals endowed with
quasi-magical attributes that enable them to solve all of society's
problems, the product of corrupt opposition governments, which
are solely responsible for these predicaments. The target audience
of this campaign is "the people," a largely unidentified mass that
has no means to solve its own problems, has been rendered immo-
bile, and has nothing more to do than applaud and wait for the
next government's handouts (Brito García, 1988:67–85).

Since 1988 constant mutual accusations of corruption and other
criminal acts have been added to the problems mentioned above.
There can be no doubt that by following this style of politics the
leadership has itself contributed to the present critical level of distrust. Throughout its democratic history, socioeconomic issues such
as inflation and unemployment have been priorities. However, since
1978, and especially during the 1992 and 1993 campaigns, the corruption of the political class has become a key issue in the electoral
debate.

In sharp contrast to the 1963, 1968, and 1973 elections, since
1978 political campaigns have become more and more characterized by constant attacks on the government, to the point that it is
no longer uncommon for the incumbent party's candidate to distance himself from the government and attack it so harshly that it
would appear as though he belonged to the opposition party. For
example, during the 1963 election, Raúl Leoni, the AD candidate,
simply promised to continue the reforms begun under AD President Rómulo Betancourt. In turn, AD candidate Gonzalo Barrios's
campaign never attacked Leoni's government but instead was based
largely on Barrios's personality. COPEI's Lorenzo Fernández's 1973
campaign presented him as the candidate both of the party and of
former President Caldera.

By 1978, however, AD candidate Luis Piñerúa had started a
trend that has become increasingly widespread. One of the most
important slogans in his campaign was "Piñerúa, ¡correcto!"—a
statement that implied that he was more honest and upright than

President Pérez (AD), who had been denounced as corrupt and immoral by the opposition. In 1983, when former President Caldera again wanted to run for office, he tried to distance himself as much as possible from the incumbent COPEI government, then headed by Luis Herrera Campíns. The other COPEI candidate, Eduardo Fernández, took this trend to an extreme, organizing a campaign wherein he was the "new candidate" taking on "old politics," which he identified as not only his major opponent, former President Carlos Andrés Pérez, but also two former COPEI presidents, Caldera and Herrera Campíns. But a Fernández television spot went too far and provoked a strong response from Herrera Campíns that was broadcast live during prime time. AD then ran several television spots questioning Fernández's trustworthiness and accusing him of betraying the principal leaders of his own party, in particular Caldera, with whom for years Fernández had enjoyed a virtual father-son relationship.

Attacking previous governments as the culprits of all common ills has thus been established as a permanent theme in Venezuelan electoral rhetoric for some years. It also has become fashionable to completely discredit one's opponents, a strategy in use even during primary campaigns. Allegations of corruption have become the weapon of choice for all levels of political campaigning. Since 1988, charges of corruption in campaign finances have become an important tool in the effort to discredit the opponent, especially since in Venezuela these matters are not well regulated (Alvarez, 1995). In fact, during the 1988 presidential race, each of the AD and COPEI candidates (Carlos Andrés Pérez and Eduardo Fernández, respectively) went so far as to insinuate that his opponent was receiving contributions from drug traffickers.

It is a fact that in Venezuela election campaigns are costly. Although parties do not divulge the actual expenditures or their sources, press statements made by both the AD's and COPEI's campaign managers confirmed that the 1988 contests cost each party over U.S.$12 million. COPEI incurred similar expenditures during the 1993 primaries. These high costs, together with undeclared contributions, are fertile ground for corruption. It is known, for example, that funds belonging to the so-called secret resources of the Ministry of Domestic Relations (charged with paying security and defense expenses) were used in 1988 to purchase utility vehicles to be used by AD campaign managers during Pérez's bid. These same vehicles later became the personal property of these managers. The revelation of this scandal forced the Attorney General to request that the Supreme Court hold a hearing on the question of whether criminal charges should be filed against former President Jaime Lusinchi and his Secretary of State.

Given that the 1979 and 1984 local political races only allowed voters to choose between specific slates or blocs of candidates, these campaigns tried to do little more than mobilize party loyalists. Those parties that won the 1978 and 1983 presidential campaigns made widespread use of the image of the president and his party but, in general, did not address specific local issues. Although 1989 was the first time that voters elected their own governors and mayors, this campaign also did not focus on local issues. Indeed, opposition leaders who won their governors' races ran campaigns that tended to emphasize the national issue that brought them to prominence, namely, corruption. By the end of President Lusinchi's term in office, the issue of administrative corruption had become a major one in the political debate. Representatives Tablante, Velázquez, and Alvarez Paz made corruption the leitmotif of their speeches during their respective campaigns for governor.

The 1992 and 1995 Caracas mayoral campaigns differed from those in other departments. The candidates from Baruta, Chacao, El Hatillo, and Sucre focused on local problems such as safety, police, land use, and traffic problems. But in Libertador, the largest Department of Caracas with the largest low-income population, national and local issues played an important role in the mayoral campaign. The main issues included the legitimacy of President Pérez's government and his removal from office, the credibility of the national parties, political instability, the eventuality of a military coup, and the impact of macroeconomic adjustments imposed at the national level. At the same time, local issues such as those dealing with police safety and the growth of a local economy were also emphasized. During the 1995 presidential race, Rafael Caldera's policies were roundly attacked in local campaigns.

The campaign waged by Caracas's present mayor, Aristóbulo Iztúriz, has been one of double entendres. His slogans "Caracas no se devuelve" and "La batalla de Caracas" may be interpreted in two ways. The first slogan not only means that Caracas will not go back but it suggests as well that LCR is not willing to give power back to AD, especially in light of the second slogan, which literally translated means the battle or struggle for Caracas.

MAS and Convergencia jointly nominated their national Secretary General, Enrique Ochoa Antich, a young party leader who was unanimously elected representative for the Federal District. Ochoa was only able to attain his position as Secretary General after defeating two of the founding but now aging members of MAS who sought the position. Ochoa, whose brother was the Minister of Defense who helped put down the 4F military rebellion, is positioning himself to be his party's candidate for president during the 1998 elections.

Conclusion

Given Venezuela's national political reality until 1988, the recent regionalization process has made local elections much more democratic and accessible. Today, the leaders of parties who are minor players at the national level can be elected locally to important offices. Notwithstanding all these changes, major barriers still restrict access to the electoral process. Three factors severely limit the effect of these democratic changes within the Venezuelan political system: 1) the high cost of campaigning, 2) unequal access to the means of communication, and 3) the lack of an automated voting procedure that has become a source of power for the party's vote-getting machinery.

Two of these factors are especially important during the campaign season: cost, and the lack of equal access to the means of communication. To compete with any realistic expectation of winning requires a budget in excess of U.S.$10 million. Coupled with this high cost is the fact that all three privately owned television stations, most of the radio stations, and most of the national and regional printed media are controlled by two multimedia conglomerates, 1BC and the Diego Cisneros Organization. Thus, access to these means of communication is limited to those whose politics agree with these conglomerates (Giménez and Hernández, 1988). But even if these hurdles are overcome, a final barrier is raised by a voting procedure that still requires the manual counting of the ballots at each polling site. A huge and unwieldy human army of nearly one hundred thousand people is the only method presently in place to assure clean voting. Since the ballots are destroyed once the vote is entered on the record, there exists little redress in case of any irregularity that may have occurred during the counting process.

No political system guarantees full, equal, and free access to the electoral process. Democracy as a political system is especially sensitive to the need to remove all possible restrictions. For all practical purposes, Venezuela still requires that a party, to be effective, must have ample money, a well-oiled machine, and a working relationship with the owners of the media. Initially, media access may seem expensive, but advertising will improve a candidate's standings vis-à-vis the national surveys, which in turn will give him access to those monies controlled by so-called political investors. The intertwining of these factors has made participation in Venezuelan politics more a function of machinery, money, and mass media than of ideology or policies.

On the other hand, all of the changes described here have been achieved within a context of severe economic crisis that recent governments have been unable to resolve. Economic measures imposed have not controlled inflation, have further skewed the nation's income distribution, and have weakened its currency. The deepening of the socioeconomic crisis has further undermined the public's trust in the national political parties and its sense of order. Table 9 showed an increasing lack of public support for any of the parties. In addition, events such as violent protests and two failed military coup attempts are deeply troubling, especially in light of the historically conciliatory role played by the parties for the last several decades. By establishing a set of clear and stable "rules of the game," the parties contained or encapsulated political conflict, thereby minimizing its effect on the general society.

The current political crisis has provoked a resurgence of open conflict at a level unknown since the outbreak of the guerrilla movement of the early 1970s. New arenas of conflict that pit regions against the center have opened up, thus destroying the existing rules. The present-day national leadership tends to view the new emergent regional leaders as a threat to its hegemony. However, all indications suggest that these new leaders, who, thanks to the opening up of the electoral process, have managed to consolidate considerable political support, hold the key to Venezuela's ability to survive the crisis. The November 27, 1992 coup attempt seems to have had the positive effect of reenforcing the populace's faith in the democratic (if not the party) system. The people apparently believe that by electing new local leaders, political change can be achieved. It is as though the voters have offered a hard compromise: substitute the old-line, centralist party leadership with new independent candidates who have proven themselves at the local and regional level in exchange for an improvement in the levels of trust and credibility afforded the government, attributes which are essential if a democracy is to survive economic difficulties.

References

Alvarez, Angel. 1987. "Los contenidos de la propaganda electoral y la protección de la racionalidad política del elector." In Manuel Vicente Magallanes, ed., *Propaganda política, partidos y sistema electoral*, 63–104. Caracas: Consejo Supremo Electoral, Colección Cincuentenario No. 2.

———. 1990. "Estrategias de propaganda y competencia interpartidista." In Manuel Vicente Magallanes, ed., *Mandato político, evolución electoral, comunicación y sociedad*, pp. 157–78. Caracas: Consejo Supremo Electoral, Colección Cincuentenario No. 9.

———. 1994. *Estrategias de propaganda electoral en Venezuela*. Caracas: Universidad Central de Venezuela.

———. 1995. "Competencia política, igualdad de oportunidades y financiamiento de los partidos." In Angel Alvarez, ed., *Reforma de los partidos políticos, financiamiento y democracia*, pp. 11–106. Caracas: Konrad Adenauer Stiftung and COPRE (Comisión Presidencial para la Reforma del Estado).

Barrios Ferrer, Gonzalo. 1995. "Cambios en el sistema de partidos venezolanos, con especial referencia a la Causa Radical." *Cuestiones Políticas* (Maracaibo) 14, no. 214: 5–18.

Bloom, David. 1980. "El desarrollo de los partidos políticos en Venezuela: Crecimiento electoral del partido social cristiano (COPEI), 1963–1973." *Politeia* (Caracas) 9 (1980):287–310.

Brito García, Luis. 1988. *La máscara del poder*. Caracas: Alfadil Ediciones.

Combellas, Ricardo. 1985. *COPEI: Ideología y liderazgo*. Caracas: Editorial Ariel.

Edelman, Murray T. 1988. *Constructing the Political Spectacle*. Chicago: University of Chicago Press.

El Nacional, January 29, 1992.

Giménez, Lulú, and Angela Hernández. 1988. *La estructura de los medios de difusión en Venezuela*. Caracas: Universidad Católica Andrés Bello.

Herman, Donald. 1980. *Christian Democracy in Venezuela*. Chapel Hill: University of North Carolina Press.

Levine, Daniel. 1973. *Conflict and Political Change in Venezuela*. Princeton, NJ: Princeton University Press.

Martz, John. 1966. *Acción Democrática: Evolution of a Modern Political Party in Venezuela*. Princeton, NJ: Princeton University Press.

————, and Enrique Baloyra. 1979. *Political Attitudes in Venezuela.* Austin: University of Texas Press.

Molina, José, and Carlos Pérez. 1993. "Venezuela, ¿Un nuevo sistema de partidos? La elección de 1993." *Cuestiones Políticas* (Maracaibo) 13, no. 199: 63–84.

Myers, David. 1975. "Urban Voting, Structural Cleavages, and Party System Evolution: The Case of Venezuela." *Comparative Politics* 7, no. 2 (October): 119–51.

Navas Blanco, Alberto J. 1993. *Las elecciones presidenciales en Venezuela del siglo XIX: Elaboración de un modelo de comportamiento electoral, 1830–1854.* Caracas: Academia de la Historia.

Njaim, Humberto. 1980. "Las prioridades de los candidatos presidenciales en la campaña electoral." *Politeia* (Caracas) 9 (1980): 133–216.

————, Ricardo Combellas, and Angel Alvarez. 1992. "Problemas de legitimidad, opiniones políticas y democracia en Venezuela." Caracas: Unpublished mimeo.

Panebianco, Angelo. 1982. *Modelli di partiti.* Bologna: Società Editrice Il Molino.

Rey, Juan Carlos. 1989. "Continuidad y cambio en las elecciones venezolanos, 1958–1988." In Manuel Caballero et al., eds., *Las elecciones presidenciales: ¿La última oportunidad o al primera?* pp. 11–120. Caracas: Grijalbo.

Sosa, Arturo, and Eloi Lengrand. 1981. *Del garibaldismo estudiantil a la izquierda criolla: Los orígenes marxistas del proyecto de A.D. (1928–1935).* Caracas: Ediciones Centauro.

Sosa, Joaquín Marta. 1993. "La abstención electoral en 1989, una señal de alerta." *COPRE* (Comisión Presidencial para la Reforma del Estado, Caracas), 3: 210–24.

Stambouli, Andrés. 1980. "Los resultados de las elecciones nacionales de 1978 y municipales de 1979." *Politeia* (Caracas) 9 (1980): 423–69.

Torres, Arístides. 1985. "Fe y desencanto político en Venezuela." *Nueva Sociedad* 77: 52–64.

Velázquez, Ramón J. 1976. *Venezuela moderna: Medio siglo de historia, 1926–1976.* Caracas: Editorial Ariel.

Vivas, Mecha. 1982. *¿Quiénes son los estudiantes?* Caracas: Ministerio de Relaciones Interiores.

Conclusion

Henry A. Dietz and Gil Shidlo

The impetus behind this volume was a series of interrelated questions. How, in what ways, and why have local urban elections in Latin America developed patterns that make them distinct from national or presidential contests? How has the emergence of independent local elections in many Latin American cities assisted or impeded the redemocratization process since 1980? And how did the so-called lost decade of the 1980s, with its accompanying socioeconomic disruption and the emergence of the informal economy and of new social movements, play out in the political arena?

As contributing chapters came in, it became clear that the individual countries had individual answers to these questions, and that what might be a fundamental problem or a crucial political issue in one might take on a different guise or have much less salience in another. Thus, not all country experiences can or will contribute equally to all of the questions set forth in the introduction. Nevertheless, enough countries have enough to say about each major question that a synthesis can offer some tentative conclusions and generalizations.

Intraurban Politics

Since many Latin American countries have primate capital cities that overwhelm their provincial competition, it is only natural that most of the authors pay close attention to elections in their capitals. It is also likely that regional differences may emerge in local elections, with one party showing strength in one region but weakness in another.

Several countries manifest such traits. For example, Caracas, Montevideo, and Lima all have had mayoral races that generated a great deal of attention apart from and independent of presidential races. Each of these cities has seen opposition parties post significant and unexpected victories, but for sometimes different reasons. Causa R's 1993 win in Caracas reflected profound disenchantment with AP and COPEI, Venezuela's two major parties, a disenchantment that also led to the impeachment of Carlos Andrés Pérez, AD's president. The 1989 victory by the Frente Amplio in Montevideo signaled the final collapse of the historical domination of the capital by Uruguay's Colorado Party. But in Lima the notable opposition victories first by the left (1983) and then by an independent candidate (1989 and repeated in 1993 and 1995) signaled not only repudiation of Peru's traditionally strong parties but also a discontent and even desperation with traditional parties of all ideologies and a swing toward nonparty candidates. In a variation on this same theme, Colombia's major cities reflect the centuries-old division of the country into Liberal and Conservative adherents, where each city, until recently, has fought municipal contests along these same lines. The most recent Colombian local elections have reflected some of the constitutional changes that came into effect in the late 1980s that allow smaller, newer, and unaffiliated parties to become active, especially in local politics.

Argentina's and Mexico's intraurban political differences do not revolve around Buenos Aires or Mexico City versus the rest of the nation as much as they do around regional and city-specific differences. In the Argentinean case, Cordoba and Mendoza both have strong local flavors; and, although local candidates who run for municipal office do so with the help of the national party, a win for a party in Buenos Aires may have little effect on the outcome in either of these two cities. In Mexico, the PRI has faced its major competition in the northern parts of the country, especially in those states bordering on the United States. The PRD victory in mid-1997 may presage even more difficulties for the PRI. In Brazil, the multiplicity of parties and great variations in regional strength make lasting dominance by one party across the country difficult. Brazilian local elections have closely followed the voting tendencies shown in presidential contests, but strong personalities also have played major roles in determining local elections. And El Salvador's recent municipal elections have followed the same general pattern. Presidential races strongly influence local races, and significant differences across the country's cities are the exception rather than the rule.

Several countries, including the Dominican Republic, Colombia, and Venezuela, have instituted new constitutions or electoral rules that should allow opposition candidates and parties access to at least local power. At the same time, regional moves toward decentralization and privatization may begin to mean that whoever wins local races will find new responsibilities—rising constituent expectations for goods and services previously carried out by national authorities—that require new financial and tax resources that may be difficult to wrest away from the national government or that will necessitate unpopular policies.

All in all, the presence of meaningful local elections in the countries under consideration here suggests that dominant capital cities can become places of political experimentation and ferment for minority and independent candidates, especially when and if: 1) formal constitutional changes create spaces for such parties; and 2) economic problems (which tend to be exacerbated in urban settings) or corruption produce broad discontent. Regional political identities and anomalies also can be intensified as democratization occurs and as decentralization and privatization efforts come on line.

Urban-National Politics

The relationship between national and urban elections varies widely in the cases examined in this book. In some countries—El Salvador, the Dominican Republic—the fit is almost exact: whoever wins the presidency wins most of the nation's cities as well. Sometimes such congruence is due to the rules of the game. The Dominican Republic, for example, holds elections concurrently for all levels of office, from the president to local city council members.

Others, however, exhibit considerable variation. In La Paz, local election outcomes have historically reflected national races, but in 1993 the MNR, Bolivia's major national party, suffered an unexpected defeat as CONDEPA, a populist following led by Carlos Palenque and composed of the city's working classes and masses, not only saw the party sweep into office in La Paz but also finish second nationally to the MNR. In Lima throughout the 1980s, if municipal elections came shortly after a presidential race, candidates running on the presidential ticket did well, but the reverse also held—that is, municipal elections that took place just before a presidential election gave opposition candidates strong victories.

Other countries showed still different patterns. For example, in Uruguay, Venezuela, and Colombia, traditional and well-entrenched parties have done poorly in recent elections, indicating that unpopular or indifferent economic performance by a president can have a direct effect on municipal elections. In Uruguay, minority parties and *sublemas* have started to appear in Montevideo and elsewhere, threatening not only the historical hold that the Colorado Party has had on the capital but also what Aidan Rankin refers to as the Colorado-Blanco duopoly of power throughout the nation. In Venezuela, the electorate's enormous displeasure with both AP and COPEI has created political space for Causa R and MAS. These are groups that in normal times would doubtless have great difficulty being anything more than ideological or regional minor parties. But given Venezuela's economic problems and the widespread perception that both major parties were equally culpable and corrupt, parties such as Causa R and MAS have been given unprecedented electoral strength. Finally, Colombia's elitist two-party hegemony has been challenged as well in municipal elections, especially in 1992, when the results suggested a pluralization of the political spectrum. In all three of these cases, historically strong two-party systems have seen their power eroded by formal changes in the electoral game as well as by discontent from below.

In sum, democratization can produce fundamental changes in the nature of the linkages between national—that is, presidential—and local elections and electoral behavior. Many Latin American cities have seen mayoral races that have gone against the grain of national politics and where either minority parties have won for the first time or presidentially dominant parties have been ousted from municipal power. It appears from the cases under study that the rules of the electoral game have a crucial influence: countries where ticket-splitting is difficult or impossible, or where national and local elections are held concurrently, show much less variation between local and national races. But many countries with such constraints are beginning to experiment with staggered elections and with less rigid ballots, and it is likely that urban-national differences will start to develop.

Formal-Informal Politics

The 1980s saw a proliferation of new social movements and grassroots groups, often in response to the currents of democratization that flowed through the region. Such movements were paralleled by the emergence of an informal urban economy that appeared as a response to the incapacity of the formal economic structures to absorb the vast surplus labor (frequently migrant in origin) present in the region's cities.

These socioeconomic processes have had political impacts on the cities. Nowhere has this success been more visible than in poor countries with large indigenous populations such as Bolivia and Peru. The success of CONDEPA in La Paz and elsewhere in Bolivia rests largely on such movements and transformations. Its self-identification as a party of *cholos* and marginals, and the clear use of Aymara symbols in the 1993 campaign, all helped to give CONDEPA a major electoral win. In Peru, in somewhat analogous fashion, both Alberto Fujimori on the national level and Ricardo Belmont in Lima were able in different ways to portray themselves as independents who spoke for the working classes and the popular masses of the capital. In the 1993 municipal elections, independents won widely throughout the country, many heading nontraditional movements that campaigned by publicly distancing themselves from Peru's formal political party system and its traditional parties. And in the Dominican Republic, a well-known television personality won the mayoral race in Santo Domingo. In contrast, Mexico has not yet seen a coherent ethnic-based political movement, despite the presence of large ethnic minorities.

Similar cases exist in other countries where poverty and indigenous groups are not major factors. In Venezuela, a community activist for Decisión Ciudadana was the first person to win as a candidate of a neighborhood community movement, running against the country's traditional major parties. And in Uruguay, the presence of street vendors in the heart of Montevideo became a major issue not only in the mayoral race but also in city-state relations.

Despite such similarities, there is no straightforward or automatic relationship between poverty, new social movements, and electoral politics. As the literature attests, many social movements consciously avoid involvement in electoral politics, thinking that such participation could endanger the strength that they have through their autonomy. Yet it is clear from the cases under study that some social movements have put forth their own candidates for municipal office and have in other ways entered into formal electoral politics. It is also equally clear in some countries that candidates and parties have discerned that campaigns pitched to the urban working classes and popular masses can generate considerable electoral strength. Numerous studies over recent decades have shown that the urban poor are not a homogeneous mass that behaves or votes in predictable or uniform ways, but their sheer numbers inevitably have made them targets for politicians now and in the future.

One effect of democratization occurring in a fluid context of economic difficulties, grass-roots movements, and widespread poverty is the likelihood that populist leaders and campaigns may reassert themselves. Max Fernández and Carlos Palenque in Bolivia, along with Leonel Brizola and Lula in Brazil, are only a few instances of politicians who have gone far with populist tactics and campaigns that often run on platforms that attack traditional dominant parties. Populism and charisma are fragile vehicles for democratic governance; and, while challenges to hegemonic parties are a necessary and welcome part of democratization, an abrupt or exaggerated swing toward populism may result in overall instability and a potentially restive military.

This volume, as mentioned, has few pretensions. It brings together eleven authors who describe and analyze developments in local elections since the onset of electoral democracy in the early 1980s. Much attention has been paid to the preconditions necessary for transitions to, and for the consolidation of, democracy. But these discussions have included very little reference to local elections and to the various roles that Latin America's cities and urban populations will play in these processes. Beyond this book lies a limitless number of questions and subjects only hinted at here: decentralization in theory and in fact, municipal governance, intergovernmental relations, municipal campaign strategies, detailed analyses of specific municipal elections, the impact of electoral rules and laws, municipal finance, and more. *Urban Elections* makes no attempt to address all of these issues; indeed, no single volume could do so. Rather, by describing and highlighting the major dynamics of the electoral process and its outcomes, this study takes the first of many steps necessary to come to a fuller understanding of municipal politics.

Local elections in Latin America have come a long way. For most of this century, the great majority of Latin American cities had unelected mayors who were responsible only to the presidents or legislatures that appointed them. That the 1980s and 1990s have witnessed a proliferation of urban elections with meaningful races and independent opposition candidates and parties is all the more remarkable for the context of economic difficulties in which it occurred. Many countries, as of this writing, are still experimenting with new rules and procedures, and what the outcomes may be remains obscure. But if the cases under study here are any guide, it is clear that democratic governance is in for a complex transition that will change fundamentally the process, outcome, and impact of urban politics in the region.

About the Contributors

ANGEL E. ALVAREZ is a political scientist at the Universidad Central de Venezuela and the director of its Institute of Political Studies. His areas of interest include elections, political communications, and political parties. He is most recently the author of *Estrategias de propaganda electoral en Venezuela* (1994).

PETER A. CALVERT, professor of comparative and international politics at the University of Southampton, UK, is the author of *The Falklands Crisis: The Rights and the Wrongs* (1982) and co-author, with Susan Calvert, of *Argentina: Political Culture and Instability* (1991).

RICARDO CÓRDOVA MACÍAS is the director of the Fundación Dr. Guillermo Manuel Ungo in San Salvador, El Salvador. A Ph.D. candidate in political science at the University of Pittsburgh, Cordova is completing his dissertation on voting behavior in Central America. His previous research focuses on electoral and party systems, voting, municipal government, and public opinion and social policy. Among his more recent publications are *El Salvador: De la guerra a la paz: Una cultura política en transición* (1995) and *Perspectivas para una democracia estable en El Salvador* (1992), both co-authored with Mitchell Seligson; and "Procesos electorales y sistema de partidos en El Salvador, 1982–1989" (1992).

EDUARDO A. GAMARRA is associate professor of political science and acting director of the Latin American and Caribbean Center at Florida International University. His major research interests include democratic transition and consolidation and civil-military relations in Latin America, especially in Bolivia and the Andean region.

GARY HOSKIN is an associate professor of political science at the State University of New York at Buffalo. Upon several occasions since 1968, he has been a visiting professor in the Political Science

Department of the Universidad de los Andes in Bogotá, Colombia, researching political parties and elections. He has contributed to numerous books and journals, including the *American Journal of Political Science, Comparative Politics*, the *Journal of Inter-American and World Affairs, Current History, International Journal of Comparative Sociology*, and *Pensamiento Iberoamericano: Revista de Economía Política*.

CHRISTOPHER MITCHELL is professor of politics and director of the Center for Latin American and Caribbean Studies at New York University. He received B.A. and Ph.D. degrees from Harvard University. Mitchell has edited *Changing Perspectives in Latin American Studies* (1988) and *Western Hemisphere Immigration and United States Foreign Policy* (1992). He has visited and studied the Dominican Republic regularly since 1975.

AIDAN RANKIN is Campaigns Press Officer for Survival International in London, the worldwide organization supporting tribal peoples. He has recently completed a Ph.D. on Uruguayan redemocratization at the London School of Economics.

VICTORIA E. RODRÍGUEZ is an associate professor at the Lyndon B. Johnson School of Public Affairs, University of Texas at Austin. Since 1989 she has been working with Peter M. Ward on a major research project on opposition governments and state and local governments in Mexico. Together they have written two volumes on the subject, *Policymaking, Politics, and Urban Goverance in Chihuahua: The Experience of Recent Panista Governments* (1992) and *Political Change in Baja California: Democracy in the Making?* (1994) and edited a third, *Opposition Government in Mexico* (1995). She is the author of *Decentralization in Mexico: From Reforma Municipal to Solidaridad to Nuevo Federalismo* (1997) and of several articles dealing with politics and public administration. Her current research interests focus upon the role of women in contemporary Mexican politics.

ANDREW J. STEIN, assistant professor of political science at Tennessee Technological University, received his Ph.D. in political science from the University of Pittsburgh, where his dissertation, "The Prophetic Mission, the Catholic Church, and Politics: Nicaragua in the Context of Central America," dealt with the impact of religion on church-state relations and political participation. He has published on Nicaragua, religion and politics, and public opinion and elections. His most recent publication is "The Church," in Thomas W. Walker, editor, *Nicaragua without Illusions* (1997).

Index

[Note: For a list of acronyms, see Abbreviations of Political Parties on pages xix–xxv.]

Abogansters, 26
Abstentionism: Bolivia, 43; Brazil, 80, 85; Colombia, 94, 96–97, 101, 102–3, 106; Dominican Republic, 135; El Salvador, 141, 152, 155; Mexico, 166, 179; Peru, 201–2, 218; Venezuela, 254, 257–58
Acción Democrática (AD, Venezuela), 243, 244, 250, 251, 253, 259, 268, 272–73, 274
Acción Democrática y Nacionalista (ADN, Bolivia), 24, 25–26, 30, 32, 33, 34, 36, 41, 47, 54, 55
Acción Popular (AP, Peru), 204–5, 206–7, 209, 212, 214, 215, 217, 218, 221
Acuerdo Patriótico (AP, Bolivia), 22, 25, 37–41, 42, 43
Alfonsín, Raúl, 1, 4, 9
Alianca Renovadora Nacional (ARENA, Brazil), 69
Alianza de Centro (Argentina), 4
Alianza Democrática-M-19 (AD-M-19, Colombia), 95–96, 97, 103–4
Alianza Nacional Popular (ANAPO, Colombia), 95, 96, 103–4
Alianza Patriótica (AP, Bolivia), 23–24, 34
Alianza Popular Revolucionaria Americana (APRA, Peru), 203, 204, 207–13, 214, 215, 218, 219, 220, 221

Alianza Republicana Nacionalista (ARENA, El Salvador), 144, 146, 147, 149, 150, 151, 155, 156–57
Alsogaray, Alvaro, 4, 12
Andrade, Alberto, 216–17
Angeloz, Eduardo, 4, 13, 14, 18
Araníbar, Antonio, 26
Argentina: elections in, 1–19
Argüello, Jorge, 5
Arias Cárdenas, Francisco, 265, 266
Attas, Ivonne, 270–71
Austerity programs: Dominican Republic, 133
Authoritarianism: Mexico, 163, 164; Peru, 206, 214

Balaguer, Joaquín, 119, 132, 135
Boleta de arrastre (Dominican Republic), 127
Banzer Suárez, Hugo, 24, 25, 26, 47
Barrantes, Alfonso, 203, 207, 209, 210–11
Barrio, Francisco, 180–81
Batlle, Jorge, 238
Batlle y Ordónez, José, 230
Batllismo, 230–31, 236, 239
Bedoya Reyes, Luis, 205
Bedregal, Guillermo, 33
Belaúnde Terry, Fernando, 204, 206–7, 208–9
Belmont, Ricardo, 212, 214, 219
Betancourt, Rómulo, 244
Betancur, Belisario, 93, 104

Blank and null votes: Colombia, 97, 98
Bolivia: elections in, 21–58
Bordón, José, 11, 14
Bosch, Juan, 119
Braga, Roberto Saturno, 67
Brazil: elections in, 63–86
Brizola, Leonel, 66, 70, 74, 77
Burgoa, Jorge, 38

Cafiero, Antonio, 6, 8
Cajías, Fernando, 39–40
Caldera, Rafael, 256–57, 267, 274
Cambio '90 (Peru), 214, 216, 217, 218, 221
Campaign costs: Venezuela, 273–74, 275
Candia, Gabriela, 55
Capra Jamio, Guido, 38, 40, 41
Caputo, Dante, 6
Cárdenas, Cuauhtémoc, 167, 185, 189
Cárdenas, Victor Hugo, 46
Catholic Church: Brazil, 64–65; Colombia, 108, 111; Dominican Republic, 134; Uruguay, 230–31
Caudillismo: Bolivia, 57; Uruguay, 237
Cavallero, Héctor, 13
Cavallo, Domingo, 7, 14
Cervecería Boliviana Nacional (CBN, Bolivia), 29
Chazarreta, Germán "Chaza", 45, 48
Chiapas uprising (Mexico), 169
Christian Democratic parties (Venezuela), 243, 258
Citizen participation. *See* Popular participation
Civic culture: Colombia, 108, 109; Mexico, 164, 179
Civil disobedience (Mexico), 180
Civil rights: Mexico, 169; Uruguay, 227
Clientelism: Bolivia, 27, 29, 30, 33; Dominican Republic, 131, 133; Mexico, 168; Uruguay, 232–33, 236–37
Clouthier, Manuel, 167
Collor de Mello, Fernando, 79–80, 81, 82

Colombia: elections in, 91–112
Comité de Organización Política Electoral Independiente (COPEI, Venezuela), 243, 250, 251, 252, 253, 259, 268, 273
Comunidades Eclesiales de Base (Dominican Republic), 134
Comunidades Eclesias de Base (CEBs, Brazil), 64–66
Conciencia de Patria (CONDEPA, Bolivia), 27, 28, 30–31, 38, 41–43, 48, 49, 51–52, 53–54, 56–57
Conservative Party (Colombia), 91, 92, 99–100, 102, 107, 111
Constitution: Brazil, 77–79; Colombia, 92, 93, 97, 104–6; Mexico, 172; Peru, 201, 216; Uruguay, 227; Venezuela, 244
Convergencia (Venezuela), 268, 275
Convergencia Democrática (CD, El Salvador), 144, 147, 151, 156
Convergencia Democrática (CODE, Peru), 210
Coparticipation: Uruguay, 231–33, 237, 239
Corporán de los Santos, Rafael, 128, 132
Corruption: Argentina, 6–7, 14; Bolivia, 37, 52, 56; Brazil, 75, 79–80; Venezuela, 272–74
Covas, Mario, 78
Cruz, Mabel, 55
Cruzada '94 (Uruguay), 236
Cuba: MIR crisis in, 47

Dalesio de Viola, Adelina, 12
Decentralization: Bolivia, 53; Brazil, 83; Colombia, 104–6; Venezuela, 267–68
Decisión Ciudadana (Venezuela), 260
De la Rúa, Fernando, 7, 10–11, 19
De la Sota, José Manuel, 6–7
Del Castillo, Jorge, 210–11
"Delegative democracy" (Bolivia), 27
Delgadillo, Walter, 26
Democracia Avanzada (Uruguay), 236

Democratic Convergence (CD, El
  Salvador), 144, 151
Democratization: Bolivia, 33;
  Mexico, 163; Peru, 222, 239
Dirty War (Argentina), 1
Domínguez, Jorge, 7
Dominican Republic: elections in,
  117–38
Double simultaneous vote:
  Argentina, 13; Uruguay, 233–34
Drug trafficking: Bolivia, 27, 28–
  32, 39, 46, 47, 48; Colombia, 109;
  Mexico, 169
Duhalde, Eduardo, 9, 14, 18

Ecclesial base communities:
  Brazil, 64–66; Dominican
  Republic, 134; Uruguay, 230–31
Economic crisis: Argentina, 6;
  Bolivia, 21, 32; Mexico, 169–70,
  174–75; Peru, 205, 206, 211, 213;
  Venezuela, 246–47, 276
Eid Franco, Oscar, 26, 47
Ejército de Liberación Nacional
  (ELN, Colombia), 109
Election monitoring: Mexico, 169,
  180; Venezuela, 251
Electoral behavior: Argentina,
  17–19; Colombia, 93–94, 103–4;
  El Salvador, 142, 143
Electoral fraud: Bolivia, 38, 40;
  Mexico, 166–67, 172–73, 175,
  179–80; Venezuela, 243, 249–50
Electoral procedures: Bolivia, 22,
  35, 58; Brazil, 69, 70–71, 78–79;
  Colombia, 92, 105–6; Domini-
  can Republic, 124, 128, 135; El
  Salvador, 145–47, 148; Mexico,
  171, 183–84; Peru, 201–2, 215;
  Uruguay, 233–34, 239; Vene-
  zuela, 248–50
Electoral reform: Bolivia, 42;
  Colombia, 104–5; Dominican
  Republic, 134–36; Mexico, 170–
  74; Uruguay, 233–34
Elite pacts: Dominican Republic,
  117
El Salvador: elections in, 141–57
Encuentro Progresista (Uruguay),
  225
Erundina, Luiza, 68, 76–77

Executive power: Argentina, 2;
  Mexico, 165, 184, 187; Uruguay,
  227

Farabundo Martí Liberación
  Nacional (FMLN, El Salvador),
  141, 144, 147–48, 149, 151–52,
  155, 156, 157
Farizano, Juan Carlos, 5
Favela Neighborhood Associa-
  tions of Rio de Janeiro
  (FAFERJ), 66–67
Favelas. See Shantytowns, Brazil
Federação de Associacoes de
  Moradores do Estado de Rio de
  Janeiro (FAMERJ), 67
Fernández, Johnny, 55
Fernández, Max, 27, 28–32, 38, 47
Fernández Mejide, Graciela, 11–
  12, 18
Fontanelle, Maria Luiza, 74
Fortún, Guillermo, 25, 47
Fox, Vicente, 178, 181
Franco Badía, Pedro, 131, 132, 134
Frente Amplio (FA, Uruguay),
  226, 229, 234, 235, 236, 240
Frente del Pueblo Unido (FPU,
  Bolivia), 23
Frente Democrático (FREDEMO,
  Peru), 205, 212–13
Frente Democrático Nacional
  (FDN, Mexico), 167
Frente Grande (Argentina), 7, 11–
  12
Frente Justicialista de la Patria
  (FREJUDEPA, Argentina), 8
Frente Justicialista de Liberación
  (FREJULI, Argentina), 8
Frente para un País en
  Solídaridad (FREPASO, Argen-
  tina), 10, 11–12, 18
Frente Unido del Pueblo (FUP,
  Colombia), 96
Fuerza Especial de Lucha contra
  el Narcotráfico (FELCN,
  Bolivia), 26, 47
Fuerza Republicana (Argentina),
  15
Fuerzas Armadas Revolucionarias
  de Colombia (FARC, Colom-
  bia), 96, 109

Fujimori, Alberto, 206, 213–14, 216–17, 219, 220, 222, 237

Galindo, Eudoro, 25
Galvez, Rodolfo, 55
García, Alan, 204, 209, 210–11, 212, 215
Grass-roots groups. *See* Neighborhood associations
Grosso, Carlos, 5, 6–7
Guerrilla groups: Bolivia, 57; Colombia, 96, 109–11; El Salvador, 141, 143; Mexico, 165; Peru, 205; Uruguay, 240; Venezuela, 245, 252
Guevara Arze, Walter, 24

Haya de la Torre, Victor Raúl, 204
Housing. *See* Shantytowns

Independientes para un Frente Nacional (IPFN, Venezuela), 252
Indigenous movements: Colombia, 111
"Informal politics" (Argentina), 16–17
Informal sector: Peru, 201, 206, 212, 219; Uruguay, 235
International Monetary Fund, 133
Izquierda Unida (IU, Bolivia), 24, 43
Izquierda Unida (IU, Peru), 203–4, 207–8, 209, 210–11, 213, 214, 215, 218, 221
Iztúriz, Aristóbulo, 265–66, 274

Kieffer, Fernando, 25–26
Kuljis, Ivo, 28

Labor unions: Mexico, 165, 168; Uruguay, 30
Labor unrest: Argentina, 17; Bolivia, 39
Lacalle, Luis Alberto, 229, 238
La Causa Radical (LCR, Venezuela), 251, 265–67, 268, 274
Land issues: Brazil, 76
Landívar, Jorge, 26
Language issues: Bolivia, 49
La Porta, Norberto, 7, 18

Left-wing parties: Argentina, 7; Bolivia, 23–27, 41–43; Brazil, 64, 65, 75, 77, 85; Colombia, 95–96, 97, 103–4; Dominican Republic, 119; El Salvador, 144, 156; Mexico, 170; Peru, 203–4, 207, 208–10, 214; Uruguay, 225, 226, 228, 236–37, 239; Venezuela, 243, 252–53, 264–65
Lema system: Argentina, 13; Uruguay, 233–34
Liberal Party (Colombia), 91, 96, 98–99, 102, 107, 111
Liga Municipal Dominicana (Dominican Republic), 131
Luder, Italo, 4
Lusinchi, Jaime, 274

Maclean, Ronald, 25, 34, 35–37, 38, 41, 44–45, 50, 51, 55–56, 58
Maders, Regino, 13–14
Maluf, Paulo Salim, 72, 81, 82
Mandato por la Paz (Colombia), 109–10, 111
Mantilla, Julio, 28, 41, 44–47, 48–49, 50, 51, 58
Marxism: Bolivia, 23, 26, 43
Massaccesi, Horacio, 11, 18
Media (press, radio, television): Argentina, 17; Mexico, 168–69; Peru, 220–21; Venezuela, 272, 275, 276
Medina, Mónica (La Comadre Mónica), 48–49, 50–52, 53–54, 55
Medina, Pablo, 265, 266
Menem, Carlos, 2, 4, 5, 10
Menezes, Gilson, 67
Mestre, Ramón, 14, 18
Mexico: elections in, 163–90
Migration, internal: Bolivia, 43; Brazil, 63–64; Dominican Republic, 125; Peru, 200–201
Military governments: Argentina, 1; Bolivia, 21; Brazil, 63, 64, 69, 71–72, 75; El Salvador, 142–43; Peru, 201; Uruguay, 227; Venezuela, 243–44
Mockus, Antanas, 108
Movimiento al Socialismo (MAS, Venezuela), 251, 253, 264, 266, 268, 275

Movimiento Auténtico Cristiano
(MAC, El Salvador), 144, 147
Movimiento Bolivia Libre (MBL,
Bolivia), 23, 26, 34–35, 43, 48,
54–55
Movimiento de Izquierda
Revolucionaria (MIR, Bolivia),
24, 25, 26–27, 30, 34, 36, 41, 47,
49, 53
Movimiento de Izquierda
Revolucionaria (MIR, Venezu-
ela), 245, 253
Movimiento de Izquierda
Revolucionaria-Bolivia Libre
(MIR-BL, Bolivia), 23, 26
Movimiento de Izquierda
Revolucionaria (Labor faction)
(MIR-Masas, Bolivia), 23, 26
Movimiento de Izquierda
Revolucionario-Nueva Mayoría
(MIR-NM, Bolivia), 26
Movimiento de Liberación
Nacional (MLN, Uruguay), 240
Movimiento de Solidaridad
Nacional (MSN, El Salvador),
144
Movimiento de Unidad (MU, El
Salvador), 144
Movimiento Electoral del Pueblo
(MEP, Venezuela), 252, 253
Movimiento Nacionalista
Revolucionario (MNR, Bolivia),
21, 24–25, 29, 30, 32, 41, 43, 45,
46, 47, 48, 49, 50, 53, 54
Movimiento Nacionalista
Revolucionario (MNR, El
Salvador), 144
Movimiento Nacionalista
Revolucionario Histórico
(MNRH, Bolivia), 24
Movimiento Nacionalista
Revolucionario Izquierdista
(MNRI, Bolivia), 24
Movimiento para Dignidad e
Independencia (MODIN,
Argentina), 12
Movimiento Popular Fuegino
(MOPOF, Argentina), 15
Movimiento Popular Social
Cristiano (MPSC, El Salvador),
144

Movimiento Revolucionario
Tupac Katari (MRTK, Bolivia),
46
Mur, Walter, 33, 36

National Front (Colombia), 91, 93
Nationalist Democratic Union
(UDN, El Salvador), 144
Nava Martínez, Salvador, 182
Neighborhood associations:
Bolivia, 53; Brazil, 64–68, 85–86;
Dominican Republic, 133;
Mexico, 168; Peru, 220
Neoliberalism: Argentina, 2–3;
Bolivia, 32, 42, 46; Mexico, 164;
Peru, 212, 213; Uruguay, 225,
231, 240; Venezuela, 256
Neves, Tancredo, 72, 85
New Economic Policy (NPE,
Bolivia), 24, 32, 33
New Liberal Party (Colombia),
98–99, 103–4
Nongovernmental organizations
(NGOs): Mexico, 169
Nueva Generación Democrática
(NGD, Venezuela), 253
Nuevo Espacio (NE, Uruguay),
229, 235

Obeid, Jorge, 13
Obleas de Torres, Ema, 34, 36
Obras (Peru), 212, 214
Ochoa Antich, Enrique, 275
Olivos Pact (Argentina), 7, 15
Opposition parties: Brazil, 70; El
Salvador, 148; Mexico, 163, 166,
170, 171–72, 173, 174–79, 184,
188; Peru, 206, 214
Organic Law of Municipality
(Brazil), 68
Ortega, Ramón "Palito", 15

Pacto por la Democracia (Bolivia),
22, 24, 32, 34, 35, 36, 37
Palenque, Carlos "El Compadre",
27, 28, 30–32, 38, 40, 42, 48–49,
57, 58
Paramilitary forces, 110, 111
Partido Acción Nacional (PAN,
Mexico), 166, 175–77, 178–79,
180–81, 185, 187, 188–90

Partido Blanco (Uruguay), 226, 229, 232, 234–37
Partido Colorado (PC, Uruguay), 226, 228, 229, 230, 232, 234–37
Partido Comunista Boliviano (PCB, Bolivia), 23, 24
Partido Comunista Brasileiro (PCB, Brazil), 81
Partido Comunista do Brasil (PCdoB, Brazil), 65
Partido Comunista Uruguayo (PCU, Uruguay), 236
Partido Comunista Venezolano (PCV, Venezuela), 243, 244
Partido da Reconstrução Nacional (PRN, Brazil), 81
Partido da Social Democrácia Brasileiro (PSDB, Brazil), 77, 82, 86
Partido de Conciliación Nacional (PCN, El Salvador), 144, 146, 147, 149, 150, 156
Partido de la Liberación Dominicana (PLD, Dominican Republic), 119, 126–27, 128, 131, 134
Partido de la Revolución Democrática (PRD, Mexico), 168, 176, 177, 185, 188–90
Partido Demócrata Cristiano (PDC, El Salvador), 144, 146, 147, 149, 150, 151, 155, 156
Partido Demócrata Mexicano (PDM), 175
Partido Democrático Boliviano (PDB, Bolivia), 25
Partido Democrático Cristiano (PDC, Bolivia), 24
Partido Democrático Social (PDS, Brazil), 69, 70–71, 74, 77, 80, 81, 82, 84
Partido Democrático Trabalhista (PDT, Brazil), 66–67, 70, 74, 75, 76, 77, 80, 84, 85, 86
Partido dos Trabalhadores (PT, Brazil), 64, 67–68, 71, 74, 75, 76, 80, 81–82, 84, 85
Partido Frente Liberal (PFL, Brazil), 72, 77, 80, 81, 82
Partido Intransigente (PI, Argentina), 4

Partido Justicialista (PJ, Argentina), 4, 6–7, 13, 14, 18
Partido Movimento Democrático Brasileiro (PMDB), 65, 69, 71, 72–73, 74, 75–76, 77, 80–81, 84, 85–86
Partido Popular Cristiano (PPC, Peru), 205, 207, 209, 210–11, 212, 214, 215
Partido Popular Socialista (PPS, Brazil), 81, 82
Partido Reformista (PR, Dominican Republic), 119, 129
Partido Reformista Social Cristiano (PRSC, Dominican Republic), 119, 126, 127, 128
Partido Revolucionario Dominicano (PRD, Dominican Republic), 118–19, 126–27, 128, 129, 131, 134
Partido Revolucionario Independiente (PRI, Dominican Republic), 126
Partido Revolucionario Institucional (PRI, Mexico), 18, 163, 166–68, 170–74, 175, 179, 180, 184–85, 187, 188–90
Partido Revolucionario Social Cristiano (Dominican Republic), 129
Partido Social Demócrata (PSD, El Salvador), 144
Partido Socialista Brasileiro (PSB, Brazil), 75, 77
Partido Socialista de los Trabajadores (PST, Mexico), 175
Partido Trabalhista Brasileiro (PTB, Brazil), 70, 72, 77, 82, 84
Partido Verde Ecologista Mexicana (PVEM, Mexico), 188, 189
Patronage: Bolivia, 38, 57; Dominican Republic, 133
Paz Estenssoro, Victor, 24, 33
Paz Zamora, Jaime, 26–27, 34, 37, 39, 41, 42, 43, 47
Peñalosa, Enrique, 112
Pérez de Cuellar, Javier, 216
Peronism, 1, 6
Peronist Popular Judicialist Front (FREJUPO, Argentina), 4

Personalism: Dominican Republic, 119; Peru, 203; Venezuela, 270

Peru: elections in, 199–222

Plurinominal deputy system (Mexico), 171, 183

Popular participation: Bolivia, 52–53; Brazil, 67–68; El Salvador, 154–55

Popular Participation Law (LPP, Bolivia), 52–53

Populism: Bolivia, 27, 42–43; Uruguay, 230, 235–36; Venezuela, 258

Pre-Columbian symbols, 42, 49

Privatization: Argentina, 2–3, 17; Uruguay, 231, 236, 239; Venezuela, 256

Proyecto Carabobo (Venezuela), 260, 264

Public works: Bolivia, 22, 29, 36, 38, 45, 51

Punto Fijo Accords (Venezuela), 244

Quadros, Janio, 72, 73–74, 75

Radical Civic Union (UCR, Argentina), 1, 3, 4, 6, 9, 18

Renewal Peronists (Argentina), 5, 6–7

Revenues: Brazil, 78, 83; Colombia, 104, 105; Dominican Republic, 129–30, 131; El Salvador, 153–54

Rico, Aldo, 8–9, 12

Ruffo, Ernesto, 181

Russak, Mario, 10

Sáez, Irene, 269–71

Salas Römer, Henrique, 264, 267

Salinas de Gortari, Carlos, 164, 165, 167, 176

Salmón, Raúl, 34, 35–37

Samper Pizano, Ernesto, 109–10

Sánchez de Lozada, Gonzalo, 24–25, 30, 40, 46, 48, 54

Sanguinetti, Julio María, 225, 227–28, 240

Santa Cruz Civic Committee (Bolivia), 26

Sarney, José, 72, 76

Sendero Luminoso. *See* Shining Path

Seregni, Liber, 234, 237, 238

Shantytowns: Argentina, 17; Bolivia, 45, 49, 57; Brazil, 65, 66, 76–77; Peru, 201

Shining Path (Sendero Luminoso, Peru), 205, 214

Siles Zuazo, Hernán, 24

Silva, Luís Inácio da ("Lula"), 70, 77, 85

Social class: Dominican Republic, 126–27; Peru, 200, 220

Socialist parties: Argentina, 6, 7, 13; Bolivia, 23–24, 43; Brazil, 75, 77; Mexico, 175; Uruguay, 229; Venezuela, 264–65

Social movements: Brazil, 64–66, 85–86; Mexico, 165–66

Social unrest: Argentina, 5, 15, 18; Bolivia, 39; Mexico, 165; Peru, 208; Venezuela, 245, 250–51, 276

Somos Lima movement (Peru), 217

Suárez Lastra, Facundo, 5

Suplicy, Eduardo, 74, 82

Two-party system: Argentina, 2; Brazil, 70; Colombia, 91, 93, 94, 101–2, 106–7; Uruguay, 226, 232, 239; Venezuela, 253–54, 259

Unemployment: Brazil, 65, 74; Peru, 201, 206

Unidad Cívica Solidaridad (UCS, Bolivia), 27, 28–32, 41, 45, 47, 54, 56–57

Unidad Democrática y Popular (UDP, Bolivia), 24

Unidad Socialista (SU, Argentina), 7, 12

Unión Democrática Nacionalista (UDN, El Salvador), 144, 147

Unión Nacional de Oposición (UNO, Colombia), 96

Union of the Democratic Center (UCEDE, Argentina), 4, 12

Unión Patriótica (UP, Colombia), 96, 97

Unión Republicana Democrática (URD, Venezuela), 243, 244, 252, 253
Unión Vecinal (Argentina), 8, 9
United States: Central American policy, 141; occupation of Dominican Republic, 117, 119
Urbanization: Brazil, 63–64; Colombia, 98; El Salvador, 150
Urban organizations. *See* Neighborhood associations
Uruguay: elections in, 225–40
Usandizaga, Horacio, 13

Valle, Luis Alberto "Chito", 47, 50
Value-added tax (IVA): Brazil, 83; Colombia, 104, 105
Vargas, Ivete, 70
Vargas Llosa, Mario, 212, 213
Vázquez, Tabaré, 225, 229, 234, 235, 236–37, 238

Velázquez, Andrés, 265, 274
Venezuela: elections in, 243–77
Viola, Adelina Dalesio de, 12
Violence: Colombia, 109; Dominican Republic, 119; Venezuela, 250–51
Voter registration: Bolivia, 37–38; Colombia, 110; El Salvador, 155; Mexico, 172, 180; Venezuela, 245

Women: Argentina, 11–12, 16; Bolivia, 48–49, 55; Brazil, 65, 74; Dominican Republic, 128, 134; Mexico, 182–83; Peru, 220; Uruguay, 226; Venezuela, 258, 266, 269

Yoshiyama, Jaime, 216–17

Zedillo, Ernesto, 187

Latin American Silhouettes
Studies in History and Culture

William H. Beezley and
Judith Ewell
Editors

Volumes Published

William H. Beezley and Judith Ewell, eds., *The Human Tradition in Latin America: The Twentieth Century* (1987). Cloth ISBN 0-8420-2283-X Paper ISBN 0-8420-2284-8

Judith Ewell and William H. Beezley, eds., *The Human Tradition in Latin America: The Nineteenth Century* (1989). Cloth ISBN 0-8420-2331-3 Paper ISBN 0-8420-2332-1

David G. LaFrance, *The Mexican Revolution in Puebla, 1908–1913: The Maderista Movement and the Failure of Liberal Reform* (1989). ISBN 0-8420-2293-7

Mark A. Burkholder, *Politics of a Colonial Career: José Baquíjano and the Audiencia of Lima*, 2d ed. (1990). Cloth ISBN 0-8420-2353-4 Paper ISBN 0-8420-2352-6

Carlos B. Gil, ed., *Hope and Frustration: Interviews with Leaders of Mexico's Political Opposition* (1992). Cloth ISBN 0-8420-2395-X Paper ISBN 0-8420-2396-8

Heidi Zogbaum, *B. Traven: A Vision of Mexico* (1992). ISBN 0-8420-2392-5

Jaime E. Rodríguez O., ed., *Patterns of Contention in Mexican History* (1992). ISBN 0-8420-2399-2

Louis A. Pérez, Jr., ed., *Slaves, Sugar, and Colonial Society: Travel Accounts of Cuba, 1801–1899* (1992). Cloth ISBN 0-8420-2354-2 Paper ISBN 0-8420-2415-8

Peter Blanchard, *Slavery and Abolition in Early Republican Peru* (1992). Cloth ISBN 0-8420-2400-X Paper ISBN 0-8420-2429-8

Paul J. Vanderwood, *Disorder and Progress: Bandits, Police, and Mexican Development*, revised and enlarged edition (1992). Cloth ISBN 0-8420-2438-7 Paper ISBN 0-8420-2439-5

Sandra McGee Deutsch and Ronald H. Dolkart, eds., *The Argentine Right: Its History and Intellectual Origins, 1910 to the Present* (1993). Cloth ISBN 0-8420-2418-2 Paper ISBN 0-8420-2419-0

Steve Ellner, *Organized Labor in Venezuela, 1958–1991: Behavior and Concerns in a Democratic Setting* (1993). ISBN 0-8420-2443-3

Paul J. Dosal, *Doing Business with the Dictators: A Political History of United Fruit in Guatemala, 1899–1944* (1993). Cloth ISBN 0-8420-2475-1 Paper ISBN 0-8420-2590-1

Marquis James, *Merchant Adventurer: The Story of W. R. Grace* (1993). ISBN 0-8420-2444-1

John Charles Chasteen and Joseph S. Tulchin, eds., *Problems in Modern Latin American History: A Reader* (1994). Cloth ISBN 0-8420-2327-5 Paper ISBN 0-8420-2328-3

Marguerite Guzmán Bouvard, *Revolutionizing Motherhood: The Mothers of the Plaza de Mayo* (1994). Cloth ISBN 0-8420-2486-7 Paper ISBN 0-8420-2487-5

William H. Beezley, Cheryl English Martin, and William E. French, eds., *Rituals of Rule, Rituals of Resistance: Public Celebrations and Popular Culture in Mexico* (1994). Cloth ISBN 0-8420-2416-6 Paper ISBN 0-8420-2417-4

Stephen R. Niblo, *War, Diplomacy, and Development: The United States and Mexico, 1938–1954* (1995). ISBN 0-8420-2550-2

G. Harvey Summ, ed., *Brazilian Mosaic: Portraits of a Diverse People and Culture* (1995). Cloth ISBN 0-8420-2491-3 Paper ISBN 0-8420-2492-1

N. Patrick Peritore and Ana Karina Galve-Peritore, eds., *Biotechnology in Latin America: Politics, Impacts, and Risks*

(1995). Cloth ISBN 0-8420-2556-1 Paper ISBN 0-8420-2557-X

Silvia Marina Arrom and Servando Ortoll, eds., *Riots in the Cities: Popular Politics and the Urban Poor in Latin America, 1765–1910* (1996). Cloth ISBN 0-8420-2580-4 Paper ISBN 0-8420-2581-2

Roderic Ai Camp, ed., *Polling for Democracy: Public Opinion and Political Liberalization in Mexico* (1996). ISBN 0-8420-2583-9

Brian Loveman and Thomas M. Davies, Jr., eds., *The Politics of Antipolitics: The Military in Latin America*, 3d ed., revised and updated (1996). Cloth ISBN 0-8420-2609-6 Paper ISBN 0-8420-2611-8

Joseph S. Tulchin, Andrés Serbín, and Rafael Hernández, eds., *Cuba and the Caribbean: Regional Issues and Trends in the Post-Cold War Era* (1997). ISBN 0-8420-2652-5

Thomas W. Walker, ed., *Nicaragua without Illusions: Regime Transition and Structural Adjustment in the 1990s* (1997). Cloth ISBN 0-8420-2578-2 Paper ISBN 0-8420-2579-0

Dianne Walta Hart, *Undocumented in L.A.: An Immigrant's Story* (1997). Cloth ISBN 0-8420-2648-7 Paper ISBN 0-8420-2649-5

Jaime E. Rodríguez O. and Kathryn Vincent, eds., *Myths, Misdeeds, and Misunderstandings: The Roots of Conflict in U.S.-Mexican Relations* (1997). ISBN 0-8420-2662-2

Jaime E. Rodríguez O. and Kathryn Vincent, eds., *Common Border, Uncommon Paths: Race, Culture, and National Identity in U.S.-Mexican Relations* (1997). ISBN 0-8420-2673-8

William H. Beezley and Judith Ewell, eds., *The Human Tradition in Modern Latin America* (1997). Cloth ISBN 0-8420-2612-6 Paper ISBN 0-8420-2613-4

Donald F. Stevens, ed., *Based on a True Story: Latin American History at the Movies* (1997). ISBN 0-8420-2582-0

Jaime E. Rodríguez O., ed., *The Origins of Mexican National Politics, 1808–1847* (1997). Paper ISBN 0-8420-2723-8

Che Guevara, *Guerrilla Warfare*, with revised and updated introduction and case studies by Brian Loveman and Thomas M. Davies, Jr., 3d ed. (1997). Cloth ISBN 0-8420-2677-0 Paper ISBN 0-8420-2678-9

Adrian A. Bantjes, *As If Jesus Walked on Earth: Cardenismo, Sonora, and the Mexican Revolution* (1998). ISBN 0-8420-2653-3

Henry A. Dietz and Gil Shidlo, eds., *Urban Elections in Democratic Latin America* (1998). Cloth ISBN 0-8420-2627-4 Paper ISBN 0-8420-2628-2

A. Kim Clark, *The Redemptive Work: Railway and Nation in Ecuador, 1895–1930* (1998). ISBN 0-8420-2674-6

Joseph S. Tulchin, ed., with Allison M. Garland, *Argentina: The Challenges of Modernization* (1998). ISBN 0-8420-2721-1

Louis A. Pérez, Jr., ed., *Impressions of Cuba in the Nineteenth Century: The Travel Diary of Joseph J. Dimock* (1998). Cloth ISBN 0-8420-2657-6 Paper ISBN 0-8420-2658-4

Guy P. C. Thomson, *Patriotism, Politics, and Popular Liberalism in Nineteenth-Century Mexico: Juan Francisco Lucas and the Puebla Sierra* (1998). ISBN 0-8420-2683-5

June E. Hahner, ed., *Women through Women's Eyes: Latin American Women in Nineteenth-Century Travel Accounts* (1998). Cloth ISBN 0-8420-2633-9 Paper ISBN 0-8420-2634-7

James P. Brennan, ed., *Peronism and Argentina* (1998). ISBN 0-8420-2706-8